THE MARROW OF THEOLOGY

THE MARROW
OF THEOLOGY

William Ames 1576–1633

Translated from the third Latin edition, 1629,
and edited by John D. Eusden

THE LABYRINTH PRESS
Durham, North Carolina

First Labyrinth Press Edition 1983
Reprinted by arrangement with the Pilgrim Press

For information contact: The Labyrinth Press
P.O. Box 2124, Durham, North Carolina 27702-2124

Library of Congress Cataloging in Publication Data

Ames, William, 1576-1633.
    The Marrow of Theology.

    Translation of: Medulla theologica.
    Reprint. Originally published: Boston: Pilgrim Press,
1968. (Milestone library)
    Includes bibliographical references and index.
    1. Theology, Doctrinal—Early works to 1800.
    2. Calvinism—Early works to 1800. I. Eusden, John
Dykstra. II. Title.
[BX9421.A4313, 1983   230'.59   82-20901
ISBN 0-939464-14-4

For Joanne

Sensu societatis vitae nostrae

The Pourtracture of the Reverend and worthy Minister of God,
William Ames D.D. sometime of Christs Colledge in Cambridge.
And Proffesor of Divinity in the Famous University of
Francker in Friesland.   Will: Marshall sculpsit.
          Printed for Iohn Rothwell at the Sunn in Paules Church yard

An engraving of William Ames by William Marshall, often found in
early seventeenth-century editions of the *Marrow of Theology*.

FOREWORD

William Ames lived through fifty-seven years of theological travail in the early seventeenth century when English Protestantism was being born. With this birth, as Christopher Dawson says, there came into being a new type of Christianity which was to become, in its diffusion over all the world, one of the great forces shaping modern times.

Ames stood in the midst of clashing systems of thought and to an unusual degree directed them, making his own contribution to the transition from medieval into modern thinking. On at least three fronts he supplied generalship. He stood with the Puritans in the liturgical revolution. (John Burgess alone uses 654 quarto pages to answer him.) He stood with the Protestants against Rome. (Vitus Erbermann, S.J., takes 393 folio pages to meet his criticism of Cardinal Bellarmine's great work.) And against every species of theology abstracted from life he stood with the *doers* of the word. (His *Conscience: Its Law or Cases* became a landmark in moral theology, going through almost twenty editions in one generation.)

His general influence is best felt in his *Marrow of Theology*, which is here, after three centuries, translated into modern English. Contemporary readers must be grateful to John Eusden for the translation and for his Introduction. He has not only given us the first essay of its size to appear originally in English on the subject of Ames and his work but he has also reproduced for us a volume which more clearly and systematically, I think, than any other sets forth the gist of Puritan thought about God, the church, and the world.

Douglas Horton

vii

PREFACE

A translation of an influential book written nearly three hundred and fifty years ago deserves more than a technical, literal presentation of the text. I have worked for the meaning of the author's words in modern English and for the sense of his argument. The Latin is given in brackets where an English expression is difficult to render, or where a word had a special meaning for late scholastic or Puritan and Reformed theology.

The biblical quotations which so liberally adorn the *Marrow* are the actual versions used by Ames. He leaned heavily on the favorite Latin Bible of seventeenth-century Reformed churchmen in the Old World and the New. The Old Testament had been translated into Latin by John Immanuel Tremellius (1510–1580), a Jewish scholar and later convert to Protestantism who taught at Cambridge and Heidelberg, and his son-in-law Franciscus Junius or Du Jon (1545–1602), professor of theology at Heidelberg. The New Testament had parallel readings, one of them by Tremellius from the Syriac and the other from the Greek by Theodore Beza (1519–1605), Calvin's successor in Geneva. Ames, however, did not follow this Latin edition slavishly. He read Hebrew and Greek easily and often made his own Latin translations from the original.

Many people have entered into the labor of this book. Particularly helpful in shaping the Introduction were the interest and criticism of fellow scholars at Williams, Yale, and Harvard: Francis C. Oakley, Sydney E. Ahlstrom, Roland H. Bainton, Douglas Horton, and Herbert W. Richardson. My father, Ray A. Eusden, read the Introduction and part of the text, always improving the style. Douglas Horton,

in addition to offering counsel on the Introduction, was a resource-
ful mentor on the text; indeed, his encouragement sustained me from
the very beginning of the task and finishing without his help would
have been difficult. Lee W. Gibbs checked against the 1629 edition,
worked on footnotes, and on many points added his expertness in
things Amesian. Raymond H. Phyles prepared the index with the demands of the reader in mind and checked Greek and Hebrew in the
proofs. Dorothy C. Hannus confirmed all biblical citations and with
diligence and humor lasted through several typings of the manuscript;
her husband Reuben R. Hannus aided in the copy editing. The Class
of 1900 Fund of Williams College stood by repeatedly to meet re-
search and clerical expenses.

When a scholar of the seventeenth century looks back at his work,
his mind's eye pictures the hours spent in reading rooms with rare
volumes — and he recalls those who were there to guide and answer.
With a sense of privilege I record my gratitude to the Houghton
Reading Room of the Harvard College Library, the Beinecke Rare
Book and Manuscript Library of Yale University, the Williams College Library, and the Folger Shakespeare Library of Washington, D.C.

John Dykstra Eusden
Williams College and
Randolph, New Hampshire
Summer 1967

CONTENTS

BOOK TWO

THE
MARROW
OF SACRED
DIVINITY,

DRAWNE OVT OF THE
holy Scriptures, and the Interpreters
thereof, and brought into Method.
BY

WILLIAM AMES, sometime Doctor and
professor of Divinity in the famous University at *Franeken* in *Friesland.*

Translated out of the Latine, for the benefit of such who
are not acquainted with strange Tongues.

Whereunto are annexed certaine Tables representing the
substance and heads of all in a short view, directing
to the Chapters where they are handled. As also a table
opening the hard words therein contained.

A Worke usefull for this Season.

1 COR. 14.26.
*When yee come together, every. one hath a Psalme, hath a Doctrine, hath a
Tongue, hath a Revelation, hath an Interpretation. Let all things be
done unto edifying.*

Published by order from the Honorable the House of Commons.

LONDON,
Printed by *Edward Griffin* for *Iohn Rothwell* at the Sun in
Pauls-Church-yard.

Title page of an earlier translation, attributed to
John St. Nicholas, London, 1643.

INTRODUCTION

The Marrow

For a century and a half William Ames's *Marrow of Theology* held sway as a clear, persuasive expression of Puritan belief and practice. In England, Holland, and New England nearly all those who aspired to the Puritan way read the book. No matter what their aspirations, undergraduates at Emmanuel College, Leyden, Harvard, and Yale had to read the *Marrow* in Latin as part of basic instruction in divinity. In a burst of enthusiasm Thomas Hooker (1586?–1647) of Hartford once recommended the *Marrow* and another of Ames's works to fellow clergymen: "They would make him (supposing him versed in the Scriptures) a good divine, though he had no more books in the world." [1] In 1717 Increase Mather preached an ordination sermon in which the only book of theology suggested for the minister's reading was the *Marrow*.[2] The present translation is probably the nineteenth printing — an extensive publishing history for an early seventeenth-century Latin book.

William Ames originally offered the *Marrow of Theology* as a series of lectures to the sons of Leyden merchants between 1620 and 1622. The first Latin edition of 1623 appeared as *Medulla theologica* under an Amsterdam imprint. Twelve Latin printings followed,

---

1. Cotton Mather, *Magnalia Christi Americana: Or the Ecclesiastical History of New England . . . 1620 unto the Year of our Lord 1688* (Silas Andrus, Hartford, 1853), I: 339–40. Hereafter cited as Mather, *Magnalia*.

2. Douglas Horton, "Let Us Not Forget the Mighty William Ames," *Religion in Life*, XIX: No. 3 (summer 1960), 434–35.

1

circulating widely in England, New England, and on the Continent. Jonathan Edwards (1703–1758) came into possession of a copy of the 1634 edition in New Haven; he twice signed it and added notes which bespeak his indebtedness.[3] Three printings of an English translation appeared between 1638 and 1643, one of them "by order from the honorable House of Commons," as stated on the title page. A Dutch translation was made in 1656.[4]

Ames wrote his *Marrow* not as a scholarly treatise but as a useful compendium for laymen and students.[5] The text is divided into two books with chapters in numbered sections, providing even a neophyte a chance to discover quickly the Amesian answer on a particular point. More than a theological check list, however, the book was a declaration of the Puritan position that theology was an art with its own rules and practice — an art for every man, not reserved for the expert or the *perfectiones*. Theology was for all men because it spoke not only to the intellect, but to the common *sensus*, or man's feeling and emotions. When Ames was fleeing his native England, a senior Puritan

3. The Edwards copy, autographed in 1721 when the owner was eighteen, is in the Beinecke Rare Book and Manuscript Library, Yale University. Jonathan Edwards also owned Ames's *Theses logicae*, or *Principles of Logic*, and likely *De conscientia et eius iure vel casibus*, or *Conscience: Its Law or Cases*. He certainly made use of the latter; see p. 65.

4. For a listing of Ames's works see Douglas Horton, trans. *William Ames by Matthew Nethenus, Hugo Visscher, and Karl Reuter* (Harvard Divinity School Library, Cambridge, Mass., 1965), pp. 278–79. Hereafter cited as Horton, *Ames by Nethenus* (or Visscher or Reuter). The bibliography is Reuter's, given in *Wilhelm Amesius: Der führende Theologe des erwachenden reformierten Pietismus* (Neukirchener Verlag des Erziehungsvereins, Neukirchen, 1940), pp. 155–57, or *William Ames: The Leading Theologian in the Awakening of Reformed Pietism*. The listing does not include the many later editions of the *Marrow* and *Conscience*. The probable eighteenth printing of the *Marrow* is a limited facsimile edition of the 1643 English translation (attributed to John St. Nicholas) issued by the Harvard Divinity School Library, Cambridge, Mass., 1964. Brief selections from the English *Marrow* were compiled by Conrad Wright in typescript copy (Harvard Divinity School Library, Cambridge, Mass., 1958).

5. John Milton (1608–74) was attracted to the form and purpose of the *Marrow*. In the preface to *Christian Doctrine*, Milton referred to "the shorter systems of divines, in imitation of whom I was in the habit of classing under certain heads whatever passages of Scripture occurred for extraction, to be made use of hereafter as occasion might require," *Works* (Columbia University Press, New York, 1933), XIV: 5. Milton quoted the *Marrow* in a discussion of the sabbath, XVII: 173, and referred to Ames in the *Tetrachordon*, IV: 102–03. The compendium style had been used before Ames by several continental Reformed theologians, but no one equaled Ames in mastery of the technique. Perhaps his nearest rival was Basel professor Johannes Wollebius, or Wolleb (1586–1629), *Compendium theologiae Christianae* (Amstelodami, 1633). Theodore D. Woolsey, "The Course of Instruction in Yale College," in *Yale College* (William L. Kingsley, ed. Henry Holt and Co., New York, 1879) II: 496–99, records that Ames and Wolleb were required reading in Latin for Yale undergraduates as late as 1779.

mentor reminded him, "Beware . . . of a strong head and a cold heart." [6] In the *Marrow*, Ames heeded this advice of Paul Baynes (d. 1617), although the sensitivity for the human situation may appear to a twentieth-century reader buried under an avalanche of arguments and biblical citations. Above all, according to the *Marrow*, theology should lead men to actual life responses, it should show them how "to live sober, upright, and godly lives in this world (Titus 2:12)." [7] Thus, the book is fundamentally a teaching document about Christian life in the Puritan style. Ames wrote it in simple, late Renaissance Latin so that it could be read by anyone with a rudimentary seventeenth-century education, be he English, French, Dutch, or German.[8] The 1967 translation into modern English, based on the third Latin edition of 1629 — the last before Ames's death in 1633 — will again give the *Marrow of Theology* a chance of being read and, it is hoped, add to our understanding of Puritanism.

The Author

William Ames was born in 1576 at Ipswich in Suffolk, that region of East Anglia where Puritanism had its tap root and where the religious persecutions of crown and bishop were least effective. His father was a well-to-do merchant with known Puritan sympathies; his mother was related to families that helped found Plymouth Plantation in the New World. Tragedy came early in life to Ames with the death of both parents. An uncle, Robert Snelling of Oxford, took William into his home and with understanding and generosity saw to his needs and education.

Ames naturally chose the center of Puritan learning, Cambridge University, over Oxford for his higher education. Cambridge was dominated during Elizabethan and Jacobean times by the teaching and preaching of such giants as Thomas Cartwright (1535–1603), William Perkins (1558–1602), and John Preston (1587–1628). One of the ancient traditions of Cambridge, not shared by Oxford, was the right to choose twelve preachers each year without the approval of the bishop. While Westminster and Canterbury fumed, many a nonconformist legally preached in the college chapels of the university. Ames entered Christ's College where he encountered the teaching and the

6. Cotton Mather, *Johannes in eremo*, or *John in the Wilderness* (London, 1695), p. 4.
7. II, ii, 17, p. 226.
8. On the use of Latin in educational circles on both sides of the Atlantic well into the 18th century, see Walter J. Ong, S. J., *Ramus, Method, and the Decay of Dialogue* (Harvard University Press, Cambridge, Mass., 1958), pp. 12–13. Hereafter cited as Ong, *Ramus*.

spirit of William Perkins who was doubtless the college's most distinguished fellow. Perkins became Ames's tutor and close friend. In a sense, Ames remained all his life under the spell of the "architect of Elizabethan Puritanism," [9] although the Amesian theology reworked much of the old and explored areas not entered by his respected teacher.

Ames received his A.B. degree in 1607 and was promptly invited to become a fellow of Christ's College. He was even in the running for the mastership of the college as a successor to Edmund Barwell in 1609. But higher authorities in state and established church interfered to prevent the election of such a strong nonconformist candidate. Ames refused to wear some of the vestments of the church and spoke against the use of the cross in baptism and other ceremonies. Valentine Cary, more dependable in ecclesiastical leanings but less endowed with talent, was selected. The situation at Christ's College deteriorated, at least in the eyes of Ames and his Puritan colleagues, and he resigned his post voluntarily, never to return to English academic life.

Ames, like many Puritan figures of the time, could move easily between the worlds of university and church. The Colchester congregation issued a call and he was happy over the prospect. But he was already a marked man in the new persecutions launched by James I and Archbishop Bancroft. Known for his teaching and preaching, Ames was also singled out because he had translated into Latin the blunt treatise of William Bradshaw, *English Puritanism*, in order that it might have a reading outside England and added for good measure a long, supporting introduction. The Bishop of London blocked ratification of the Colchester call. Ames soon found that he was actively sought by the authorities. About to be "harried out of the land" or imprisoned, Ames finally made the hard decision to leave England for Holland. He was encouraged by the knowledge that Bradshaw had just escaped and that many others were planning the same course of action. Aided by one Richard Brown, Ames and a friend, Robert Parker, were taken to Gravesend and thence across the North Sea at the very time "when they were pursued by some that would willingly have shortened their journey." Archbishop Bancroft wrote in 1611, "If he (Ames) were here amongst us . . . some exemplary punishment would be his reward." [10]

Ames arrived in Holland in 1610 to begin a new life that would bring him fame, conflict, the death of his first wife, financial insecurity, continued interference from English authorities, and his own

9. See William Haller, *The Rise of Puritanism* (Columbia University Press, New York, 1938), pp. 91–92.
10. Horton, *Ames by Visscher*, pp. 40, 35.

death at age fifty-seven. He tarried briefly in Rotterdam where he met John Robinson (c. 1576–1625), pastor of the separatist English congregation at Leyden — some of whose members were soon to establish Plymouth Plantation in the New World and be known as the Pilgrims. Robinson and Ames did not see eye to eye on the Puritan structure of the church; in fact, Robinson made a play on his fellow clergyman's Latin name, Amesius, and labeled him "Mr. William Amiss" in an earlier treatise. Robinson held for the Brownist interpretation that the Puritan churches should separate "root and branch" from the Church of England; Ames on the other hand argued the nonseparatist position, namely, that the new churches should be considered as independent congregations within the established church, working for its reformation. In Rotterdam and Leyden, Ames was able to persuade Robinson to drop some of his rigid ways. At least the Pilgrim pastor admitted that churches other than separatist were true churches, that his own members could in good conscience attend the services of other Reformed congregations, and that members of other congregations could be allowed to partake of the Lord's Supper in his church. Robinson came only part way, however, for he maintained stoutly that participation by his parishioners in the sacraments of other Puritan and Reformed churches was invalid. As a result of Ames's influence, Robinson can rightly be called a semiseparatist, or as the Dutch scholar Hugo Visscher puts it, a "semist." [11] Ames's partial persuasion of Robinson helped to account for the generally good relations existing later in New England between the Plymouth settlers and the Salem-Boston Puritans who followed the Amesian way of nonseparating Congregationalism.

During the first years of exile, Ames supported himself by offering his ministerial services to one of the several large communities of Englishmen living in The Netherlands. These communities were composed of the English Merchant Adventurers who had been chartered since the fifteenth century to handle trade between England and the Low Countries, officers and men sent in the 1580's to help the Dutch maintain their new independence from Spain, members of the diplomatic corps, and religious exiles.[12] Ever since the Marian persecution of the 1550's, English nonconformist ministers in exile had always been able to find professional employment, although usually at a bare subsistence level. Supported by Colonel Horatio Vere, a Puritan sym-

11. For the Ames-Robinson confrontation, see the documented account in Horton, *Ames by Visscher*, pp. 41–42, 48. See also Robert S. Paul, ed. and intro. *An Apologeticall Narration* (United Church Press, Boston, 1963), pp. 63–66, for a discussion of "the Congregational way" and Robinson.

12. See Raymond P. Stearns, *Congregationalism in the Dutch Netherlands* (The American Society of Church History, Chicago, 1940), p. 12.

pathizer, Ames succeeded John Burgess in 1611 as chaplain to the British community at The Hague. He found time for courtship and married Burgess' daughter, but she died soon afterwards leaving him childless. The long arms of bishop and king reached across the North Sea, however, and Lord Vere was forced to dismiss Ames from his post in 1618. His professional life continued to be precarious until his appointment to a professorship at the young University of Franeker in north Holland. Although his recommendation in 1619 by the Synod of South Holland was enthusiastically received by the trustees of the new Friesland university, Ames was not able to deliver his inaugural address until 1622. The English authorities spared no effort to prevent his taking the post and would likely have been successful had it not been for the direct intervention of the Dutch Prince Moritz. They were successful in the case of the University of Leyden whose faculty had been making serious overtures to Ames. These were years in which Ames encountered deceit and intrigue; people whom he counted as friends, such as British Ambassador Carleton, turned out to be informers to his enemies across the Channel.

Despite this array of personal misfortune, Ames's voice was still one of the most influential in the theological development of the Puritan and Reformed churches in England and The Netherlands. From discussion of church polity with Robinson, he turned to dispute with continental theologians. The points of argument were all related to Arminianism, the great theological issue of the early seventeenth century. Very soon after his arrival in Holland, Ames was enlisted on the side of the so-called orthodox party which was standing its ground, none too well, against the position of the followers of the late Jacobus Arminius (1560–1609), theological professor at the University of Leyden from 1603 to 1609. The Arminians, or Remonstrants as they were better known, opposed the rigid Calvinism of the Dutch Reformed churches — a rigidity also shared by most English Puritans. The Remonstrants argued two main points: that the human will played a significant, if not controlling, role in salvation and that Christ died for all men, not just the elect. On the second point, Arminius had made a special attack on the theory of predestination held by William Perkins, Ames's respected Cambridge tutor. Ames did battle in several tracts with Jan Uitenbogaert (1557–1644), Simon Episcopius (1583–1643), and especially Nicolaas Grevinchoven (1593–1632), influential Remonstrant minister in Rotterdam. The *Coronis ad collationem Hagiensem*, or a *Finishing Touch to the Hague Conference*, published in 1618 as a strong affirmation of the orthodox ministers, presented forcefully the Amesian answer to the Remonstrants. In the winter of 1618–19, the whole Arminian dispute reached a climax in the famous Synod of Dort to which Reformed theologians came from England, Holland, France, Switzerland and Germany. As an exile and alien in a new land, Ames was not an official delegate to the conference which was to condemn the Remonstrant movement. He did serve, however, as a consultant to the moderator of the synod at a salary of four guilders a day.

One of Ames's biographers, looking back on the Remonstrant debates with a supralapsarian gleam in his eye, wrote, "Ames plainly deserved our saying in his honor what the mothers of Israel once said in honor of David: 'Other theologians have slain their thousands, but Ames his tens of thousands!' " [13] Ames was thought to be something of a giant killer in theological debate. What disturbed him about the Remonstrants was their failure to give the sovereignty and working power of God a primary place in theology; they had, in his mind, placed the Almighty at the beck and call of man. For this they surely deserved censure. But Ames, almost alone in the orthodox party, found that the Remonstrant insistence on man's response in the drama of salvation was a needed corrective for Reformed theology. In the *Marrow* he parallels one thrust of the original 1610 Remonstrance: "True Christian faith . . . always leans upon divine testimony . . . But this testimony cannot be received without a genuine turning of the will towards God. John 3:33, *He who receives his testimony has sealed that God is true*." [14] The Amesian view on the relation between man's act and God's grace in salvation will be dealt with later; it should be said here that Ames did not believe a sweeping, syllogistical declaration of the sufficiency of God settled the problem of salvation. There was much that man had to do; "spiritual preparation" was called for if grace was to be experienced. He differed from such straight-arrow, orthodox theologians as Franciscus Gomarus (1563–1641) and Johannes Maccovius (1588–1644), his colleague at the University of Franeker, both of whom were seemingly unconcerned with the human side of the religious life. Even in the matter of predestination Ames was not completely orthodox, although he was far from agreeing with the universal salvation concept of the Remonstrants (another point for later consideration). It is not being suggested here that Ames was an Arminian-within-the-gates, or a quasi Remonstrant, but it is true that among orthodox theologians he was the most sensitive to the criticisms advanced by the opposition party.

Finally it should be noted that Ames did not call down the usual orthodox vituperation on his opponents. In the *Conscience* he asks if the Remonstrants are heretics and gives this answer: "The position

13. Horton, *Ames by Nethenus*, p. 18.
14. I, iii, 5–6, p. 81.

of the Remonstrants, as held by most that favor it, is not properly a heresy but a dangerous error in the faith, tending to heresy." He goes on to say, however, that when the Remonstrant view on the role of the will is pushed too far, it does become a heresy — "a Pelagian heresy, because it denies the effectual operation of internal grace to be necessary for the effecting of conversion and faith." [15] Here the line must be drawn.

Ames began his work as professor of theology at Franeker happily in 1622. He found, however, that he could join Maccovius and Sibrandus Lubbertus (1557–1625) on the theological faculty only in formal colleagueship, never in mind and spirit. With Maccovius, especially, he found that his relationship was one of steady deterioration. The Polish-born theologian followed a strict Calvinist position on the issues raised by the Remonstrants and, more important, presented what was to Ames a desiccated version of the Christian faith. Maccovius depended heavily on Aristotelian logic and scholastic definition to establish the all-powerfulness of God, his wisdom, and even his love. Faith was the acceptance of the findings of these disciplines and theology was basically a kind of specialized skill — points at great variance with the Amesian view. The two could not be expected to join hands, for Ames was at home in the world of evangelical English Puritanism and a stranger in the world of Maccovius — the latter being founded on an intellectualization of faith widely held by orthodox continental theologians, such as Bartholomaeus Keckermann (1571–1609), Maccovius' teacher at Heidelberg.

Ames also found personal grounds for criticism of his colleague who, in some ways, must have been the faculty character at Franeker. When the syllogisms got a little heavy and the premises a little grim, Maccovius would cast them aside and go off on a large bender. Douglas Horton gives this description. "The students, knowing this man's gift for imbibing, would sometimes give him a chance to exercise his talent to the full, and then, under the pretext of carrying him home, deposit him at the gates of some remote village whence he would not have time to return for his next lecture." [16] Ames was not an abstainer, but he did believe there was a connection between being a theologian and living rightly. He often touched on the matter of Christian right

15. *De conscientia et eius iure vel casibus: libri quinque* (Amstelodami, 1630), or *Conscience: Its Law or Cases, Five Books*, IV, iv, 10. My translation. Hereafter cited as Ames, *De conscientia*. The original English translation, *Conscience with the Power and Cases thereof: Divided into Five Books* (London, 1643), has been reproduced with the *Marrow* in a limited facsimile edition, Harvard Divinity School Library, Cambridge, Mass., 1964.
16. "Let Us Not Forget the Mighty William Ames," *Religion in Life*, XIX: No. 3 (summer 1960), 440–41.

living in addresses to students. His speech on the motto of Franeker, *Christo et Ecclesiae,* For Christ and the Church, which was to become the first motto of Harvard, was a sympathetic, unstrictured description of the good life for students.

The Franeker years were Ames's most productive. During their span he continued to write about the Arminian crisis, brought forth a long polemic against a leading Roman Catholic thinker, *Bellarmine Disarmed,* and wrote his second most popular work, *Conscience: Its Law or Cases.* The latter was reprinted many times and was translated, like the *Marrow,* into English and Dutch. A German edition also appeared in 1643 and 1654. The University of Franeker had, on the whole, treated its luminary well. Midway through his tenure Ames was made *Rector magnificus;* the trustees and many colleagues continually, and for a while successfully, urged him to continue in service. He had reasonable financial security, compared at least to his immediate past. But in the late 1620's Ames began to feel strongly that he must leave. Not only was the rigid orthodoxy and perhaps the isolation of the Friesland university becoming more difficult, but like was calling to like. Ames had received correspondence from his English Puritan friends who urged him to join their New World endeavor as a pastor, or teacher, or school or academy head. His Franeker colleague Meinardus Schotanus spoke in 1628 of letters written so movingly "that they really forced tears to the eyes and could move a heart of iron." [17] Ames received these overtures sympathetically — and so did his second wife, an Englishwoman who longed to be with her kind. In December 1630, he wrote to John Winthrop, newly arrived in Massachusetts Bay Colony, that he would follow in the very near future: "My daily prayers unto God shall be for the good success of the business you have undertaken. And for myself, I long to be with you, though I do not see how I should satisfy the opinion and expectation which you have conceived of me." [18]

But William Ames was never to sail for New England. In Cotton Mather's expression, he "was upon the wing for this American desert, but God then took him to the heavenly Canaan." [19] Ames went to Rotterdam in 1632, answering a call to serve an Independent congregation as co-minister with his friend Hugh Peter, or Peters (1598–1660). This fast-growing church intended at the time to start an academy of which Ames would have been the principal teacher. Undoubtedly Ames looked forward to the freer, more convivial air of Rot-

17. Horton, *Ames by Visscher,* p. 61.
18. *Winthrop Papers* (Massachusetts Historical Society [Boston], 1929–47), II:180.
19. Cotton Mather, *Johannes in eremo* (London, 1695), p. 4.

terdam (his young friend Thomas Hooker was there) and to the new responsibilities which would offer him a chance to replenish his finances and otherwise make ready for the journey across the Atlantic. In October 1633 the River Maas flooded. Water coursed into the Rotterdam home of the Ames family, abruptly rousing all members. Ames suffered drastic exposure to cold water and cold air and contracted a high fever which his weakened heart could not stand. Medicine and doctors were to no avail; his family and friends watched his courageous spirit endure to the end which came within a few days. The straightened, disconsolate plight of the Ames family was tended to by many, but especially by Hugh Peter. Largely because of his persuasion, the magistrates of Rotterdam presented Ames's widow with the modest sum of two hundred guilders and made it possible for her to publish his *Lectures on the One Hundred and Fifty Psalms of David*. Ames's last book, *A Fresh Suit against Human Ceremonies in God's Worship* with a preface attributed to Thomas Hooker (who had just left for the New World) was also released. Travel plans had been made before Ames's death and the widow was convinced they should be carried out. In 1637 she arrived with her three children at Salem in the Bay Colony. Her new beginning was aided by a gift of forty acres from the town of Salem and forty pounds from the Bay Colony. Mrs. Ames came with little of this world's goods, but she did come as the widow of the loved and revered Amesius — a matter which made for a warm reception amid the rigors of the New World.

Thus, he who was to be of perhaps greatest influence in the intellectual history of early New England was never to arrive. If he had made the journey to America, he might well have become Harvard's first president.[20] But speculation is not required to establish his place in New England history — let alone the impact he left on theological circles in Holland and England. According to Daniel Neal, the "first furniture" of the Harvard College Library "was the books of Dr. William Ames, the famous professor of divinity at Franeker." [21] All his

20. See Ong, *Ramus*, p. 12. A portrait of Ames, finished in the year of his death, now hangs in the Houghton Reading Room of the Harvard College Library and is reproduced here as the frontispiece.

21. See Samuel E. Morison, *The Founding of Harvard College* (Harvard University Press, Cambridge, Mass., 1935), p. 267. In the original library of John Harvard (1607–38) were *Coronis ad collationem Hagiensem* (Lugduni Batavorum, 1618), or *A Finishing Touch to the Hague Conference; Bellarminus enervatus* (Oxoniae, 1629), or *Bellarmine Disarmed; De conscientia* (Amstelodami, 1630); *Medulla theologiae* (Amstelodami, n. d.); and *Utriusque Epistolae divi Petri Apostoli explicatio analytica* (Amstelodami, 1635), or *An Analytical Exposition of Both the Epistles of the Heavenly Apostle Peter*. Other editions of Ames's works were added as soon as they became available; much of the Harvard Amesian collection was lost in the library fire of 1764 and later replaced. On the disposition of Ames's personal

American contemporaries and immediate followers spoke of him with respect and feeling. The *Magnalia* of Cotton Mather (1663–1728), biographical essays on New England founders, called him (in good Mather hyperbole): "That profound, that sublime, that subtle, the irrefragable — yea, that angelical doctor." [22] John Cotton (1584–1652) referred to him often and freely used his thought.[23] When John Norton (1606–63) was asked by his colleagues to prepare a tract to answer British critics of New England church polity, he turned to William Ames as his chief authority.[24] The 1648 Cambridge Platform propositions on the theory and structure of early American Congregationalism was, according to its subtitle, "Gathered out of the Word of God," but much of it was reaped from the *Marrow* and Ames's writings on polity. Each ship from England or Holland brought new editions of his books, which were to be added to libraries for the college and university education of early American generations. As late as 1815 two of his Latin works were among the acquisitions of twenty-two-year-old Williams College.

Only when Puritanism radically changed its character to a semiarid legalism in the late seventeenth century did his name cease to appear with regularity in New England theological annals. Samuel Willard (1640–1707), publishing the *Complete Body of Divinity* and works on the covenant in the 1680's, found no room for Amesian thought. But the *Marrow* and the *Body* represented different strands of Puritanism. Whenever a new interest occurred in the early Puritan concern for religious experience and for covenant as an expression of grace, Ames once again became a point of departure. Jonathan Edwards (1703–58) often began with the thought of the Franeker professor. In early American theological and intellectual history, William Ames was without peer.

library, see Morison (above citation) and Raymond P. Stearns, *The Strenuous Puritan: Hugh Peter, 1598–1660* (University of Illinois, Urbana, 1954), pp. 84–86. Most of the library was undoubtedly sold in Holland by Mrs. Ames before departure for the support of herself and her children.

22. Mather, *Magnalia*, I: 236. See Keith L. Sprunger, "William Ames and the Settlement of Massachusetts Bay," *New England Quarterly*, XXXIX: No. 1 (March 1966), and "Ames, Ramus, and the Method of Puritan Theology," *Harvard Theological Review*, LIX: No. 2 (April 1966).

23. Larzer Ziff, *The Career of John Cotton: Puritanism and the American Experience* (Princeton University Press, Princeton, 1962), pp. 199–200.

24. Douglas Horton, ed. and trans. John Norton, *The Answer to the Whole Set of Questions of the Celebrated Mr. William Apollonius* (Harvard University Press, Cambridge, Mass., 1958), pp. xvi–xvii.

The Theology of William Ames

AUGUSTINIAN AND SCHOLASTIC ROOTS · Ames stood within
the central tradition of the early Reformation by developing much of
his thought within a framework established by St. Augustine (354–
430). Although the *Conscience* and the *Marrow* have only a few direct
references to the *Confessions* and *City of God*, the Augustinian approach is clearly present when Ames speaks of the nature of man, the
meaning of sin, the importance of the will in conversion, and the
problems of war.

Ames turns to Genesis 1:26 as a necessary beginning for any discussion of the nature of man. Following the lead of all Catholic and Reformed thinkers who found a source in the writings of Augustine,
Ames divides the passage into the sections "Let us make man" and
"In our image, after our likeness." It is significant, he points out, that
the biblical account does not say, "Let there be man," as was said
for the light, the firmament, and the dry land. "Let us" points to a
uniqueness for man among all the objects of creation; it implies that
man was brought forth with greater deliberation and care than were
other created things. Ames notes that this deliberative creation of man
was the final creating act of God, a point which argues that man is
the climax and the summary, or compendium, of all creation. The
meaning of the climactic action of God in man is found in the second
part of the passage. To be "In our image, after our likeness" is to
have a natural conformity to the perfection of God. The conformity
is partly construed as a form of obedience, but for Ames it is also
understood in the more general sense as a desire or drive to be like
God — always within the limits of human existence. Conformity is
not perfect in man, not even in the greatest saint; a perfect image has
been reserved for the Son of God (Col. 1:15, Heb. 1:3).

The drive to be like God, given to man as the chief mark of his
uniqueness, is seen in his body and in his mind or soul. Man can
think, decide, and will in such a way that he may live in holiness,
wisdom, and righteousness and thus be brought close to the nature of
God. In the proper use of his body man is also brought close. Ames
chooses to speak about sex in this connection and, although he shares
the medieval negative attitude, he expresses the positive biblical note
often suppressed by Christian thinkers (and too often overlooked in
estimates of Puritanism). It is natural and good that "a man leaves
his father and his mother and cleaves to his wife, and they become
one flesh. (Gen. 2:24)," for the comeliness of the body has been ordained that it might be an aid to righteous living. Marriage and bod-

ily communion have their end not only in propagation and the control of carnal desire, but in mutual comfort and help. Even in the dark writings of St. Paul on this subject, Ames finds — in a momentary abandonment of Augustinian thought — corroboration for expressing the sense of image or conformity in sex relations. "Yield yourselves to God as men who have been brought from death to life, and your members to God as instruments of righteousness (Rom. 6:13)." [25]

Ames wishes to stress the actual situation of man as he lives in the image of God. All men are given an aspiration toward perfection by the creating power and wisdom of God, but men are continually destroying this part of the image. Ever since Adam, mankind has fallen away from the image, rather than attempting to realize it. Something of the original promise has been lost in every man. Like Augustine, Ames does not wish to hold God responsible for the erosion; the blame is rather placed on man's will and actions. God has an indirect part — not that he commanded man to fall away, but that the possibility of such human action must have been implicit in the kind of perfection to which man was ordained. Ames attempts to solve the old problem of God's responsibility for human transgression by saying that man is imperfect not because of God's deprivation, but because the negative possibility of imperfection and disobedience was present in original creation. To be a human being is to know this negative possibility in one's actions and its great controlling power in one's will. Ames is convinced, like Augustine and Luther, that all of us are aware of this dark side of our lives and that we live much of the time in its shadow.

Perhaps the most moving section of the *Marrow* is a description of what Ames calls spiritual death, his term for the sense of sin. Here for the only time he drops his usual didactic style and speaks repeatedly in the first person plural: "We refuse to subject our wills to the will of God and attempt to make his will subject to our lust." [26] In the case of those who deny God altogether there is a lack of any feeling for justice and love — even the natural conscience in such a state offers scant guidance and sustenance. Spiritual death also occurs among those who confess the Christian faith, seen in the many acts of temptation to which the godly succumb. A righteous man makes a trial of God's perfection or power or knowledge by setting a time and space limit on divine activity. A faithful man tempts God by living in despair and not in hope. A hopeful man tempts God by not using the

25. For the treatment of Genesis, see I, viii, 61–80, p. 105. Ames discusses love and marriage further in II, xix, 25, 39, 40, and 42, beginning p. 318.

26. II, xii, 14, p. 276. The same usage occurs in II, xii, 1, 15, 16, beginning p. 275. For another vivid discussion of sin, see I, xiv–xvii, p. 121.

means that are necessary for the goal of his hope. If he looks for a restoration of health he refuses medicine and food. Or if he wishes for inner strength, he does not reflect upon the meaning of the sacrament or study the word of God. All men know or have known spiritual death in some degree. Echoing the bishop of Hippo, Ames says that human pride is the cause of this death. In our inevitable arrogance we refuse to listen to God's will for us, or we try to make his will subject to our schemes and even our lust. We are like the supposed good King David whom Nathan rebuked, "Why have you despised the word of the Lord in doing what is evil in his eyes (2 Sam. 12:9)?" [27]

The picture of man's nature is best set forth in the biblical account of Adam. The first man of the Genesis story is not regarded primarily as a private person like the angels (although Ames is convinced that Adam was the first historic human being). He is above all a public person, representing the head or epitome of man's nature. He stands as a symbol of both the image of God given to man and the actuality of man's sin and evil. Adam can be said to be a cause of man's later punishment, exacted because of the original disobedience. But Adam's real significance is not as a cause but as a type. He stands for all men who fail to trust God and repeatedly yield to the temptations of lesser powers and attractions. The Genesis account graphically personifies temptation in the form of the devil. Ames, like Augustine, does not see any great cosmic battle between creator and devil looming in the biblical story. The devil — sometimes Ames speaks of devils — represents in Genesis' stark and vivid language man's constant potential for exercising his pride in sin and turning away from God. Adam is everyman.[28] In the *Conscience*, Ames lays it down that each decision should be preceded by an examination of one's state which includes a grasp of the means of grace but, first, a knowledge of the Adamic ambiguity in one's self.[29]

In his discussion with the Remonstrants, Ames considers the role of the human will and displays, perhaps more than anywhere else, his indebtedness to St. Augustine. It is the will that must be changed in order to control the pervasive sin of man; the enlightening of the mind is not enough. Ames follows the argument of the *City of God* that a man is known by what he loves. A man may be an earthly citizen and live in godless love of self or a heavenly citizen and live in selfless love of God, or he may find, as the honest, faithful man usually does, that he has a dual citizenship. The kind of love that prevails and dominates is determined by what a man wills. Ames's dispute with the

27. II, viii, 23, p. 256.
28. See I, x, xii; II, viii, 28; and II, xii, 26, pp. 110, 116, 257, 277.
29. *De conscientia*, II, i, p. 34.

Remonstrants, like Augustine's with the Pelagians, centered on the insistence that only God can work effectually to change a man's will. There is no inner power by which the will converts itself. The prime responsibility of the religious life is to open the will to the possibility of God's restoring activity. A persistent theme in all the Amesian writings is that God is truly engaged in converting the will of man. "It is God that works in you both to will and to do his own good pleasure (Phil. 2:13)." [30]

Last, in an area of social thought, Ames takes almost point for point an Augustinian position espoused by most medieval Catholic theologians, Renaissance humanists, Luther, and Calvin. In book two of the *Marrow* he discusses the conditions under which Christians may participate in war. He advances Augustine's theory of the "just war." Participation is lawful only when there is a just authority commanding the action, a just intention, a just manner, and a lawful cause. Like Augustine, Ames is convinced that all these categories of justness can be weighed accurately and fully by men. When everything is properly analyzed it will be discovered that the war is just for only one side; if that side is yours, there can be no guilt over participation even if it involves the taking of the enemy's life. [31]

The late scholastic tradition from the thirteenth to the seventeenth centuries is also source material for William Ames. His opposition to papal authority, to the Roman Catholic doctrine of the church and sacraments, and to the Thomistic stress on the importance of intellect and logic do not prevent a partial dependence on late medieval theology. A reader of the *Marrow* and the *Conscience* notices especially Ames's respect for the analytical skill of Thomas Aquinas, although the Puritan divine and the angelic doctor part company on such basic considerations as the nature of theology and the meaning of the religious life. Ames even finds Aristotle, the venerated Philosopher of the *Summa theologica*, and the Peripatetics, to be dependable aids in his search for consistency and order in theology. The Protestant writings of the early seventeenth century frequently dismissed Aristotle as a protopapist. Ames, too, is critical of Aristotelianism, finding his orientation in another logician and philosopher, Peter Ramus (1515–72), but he is not prepared to dismiss the force and relevance of Aris-

30. I, xxvi, 23, p. 159. See Horton, *Ames by Reuter*, pp. 184–85, 202.
31. II, xviii, 43–46, p. 317. Ames stresses that intention is the most difficult, but the most necessary, to assess. A ruler and a participant must sincerely intend to vindicate justice and restore peace. On the whole subject of the just war, see Robert P. Adams, *The Better Part of Valor: More, Erasmus, Colet, and Vives on Humanism, War, and Peace*, 1496–1535 (University of Washington Press, Seattle, 1962), and Roland H. Bainton, *Christian Attitudes toward War and Peace* (Abingdon Press, New York, 1960).

totle's thought. A form of Aristotelian syllogism is used occasionally in
the *Marrow*, more often in the *Conscience* and in the polemical works,
especially *Bellarmine Disarmed*.[32]

To the perennial question of "Who is my neighbor?" Ames offers
essentially the answer of Thomas Aquinas. Ames speaks occasionally
as a Luther, maintaining that every person is a neighbor and that
neighbor love falls under the general, categorical demand to be a
Christ to one's brother.[33] But in practical living a moment of calcu-
lation must enter — even a moment of shrewdness. We should love
our neighbor according to certain orders of comparison inherited from
the scholastic tradition — blood kin more than strangers, among kin
those nearest to us more than those removed, a special friend more
than ordinary kin. Those who have done good things to us, especially
those who have helped us in things of the spirit, are more to be loved
than those who have not; Ames refers to Galatians 6:6 in this connection, "Let him who is taught the word communicate to him that
taught him all good things." [34] Ames does not espouse the Thomistic
point that we should love most of all those who are most pleasing to
us, but without question he avoids any insistence on the absolute, im-
possible-to-be-fulfilled character of the second great commandment.
The love of neighbor is chiefly an injunction to those of a particular
community, to be applied within that community. The Amesian interpretation provides a basis and a clue to the early American zeal for
taking care of the household of faith even to the neglect of those outside, no matter what their suffering and plight.

Ames leans heavily on Thomas in sections of the *Marrow* and the
Conscience which develop a personal economic ethic, especially in
book five of the latter where contracts, interest, and profits are discussed.[35] A contract is based on a freedom of agreement between two
parties mutually pledged to obey the stipulations of the contract and
is expressed by means of an outward sign. Ames notes that exorbitant
usury is condemned by the Bible but that all forms of interest or profit
making from the loan of money are not prohibited. The Jews were
allowed to lend money with interest to the Gentiles (Deut. 23:20).
The New Testament parable of the talents has primarily a spiritual
meaning, but the words of the master to the servant should be construed as condoning a kind of usury: " Then you ought to have in-
vested my money with the bankers, and at my coming I should have
received what was my own with interest (Matt. 25:27)." The profit

32. For an example in the *Marrow*, see I, vi, 8, p. 92. The use of syllogism is discussed below in the section on Ramist logic, pp. 37–47.
33. II, xvi, 3, p. 246.
34. II, xvi, 28, p. 249.
35. *De conscientia*, V, xliii–xlv, p. 284.

from money loans should depend on the success or failure of the venture engaged in by the borrower; there should be no set figure by the lender. The loaning of money at interest is primarily a way of helping the neighbor (Deut. 24:10–13), not a true vocation. Ames, like Thomas, surrounds an acceptance of usury with strictures about the use of wealth, the definition of money, and the meaning of honest employment.[36]

The library of William Ames contained a surprising number of medieval Roman Catholic authors. Ames used these books not only to dispute and challenge, as in the case of Bellarmine's works, but to instruct and amplify his own teachings. Peter Lombard (1100?–1164), Bonaventura (1221–1274), Duns Scotus (1265?–1308?), William of Paris (fl. 1310), Thomas Cajetan (1469–1534), Francisco Suarez (1548–1617), and especially the author of *sacra doctrina*, Thomas Aquinas (1225–74), were his helpmates. In "To the Reader" of the *Conscience*, Ames admits that these authors have "veins of silver from which, I suppose, I have taken some things not to be despised." Ames mined extensively — his theory of law depends heavily on his findings in Suarez. Nevertheless, he goes on to say, their teaching is often without life. The schoolmen did not influence him mightily; Ames was not of their inner spirit. His deepest inspiration and continued guidance came from the great Puritan fathers in England. With them he felt himself to be one in mind and heart.

ENGLISH PURITANISM — THE AMESIAN MARROW ·

SIGNS OF A PURITAN · While a student at Christ's College in Cambridge, William Ames began an exhaustive reading in Latin and English of Puritan works. Books by Henry Ainsworth (1571–1622 or –23), William Bradshaw (1571–1618), Nicholas Byfield (1579–1622), Thomas Cartwright (1535–1603), John Dod (1549?–1645), George Downham (d. 1634), John Downham (d. 1652), Arthur Hildersam (1563–1632), William Perkins (1558–1602), John Rainolds, or Reynolds (1549–1607), and Samuel Ward (1572–1643) formed a sizeable part of his permanent library in Holland. He hoped that his own writings would carry out the major themes of this extensive Puritan corpus. In the opening of *Conscience: Its Law or Cases*, Ames writes that he plans to emulate the approach of his teacher Perkins and

36. In commentary on Ps. 15, *Lectiones in CL Psalmos Davidis* (Amstelodami, 1635), or *Lectures on the One Hundred and Fifty Psalms of David*, Ames argues that one may rightly seek gain in aiding another. But he decries a *usuram mordentem, rodentem*, a biting, gnawing usury, which can hurt another (nearly identical words are used in *De conscientia*, V, xliv, 12, pp. 288–89). See John T. Noonan, Jr., *The Scholastic Analysis of Usury* (Harvard University Press, Cambridge, Mass., 1957).

will emphasize the practical side of theology. But Ames also wrote
as a creative individual and often broke with his colleagues in
the Puritan brotherhood. In the *Conscience* reference to Perkins,
Ames immediately says that he views conscience as an act of practical
judgment not, like Perkins, as a faculty. He often departs from his
venerated teacher — most notably, as we shall see, in the interpretation of predestination and in the use of Ramist logic. We shall discuss both his stand within the tradition and his boldness in stepping
outside. The latter point is the minor of the two, for Ames was to his
very end an English Puritan.

At least one of Ames's differences with his Puritan colleagues ended
in permanent misunderstanding and acrimony. In section eleven of
book two, the *Marrow* deals with lots, or the casting of a die to settle
a dispute between two parties. Ames holds that a lot can be rightly
employed after all reasonable attempts to solve the issue have been
employed and after both parties agree to treat the result of the lot as
a final decision. Under such conditions, a lot will express the special
providence of God, whose will it always is that a dispute be settled.
"The lot is cast into the lap, but the whole judgment is of the Lord
(Prov. 16:33)" [37] This curious, belabored point in the *Marrow* is in
part an answer to Thomas Gataker (1574–1654), influential London
divine and lecturer at Lincoln's Inn, who first set forth his position
several years after Ames left England. Gataker amplified his views in
two later tracts, speaking against all lot throwers, astrologists, and
other predictors. Such persons, he declares, cannot be depended upon
"for discovery of God's will and purpose, either what he would have
done by us, or determineth himself to do." [38] The will of God, continues Gataker, is found only in a critical study of the Scriptures; even
in the Bible there is no guarantee that particular disputes between persons can be arbitrarily decided. Ames was upholding a peculiar position — one which he felt evolved not only from God's general sovereignty, but from his actual working power in everything. It was a
common opinion among continental Reformed theologians. But to
many fellow Puritans and later followers, the Franeker professor appeared artificial and erroneous.

William Ames bore the usual marks of the early seventeenth-cen-

37. II, xi, 1, p. 271.
38. Thomas Gataker, *A Discourse Apologetical* (London, 1654), p. 21.
Gataker's earlier tracts on the subject were, *Of the Nature and Use of Lots*
(London, 1619) and *Antithesis, partim Guilielmi Amesii, partim Gisberti
Voetii de sorte thesibus reposita* (Londini, 1638). The practice of determining
divine will by casting lots continued to be used, especially in America. The
First Church of Christ in Middletown, Conn., cast a lot in 1715 to settle
the location of its meeting house.

tury English Puritan. He had, first of all, a zeal for church reformation. The Amesian view, to be examined in detail later, held for the abandonment of the hierarchy of the Church of England and the substitution of a system of independent but associated congregations as polity for the established church. He also called for a return to simplicity in worship, involving the elimination of kneeling, images, and all "superstition." [39] He was a sabbatarian. The most documented chapter in the *Marrow* deals with the sabbath, arguing that a day of rest and worship has its foundation not only in the Old and New Testaments, but in classical Greek and Latin writers as well. For Ames, the sabbath was more than a demand to cease from labor and worldly pursuits. It was primarily an enabling decree, for it offered man a stated time to participate in public worship to reflect on the resurrection of Christ — that event particularly solemnized by the Christian sabbath.[40]

THE REFORMED TRADITION. CHRISTOLOGY · The genius of English Puritanism which Ames shared and perpetuated is known by characteristics other than those commonly associated with the name "Puritan." The English movement of the late sixteenth and seventeenth centuries is above all a form of evangelical Calvinism. Its leaders depended heavily on the thought of the *Institutes of the Christian Religion* and the Genevan reformer's commentaries. Perkins, George Downham, Bradshaw, Ames, and the others also turned readily to Calvin's immediate followers such as Beza, Bucer, Rollock, and Bullinger. Ames and his colleagues stand within a broad theological tradition that bound together a host of reformers in Switzerland, France, Holland, England, and Scotland.[41]

39. II, xiii, 23 ff., p. 280. See Ames's last work, *A Fresh Suit against Human Ceremonies in God's Worship* (Rotterdam, 1633).

40. II, xv, p. 287. Two editions of Ames's tract, *Sententia de origine Sabbathi et die Dominico,* or *An Opinion on the Origin of the Sabbath and the Lord's Day,* were brought out posthumously: the one (Amstelodami, 1658) by Nathaneal Eaton (1609?–1674), student of Ames at Franeker and later the strange first head of Harvard, and the other by Christianus Schotanus (1603–71) with intro. (n.p., n.d.). See Horton, *Ames by Visscher,* pp. 133–40. Eaton also wrote a thesis under Ames's direction, *Inquisitio in variantes theologorum quorandam sententias de sabbato* (Franekerae, 1633), or *An Examination of the Diverse Opinions Held by Certain Theologians concerning the Sabbath.* Ames differed only in minor detail from other sabbatarians in the Reformed tradition, e.g., Bownd, Perkins, Teelinck, Walaeus. All of them depended heavily upon the findings and arguments of the late scholastics, especially Francisco Suarez (1548–1617).

41. For the Calvinist core of English Puritanism and the Reformed tradition see my *Puritans, Lawyers, and Politics in Early Seventeenth-Century England* (Yale University Press, New Haven, 1958), pp. 9–40. For a view that denies an distinct theological identity to Puritanism see Charles H. and Kath-

A reader of the early seventeenth-century English Puritans is soon aware that he is confronting material quite different from that found in the writings of Martin Luther.[42] We have already noted that Ames held a concept of neighbor love less radical than that of Luther, a position typical of English Puritanism. We could also point to the differing views which Luther and the Reformed tradition held on the relationship of law and gospel; the Reformed was inclined to make a greater positive use of law, both in its scriptural and civil form, whence a legalism as seen, for example, in decrees about the sabbath.[43]

Perhaps the greatest contrast occurs, at least when one reads Ames, in concepts about the person and work of Christ. The Christocentrism of Martin Luther is not shared by most English Puritans. Christ for them was a necessary part of the divine-human drama, but they did not feel a deep, confessional attraction towards him as a divine person. The best Puritan New Testament commentary was not on the gospels, but on the Book of Acts and the letters of Paul. Luther also commented extensively on Paul, but at the same time he wrote much, in perhaps his most moving style, on the Word in the the gospels. One of his longest commentaries deals with just the first four chapters of the Gopel according to John. The Puritans did not walk on the Lutheran *via crucis*; or, if they did, they traveled hurriedly and often without imagination. The incarnation for the Puritans was not a mystery in which man should lose himself; it was to be explained and placed before man as an article of faith. Ames's favorite device for representing the two natures in Christ was to choose biblical passages describing a unique quality or action of Christ and conclude that Christ must be both man and God. For example, in the scriptural presentation of Christ as a sacrifice it is necessary that Christ be God so that the sacrifice should have sufficient force, but also that he be man so that the sacrifice would be suitable.[44]

---

erine George, *The Protestant Mind of the English Reformation, 1570–1640* (Princeton University Press, Princeton, 1961). An interpretation critical of the Georges is taken by John F. H. New, *Anglican and Puritan: The Basis of Their Opposition, 1558–1640* (Stanford University Press, Stanford, 1964), and by David Little, "The Logic of Order: An Examination of the Sources of Puritan-Anglican Controversy . . ." (unpub. diss., Harvard, 1963).

42. No work by Martin Luther is listed in the *Catalogus variorum et insignium librorum clarissimi et celeberrimi viri D. Guilielmi Amesii* (Amstelodami, 1634), or *Catalogue of the Varied and Significant Books of the Most Illustrious and Celebrated Dr. William Ames.*

43. See E. Gordon Rupp, "Luther and the Puritans," in *Luther Today* (Luther College Press, Decorah, Iowa, 1957), for Luther's relationship to selected Continental reformers (not the English Puritan fathers).

44. I, xix, 20, p. 133. Ames presents basically an Anselmic interpretation of the atonement, stressing Christ's "satisfaction." See n. 116, p. 53.

The Calvinist understanding of the three offices of Christ as prophet, priest, and king supplied further general categories within which the incarnation could be understood. Luther chose to present the incarnation more simply, yet more profoundly, as the offering of divine love before which sinful men stood in awe and in thanksgiving. He would have understood the thrust of the remark that he who says he knows all about the incarnation knows nothing about the incarnation. Finally, Ames and his associates were more concerned with the ascension and exaltation of Christ than with his presence on earth as the God-man. The glory of Christ was the ultimate point for the Puritans to emphasize in Christology, not divine participation in a humble life, the agony of the cross, or the role of suffering in redemption.[45]

The Calvinist core from which Puritan thought emanated with variations is further distinguished by its thought on the nature and knowledge of God, divine sovereignty, predestination, and the stages of salvation. And English Puritanism is identified by at least one other characteristic, connected with the Reformed tradition, but uniquely Puritan in elaboration: a stress on the work of the Holy Spirit in religious experience.

NATURE AND KNOWLEDGE OF GOD · Ames warns his readers that they must be aware of inescapable limitations in their search for an understanding of God. Like Calvin (and Luther, Hugh of St. Victor, Peter Lombard, and Augustine), Ames speaks of God as both *revelatus,* revealed or known, and *absconditus,* hidden or unknown. In this life we are confronted mainly by *Deus absconditus* — not that God is withdrawn, but that he is veiled and always beyond our powers of conception. We shall know of him but not about him. It will be with us as it was with Moses: "And the Lord said, 'Behold there is a place by me where you shall stand upon the rock . . . and you shall see my back parts; but my face cannot be seen (Exod. 33:21–23).'" Yet, some things can be said about God, granted human limitations. We can truthfully proclaim in the language of the New Testament that God is a spirit (John 4:24). The God of Christian faith is a special kind of spirit — he is, says Ames, a spirit living from himself. The sufficiency and living quality of God are the characteristics which set him apart from all idols and other representations of divinity. Ames insists that God is not only a life-having spirit, but a life-producing spirit. His creative, life-producing power has no limitation of space or time; this assertion, Ames believes, is the foundation of the Christian belief in eternal life. In faith we apprehend a life everlasting be-

45. I, xxiii, p. 144.

cause of its creation by an eternal living spirit, a life in which the
present form is but one phase.[46]

Human virtues may be used in speaking about God, but only those
virtues towards which we aspire, not those which are concessions to
human pride, such as humility, self-control, and shamefacedness. We
may speak of God's perfect goodness and wisdom. The story of creation, especially, displays these qualities of God: His goodness is shown
in his creation of plants, herbs, and trees before the sun which was to
be a cause in their growth; domiciles before inhabitants; food before
animals; and things useful to man before Adam. Divine wisdom is
seen in the structure and logic of creation, for those things were created first which only have being, next those with being and life, and
then those which have being, life, and sense, and finally those which
have being, life, sense and reason.[47]

Philosophical terms may also be used to adumbrate the nature of
God. Using a scholastic pattern familiar to the Reformed tradition,
Ames writes of three modes of divine being. God is known in his essence (*essentia*), his subsistence (*subsistentia*), and his efficiency or
working power (*efficientia*). The first two are usually linked together
in the *Conscience* and the *Marrow* and are held to comprise God's
sufficiency, or divine completeness. God's essence receives the least
emphasis, for it is the least likely to be grasped by human minds —
and by practical theology. It represents "that by which he is absolutely the first being," not only because of his eternity but because
of his oneness, his uncausedness, and his immutability.[48] The subsistence of God is his being in its quality of making itself known.
Divine subsistence is expressed through the persons of the Trinity
which represent different forms or "properties" of one and the same
God. Ames uses a traditional description of the Trinity presented in
the *Institutes of the Christian Religion*. The Savior-Son is begotten in
spiritual generation from the Creator-Father and the Sanctifier-Holy
Spirit proceeds from both Father and Son. Spiritual generation is not
the same as physical or temporal generation. Father, Son, and Holy
Spirit are of God eternally and equally; there was not a time when
one existed without the others. They comprise, each in his own way,
the subsistence of God known to man in creation, salvation, and
spiritual maintenance.[49]

The third mode of divine being, efficiency or working power, receives Ames's greatest attention. Although briefly presented in book

46. See I, iv, especially 3, 33–37, 46–49, beginning p. 83.
47. I, viii, 57–58, p. 105.
48. I, iv, 13–32, p. 84.
49. I, v, p. 88.

one, it is a major unifying theme throughout the *Marrow*, the *Conscience*, and his commentaries. Scholastic philosophy insisted on two considerations, or actions, which must be distinguished in the understanding of anything, including God: *esse* and *operari*, being and performing or functioning. Ames was always more concerned with the action or the performing of God. The supreme nature of God is to act in an all-powerful fashion. The effect of God's power on us is what enables us to know anything about God. The nature of God's mercy is to show mercy and of God's love to love. The concept of God with which Ames is most content is that God is single, most pure, most simple act (*actus*). All other so-called attributes flow from this consideration. God's omnipotence, in short, is his efficiency.[50]

The *Marrow* presents a God who, in good Reformed theology, suffers no impediment to the carrying out of his will. Ames offers, for example, a brief exegesis of Christ's healing the leper in Matthew 8:1–4. He considers the point of the miracle story to be a demonstration of God's unquestioned ability to move from will to power: " 'Lord, if you will, you can make me clean.' And he stretched out his hand and touched him, saying, 'I will; be clean.' And immediately his leprosy was cleansed." Ames speaks out against *velleitas*, or "woulding," a position on God's will held by a few scholastics, who maintained that God would do certain things if certain conditions were present. Ames rejoins, "This does not agree with an omniscient, omnipotent, and infinitely blessed nature." God's will and power are unconditional, not dependent upon the power or even existence of anything else. To be sure, God can will that one thing be an instrument for another, but this does not mean that the first causes the second or that the first causes God to will the second. God willed and acted so that the sun and stars should exist for the generation, conservation, and corruption of "things below." But the sun and stars have no willing power of their own and they did not cause God to will that things below be generated, conserved, and corrupted; they were only sequential means of carrying out the divine will.[51]

Ames uses a traditional distinction between *potentia absoluta* and *potentia ordinata* to explain why God does not do certain things if, indeed, he has the power. The absolute power of God is his ability to do all things, even though some shall never come to pass. "God is able from these stones to raise up children unto Abraham (Matt. 3:9)." God has the power to raise up such children, but he has not chosen to do so. The human mind even when enlightened by Christian faith cannot know why God in his absolute power has chosen to

50. I, vi, p. 91.
51. I, vi, 8; vii, 42, 40, beginning pp. 92, 98.

will and do certain things and not to will and do others. The word *ordinata* means more to Ames than "ordained," indicating in the traditional sense the power of God operating through the laws he has decreed. *Potentia ordinata* relates to the sure, present power of God in offering salvation to men. The word "ordaining" is a better translation; Ames himself at the introduction of the term writes " or actual" (*ordinata sive actualis*). Man should rest in the ordaining power of God which he can know and trust. This power is not dimly stated in an hypothesis that God can do whatever he wills, but is fully known in the assurance that he always wills and does certain things. He is always acting to redeem and restore men; he always acts to comfort and protect. " This was according to the eternal purpose which he has realized in Christ Jesus our Lord, in whom we have boldness and confidence of access through our faith in him. So I ask you not to lose heart (Eph. 3:11–13)." Let man not limit the ordaining power of God, for he who is " at work within us is able to do far more abundantly than all that we ask or think (Eph. 3:20)." [52]

DIVINE SOVEREIGNTY. POLITICAL THEORY. PREDESTINATION · Ames found, as did Calvin, that much of God's ordaining power can be expressed in a concept of divine sovereignty. God's governing power or his rule must be acknowledged in society as well as in the religious life of individual men. Ames supported his Puritan colleagues in England who, holding a vivid belief in the rule of God, fought against the absolute rule of James I and Charles I. Because God ruled everywhere, the Puritans claimed, no mortal king had an unlimited right to govern. Nor could a king assert, let alone implement, a "divine right" kingship, as James set forth in *The True Law of Free Monarchies*. The early English Puritan concern for divine sovereignty in the body politic stressed a relationship between institutions. The individual was not given central political consideration, nor were the "rights of man" — this emphasis was to come later in the Puritanism of the Great Rebellion, greatly aided by secular political thought which claimed little association with divine sovereignty. The great political contribution of pre-1640 Puritanism was the insistence that all institutions depended

52. I, vi, 18–20, p. 93. On the classic distinction between *potentia absoluta* and *ordinata*, see Heiko A. Oberman, *The Harvest of Medieval Theology: Gabriel Biel and Late Medieval Nominalism* (Harvard University Press, Cambridge, Mass., 1963), pp. 36 ff., and the helpful "Nominalistic Glossary," pp. 459–76, containing many other terms used by Ames; also Francis C. Oakley, *The Political Thought of Pierre d'Ailly: The Voluntarist Tradition* (Yale University Press, New Haven, 1964). Albertus Magnus (1193?–1280) was the first to make a systematic distinction between the two powers, although the terms had been employed before, e.g., by the canonist Innocent IV (pope 1243–54).

on the rule of God known in the Bible, rightly understood and applied, and in his rule in the law of the land, or the English common law tradition. The crown could not lord it over the common law courts or Parliament or the church. Nor could the powerful Long Parliament rule without limit, even in war time. Each institution owed supreme allegiance to God, not another institution; each had its distinct role to play; each was needed in the life of the commonwealth. The Puritans fashioned, with their allies the common lawyers, a theory about institutional independence based on a division of power.[53]

Ames encouraged this line of thought and the revolutionary action to which it led. He pointed out in the *Conscience* that no magistrate, whatever his office, had unlimited power to govern. A ruler was limited by the will of God and the will of man, both of which included the laws on which the power of a particular dominion was founded. Ames warned against the evils of an unbounded kingship, referring to the hard words found in 1 Samuel 8:11–7: "These shall be the ways of the king who will reign over you: he will take your sons and appoint them to his chariots . . . he will take your daughters . . . he will take the best of your fields and vineyards . . . the best of your cattle . . . and you shall be his slaves. And in that day you will cry out because of your king." [54] In the *Marrow* Ames writes that obedience to superiors must never be blind. The responsible Christian citizen is called to examine the reason for obedience, to see if that which is commanded is lawful and binding.[55] Had Ames stayed in England, he undoubtedly would have been drawn into greater political expression and action as were his friends Baynes, Bradshaw, Preston, and Gouge.

Removed from the political conflicts of his native land, Ames turned his attention more to the religious meaning of divine sovereignty. For individuals the rule of God was most vividly known in the idea of predestination. This ancient idea, emphasized by John Calvin, Ames found useful but also in need of change. In the last edition of the *Institutes of the Christian Religion,* Calvin put down his theory of double predestination in decisive language. God had willed some to eternal salvation and some to eternal damnation; these were decrees of a sovereign God which would be carried out. One tends to forget that the Calvin of the earlier *Institutes* did not consider predestination to be a central theological concern. Even in his later life Calvin insisted that double predestination was not rashly to be proclaimed; its harshness and essential mystery did not make it a fit subject for

53. A thesis of my *Puritans, Lawyers, and Politics* (Yale University Press, New Haven, 1958).
54. *De conscientia,* V, xxv, 3, 4, p. 235.
55. II, xvii, 56, p. 312.

preaching; and it should never be included in children's catechisms. William Ames could speak as decisively about predestination as did the later Calvin and a possible interpretation is to say that he only echoed the predominant thought of the Genevan reformer. Ames supported all those who defended predestination against the Remonstrants. On the title page of his book, *Disputatio theologica de perfectione SS. Scripturae*, or *A Theological Discussion on the Perfection of the Holy Scripture*, appears a reference to William Barlee, minister in Northamptonshire, who wrote a widely read orthodox book on predestination. The *Marrow* describes three definite steps for both election and reprobation: the determination of the divine will, the appointment of certain men, the preparation of the proper means to carry out the divine decision. Ames writes that God knows not only how many shall be saved, but who the actual men are. He cites Romans 9:13 and Mal. 1:2–3 many times as the scriptural basis for double predestination: "As it is written, 'Jacob I loved, but Esau I hated.'" [56] Yet, when all of Ames's views on predestination are weighed, it is discovered that questions and qualifications are more important than any bald statement of the theory.

In the *Marrow* and the *Conscience*, predestination is not presented as the warp and woof of theology. In orthodox Reformed thought, predestination was often the primary consideration in a dogmatic system, other points being deduced from it. Ames refuses to say that a believer, or would-be one, must confront the division among men made by the eternal decree of God before considering other parts of the Christian proclamation. As we shall see, the meaning of faith and an understanding of the spiritual life come first. The single chapter on predestination in the *Marrow* occupies a peculiar position compared with most Puritan and Reformed treatises. It is found nearly two thirds of the way through book one, following the chapters on faith, the nature of God, sin, and the person and work of Christ. There is no mention of predestination until its separate consideration in chapter twenty-five — not even in the long chapter which deals with the decree and counsel of God. Chapter twenty-five precedes the chapters dealing with vocation, justification, adoption, sanctification, and glorification. William Perkins, in the *Golden Chain: Or the Description of Theology*, following Beza, had discussed predestination under the general heading of the work of God. Ames did not follow his teacher, but considered predestination as a transitional theme between the work of Christ and the description of the Christian life. This positioning is important, for it shows that Ames believes predestination to have chiefly an instrumental value. It leads and points to the Chris-

56. I, xxv, especially 20–24, p. 152.

tian life. It is a way of assuring the believer that he can expect the
blessings of the Christian life which are then presented in the chapters which immediately follow.

In Ames's concern with election, almost to the neglect of reprobation, predestination is set down as a hopeful promise. Election to salvation is sure and, therefore, one can rightly expect the "application"
of the work of Christ. God's election is clearly *pre*-destining; it does
not follow, confirm, or depend upon anything. The Remonstrants
depicted election as a sequence or as a result of man's faith and good
works. But election is always prior in the sense that it sets before us
our destiny. By virtue of God's decree we are made ready to become
what we were intended to be from eternity. The believer should view
predestination as an incentive to introspection and personal spiritual
testing. Although it comes from eternity, the decree of God has no
effect on the predestined person until Christ's saving work is known
and the Christian life is being lived. Predestination should lead a man
to inquiry about calling and regeneration and to searching for the way
in which the Christian life can be known. Predestination is an invitation to begin one's spiritual pilgrimage — with the implicit warning
that the certainty of God's decree shall not be known until one does
begin. Thus predestination is not primarily a theory about foreordina-
tion; it is a statement of surety to those who have already been saved
by God's gracious act. It is ultimately an expression of the beneficent
will of God, not an inquiry into the divine mind and reason. The doctrine of predestination assures men that God has willed and is acting
in his power to restore and justify them through his love.[57] It is, in
short, a "comfortable doctrine."

But not all men can be expected to experience the surety of God's
saving decree, for some have been appointed to reprobation. Ames
does not consider the state of damnation in a separate chapter as did
most of his contemporaries; it is found in the brief, concluding eleven
sections (out of forty-one) in the single chapter on predestination.
One comes upon it in the *Marrow* almost as a reluctant appendage.
It is the dark shadow of election. The differences between Ames and
his teacher Perkins and the leading Reformed continental theologians
are pronounced. First, Ames at no point speculates on the state or
condition of the reprobate either in this life or in eternity.[58] Second,
reprobation is not connected with the mediation of Christ who came
only to save men and in no sense to deny and punish. Third, God's

57. See Horton, *Ames by Reuter*, pp. 248–54.
58. See William Perkins, *A Golden Chain: Or the Description of Theology*, in *Works* (London, 1616), I: 105–12. Also consult *A Treatise Tending
unto a Declaration whether a Man Be in the State of Damnation, or in the
State of Grace*, in *Works*, I: 351–420.

decree in reprobation results from divine omission, not commission. Election may be called an action and decree of God, but Ames finds it difficult to use such terms in the case of reprobation. He writes that God has merely not bestowed on some the good he has graciously conferred on others. Nowhere in this brief section is there a picture of a God who in vengeance or wrath appoints certain men to destruction. He is shown rather as a withholding God. Because he withholds from some, "He is *said* to hate them"; [59] but reprobation does not truly imply a God of hatred. Nor is God represented as the cause of the sin and evil which is in the reprobate (again in contrast to Perkins). All men sin and sin mightily, whether elect or reprobate. As with sin in general, God's withholding in reprobation is antecedent in that it permits actual transgression; God no more causes the sin of the reprobate than he causes the sin of the elect. To be sure, he punishes the sins of the reprobate whereas he forgives the sins of the elect, according to the mystery of his own counsel and will.

Ames is typically concerned with the meaning of reprobation in the personal lives of men. He finds it, in sum, to be of little or no account for the actual living of the Christian life. Indeed, its chief uses are a warning to the elect and an exhortation to charity and humility. In book two, Ames writes that in this life God never reveals to those who shall not be partakers of grace and glory their actual condition. All men should act as if they were members of the elect; they should not be despondent over what they might feel to be a state of damnation. Despair over one's ultimate condition is a sin for which one needs to ask God's forgiveness.[60] Ames admonishes those who think they can tell when another is in a state of reprobation. In the chapter preceding his discussion of predestination, he writes that the temporal benefits of Christ's work apply to all, that is, the teaching, death, and resurrection of Christ have relevance and meaning for elect and reprobate. The benefits of the glorified and exalted Christ do not have equal application, for Christ will plead before the Father only in behalf of those appointed from eternity. But since "these counsels of God are hidden to us," it is well for us to make no distinctions between elect and reprobate in this life and "it is the part of charity to judge well of everyone." [61] Finally, in our prayers we should not reject any man from spiritual communion "for conjectures or probable signs of reprobation," although we may not pray that all men be saved for we know that some have been determined by God not to be.[62]

59. I, xxv, 37, p. 156. Editor's italics.
60. II, vi, 30, p. 249.
61. I, xxiv, 8–9, p. 150.
62. II, ix, 71, p. 264. Among English Puritan colleagues, Richard Sibbes (1577–1635) stands closest to Ames in qualifying reprobation.

In the midst of these radical departures, why does Ames still cling to the idea of reprobation? If the major point in predestination is that God leads men to the Christian life and assures them by election, how can the same God be one who also withholds and omits? An answer is that reprobation is held to be part of the unlimited sovereignty of God whose will must be completely free. No Reformed theologian would accept qualification of God's rule — even when given a minor place, reprobation corroborates the basic canon. Ames followed Calvin in finding scriptural support for the connection between reprobation and divine sovereignty. They both turned to Paul: "Has the potter no right over the clay, to make out of the same lump one vessel for beauty and another for menial use? What if God, desiring to show his wrath and to make known his power, has endured with much patience the vessels of wrath made for destruction, in order to make known the riches of his glory for the vessels of mercy, which he has prepared beforehand for glory (Rom. 9:21–23)." [63] But for Ames reprobation was shrouded in greater mystery than it was for Calvin and his most direct descendants. God's withholding and omission were part of God's absolute power, forever beyond the ken of man — and even beyond man's concern. It would never be known fully why God does not save all men; surely he has the power to do so, just as he has the power to raise up children to Abraham from stones, but he has chosen not to. God's election and salvation, on the other hand, were part of God's ordaining power which was known fully and rejoiced in by men. Several generations of theologians would live, write, and die before it could be said that reprobation was unnecessary for divine sovereignty and that assurance in election compromised God's total action towards men. The Franeker professor would have denied such assertions. But more than any other theologian in the early seventeenth-century Reformed tradition, William Ames was tending toward these ideas of the future.[64]

STAGES OF THE CHRISTIAN LIFE. THE CALLING · Ames's description of the Christian life is essentially a long exegesis of a key passage for Reformed theology: "And those whom he predestined he also called; and those whom he called he also justified; and those whom he justified he also glorified (Rom. 8:30)." The good doctor exceeds St. Paul by speaking of five states rather than the original three, although the two added, adoption and sanctification, are discussed by Paul in other

63. I, xxv, 30, p. 155. 2 Thess. 2:12 and Jude 4 are also cited.
64. Gottlob Schrenk, *Gottesreich und Bund im älteren Protestantismus vornehmlich bei Johannes Cocceius* (C. Bertelsmann, Gutersloh, 1923), pp. 44, 52, maintains that wherever covenant thought predominates, a weakening of predestinarian ideas takes place.

places. Ames generally follows the simplicity of presentation found in
Calvin and the English Puritans; he is unconcerned with an elaborate
proliferation of stages, such as is found in Amandus Polanus (1561–
1610) and Hermann Witsius (1636–1708) who speculated, respec-
tively, on nine and ten steps.[65] William Perkins spoke simply of effective calling, justification, sanctification, and glorification. His pupil
was of almost the same mind.

Ames describes calling, or vocation, as an effective spiritual relationship with Christ. He uses the word "union" in speaking about
this first stage, whereas the word "communion," or participation, is
used in the discussion of the other four. The point of the distinction
is that in calling a believer is subjectively drawn to the person of
Christ and that in the other stages he objectively shares the benefits
of the work of Christ.

Ames does not use the word union in a mystical sense; not once
does he refer to the famous Pauline words, "It is no longer I who
live, but Christ who lives in me (Gal. 2:20)," although he does mention the eucharistic saying in John 6:56, " He abides in me, and I in
him." Union means to Ames, first, the attraction which men naturally have for the person of Jesus Christ. Men are said to be in union
as they desire to know more about Christ and his way. Believers do
not lose their own unique, concrete existence by dwelling in some new
form in Christ. Rather, in the spirit of St. Paul in Galatians, they
seek after Christ: "For as many of you as were baptized into Christ
have put on Christ (Gal. 3:27)." To be in union with Christ also
means to be gathered unto Christ, to experience along with other men
a living bond with the risen Lord. Ames finds that the sense of being
gathered is an identifying mark of the church, the people of God
come together because of their bond to Christ (but he insists that the
idea of being gathered must first be grasped in the lives of individual
members). Once in union the believer comes to know the enfolding
power of God's love in the life, suffering, and resurrection of Christ.
Union in calling, then, refers to what Ames considers to be the in-
eluctable pull of Christ on men and to the knowledge of God's grace
that men have when they acknowledge the call of Christ.

In order to discuss the implementation of calling, or how it is possible for that union to take place, Ames divides calling into two parts:

65. *De conscientia* discusses the stages in a slightly different order and
terminology: effective vocation, faith, justification, adoption, sanctification, and
glorification (II, v–xiii pp. 39 ff.). The *Marrow* reserves faith for a separate
and more emphatic discussion. See Horton, *Ames by Reuter*, pp. 247–48, 268.
On the whole subject of the stages, or the order of salvation, see Norman Pet-
tit, *The Heart Prepared: Grace and Conversion in Puritan Spiritual Life* (Yale
University Press, New Haven, 1966).

the offer of Christ and the receiving of him.[66] The first is God's bestowal of Christ as a sufficient and necessary means to salvation. As Peter once preached, "There is no other name under heaven given among men by which we must be saved (Acts 4:12)." However, Ames is more concerned with the second wherein, he asserts, Christ is joined to man and man to Christ. Receiving depends primarily upon the action of God, "None can come to me, unless the Father . . . draws him (John 6:44)," but it is not unconnected with man's free response. Ames consistently emphasizes the "action of God moving before and stirring up" as the crucial part of calling. He is not one to minimize, as we shall see, the need for spiritual preparation and discipline — at the end of the chapter the necessity of repentance is heavily stressed — but he is constrained to show that even the faith needed in union with Christ is the gift of God. Ames never doubts that, because of the grace of God, receiving will take place. In a typical note of assurance he refers again to the fourth gospel: "Whoever my Father gives me will come to me (John 6:37)." [67]

The idea of the calling in Calvinism and Puritanism has been the subject of extensive investigation ever since 1904–05 when Max Weber offered his interpretation of the rise of the spirit of modern capitalism. The "Weber thesis" and the ever continuing counter and qualifying statements which it has produced will not be reviewed here — enough to say that the German historian-philosopher-sociologist considered the Calvinist and Reformed concept of calling to be crucial in the connection between Protestantism and capitalism. Man was called to labor hard in a particular work in order to glorify the God who had saved him. The elect are to reflect God's glory in work because God had predestined them to eternal salvation. Productive work was both the discharge of man's duty to lead a holy and a righteous life and a way in which man showed his thankfulness to God. A believer must organize his life in the world and choose the most effective, efficient means of glorification. If a man doubted his election (and the decree was, of course, known only to God), he could reassure himself through the "signs" of hard work and a life of self-denial amid the temptations of the world. Weber argued that because of the calling "the moral conduct of the average man was thus deprived of its planless and unsympathetic character and subjected to a consistent method of conduct as a whole." [68] This plan had profound impli-

66. A similar division had been made by Robert Rollock (1555?–1599), A *Treatise of Our Effectual Calling*, in *Select Works* (William M. Gunn, ed. Wodrow Society, Edinburgh, 1849), I: 29–30.

67. I, xxvi, 27–28, p. 159.

68. *The Protestant Ethic and the Spirit of Capitalism* (Talcott Parsons, trans. Charles Scribner's Sons, New York, 1958), p. 117. This passage is

cations for the "rational" or systematic ethos required in modern capitalism.

The Weber analysis of the calling rings true in the case of late English and American Puritan thinkers, for example, Richard Baxter (1615–91), Samuel Willard (1640–1707), and Samuel Sewall (1652–1730). But such a conception is not presented by the *Marrow of Theology* or in the writings of Ames's contemporary Puritan colleagues. Man's glorification of God is not a generative ethical or theological idea for Ames; it is mentioned as a subsidiary point in several chapters, principally those dealing with creation and reprobation. In early Calvinism man's glorification of God is a seminal principle, even a command, put forth clearly in the *Institutes of the Christian Religion*. And the later Westminster Shorter Catechism of 1647 begins with a reference to man's chief end which is "to glorify God, and to enjoy him forever." The meaning of glorification for Calvin, the Westminster authors, and later Puritan preachers cannot be discussed in detail here. The thrust of the idea, as Weber pointed out, was that man should tend towards the glorification of God by the careful organizing of his life, especially by what he did in his work (a point more central in the later Puritan tradition than in Calvin).

Ames always uses the word calling in the Lutheran sense of the call to be a Christian, the particular Amesian interpretation of which has just been described. He does not follow Luther, however, in speaking of "particular vocation," or the work that a man does. Ames has no developed doctrine of the callings. In book two, he questions those theologians who think that "a man's particular life occupation" can be called a vocation (the only exception is the Christian ministry in which "a minister of the word is set apart to fulfill the work of the ministry"). What one does for work depends, in a common sense way, on one's inward endowments and inclinations and to a degree upon outward circumstances. "As each has received a gift, employ it for one another, as good stewards of God's varied grace (1 Peter 4:10)." [69] Work is important, but Ames did not equate it with calling or vocation. Calling was man's relationship to the saving act of God in Christ. If a man entered into union with Jesus Christ, he would work, of course, but there was no attendant imputation of spiritual qualities to labor. Lastly, calling was not tied with predestination in the way which Weber interpreted, at least in the thought of

quoted in Edmund S. Morgan's penetrating review of Kurt Samuelsson, *Religion and Economic Action* (E. Geoffrey French, trans. from the Swedish, Basic Books, New York, 1961), in *William and Mary Quarterly*, 3rd series, XX: No. 1 (Jan. 1963), 135–40.
69. II, xx, 29, 27, pp. 323, 322.

William Ames. The function of predestination was not to impel man into an organized, efficient life in the world, an "inner worldly asceticism." It was rather, as we have seen, an incentive to spiritual introspection. The point of predestination was to lead men to the stages of the Christian life; it was an invitation to sinful and anxious men that they should begin their pilgrimage of faith; and it was assurance that they had been placed on their pilgrimage by God. The Weber thesis, for all of its insight and application to other Protestant thinkers, does not fit the essential pietistic nature of the early seventeenth-century Puritan idea of calling.[70] In speaking about union with Christ in calling, Ames chose in one place the words of 1 Peter 2:4, 5, words that have little to do with the spirit of capitalism, "Come to him, to that living stone, rejected by men but in God's sight chosen and precious; and like living stones be yourselves built into a spiritual house." [71]

Justification and adoption refer to specific actions of God in the drama of redemption. In justification, God accounts a man righteous because of the work of Christ. A Pauline passage illustrates the main point: "They are justified freely by his grace, through the redemption which is in Christ Jesus, whom God put forward as an expiation by his blood, to be received by faith (Rom. 3:24, 25)." The divine act not only takes away any deserved punishment of sin but also has an

70. See Robert S. Michaelsen, "Changes in the Puritan Concept of Calling or Vocation," *New England Quarterly*, XXVI: No. 3 (Sept. 1953). The genius of the Weber thesis is an identification of the practical tendency in Puritanism and an imaginative demonstration of the process and social impact of secularization in religious ideas and institutions. See H. Stuart Hughes, *Consciousness and Society: The Reorientation of European Social Thought*, 1890–1930 (Vintage Books, New York, 1958), pp. 314 ff. See also David Little, "The Logic of Order: An Examination of the Sources of Puritan-Anglican Controversy . . ." (Unpub. diss., Harvard, 1963), for a development of the more general Weberian point that religion follows its own independent laws or "logic" and that religious beliefs have always been an instrumental force in fashioning social responses and action.

The Amesian understanding of calling as an examined and experienced union with Christ gave way to an insistence on an organized life in the world which, in turn, led to a stress on productivity and efficiency with few theological overtones. Sydney E. Ahlstrom, "Thomas Hooker — Puritanism and Democratic Citizenship," *Church History*, XXXII: No. 4 (Dec. 1963), p. 427: "Ineluctably, however, the doctrine would be secularized. By a steady, half-noticed process it would be drained of its corollaries in piety," and "The Puritan Ethic and the Spirit of American Democracy," in George L. Hunt and John T. McNeill, eds. *Calvinism and the Political Order* (Westminster Press, Philadelphia, 1965). The Yankee gospel of work and the Gilded Age's gospel of wealth do come out of early 17th-century Puritanism. But what is present at the end cannot be claimed indiscriminately for what was there in the beginning. Looking back to Calvin and the early Puritans, Weber tries to make the claim.

71. I, xxvi, 4, p. 155.

effect on man's guilt. The latter is not completely removed, but man no longer has the pursuing thoughts or the "deadly effects" of guilt. In adoption, God grants the dignity of sons to the faithful. "As many as receive him to these he gives the right to be made the sons of God, to those who believe in his name (John 1:12)." The fruits of sonship for man are Christian liberty wherein man is free from the bondage of the law, sin, and the world; a partaking of the dignity of Christ so that the faithful bear witness to God as prophets, priests, and spiritual kings; and finally a rightly exercised dominion over the creatures.[72]

Sanctification, a favorite Puritan term, is a subject for more detailed and imaginative analysis. In the discussion of justification and adoption, Ames speaks about the "relative" change in the believer, or a change which relates to the believer, but which has taken place outside of him in the will of God to justify and adopt. The remaining chapters on the stages deal with "absolute" or "real" change in the believer, or what happens within the believer as a result of God's action. Ames is seen returning again to his major concern with the actual human condition of the life of faith. When one has been made a son of God he can expect a new orientation; he will "Put off that which pertains to the old conversation, that old man, corrupting itself in deceivable lusts, and be renewed in the spirit of your mind. Put on that new man who according to God is created to righteousness and true holiness (Eph. 4:22–24)." [73] Ames employs the usual Puritan terms of mortification and vivification to describe the change. He insists that the new man of vivification will come to know the original sense of being in the image of God.

In perhaps the most striking part of the discussion, Ames carefully describes what the faithful should and should not expect in sanctification. He mentions "the dreams of some fanatics" who imagine a perfection of sanctification. There is no perfection possible in this life because all men live under the double form of sin and grace. The words of 1 John 1:8 are a warning and a true description of man's experience, "If we say we have no sin, we deceive ourselves, and there is no truth in us." The *Marrow* and the *Conscience* are full of the restrictions and impossibilities which must be realistically confronted in Christian life. Neither the great positive command of obedience, "You shall love the Lord your God with all your heart," nor the great negative, "You shall not covet," can be realized in sanctification by even the most faithful. As Paul observed in Romans 7:14, we cannot render full obedience even to a spiritual law. "The desires of the flesh are against the Spirit, and the desires of the Spirit are against the flesh

---

72. I, xxvii, 10, 21; xxviii, 1, 25–27; pp. 162, 163, 164, 167.
73. I, xxix, 4, p. 168.

(Gal. 5:17)." A man must be honest about the warfare that rages within. But, we can expect spiritual growth and maturation in sanctification. The imagery of 1 Corinthians 13:11 raises legitimate hopes, "When I was a child, I spoke like a child, I thought like a child, I reasoned like a child; when I became a man, I gave up childish ways." We may be able in God's grace to grow into a new kind of spiritual man.[74]

Ames warns against any self-glorification by those who judge themselves to have a successful spiritual growth. Sanctification does not allow any separation from ordinary practice nor does it admit of "consecration to some special use." The believer can never bask outwardly in his righteousness, if indeed there be any; he may never have a holier-than-thou attitude — he is rather to manifest a joy over the love and promises of God. Furthermore, on a practical note, the faithful should be far too busy with their own inner struggle to make outward declarations.[75]

Some Reformed theologians considered glorification to be a stage of the Christian life which believers reached after death. In chapter thirty of book one, Ames mentions the eternal aspect of glorification, but he is primarily concerned with the meaning of the term in this life. Glorification is the stage in which the ambiguity about redemption, known to every man in sanctification, is resolved. Although realistic about the grasp of both sin and grace, Ames also insists that certain marks of redemption can be expected and known. The certainty of glorification is known, first, in a spiritual sense through which the grace of God is personally experienced in some way by the believer. It is also known in one's ability to discern a true, inner working of grace from an outward show of it. Finally, the believer may infer from the "discourse and testimony of conscience" that a state of surety has been reached. The usual Amesian caution and admonition are still present in discussion of glorification: Spiritual assurance does not always mean "certainty in the subject," that is, it may not be sensed at all times by those in the state of glorification.[76] An ebb and flow is to be expected. He warns his readers that true glorification will never be known if a man confuses it with presumption, or makes an outward profession of his confidence. Nor shall glorification be known to the man who neglects the spirit and acts of continual repentance. In this chapter and in corresponding parts of the *Conscience*, Ames assures believers that they can expect some definite signs of redemption within themselves, but he also presents the spiritual life as an unremitting struggle.

74. I, xxix, 29; II, xxii, 20–22; pp. 170, 143.
75. I, xxix, 6; iv, 45; pp. 168, 86.
76. I, xxx, 15, 13, pp. 173, 172.

THE HOLY SPIRIT · A final characteristic of Ames's theology which
illustrates his attachment to the Calvinist core of English Puritanism
is his concern with the work of the Holy Spirit. It is often said that
the major formulators of Western Christian thought can be charac-
terized and initially understood by asking which person of the Trinity
appears to receive the most creative interpretation in their writings.
Augustine was especially attracted to the place and role of the Father
in the Trinity; the problem of creation and of time and eternity were
among his major theological concerns. Luther stood always in the
shadow of the Son of God on the cross; the meaning of the incarnation, suffering, and God's redeeming act were crucial problems to
which he directed his mind and spirit. For Calvin, most Reformed
theologians, and the Puritans the work of the Holy Spirit was central;
they were concerned especially with the present action of God in the
lives of men; they were physicians of the soul analyzing symptoms of
spiritual decay and prescribing ways in which religious experience and
renewal could take place. Some of Calvin's most poetic language in
the *Institutes* is found in the sections dealing with the Holy Spirit,
described now as the water which washes clean and refreshes and now
as the fire which purges and makes bright.

Ames is clearly within this tradition. It is the Holy Spirit that leads
men from calling to glorification; through all the stages of the Christian life men should search out the Spirit's presence and apprize themselves of his work. "Try yourselves, to see if you are in the faith.
Examine yourselves (2 Cor. 13:5)," one of Paul's commands, is a true
saying for Ames. The Christian is always called to look for what God
is doing in the lives of men. A man will not be disappointed, for "The
Spirit himself witnesses with our spirit that we are sons of God (Rom.
8:16)." [77] In his small work, a *Theological Discussion on the Perfection of the Holy Scripture*, Ames offers these further observations:
The Holy Spirit alone produces whatever blessedness is possible in
this life; the work of the Spirit is to penetrate our minds and consciences so that we can execute the will and commands of God; we
are daily refreshed in spirit and body by his nurture; and finally the
Holy Spirit leads us to the end of our hope which is a communion
in this life with all the persons of the Godhead. "My soul thirsts for
God, for the living God. When shall I come and behold the face of
God (Ps. 42:2)?" That perennial religious question of man can only
be answered by the work of the Holy Spirit.[78]

77. I, xxx, 15, p. 173.
78. *Disputatio theologica de perfectione SS. Scripturae* (William Barlee,
ed. Cantabridgiae, 1646), p. 11, or *A Theological Discussion on the Perfection
of the Holy Scripture*. Hereafter cited as Ames, *Disputatio de perfectione*.

UNIQUENESS WITHIN A TRADITION · William Ames shared the basic insights of the early seventeenth-century Puritans. The intellectual and spiritual house built by his English mentors and colleagues was his domicile, although he was to suggest and carry out some changes, as we have seen, in its design. But Ames also stepped out of this house, neither forgetting whence he had come nor unwilling to acknowledge it as his true home. His imaginative freedom helped to account for the decisive role his writings played in England and America. Ames's extensive use of the new Ramist logic, his conception of "living to God" and of faith, his interpretation of covenant, his theory of the church, his understanding of biblical authority — all these display a searching mind and a new sensitive spirit at work.

USE OF RAMIST LOGIC · Peter Ramus, born in 1515, was a Reformed continental philosopher who perished in the prime of his life in 1572 during the St. Bartholomew's Day massacre in Paris. One of his major scholarly concerns was the formulation of a new logic which he believed would augment, perhaps supplant, formal Aristotelian logic. Only recently through the works of Perry Miller and Walter Ong has Ramus' immense influence on the intellectual history of the sixteenth and seventeenth centuries been grasped.[79] His Latin books circulated widely on the Continent and were translated into all the languages of Western Europe. In England many tutors at Cambridge and Oxford were attracted to his philosophy and logic. At Christ's College in Cambridge the succession of Ramist teachers ran Laurence Chaderton (1536?–1640), Gabriel Harvey (1545?–1630), William Perkins (1558–1602), George Downham (d. 1634), Ames, William Chappell (1582–1649), and John Milton (1608–74).[80] In general, however, Ramism found its best reception at continental centers of learning where Ramus' disciples and followers were in greater abundance. Among English Puritans, Ames was undoubtedly the most deeply immersed in Ramist thought. Fr. Ong writes, "English Ramists are outdistanced by the Germans and the Dutch. The one Englishman under Ramist influence who stands out as a possible competitor is William Ames . . . who lived for a long time in the Netherlands."[81]

Ames's technical treatises on logic and philosophy, published post-

79. Ong, *Ramus,* and Perry Miller, *The New England Mind* (Harvard University Press, Cambridge, Mass., 1954), I: 300–30, 493–501.
80. Wilbur S. Howell, *Logic and Rhetoric in England, 1500–1700* (Princeton University Press, Princeton, 1956), pp. 211–12.
81. Ong, *Ramus,* p. 304. See Paul Dibon, *L'enseignement philosophique dans les universités à l'époque precartésienne, 1575–1650* (Elsevier Publishing Company, Paris, 1954).

humously and known as the *Philosophemata*, or *Philosophical Presuppositions*, were all done in Ramist style: *Technometria omnium et singularum artium* (1633), or *The Technometry of Each and Every Art*; *Alia technometriae delineatio* (1646), or *Another Delineation of Technometry*; *Demonstratio logicae verae* (1646), or *Demonstratio of True Logic*; [82] *Disputatio theologica adversus metaphysicam* (1646), or *A Theological Argument against Metaphysics*; and *Theses logicae* (1646), or *Principles of Logic*. In book two, chapter two of the *Marrow*, Ames refers to Ramus as "the greatest master of the arts." The English Puritan was attracted to the French philosopher chiefly for the latter's skill in the art of thinking, but also because he sensed a mind of kindred theological bent. Ramus had adopted French Calvinism as his own personal belief and became one of the very first in the French Reformed tradition to stress the Calvinist concern for instruction and practical theology — the heart of the matter for Ames. Ramus used the phrase, *Deo vivere*, living to God, which Ames was later to advance as part of his definition of theology. The longest quotation of the *Marrow* gives Ramus' view on religious education; the central point is that children should be taught "out of the gospel by a learned theologian of proved character [rather] than out of Aristotle by a philosopher." [83] Even in the matter of polity there was a connection between the two men. Ramus was not only a Protestant but an incipient Congregationalist who acceded to the arguments and persuasion of Jean Morely, a French Reformed writer and teacher, who stood for Congregational ideas against the Presbyterian Theodore Beza (1519–1605).[84] It is fair to say that Ames considered Peter Ramus, whom he never met, to have wielded an influence on his life nearly equal to that of William Perkins.

Simplicity and applicability were Ramus' concerns in his new logic. Although his books were crammed with details, often presented in complicated style, his aim was to advance certain key ideas which would enable men to think correctly and easily. Ramus began his analysis with an assertion that among the three parts of philosophy

---

82. The *Demonstratio* was later published as a type of commentary, or parallel text, with Ramus' *Dialectic*. *P. Rami Veromandui Regii Professoris, dialecticae libri duo: quibus loco commentarii perpetui, post certa capita subjicitur, Guilielmi Amesii demonstratio logicae verae* (Cantabridgiae, 1672), or *The Two Books of Dialectic of P. Ramus, French Belgian Royal Professor: To Which by Way of a Running Commentary Is Added William Ames's "Demonstration of True Logic" under Given Heads.*

83. II, ii, 18, and n. 11, pp. 226, 227. For another criticism of Aristotle see II, ii, 14, p. 225.

84. See Robert M. Kingdon, "Calvinism and Democracy: Some Political Implications of Debates on French Reformed Church Government, 1562–1572," *American Historical Review*, LXIX: No. 2 (Jan. 1964), pp. 393–401.

— dialectic, physics, and ethics — the mind must rely on dialectic in its search for the right thinking that will lead to a fruitful life. One moves to dialectic by advancing through the substages of grammar and rhetoric. Grammar is the beginning level of communication and understanding in which the necessary words are simple, being formed with relatively few letters and sounds. A person starting a foreign language, for example, finds himself in the grammar stage. Rhetoric goes beyond minimal understanding and communication: Men attempt to present in language, written and spoken, all the variety which they observe in things. There is no end to this effort. Rhetoric is the stage in which men strive to present subtleties and intricate ideas; it includes figures of speech and poetry. Dialectic, on the top rung of the ladder of understanding and communication, gives a measure and a sense of order to rhetoric. As Fr. Ong writes, "dialectic rules the organization of the art of rhetoric." [85] Properly used, it gives man an opportunity to rid himself of distracting and irrelevant ideas, to concentrate on the problem at hand, and to reason his way to a conclusion. Dialectic does its work mainly through the resolution of problems put in the form of questions which man has formulated from real-life situations.

Ramus followed the lead of Rudolph Agricola (1443–1485), a predecessor in the departure from Aristotelian forms, by arguing that dialectic consists of invention and judgment. An example will best show the Ramist understanding and application of invention, considered the more important part of dialectic. One might wish to know if, in fact, man had the power to be dialectical, or to bring order into his thinking, and hence the question occurs, "Is man dialectical?" [86] To obtain an affirmative or a negative answer to this question, one need not go to the famous Aristotelian theory of predication or categories. To a man unskilled in Aristotelianism, the categories often represented another field of learning which he must master before returning to his question. Predication likewise ran the risk of detachment, for it assigned qualities and a classification scheme to things on the basis of assumptions that might not apply to the question being asked. Was there not a simpler and more genuine way of reaching an answer? One had only to search for a way of joining the "minor part" of the question, man, with the "major part," dialectical. If no joining were possible, the question was to be answered in the negative. In this case a connection can be made by "inventing" or finding a term linking man and dialectical. The Ramists called such a link an "argument" or middle term. In the new logic, an argument was not a force-

85. Ong, *Ramus*, p. 189.
86. Based on Ong, *Ramus*, pp. 182 ff.

ful point to be used in a controversy; it was that which described an essential relationship between things. Man's task in thinking — in solving the problems and in answering the questions which life presents — is one of finding the true connection between the given minor and major parts of any question. The heart of logic is man's search for the right argument or link.

The argument which suggests itself in the question at hand is "rational." One now uses the argument in a simplified syllogism (this much of Aristotle was kept): Whatever is rational is dialectical; every man is rational; therefore, man is dialectical. The original question has an affirmative answer.

The problem, of course, is how the argument can be discovered or invented. Ramus proposed a list of topics or "places" (sometimes called generic arguments) where, he believed, all possible middle terms or arguments were to be found. His first list of topics totaled fourteen in the 1543 *Training in Dialectic* and had two divisions: those known as "primary" topics or places (causes, effects, subjects, adjuncts, disagreeings), and those which are "derived" (genus, form, name, notations, conjugates, testimonies, contraries, distributions, and definitions). With the original question in mind, one examines the topics and comes to "form," which might also be known as species, and remembers that man's specific and identifying nature is rationality. The same quality is also a basic constituent of dialectic. A link between the minor and major part of the question is now formed with the argument "rational." The middle term can also be procured in a secondary, speculative way: If man were dialectical, his being a rational animal would be a "cause" of his ability to be dialectical. The topic cause confirms the argument drawn from form. By either route the middle term rational has emerged and is now ready for use in the syllogism. Sometimes the argument will naturally spring to mind and the topic list need not be consulted or the syllogism used, but usually topics and syllogism must be employed.

In later works, Peter Ramus revised and enlarged his list of topics or places wherein the arguments or middle terms were to be discovered. As Fr. Ong points out, his followers carried on the expansionist tendency with the result that Ramist writers and editors, such as Johann Alsted (1588–1638), were to produce the first modern encyclopedias "as a kind of ultimate elaboration" of places and generic arguments.[87]

Judgment, the second part of the art of dialectic or the "putting into effect," has three steps, which are chiefly amplifications of the process required for invention. Ramus called the first step "syllogism"

87. Ong, *Ramus*, p. 183.

or, more accurately, the art of distinguishing and comparing the minor and major parts of any question. This includes the proper use of induction and example as well as syllogistic reasoning. The second step is skill in the use of the topics or places, including a judicious freedom to expand the basic list when experience warrants. Third, religious teaching may be used in order to develop in the questioner the insight and sense of order needed in the new reasoning process.

The most obvious indication of Ramist influence in the *Marrow* and the *Conscience* is the use of logical terms borrowed from the *Training in Dialectic* and the *Dialectic*. Ames speaks again and again, for example, of a "metonymy of the adjunct," or a figure of speech in which a connected or derived part is mentioned instead of the subject or that from which it is derived. (A "metonymy of the effect" is possible, in which the effect is put for the cause.) Hope is an adjunct of faith, for example, and often hope alone is referred to in the New Testament when faith is really meant: "We are saved by hope (Rom. 8:24)." [88] Adjunct is a Ramist topic or place which reminds one of any very close relationship — such is the situation between faith and hope. When the relationship is grasped the two may be interchanged without confusion.

Ames also relies on Ramus' schemes of division. The simplest and most logical way to conceive an area of knowledge, according to Ramus, is to be mindful of its subordinate parts. One begins with the two major components of the area in question. Each of these components has two components, and these two, two more each, and so on, until the original term is laid out in an extensive series of coupled parts — a kind of reverse tennis tournament chart. Dialectic, for example, divides into invention and judgment, as we have seen, invention into artificial (meaning "natural," or ways of invention which an individual as an artificer makes or reduces) and inartificial (meaning ways of invention taken from the testimony of others or from a tradition). The divisions go on and on. The components do not stand for rigid compartments, but rather different (yet vitally connected) perspectives of the idea to which they are subordinate. The scheme of coupled components displays the ultimate scope of dialectic: If one understands the parts one will be able to think rightly and use effectively the places or topics in searching for an argument or middle term. Ames employs a similar division with a similar purpose in his "area," namely, theology. The first two components are faith in God and observance, which immediately divide into other parts. The chart

88. On "fear of God" used in a metonymy of the adjunct for faith see I, ii, 3, p. 79. For a metonymy of the effect, "miracle" being put for God's extraordinary providence, see I, ix, 11, p. 108. See n. 7 in text, p. 79.

at the beginning of the text shows an elaborate array of successive, coupled components. Nothing could be more Ramist. And just as an understanding of the components in dialectic leads to right thinking, so Ames urges that an understanding of theology's parts leads to a grasp of the Christian life. Ames believes with Ramus that a scheme of division and interrelationship offers man a sure way, a method (*methodus*).

The French philosopher gave more to Ames, however, than terminology and schemes of division. The root meaning of dialectic itself was the aspect of Ramism most crucial to Ames; it was seized and applied in a new and forceful way to the Puritan style of life. The Franeker professor also added clarity and a sense of definition to this central term which most Ramists were content to leave in an ambiguous, if not confusing, state.

Ames readily agreed that dialectic brought order to the art of rhetoric. It enabled man to reason simply and effectively, to make comparisons, and reach conclusions. Ames especially agreed with the Ramist insight that dialectic was concerned with questions that arose in actual life situations; he developed this side of the Ramist analysis by stressing that the main point of using dialectic was to discover something immediately pressing. Rightly used, dialectical thinking could answer questions raised by a man about his spiritual condition; it could help a man meet the problems that crowded in when an important decision had to be made; and it could settle ambivalence over various courses of action.

Conscience: Its Law or Cases is really an attempt to apply the Ramist dialectic to what Ames considered the key problems of social and personal life in the early seventeenth century. All five books of the *Conscience* are written in a question and answer style (save the very beginning of book one); even the *Marrow* with its many numbered sections suggests that a series of answers are being given to assumed questions. Ames seldom, however, uses the word dialectic; he prefers his own word "conscience" which he views as the dialectical method in action inescapably tied to the issues of the moment. According to Ames, conscience is not a faculty (despite William Perkins); nor is it a habit, as some of the scholastics held; nor is it a contemplative judgment. Conscience is rather "a practical judgment whereby that which a man knows is particularly applied to his good or evil so that it becomes a rule to direct his will." [89]

Ames divides conscience (as a Ramist would) into two parts, natural and enlightened. "Natural conscience is that which acknowledges for law the principles of nature and the conclusions arising from

89. *De conscientia*, I, i, 3, p. 89.

them." [90] The Ramist processes of invention and judgment, Ames would say, are part of the natural conscience possessed by all men. But he is most concerned with the enlightened conscience, which is a dialectic available only to those who are in union and communion with Christ. "Do you not know that all of us who have been baptized into Christ Jesus were baptized into his death? We were buried therefore with him by baptism into death, so that as Christ was raised from the dead by the glory of the Father, we too might walk in newness of life (Rom. 6:3, 4)." The enlightened conscience possessed by those in "newness of life" is what Ames has in mind with his opening, oft-repeated definition: "Conscience . . . is a man's judgment of himself according to God's judgment of him." [91] "Man according to God" is the crux of conscience; once that relationship has been grasped, judgment or the action of dialectic can be accomplished. The fundamental task of conscience in the Christian faith is to examine the relationship between man and God and therein to find answers to genuine questions and to produce grounds for decision and action.

Like Ramus, Ames always asked the questions of "where" and "how." Man's relation to God can be discovered in the biblical proclamations. Indeed, Ames believes that the Bible provides the "places" or topics from which all the arguments needed to relate God and man can be taken. The Scriptures produce middle terms for all conceivable questions about "man according to God." The Bible speaks to such problems as the nature of man's life, the meaning of right conduct and decision, and the action of God in the world. Its reading even presented men with the questions that should be asked and challenged them to ask still more. Ames often points to the startling use of questions by biblical writers.

The Scriptures provided arguments or middle terms for man's questions about relationship to God in two ways. In the *Marrow* and the *Conscience*, Ames often considers the Bible in what might be called a broad Ramist method. The Scriptures offer general arguments that provide a connection between man and God. One might ask, for example, "How does God love us?" The question would be handled by searching for major themes in the Bible which would relate God and man within the confines of the query. Paul's Letter to the Romans would be such a "place." The general argument of Romans is, "But God commends his love towards us in that when we were yet sinners Christ died for us (Rom. 5:8)." Christ's dying for us demonstrates most powerfully the purpose and the way of God's love.[92] So an an-

90. *De conscientia*, I, ii, 7, p. 3.
91. *De conscientia*, I, i, preamble, p. 1.
92. See the use of Rom. 5:8 in I, xviii, 2, p. 128.

swer to the question, or at least assurance, is given by the main argument of the book of Romans which casts light on a particular question of "man according to God."

Ames insists on "inventing" or finding general arguments in the Scriptures; such a search is vastly more important than an ability to cite chapter-and-verse answers on various points. The major themes of the Bible dealing with the basic relationship of God and man are the foundation of scriptural authority. God's sense of order and creating wisdom are more significant than the details of the creation story in the beginning of Genesis; [93] man's condition as a sinner is the main point to be grasped in the story of the expulsion from the Garden of Eden; and God's covenant is the thing to be extricated from the myriad happenings in the accounts of Noah and Abraham. So Ames's Ramist advice is to look first for general arguments or broad middle terms or assertions which emerge from blocks of Scripture or biblical "places" and relate God and man.

Conscience is related to the Bible, secondly, in a more particular way. Individual believers raise pressing, personal questions about "man according to God." These are quite different from the more academic queries that man-in-general asks, such as, "How does God love us?" Conscience or dialectic must deal with the subjective, pinpointed questions as well as with the objective and detached. To reach an answer to such questions, a syllogism must be used — a syllogism adapted to conscience operating in the light of biblical arguments. At this point, we see Ames going beyond Ramus, for he rethinks the terminology and usage of this ancient form of logic. What had traditionally been called the major proposition of the syllogism becomes a "light" or a "law"; the minor proposition becomes a "witness," an "index," or "book," or "review" (sometimes an "assumption," using the Aristotelian term); and the conclusion becomes a "crisis," a "judge," or a "judgment." [94] Most important, the syllogism is used to produce the needed argument or middle term between the minor and major parts of the question; the argument is not discovered and then put into a syllogism, as it was for Ramus. In other words, the syllogism, Ames suggests, can help the questioner find the middle term.

In the beginning pages of the *Conscience* Ames offers an example of this kind of reasoning. A particular man might wish to know — and a believer certainly would — "Do I have eternal life?" The "light" of Scripture which emerges is "Whoever believes in Christ shall not die, but live." The "witness" is "I believe in Christ." The

93. See I, viii, p. 100.
94. *De conscientia*, I, i, 8–9; viii, 1–2; ix, pp. 2, 14–15, 16 ff.

"judgment" follows: "Therefore, I shall not die, but live." The syllogism helps to produce a middle term or argument which shall link the minor part "I" with the major part "eternal life"; the link is found in both the light and witness, "Believe in Christ." If I wish to have eternal life, I must believe in Christ. Most often the syllogism is tied with sections of the Bible which raise problems of ethical relevance for contemporary life. The major issue, for example, in chapters nine and ten of 1 Corinthians is the question of giving offense to others by the proclamation of the gospel. "Am I not free?" asks Paul at the beginning of chapter nine — meaning in a wider sense, "Am I not free as an apostle to give offense to anyone?" Yes, answers Paul, but he goes on to confess that he has "become all things to all men, that I might by all means save some (1 Cor. 9:22)." The question "Am I not free?" is not one, argues Ames, for only the first-century apostles; it is a question raised by each individual Christian as he decides the delicate issue of adopting or denying the ways of the world about him. The question becomes, "Am I not free as a Christian to break and abandon all practices of the times?" The light is given in 1 Cor. 10:31, "So, whether you eat or drink, or whatever you do, do all to the glory of God." The witness occurs in the words, "I do it all for the sake of the gospel (1 Cor. 9:23)." The judgment is, "I would rather die than have any one deprive me of my ground for boasting . . . Woe to me if I do not preach the gospel (1 Cor. 9:15–16)." This time the argument which connects the minor part "I" with the major part "free" is found in the judgment, "Preach the gospel." Ames's interpretation is that Paul, by adapting himself to some of the practices and customs of others, rather than making a radical break, has found a greater opportunity for his ministry. Paul has shown himself willing to use what he can in the life around him as he witnesses to the gospel.[95] And so it is for each Christian who asks the question "Am I not free?" He must inquire what in his judgment, under God's judgment, can be used. Certainly insult, separation, calumny, or an arbitrary "againstness" will not further the gospel.

It is characteristic of Ames to lay great stress on the second step of the syllogism, or the witness. The light or law of the scripture, the first step in the syllogism, is meaningless unless it can be established and applied in the second. Hence the traditional assumption or minor proposition is called an index or book or review, meaning that it must have the certainty of something that is written down and imprinted in a person's life. If there is no surety in the witness,

95. *De conscientia*, III, xvii, 9, pp. 100–01. Later in the same section Paul's decision to stay unmarried is explained by a similar reasoning process.

the judgment or conclusion has no force.[96] To explore the witness and to produce assurance is the task of the religious life. It is comforting to say that all who believe in Christ shall have eternal life, but it is only a banality unless one can say that he surely *does* believe in Christ. It is good news to know that you may drink or eat or "whatever you do" in adopting the world's ways, but it is false advice unless the witness is a certainty, "I do it all for the sake of the gospel." Ames invites and challenges his readers to search within themselves to see if they have the strength and assurance required in the witness. He warns them, "A bare and naked knowledge is not sufficient . . . things must be weighed over and over." [97] In the process of weighing and searching, a Christian may find the biblical argument or middle term which will answer the particular question he has raised about "man according to God." Theology must teach him how to search and weigh.

So in Williams Ames we confront a Ramist dialectician of Puritan style. He agreed with the French logician that dialectic could lead men to true understanding and action. Dialectic as reasoning power brought order to the babel of tongues known in rhetoric; it answered the true questions men had in life; it offered a simple, reliable way of reaching a conclusion through a middle term or argument which linked the minor and major parts of any question; and it produced sure grounds for decision. Ames theologized the dialectic and associated it with conscience. What Ramus had envisioned for dialectic Ames saw as the purpose and power of conscience. But William Ames saw an additional and more significant function: the ability of conscience to illumine the relationship between God and man. Conscience, he believed, produces its illumination chiefly by using biblical ideas. The Bible is the seat of all places or topics from which arguments of conscience are to be drawn — they are not to be found in a list of philosophical terms, as Ramus had suggested. The arguments of the Scriptures emerge, on the one hand, as great proclamations which answer real-life questions about "man according to God." The *Marrow* unabashedly gives partial quotations from the Bible, sometimes only bare citations, as if to say, "Here is a connection between the parts of your question," or "Try this for a link." On the other hand, more

96. I, iii, 22, p. 83, "firm assent leans on the trust of the heart as a middle or third term [*argumentum*]." Ames sometimes calls the judgment or conclusion the second term in which case the witness or middle term becomes the "third term." The word *argumentum* meant for Ames not only term or argument but, in the case of the witness, proof or foundation. See I, vi, 8, p. 92, for stress on the witness in a syllogistic reference to God's will as crucial for God's working power.

97. *De conscientia*, I, viii, 1, pp. 14–15.

often the biblical argument, especially that needed in immediate, personal questions, will be found only by putting together carefully the thread of a scriptural account and using the logical device of a syllogism.

Ames did not have the optimism about conscience which Ramus had about dialectic. Conscience depended in the end on what a person found within himself; the system alone did not guarantee results. So William Ames urged his fellow believers and would-be believers to wrestle and struggle that they might inwardly appropriate the truth glimpsed in the word of God. A discernment, a syllogism, even the extrication of an artful middle term was not enough.

LIVING TO GOD, OR THE LIFE OF FAITH · The *Marrow of Theology* begins with the words, "Theology is the doctrine or teaching of living to God." With this opening definition Ames placed himself, once more, in the company of Calvin, Bucer, Perkins and the English Puritans, and Peter Ramus. Calvin laid it down in the Geneva Catechism that nothing worse could befall a man than not to live to God. The serving and honoring of God by a pious and righteous life was a Calvinist charge to all the faithful. Ames carried this emphasis to a climax in becoming the first to commence a book of theology with a ringing assertion of living to God, rather than with the usual exposition of man's knowledge of God or with a declaration of the authority of the Scriptures.

Both books of the *Marrow* are concerned with the marks of living to God. "Observance" is hailed as a necessary part of theology and the Calvinist call to good works and deeds is sounded. Ames assured his readers that a concern for works in no way jeopardizes the life of faith, for works add life and meaning to faith inasmuch as they naturally flow from it. Yet the *Marrow* and the *Conscience* wish to correct a misleading point often made in Reformed theology. Living to God, says Ames, means living rightly; it does not mean living blessedly. Perkins had described theology as the knowledge or the skill of living blessedly for eternity and Ramus had even formed a school of Reformed thought whose aim was to propagate the formula of living to God rightly and blessedly.[98] For Ames the end of theology was never to produce blessedness, which he felt related chiefly to man's ultimate aspiration and desire. In a search for his own blessedness, man could miss God, the very object of his living rightly. The search, moreover, could produce inordinate introspection, detachment, and anxiety. Man should contemplate his own salvation, but theology

98. Horton, *Ames by Reuter*, pp. 171–72, 198.

should never lead to a condition of assumed beatitude in which we
frustratingly attempt to live by ourselves. It is rather the good life
whereby we live to God: emphasis falling on the directional, teleo-
logical phrase, "to God." [99]

In living rightly to God, Ames admitted the characteristic marks
of the active Calvinist life — the acceptance of a rule of life, the
honoring of God through ecclesiastical communal responsibilities, the
serving of the neighbor's need, and an upright personal conduct.
These were needed, but they were not the foundation of living to
God. Indeed, these marks produced no assurance, even in the case
of those who practiced them the most.[100] Ames was primarily concerned with living to God in faith. Other Reformed theologians held,
of course, for the centrality of faith, but Ames returned to this Protestant concept with new emphasis and passion.

He chose to speak to men about how they could live faithfully
toward God now. Consequently, after preliminary observations, Ames
begins his *Marrow* with a discussion of faith — ahead of any consideration of God, creation, providence, sin, Jesus Christ, or the
Scriptures. He attacks those who view the issue of Christian faith as
an intellectual problem. He has in mind not only Roman Catholic
but Reformed theologians such as Theodore Beza (1519–1605), Bartholomaeus Keckermann (1571–1609), and his own Franeker colleague Maccovius. He refers to such interpreters when he writes, "To
believe signifies ordinarily an act of the understanding as it gives
assent to evidence." [101] The "assent" theory of faith took one of two
forms: It could be a faith which took the findings of religious
philosophy and logic as that which is to be believed, or it could be
a faith which took the pronouncements of Scripture as the data for
belief. In each case, faith results when credence is given, or acceptance
is granted, to what is presented. Either approach, says Ames, is an
act of the mind and is an incomplete conception of faith — plainly
erroneous when put as the starting point of faith.

The *Marrow's* description of faith is close to that of Calvin in the
Institutes and to William Perkins in the *Golden Chain: Or the Description of Theology.* Following his teachers who stood in a tradition
as old as Augustine and Paul, Ames held that faith was something
beyond understanding and knowledge, far exceeding the capacity
of human knowing. Faith is that which claims the heart and the
whole being of a man. It cannot be approached with an assent or cred-

99. I, i, 8, p. 78. Ames sees a unified structure in living rightly; there
can be no compartmentalization of right thinking and right doing (II, ii,
p. 224). They flow together in living to God.

100. II, xvi, 11–12, p. 302.

101. I, iii, 2, p. 80.

ence given only by the mind. Ames wished, however, to push further than Calvin and Perkins, both of whom had favorable views on the place of *cognitio*, or knowledge, in faith. Calvin wrote in the *Institutes*, "Now we shall possess a right definition of faith if we call it a firm and certain knowledge of God's benevolence toward us." [102] And Perkins in the first chapter of the *Golden Chain* had defined the blessed life as that which exists through the knowledge of God. Calvin was on guard, of course, to protect himself from the Roman Catholic charge of "infolded faith," or a faith that is so personal and interior that it cannot be discussed objectively or communicated. Ames, apparently, did not fear counter charges from Rome or any other quarter; boldly he asserts in book one, chapter three, that faith must be understood in connection with the will. Later he is to say that it is primarily based in the will.[103]

A man must have a knowledge of the gospel, to be sure, but this knowledge is not saving in itself. One need only examine how faith works in order to discover where its roots lie. First, in a passive sense, faith "comes by the good which then becomes ours through faith"; secondly and more important, faith operates as an act of election, "a single virtue . . . not partly of knowledge and partly of the affections (1 Cor. 13)." Faith is a decision. It is choosing to trust an all-sufficient God to whom and through whom we are able to live. Faith is directed towards "the living God, who is the preserver of all men (1 Tim. 4:10)." [104] The object of faith is not the Bible (only through a "metonymy of the adjunct" can it be so considered), nor is it the church. The emphasis is squarely put in the opening words of the chapter, "Faith is the resting of the heart on God." But how — to raise the usual Amesian question — do our hearts rest on God? They rest on God's revelation which gives that which is to be believed and they depend on the inner force and work of the Holy Spirit which produces within us the act of believing.

Ames is wary of natural theology as well as intellectual faith. Theology and faith always deal with revelation, as laid down in the first chapter of the *Marrow*: "A discipline which derives not from nature and human inquiry, like others, but from divine revelation and appointment." Faith, then, is also a specific trust or hope. It is a decision to trust a providing God whose life-giving nature is

102. Jean Calvin, *Institutes of the Christian Religion* (trans. Ford L. Battles, ed. John T. McNeill, Westminster Press, Philadelphia, 1960), Vol. I, 551 (III, ii, 7).

103. And thus he places himself in the company of Anselm, St. Francis, Henry of Ghent, and other "voluntarists"; see Horton, *Ames by Reuter*, pp. 185, 202.

104. I, iii, 3, 22, 7, pp. 80, 83, 81.

known in revelation and who acts through the Holy Spirit in the lives of men.

How does one prepare for the beginning of salvation which can be known only in faith? Ames did not follow the prevailing orthodox line and hold that man can do little or nothing. Maccovius, for example, insisted that man in his fallen state was incapable of preparing for faith and conversion. Any steps which led to faith were associated with God's regeneration and could not be connected with man's efforts at salvation. For Ames the orthodox Reformed position was artificial. Surely it was true that any signs of progress towards a life of faithfulness were signs of God working within, but man was conscious in his actual life of much that he was doing — or of much that he should do. To let the matter rest with the assertion that God was the giver of faith was not only to remove responsibility from man but to take away the inescapable dynamics of religious life. Ames wished to stress the actual nature of the religious life that trusted in God, or the empirical quality of faith. The experience of faith was a sense of certainty or assurance. As Ames put it, we must be able to speak not only of "a fruit of the Holy Spirit," but also of "our fruit." [105] To say that surety related only to God's juridical act in justification, as many contemporary theologians did, was to obscure the struggles of the religious life and also to remove its experiential rewards and blessings.[106] Spiritual assurance can only grow out of the living of faith and the evidence which follows. If there is no practice or discipline, faith and certainly assurance diminish and may even be lost.[107] So Ames raised the question of what man should do to receive the gift of God. Man's paramount task was to make himself spiritually ready so that faith would actually occur and its experience might be truly his.

In Ramist fashion Ames saw the issue of preparation as a question which every honest man faced: "How can I be faithful?" The "I" and "faithful" could be linked by arguments or middle terms of Scripture which dealt with this problem of "man according to God." The location was chiefly the gospels where Jesus spoke often about the nature of man's religious life. Man should repent and confess, as Christ repeatedly urged; man should offer his unsure, ambivalent will to God in prayer that it might be informed and enlightened; he should do what he understands to be the will of the Father; and he should expose himself to the proclamations of the law and the prophets.

105. II, ii, 22, p. 227.
106. See Ames, *Bellarminus enervatus*, or *Bellarmine Disarmed* (Amstelodami, 1630), IV: 111–20.
107. See Ames, *Coronis ad collationem Hagiensem*, or *A Finishing Touch to the Hague Conference* (Londini, 1630), pp. 286 ff.

Even a ready mind and spirit are counted as preparation; as St. Paul wrote, "If there is first a ready mind one is accepted according to what he has (2 Cor. 8:12)." [108] Ames's insistence on preparation was taken to heart by his younger Puritan colleagues. Thomas Hooker, friend and admirer in England and Holland, carried out the Amesian idea in the New World and became, perhaps, the leading seventeenth-century physician of the soul.

When a man attempted to rest the heart on God in faith, Ames was persuaded that he would experience God's faithfulness which is the ground of Christian surety. "Lét us draw near with a true heart in full assurance of faith . . . for he who promised is faithful (Heb. 10:22–23)." [109] In John 1:45–51, the account of Nathaniel's call as a disciple, Christ criticizes Nathaniel for a faith which was only an "assent." Nathaniel answered him, " 'Rabbi, you are the Son of God! You are the King of Israel!' Jesus answered him, 'Because I said to you, I saw you under the fig tree, do you believe? You shall see greater things than these.' " [110] The greater thing of faith is a certainty of God's faithful love towards men. To instruct men to live in this certainty is the ultimate task of theology which is, as the opening words of the Marrow say, the teaching of living to God.

COVENANT OF GRACE · What man could expect in a life of faithfulness was best described, Ames believed, in the idea of covenant. The Marrow discusses covenant in many places, but especially in book one, chapters 10, 24, 32, 38, and 39 which deal with the governing of men and angels, the "application" of Christ, the organized church, and the meaning of covenant itself. It is clearly one of the central concepts in Amesian theology and its use and interpretation mark Ames again with a uniqueness among early seventeenth-century Puritans.[111] The idea of covenant was known in the Old Testament, of course, and beyond that in the treaties and political agreements of the Hittite empire.[112] Irenaeus in the late second century was probably the first Christian thinker to use covenant ideas in a discussion of basic relations between God and man. Calvin, John Knox, and a host of other Reformed thinkers were to depend on covenant as a key to the understanding of many theological and social issues.

108. II, iii, 26, p. 235.
109. II, vi, 21, p. 248.
110. I, iii, 20, p. 82.
111. Ames's use of covenant is overlooked by Reuter and Wilhelm Goeters, *Die Vorbereitung des Pietismus* (J. C. Hinrichs'sche Buchhandlung, Leipzig, 1911).
112. See George E. Mendenhall, "Law and Covenant in Israel and the Ancient Near East," *Biblical Archaeologist*, XVII: Nos. 2, 3 (May, Sept. 1954).

For Ames, however, the covenant idea finds its principal meaning and reaches its apex in the covenant of grace, referring to man's individual relation with God and to the life of the church. No previous thinker in the Calvinist-Puritan tradition analyzed the covenant of grace with an acuteness comparable to that of the Franeker professor.[113] Many follow in his train and add greater structure and detail, such as Johannes Cocceius (1603–69), Ames's student in Holland, and John Cotton (1584–1649) in America.

At the outset, it should be noted that Ames finds little use for covenant thought in the political realm. A common decision among a group of men "to make a city or some civil society when their immediate concern is for the common civil good" [114] could be called a covenant, but this is in the sense of merely an agreement to form a body politic. Certainly the covenant idea does not lead in Ames's thought to a juridical, political notion of contract on which all governments are founded, as Locke was later to assert. Governments are based rather on the commandments and precepts of the Bible, rightly understood and applied, the principles of natural law, and the time-tested legal customs of men, particularly the common law tradition of England. Ultimately a government depended on the judicious response of people and governors to the rule of God. A contractual theory of government, advanced as an application and subdivision of covenant theology, was found principally in eighteenth-century Puritanism when the seminal thought of Ames was no longer at work.[115]

Ames associates covenant, on occasion, with the legalistic relation between man and God known as the covenant of works. In I, xxxix, 9, he speaks of the covenant of works as a government of the law which held the "ancient people" in bondage. He first mentions such a covenant in I, x, 9, as a divine command and a threatening, accompanied by promise of reward and fulfillment if man is obedient. Such a covenant is a contract involving a *quid pro quo*, and Ames understandably prefers the word "transaction." The covenant of works is treated at greater length in the *Conscience* where it is connected with the discussion of law. The transaction concept which presents God as a lawgiver whose beneficence depends on man's action is not, however, the ultimate scriptural conception of God's work. Both the *Marrow* and *Conscience* distinguish sharply between the covenant

113. Ames surpassed his teacher Perkins and other English Puritans of the early 1600's in the use of covenant. See Perry Miller, *Errand into the Wilderness* (Harvard University Press, Cambridge, Mass., 1956), p. 58.

114. I, xxxii, 18, p. 180.

115. See my "Natural Law and Covenant Theology in New England, 1620–1670," *Natural Law Forum*, V (1960).

of works, a beginning and incomplete form of God's dealing with men, and the covenant of grace where the culminating fullness of God's relation to men is known. We read Ames best if we reserve the word covenant for the latter meaning. The transaction idea is necessary, for God does expect men to obey his commandments, as he has ever since the beginning of the covenant of works with Adam in Eden. But the lesser must give way to the greater. The whole weight of the Bible is against any final consideration of God as a party to a bargain with men. God is fundamentally a promiser and performer, regardless of what man does — and it is this action of God which Ames makes central in his covenant theology.[116]

In book one, chapter twenty-four, Ames compares transaction, often called the old covenant, with the covenant of grace. In the first, man and God promise together, but in the second man who is deep in sin can promise nothing, so God assumes the initiative; in the one God uses his justice and counsel, but in the other only his mercy; the first stresses man's ability to perform, but the second the strength of God's word; obedience and works are required in transaction, but nothing is stipulated for man in the covenant of grace (although man's faith is held to be a necessary means of appropriating the promise); the former commands what is righteous, but the latter bestows righteousness; and the one is a dead letter, but the other a quickening spirit. Ames lays the groundwork for what Peter Bulkeley (1583–1659), John Cotton (1584–1652), Thomas Hooker (1586–1647), Thomas Shepard (1604–49),[117] and other American covenant preachers are to call the unconditional covenant of grace — the conditional covenant being equated with the transaction, the old covenant, or the covenant of works. Ames preferred to describe the covenant of grace as a testament, meaning God's freely given word of assurance and salvation. The covenant of grace was that which a man sought to experience as he lived to God. It was the goal of religious discipline, repentance, and faith. It made possible the five stages of the Christian life, from calling to glorification, through which each man hoped to progress. The covenant of grace was the saving promise of a God whose initiative and

---

116. Ames does present God and Christ, however, in a contractual relationship, advancing a juridical concept of the atonement, I, xx, 4 ff., p. 135. See n. 44, p. 20. Still, in Christ's satisfaction or atoning work "the greatest justice and the greatest grace are shown forth together and work for man's redemption," I, xx, 17, p. 136.

117. Ames's New World followers were not all out of the same mold. Anne Hutchinson thought Cotton, for example, to be a faithful expositor of the covenant of grace whereas she suspected, with reason, a legalism in the covenant thought of Bulkeley. See Perry Miller, The New England Mind (Harvard University Press, Cambridge, Mass., 1953), II: 58–60, on Cotton and Hooker.

love bade him proclaim, "I will be their God, and they shall be my people (Jer. 31:33; Heb. 8:10)." [118]

Ames sees the unconditional covenant of grace as perhaps the single most important biblical teaching. It was the property of both the Old and New Testaments, having its beginning in Genesis 3 with the promise that Christ, or the seed of Eve, would overcome the evils of sin, estrangement from God, and death. This covenant found repeated expression in the lives of Old Testament figures of whom Abraham was regarded as chief. God had said to Abraham, "And I will establish my covenant between me and you and your descendants after you throughout their generations for an everlasting covenant, to be God to you and to your descendants after you (Gen. 17:7)." The covenant reached its climax in the New Testament with God's offering of himself in the life, death, and resurrection of Jesus Christ. The clearest expression of the covenant is found in Paul's letter to the Romans, where the main "argument" to be grasped, as we have seen, is "When we were yet sinners Christ died for us (Rom. 5:8)." Romans is by far the most-quoted biblical book in the *Marrow*.[119] Thus Ames considers the Christ event to be the dividing line between old and new forms of the covenant of grace. The Old Testament promises that Christ is to come and the New testifies that he has come.

Other differences follow: The Old Testament covenant is marked by ritual and ceremony, but the New by spiritual obedience; the Old runs the risk of bondage to works, but the New proclaims freedom in faith; the Old is restricted to the Jews, but the New is for all people; and the Old tends to be oppressive and heavy, but the New is inviting and lively. Yet, the nature and substance of the covenant is the same in both Old and New Testaments; the differences are in administration and application. Ames sees, for example, parallel meanings in the Old and New Testament stages of life made possible by the covenant of grace. "*Calling* came in the leading of Abraham from Ur of Chaldees to a certain new and heavenly

118. I, xxiv, 10–12; xxx, 16; pp. 150, 173.
119. 242 times. The Letter to the Romans was dear to the Reformed tradition. The 1605 translation of the Genevan Bible ("Barker's Bible") has this marginal note: "This Epistle to the Romans called by many holy men the marrow of divinity and the confession of the churches because of the excellency and fullness of it." In a sense, Ames's *Marrow* was a commentary on St. Paul's "marrow." William Ames stands in a line of Reformed Pauline interpreters, stretching from Calvin to Karl Barth.
Other biblical books cited or quoted with frequency in the *Marrow* are:

1 Cor.	156	Eph.	109
Matt.	128	Acts	94
John	128	2 Cor.	78
Ps.	121	Gen.	71
Heb.	117	Deut.	62

country . . . *Justification* was illustrated by the express testimony of God that faith was reckoned to Abraham for righteousness." [120] These terms as well as the words adoption, santification, and glorification are not the sole property of St. Paul in the New Testament. Still, the dividing point of the Christ event was definite. In the Old Testament the word had not become flesh and in the New it had. There could be no reading back of the person and works of Christ into the Old Testament. Moses was not really a Christ as he mediated between God and the people during the exodus; he was a figure chosen by God to administer the covenant of grace according to the old dispensation. Certainly the idea of a climax to God's promise, protection, and salvation to be known in Christ was longed for, pointed to, and even predicted in the Old Testament. But Christ and his dispensation of the covenant were only known fully in the new fullness of time chosen by God. Thus, Ames seldom makes a "typological" interpretation of the Bible in which the events and figures of the Old Testament were interpreted principally as types of Christ. From Genesis to Revelation, God's promise and assurance took the form of the covenant of grace, but significant changes did occur. Ames sees scriptural unity in the covenant, but also realistic disjunction.

In America, preachers and writers in the Puritan tradition were to write extensive tracts on covenant theology. On the Continent, Johannes Cocceius (1603–69) would found a similar school. Together they stood in distinction to English Puritans of the early 1600's who never expressed the covenant of grace at full strength.[121] Ames is a transitional figure — one of the very first in the Reformed tradition to seize upon the centrality of the covenant of grace. He bequeathed his enthusiasm to those whom he taught who were in turn to make the covenant of grace a theological hallmark of mid- and late-seventeenth-century Puritanism.

THE CHURCH. THE MAGISTRACY · In Amesian thought the covenant of grace is inextricably bound up with the life of the church. Although the meaning of covenant is alluded to early in the *Marrow*, its major treatment is reserved for the chapters following the discussion of the church. Ames insisted that it was impossible to separate a knowl-

120. I, xxxviii, 14, 15, 24–25, pp. 203, 204. Editor's italics.
121. Most English Puritans (e.g., Perkins, Sibbes, Preston, Ball) spoke of "the Covenant of Grace as having a twofold nature, that is, it was conditional and it was absolute," John von Rohr, "Covenant and Assurance in Early English Puritanism," *Church History*, XXXIV, No. 2 (June 1965), pp. 199–200, 202. Ames does not accept the conditional, contractual aspect of the covenant of grace.

edge of the covenant of grace from life within the church — the *Marrow* and the *Conscience* typically speak of how something takes place before turning to its definition. So the church is discussed before the covenant, being the place where the covenant is grasped. Ames shares the Lutheran and Calvinist conception of the church. He agrees with Luther's basic assertion (against the distinctions of Rome) that the church existed where the word was preached and the sacraments were celebrated; he accepts the later Calvinist insistence that the church engages in instruction or edification. Ames adds to all this the point that the church must be the place where the covenant of grace is experienced. He uses the idea of the church as a group of people living in the covenant of grace to explain the Old and New Testament presentations of the covenant. In the Old, the church was an infant, destined for much, to be sure, but not yet in its maturity — hence its legalistic if not servile condition. In the New, the church is an heir and is free for a full spiritual life. "If you are Christ's, then you are Abraham's offspring, heirs according to promise. So long as the heir is an infant he differs not at all from a servant, though he be lord of all (Gal. 3:29–4:1)." [122] Ames could write about the covenant of grace only as a church theologian.

Karl Reuter has called attention to the pronounced empirical tone of Ames's discussion of the church. A community of believers now in existence, or those presently in communion with Christ, make up the church. "God's action in history, and not God's thought before history, constitutes the church immediately as it is." [123] In the *Marrow*, Ames depends on a distinction between *materia*, material or basic matter, and *forma*, constitutive force, first offered in his *Principles of Logic*. The *materia* of a thing can be examined, in which process the thing under consideration is treated in a passive sense as an object. Or, the constitutive force may be examined, in which case the thing is viewed as a subject with attention focused on its living form or ability to give itself shape and power. Ames prefers to discuss the church as a subject or to concentrate on its *forma*. The *materia* of the church is the people, called together by God's will and providence the operation of which he has already discussed in the *Marrow*.

The single most important mark of the church as a subject is the faithful response of its members to the covenant of grace. They respond in a church covenant which is the promise to accept and abide by the faithfulness of God known in the covenant of grace. The identifying mark of the church covenant is its call for a special bond among believers. Ames found passages in Hebrews especially

122. I, xxxviii, 7–10, p. 202.
123. Horton, *Ames by Reuter*, p. 216.

fitting: "Let us consider how to stir up one another to love and good works, not forsaking the assembling of ourselves together, as is the habit of some, but encouraging one another (10:24–25)." [124] The church covenant binds people first to God and then to each other. It is the duty of the ministry to remind the people of the church covenant; it should be renewed in public profession from time to time, perhaps on each occasion of worship.[125] The church as sub- ject does not require professions of individual religious experience or faith, as later New England theologians were to insist.[126] What is required is that the existing body of Christ makes a promise to God's promise. Ames is not concerned over the particular format of the church covenant; he views simplicity and Paul's advice of order and decency (1 Cor. 14:40) as guides.[127] He would have happily accepted — he might even have suggested — the 1629 covenant of the Salem church in Massachusetts Bay Colony: "We covenant with the Lord and one with another, and do bind ourselves in the presence of God, to walk together in all his ways, according as he is pleased to reveal himself unto us in his blessed word of truth." [128]

Ames holds the two sacraments of baptism and the Lord's Supper to be individual appropriations of the covenant of grace within the life of the congregation. The church covenant has meaning for the corporate body of Christ but the sacraments apply in a singular way to the members. A sacrament is conceived in the *Marrow* and the *Conscience* in one or more of three ways: a sign or seal of the covenant of grace, a profession of love and faith flowing from union with Christ, a bond strengthening the faithfulness of members to each other. Baptism is thought of primarily as a seal. It is the first sign of the covenant of grace presented to a believer, and it should be made available to all men in their infancy. Ames does not see the force of baptism to be its connection between the sin of the individual believer and the death and resurrection of Christ, as put by Paul in Colossians 2:12, "You were buried with him in baptism, in which you were also raised with him." It is rather a profound symbol of the very heart of the unconditional covenant of grace. The promise

124. I, xxxii, p. 178.
125. The church covenant could be implicit, requiring no direct reference in worship, but Ames strongly preferred the explicit.
126. On the New England innovation, see Edmund S. Morgan, *Visible Saints: The History of a Puritan Idea* (New York University Press, New York, 1963), where it is argued that the testing of religious experience originated in Massachusetts Bay Colony, spread to Plymouth, New Haven, and Connecticut, and back to England.
127. II, xiv, 20, p. 285.
128. "Salem — 1629, 1812, 1962," *Pilgrim State News* (March 1962), p. 1.

of spiritual regeneration and acceptance into the life of the church offered by baptism have no condition or requirement. The parents, of course, must understand their act and must sincerely desire for their child the promise offered. But no good works are stipulated, no creedal statement is to be made, no proof of faith and repentance is to be adduced by parents on behalf of children. "Faith and repentance no more constitute the covenant of God now than in the time of Abraham . . . the lack of these ought not to prevent infants from being baptized any more than it prevented them from being circumcised." [129] Baptism points to God's gracious covenant to protect, save, comfort, and renew. Man receives the symbol of the promise appropriately at the earliest point in life, when the passivity required in the covenant is the only response possible.

The Lord's Supper requires a more active role for the recipient. Surely a person must be in vocation, or striving for union with Christ, and be willing to contribute to the fellowship of the congregation. The central meaning of the sacrament is symbolic: It is the sign of God's offering himself in the climax of the covenant of grace, namely, the life and death of Christ. The believer partakes with thankfulness and a promise to lead a life of renewed faithfulness towards God and fellow man. The act is a moving reminder to the congregation of the promise they have received and of their mutual responsibility.

Ames speaks out against transubstantiation as a "blind and stupid superstition." [130] Christ is not bodily present in the bread and wine. He is spiritually present with those who receive in faith. To hold otherwise is to misunderstand the language and testimony of Scripture; to misjudge Christ's human, physical, and historical nature; and to depreciate Christ's glorification. The phrase, "This is my body," found in the gospels and in Paul (Matt. 26:26, Mk. 14:22, 1 Cor. 11:24) is to be interpreted like all other sacramental expressions in the Bible. Vivid language is used to point to a spiritual truth. For example, in the reference to circumcision in the Abraham story, the words appear, "This is my covenant." The text goes on to make the fundamental point for Ames: It shall be "a sign of the covenant between me and you (Gen. 17:10–11)." Just as circumcision was not the covenant, but a symbol, so the body of Christ is not the covenant, but a symbol.[131] Ames asserts that Christ believed his body, his very life and impending death, to be a sign of the covenant — indeed, the most precious and esteeemed sign, which the sacrament of the Lord's Supper places before individual believers once more.

129. I, xl, 13, p. 211.
130. I, xl, 22, p. 212.
131. I, xl, 25–31, p. 212.

In book one, chapter thirty-two, Ames offers a traditional, Augustinian distinction between the invisible and the visible church. The former is unseen, pure, essentially unknowable, including all people living, dead, or yet unborn whom God has chosen for salvation; the latter is visible, not entirely pure, and consists of only the living. In this and in later sections on the church, he is most concerned with the visible body of Christ, or the local, instituted congregation.

The function of the visible church as it perpetuates the covenant of grace is to serve the needs of people. The church is never justified because it continues a tradition.[132] Ames believes that Congregational polity is not only scriptural, but runs less risk of being shackled to prior inventions and practices of men. It is freer in its simplicity to sense the spiritual concerns of the community and to present the covenant of grace in new ways. Ames sees this as an opportunity and warning, the latter directed especially to the clergy. Preachers should orient their sermons towards the "arguments" or middle terms that speak to the questions being asked by parishioners. The rhetorical, baroque style of Anglican preaching was often concerned with the questions nobody was asking. In the dialectical preaching which Ames calls for, "Men are to be pricked to the quick so that they feel individually . . . that the word of the Lord is a·two-edged sword, piercing to the inward thoughts and intentions and going through to the joining of bones and marrow. Preaching, therefore, ought not to be dead, but alive and effective." Displays of learning, quotations in Greek, and long, resonant sentences run counter to Paul's words, "My speech and my message were not in plausible words of wisdom, but in demonstration of the Spirit and power, that your faith might not rest in the wisdom of men but in the power of God (1 Cor. 2:4–5)." [133]

The discussion of church-state relations in the *Marrow* and the *Conscience* emphasizes the themes of independence and mutual dependence. William Ames, all too familiar with the union of bishop and king in England, rejects any notion of state control over the body of Christ. He plainly dissociates himself from Dutch Reformed leaders who concede the right of the state to confirm ministers chosen by local congregations.[134] Nor, on the other hand, is the church to exercise any direction over the state and its officials. (Ames, writing in the 1620's, usually speaks of civil rules or magistrates

132. See Ames, *Paraenesis ad studiosos theologiae, habita Franekerae, anno 1623* (Amstelodami, 1631), or *An Exhortation to the Students of Theology, Delivered at Franeker, 1623.* Douglas Horton has translated this remarkably modern counsel to theological students (private printing, 1958).

133. I, xxxv, 46, 54, p. 193.

134. Horton, *Ames by Reuter*, pp. 224, 229.

rather than of the state conceived as a political institution.) The *Marrow* discusses the uniqueness of Christ's role as king, but insists that Christ is a spiritual lord and heavenly governor.[135] The rulers of nations are not subject to his kingship through the church; princes, magistrates, and all ruling bodies are subject to divine sovereignty, known in the general affirmations of scripture and in the law of the land. Divine sovereignty, however, is not applied and interpreted by the church. It may even happen that an enlightened official of the state may inform the church about the nature of divine sovereignty at a particular point.

The magistracy, according to Ames, is a human response to a divine commandment. As authority he cites 1 Peter 2:13, "Be subject for the Lord's sake to every *human* creature, whether it be to the emperor as supreme, or to governors" which, he feels, can be reconciled with Romans 13:1, "Be subject to the governing authorities. For there is no authority except from God, and those that exist have been instituted *by God*." [136] The point is that magistracy is a human institution based on an ordinance of God to control evil and greed. A particular government is to be devised by men, for only government in general is commanded by God. Magistrates have no divine appointment or God-given status, although their response to the divine commandment should afford men an opportunity for service and structured obedience to God.

The ministry, on the other hand, is the result of a direct, particular call from Christ. A minister depends on and must be inwardly persuaded of his divine commission. A magistrate, compared with a minister, has considerable freedom in his activities: He can interpret laws, or ordain new ones; and he can decide methods of administration — all subject to the prescribed limits of his rule. But a minister can do only those things which Christ has commanded and which are set forth directly or by implication in the Scriptures. Ames envisions the magistracy working within a broad realm to direct the body politic, whereas the function of the ministry, being spiritual, is more specialized and limited.

Thus there should be a separation between church and state because of basic functions, but the line can never be drawn sharply or with finality. For "there is no thing, person, or cause so ecclesiastical that it does not belong in some way to the jurisdiction of the magistrate, and there is no action so secular . . . concerning obedience to God, that the church may not take notice of it." [137] To say that

135. I, xix, 31, p. 134.
136. II, xvii, 48, p. 311. Editor's italics.
137. II, xvii, 49, p. 312.

the church is concerned solely with spiritual matters, or that religion should not be part of public life, or that the state is unconcerned with the contribution of the church to the body politic, or that state and church do not cooperate in some way to make a commonwealth — all these, according to Ames, are artificial, inflexible positions which undermine the life of a community.

AUTHORITY OF THE SCRIPTURES · Matthew Nethenus (fl. 1665), William Ames's most enthusiastic biographer, wrote that the Amesian writings contained "solid, sinewy, and accurate practical theology, drawn not from the muddy pits of human systems and traditions, but from the limpid springs of Israel." [138] Nethenus was right in his judgment that Ames was a biblical theologian par excellence in a biblically minded age. The Marrow, the Conscience, and the other writings display a knowledge and approval of medieval and ancient philosophical systems. But Ames is wary of any ultimate dependence on secular philosophies, for they often "talk of principles without foundation and actions without end." [139] They do not give practical guidance, he feels, nor do they speak with power. Philosophical writings at their best can be used to amplify biblical themes — the ten great Aristotelian virtues, for example, are a convenient summary and artful exposition of marks of the good life commended in the Scriptures.[140] In his writings against Bellarmine, Ames puts his wariness this way: "We venerate the judgment of the ancient councils as decrees of the senate . . . we piously follow the writings of the learned as responses of the wise freely given for our thought: But in all these things our dove (I mean faith) finds no rest for the sole of her foot, so it returns to God in the ark of the Scriptures, since the waters of error are on the face of the whole earth." [141]

More than any other Puritan of the time, Ames directs himself to the questions of the Bible's authority and sufficiency. His Theological Discussion on the Perfection of the Holy Scripture is devoted to this task, as are extensive sections of the Marrow and the Conscience. Ames agrees with the usual Reformed assertion that the Bible should be reckoned as "perfection." But to Ames, this statement alone begs the question, for what is the precise nature of the perfection? The Scriptures must, first, be understood as perfect in themselves. This signifies to Ames that the Old and New Testaments are infallible when they represent God's will in faith and observance.

138. Horton, Ames by Nethenus, p. 15.
139. Ames, Disputatio de perfectione, p. 14.
140. Ames, Disputatio de perfectione, pp. 15–20.
141. Horton, Ames by Visscher, p. 118.

The Bible's infallibility for the religious life is a direct consequence of God's revelation to biblical writers.[142] The perfect-in-itself theme does not occupy Ames for long — he is not disposed to advance a theory of plenary, detailed inspiration, or a belief that each word of scripture is part of God's oracle for all time. But it is clear that he feels that God has chosen to reveal himself to Isaiah, Matthew, Job, Paul, and the other writers when they are dealing with the essentials of the life of faith.

The perfection of the Scriptures is known, second and more significantly, "in regard to our direction and instruction." [143] The Bible is perfect in the sense that its major teachings have guided the faithful of all ages and have achieved timelessness. Such perfection is the reason why the Letter to the Hebrews, for example, freely invokes the words of Solomon taken from an ancient era: "And have you forgotten the exhortation which addresses you as sons? 'My son, do not regard lightly the discipline of the Lord, nor lose courage when you are punished by him. For the Lord disciplines him whom he loves, and chastises every son whom he receives (Heb. 12:5–6; Prov. 3:11–12).'" [144] The teaching of the Bible has abided because it deals with the central problems of man's existence: the nature and way of God's revelation, man's sinful condition, the good life, the place of faith.[145]

The Scriptures give light to themselves and he who diligently applies himself will be led into the meaning of the teaching. Ames comes down hard on the point of study. It is good to know the original languages of the Bible. A man must understand that the revelation given to each of the biblical writers accords with particular circumstances. In the *Theological Discussion on the Perfection of the Holy Scripture*, he speaks of the "most agreeable tempering" of words to the person and condition of the writer.[146] St. John of the Apocalypse and St. Paul of Colossians not only write differently, but they have different concerns which the reader must understand. A student of the Scriptures must pay attention, above all, to the kind of language used by the Bible. He must not leap at picturesque and didactic detail and claim it as the very words of God. He must understand the vivid use of allegory, parable, analogy, and hyperbole in the Bible — all of which contribute to the force and life of the Scriptures. The point of the six days of creation is to show that creation was not accomplished all at once and that the particular events of creation had a beneficent sequence.[147]

142. I, xxxiv, p. 185.
143. Ames, *Disputatio de perfectione*, pp. 1, 3.
144. I, xxxiv, 14, p. 187.
145. Horton, *Ames by Reuter*, pp. 209–10, 226.
146. Ames, *Disputatio de perfectione*, p. 2.
147. I, viii, 28, p. 102.

The two trees in the Garden of Eden are essentially symbols; man must always have symbols to perceive a religious truth. God in his wisdom has chosen the tree of life to be a sign for the obedient life and the tree of the knowledge of good and evil to be a sign for disobedience. Ames is willing to call the first the sacrament of life and the second the sacrament of death.[148] If one wishes to say that the Ten Commandments were written by the finger of God in tablets of stone, he must understand he is using a powerful figure "to declare their perpetual and unchangeable duration" and sufficiency.[149] The miracles described in the Scriptures are never in themselves grounds for acceptance of the teaching (Deut. 3:1–3), and "doctrine which does not agree with the known will of God ought not to be accepted, although it might seem to be confirmed with miracles." [150]

Ames's practical advice to his readers is to study the Scriptures as good Ramists. They should approach the Bible with genuine questions about the religious life — in fact, the provocation of Scripture is so great that they should expect more questions to arise before discovering answers. Reading, thought, and prayer should lead the faithful in a search for the vital argument or middle term which will join the parts of questions arising from their own experience. Ames is assured that the Bible has an abundance of all possible arguments linking man and God. In the *Marrow* he often uses another word to denote the Bible: "In the Scriptures, or promises." [151]

Ames can argue skillfully the rational basis of the Bible's perfection for "our direction and instruction," but in the end his assurance is a confession of faith. He sides with John Calvin: The Scripture is perfect in its operation in us because it is the vehicle of the Holy Spirit.[152] To be sure, one confronts the Holy Spirit elsewhere — in nature, in man's sense of mystery, and in the human experiences of work, friendship, and love. These are important witnesses, but they do not suffice and often their very meaning can only be explained by the summary action of the Holy Spirit speaking through prophet, apostle, and evangelist. On what basis can it be said that the Scriptures are the chief instrument of the Holy Spirit? Ames answers experientially, as might be expected. Nothing has spoken so clearly and forcefully to the problem of "man according to God" as the Bible. This has been true historically and it is true in man's present religious life. An ultimate answer for Ames is that God has chosen to reveal himself through the Spirit in the word. This he does not attempt to argue, being a state-

---

148. I, x, 33, p. 113.
149. II, xv, 11, p. 291.
150. I, xxxiii, 35, p. 185.
151. E.g., I, iii, 9, p. 81.
152. Ames, *Disputatio de perfectione*, p. 3.

ment of conviction. It is conceivable that other main channels for the Holy Spirit may appear in the future, but Ames is doubtful. At most, there may be other "extraordinary ministers" like Wyclif, Luther, Zwingli, and Calvin who will make new and needed applications of biblical insights.[153] Ames finds the authority of the Scripture in the New Testament words, "Men moved by the Holy Spirit spoke from God (2 Peter 1:21)."

The *Theological Discussion on the Perfection of the Holy Scripture* points to the freedom and responsibility which both the believer and the gathered church have as the Holy Spirit is sought in the Bible. Men are free to transgress ecclesiastical restrictions (particularly those of pope and bishop), if they find the witness of Scripture to be contrary. But the faithful must strive for consensus in the biblical understanding of the point in question. A multitude of interpretations reduces the word of God to babel. Biblical study and commentary, including the works of many a Roman Catholic scholar, have produced a tradition that must be heeded. The same passage that proclaims the Holy Spirit speaking through the writers of the Bible issues a warning: "You must understand this, that no prophecy of Scripture is a matter of one's own interpretation (2 Peter 1:20)." [154] Ames urges his readers to search in the company of others and to be mindful of the historic community of learning which has attempted to bring forth the witness of the Holy Spirit in the word.

CONCLUSION · What can be said of this man who wrote his books in Renaissance Latin and who died in his prime, rudely cut off from a career in the New World? To some he stands as one among many Puritan thinkers whose special contribution lay in the skillful handling of practical questions. He is often presented as a Protestant casuist or Puritan precisionist.[155] Such an interpretation does not grasp the essential meaning of the *Conscience* and pays little attention to the purpose of the *Marrow* and other writings. Sometimes he is given only passing reference in histories of dogmatics; Albrecht Ritschl views him primarily as a transitional figure to later German and Dutch Pietism.[156] William Ames was certainly not a Luther or a Calvin, but in the New

153. I, xxxiii, 38–39, p. 185.
154. Ames, *Disputatio de perfectione*, pp. 1, 2.
155. See George L. Mosse's works, especially "The Assimilation of Machiavelli in English Thought: The Casuistry of William Perkins and William Ames," *Huntington Library Quarterly*, XVII: No. 4 (Aug. 1954), and *The Holy Pretence: A Study in Christianity and Reason of State from William Perkins to John Winthrop* (Blackwell, Oxford, 1957).
156. Albrecht Ritschl, *A Critical History of the Christian Doctrine of Justification and Reconciliation* (John S. Black trans. Edmonston and Douglas, Edinburgh, 1872), refers to Ames as a minor theologian who points to the more important thought (so he believes) of Voetius. Ritschl's *Geschichte des*

England to which he was going he was to be cited more often than either. And in the Europe where he died, his insight molded what was to abide of Luther and Calvin. Ames had his greatest influence, without question, in America where his covenant theology, church polity, Ramist thought, understanding of the Scriptures, and conception of faith and religious experience were accepted as canonical.[157] Jonathan Edwards (1703–58) found his discussion of personal faith to be crucial, especially the Amesian insistence on sincerity and humility in the believer [158] — but also Ames's concern for the marks of "observance" which were to shine forth in the life of a true believer. In his homeland, the *Marrow* and the *Conscience* were under ban until the action of the Long Parliament in the 1640's, but Ames was looked upon *in absentia* as a father of the Puritan movement. In the Great Rebellion and the post-Restoration period Ames was widely read and acknowledged as one of the masters of the Puritan and Nonconformist way.

On the Continent, particularly in Holland, he had a host of followers and successors. Gisbertus Voetius (1589–1676), professor at Utrecht whom Ritschl calls the leader of the Reformed pietistic movement, used the experiential ideas of Ames (although Voetius stayed primarily in the orthodox camp as an exegete of the doctrine of God in Scripture).[159] Johannes Cocceius (1603–69), Ames's student at Franeker added to Amesian covenant theology, giving it a sure place in Reformed thought and analyzed afresh the meaning of living to God. Peter von Mastricht (1630–1706), professor at Frankfort, Duisburgh, and Utrecht — a favorite of Jonathan Edwards — and Friedrich Lampe (1683–1729), Utrecht professor, continued to insist on the covenant ideas of Ames and Cocceius in a time of great theological change. These theologians, let alone generations of Dutch pastors who spoke warmly of Ames,[160] attest to the imprint left by the Franeker professor in his land of refuge.

The influence of William Ames goes beyond the seventeenth and

---

Pietismus in der reformierten Kirche does not mention Ames. D. August Lang, *Puritanismus und Pietismus* (Buchhandlung des Erziehungsvereins Neukirchen Kreis Moers, 1941), gives him scant and misleading notice.

157. See Roland H. Bainton, *Yale and the Ministry* (Harper, New York, 1957), pp. 9, 39.

158. Jonathan Edwards, *A Treatise concerning Religious Affections* (John E. Smith ed. and intro. Yale University Press, New Haven, 1959), pp. 67–68. The references in the text are to Ames's *De conscientia*.

159. See John W. Beardslee, III, ed. *Reformed Dogmatics: J. Wollebius, G. Voetius, F. Turretin* (Oxford University Press, New York, 1965). Voetius relies on *De conscientia* and often describes Ames as a casuist, pp. 272, 292, 301.

160. The Dutch pastor Reinerus Vogelsangius, or Voglesangh, wrote a laudatory, 14-line Latin poem about Ames, published in the front matter of *Works* (Cantabrigiae, 1646), a small volume containing Ames's Latin treatises on logic and philosophy.

early eighteenth centuries. It cannot be proved whether or not Friedrich Schleiermacher (1768–1834), the empirical German theologian and philosopher, read the *Marrow* and the *Conscience*. In the case of the *Marrow*, the possibility exists, for the work was widely circulated in Germany. If one may not speak of direct influence, one may refer to parallel concern and Ames's anticipation. Schleiermacher found the task of theology to lie in the presentation of a living relation to God. Like Ames, he deplored a heavy concentration on biblical exegesis which, he felt, would have meaning only for those firmly and even blindly within the Christian faith. Dogmatizing, even out of the Bible, always left one empty. The message of the gospel must be broken out of the ever fresh ground of human experience; here alone true religion could be known and faithful living become a reality.[161] Schleiermacher like Ames was concerned with the life of the church and found a "plurality of evangelical church societies" to create necessary vital contacts between believers.[162] Schleiermacher no doubt carried the Amesian understanding of living to God to an extreme which the Puritan would not have accepted. Gone is the Reformed concept of a God of history and institutions, also a God of promise and covenant; instead there is a subtle, indwelling God known subjectively. The Christian is urged to depend on God, but he is not called by God in word, Holy Spirit, and sacrament. Nor does Schleiermacher see the Christian life as conversionist, as well as pietistic. Yet the main connection abides: Both Schleiermacher and Ames stressed the empirical and voluntaristic nature of the Christian faith.

Among the many books that he read, William Ames was most deeply moved by St. Paul's letter to the Romans. Were Ames to present the *Marrow of Theology* to twentieth-century readers, he might, in Puritan style, put these words on the title page: "May the God of hope fill you with all joy and peace in believing, so that by the power of the Holy Spirit you may abound in hope (Rom. 15:13)."

---

161. See Richard R. Niebuhr, "Schleiermacher: Theology as Human Reflection," *Harvard Theological Review*, IV, No. 1 (Jan. 1962), and *Schleiermacher on Christ and Religion* (Charles Scribner's Sons, New York, 1964), especially pp. 142–43, 192–94.

162. Horton, *Ames by Reuter*, pp. 275–77.

Dedicatory Epistle

To the pious and benevolent merchants who, at their own expense, have liberally provided for the studies of poor youths intending to enter the holy ministry:

DAVID NUITS · DAVID DE WEERT · JOHN DE MAREES · ANTHONY GOMMARIS · LAURENCE DE GROOT · WILLIAM VANDER ELST · MICHAEL FAIS · PETER DE VOS · JOHN DUITS · JAMES VAN HOREN · JOHN VANDER MARCK · AND OTHERS HELD IN THE SAME ESTEEM.

I do not doubt, honored gentlemen, that you take with utmost seriousness our Lord's divine warning: *Take heed that you do not your righteousness before men to be seen by them. . . . When you give alms, do not sound a trumpet before you. . . . Let not your left hand know what your right hand does*, Matt. 6:1–4. To be honest, I have a scruple and a grave doubt whether I should bring to the public what you have done in secret (following the Lord's teaching). But since the chief apostle of the Lord did not hesitate *To make known to all the grace of God bestowed on the churches of Macedonia*, 2 Cor. 8:1, and since the present state of the church seems to demand that that grace be promoted in every way, I consider it better to do some violence to your modesty than to fail in my duty. As a result, it may be, as the apostle declares of the Corinthians, that *Your zeal will incite many others*, 2 Cor. 9:2. There is more glitter and prospect of worldly gain in ordinary commercial enterprise. But when all things are carefully weighed, the trade of neither of the Indies can be compared with the heavenly commerce where earthly and perishing goods are put on the market and spiritual blessings are received. The latter will endure, for we have the Lord's word: *Make friends for yourselves by means of the mammon of unrighteousness that when you fail they may receive you into everlasting dwelling places*, Luke 16:9.

What I have said is good reason for wishing your names to appear in this dedication. And it should be added that seven years ago you committed to my care some of your charges, which was the first occasion of drawing out this "marrow of theology" — so that it might serve them. I hope that the progress of some under this method of instruction has shown that success was not altogether lacking in the plan.

When I asked myself about this little book's customary dedication, I thought it should be to you, for you were, so to say, the first authors of the attempt. I earnestly pray that you may consider the work fair and reasonable. *Now he that gives seed to the sower and bread for food will . . . multiply your seed and increase the fruits of your righteousness. You will be enriched in everything for great bountifulness, which through us produces thanksgiving to God,* 2 Cor. 9:10, 11.

Your most devoted,

William Ames

A Brief Forewarning of the Author
concerning His Purpose

I do not assume that I know all the thoughts of my critics. Yet, the age being what it is, I foresee several points which will be brought against my well-intentioned endeavor, and I propose now briefly to meet the chief objections.

Some people, including those not unlearned, dislike this whole manner of writing, that is, of placing the main body of theology in a short compendium. They ask for great volumes in which they may establish themselves or wander about as they will. But I intend this for all those who have neither the ample leisure nor the great skill to hunt the partridge in mountain and forest. Their situation calls for showing them the nest itself, or the seat of what they are pursuing, without ado.

Others do not dislike the manner as long as the chief heads are treated in a broad rhetorical way — they think that details cannot be handled point by point. Yet when language flows on in a swift stream, carrying with it many things of many kinds, the reader can catch and hold fast to very little. He cannot find a resting place. But when certain directions are laid down, the reader has at every step, as it were, a spot marked where he may set his foot.

There will be some who condemn the precision of method and logical form as curious and troublesome. But we wish them sounder reason, for they separate the art of learning, judging, and memorizing from those things which most deserve to be learned, known, and memorized.

On the other hand, there will be those who desire a more exact use of the art of logic. These I could not satisfy fully even if I would, because of my own imperfection; neither would I, even if I could, because of the shortcomings of others.

I imagine also that there will be not a few who believe that to set forth such teachings as these, after the labors of so many learned men in the same vein, is superfluous, and doing only what has been done before. I should be of the same opinion if anything of this kind were available which pleased everyone in all respects. I hope it will not be judged that I expect to please all by this work. My hope is, however, that at least two or three may presently come upon this endeavor and find in it something which is better suited to instruct, to stir conviction, than what they have found in the more learned writing of others. If this proves a sound conjecture, I shall consider that I have been well paid for my labor.

I expect to be accused of obscurity by those who are relatively unskilled in theology. I wish they would learn from Cyrus that the sight of the sun's rays, αἱ διάφασεις, shining through a window loses its charm if the window is too large.[1] A contracted light, although it may appear small, is more enlightening (if a man comes near and observes) than one which is, as it were, dissipated by too much enlargement.

The dryness of style and the harshness of words will be criticized by the same persons. And I confess that I share that heresy which bids me, when teaching, not to say in two words what may be said in one and which allows me to choose the key which best opens the lock. The key may well be of wood if the golden key does not work.

Finally, if there are some who desire to have practical matters better explained, especially those of the latter part of this *Marrow*, we shall attempt, God willing, to satisfy them in a special treatise, which I mean to write, dealing with questions usually called "cases of conscience."[2]

If there are some who criticize or desire other things, I ask that they candidly give me their thoughts, so that I may make just apology or due amendment.

Finis

1. Probably an Amesian paraphrase of a section of Xenophon's idealized life of Cyrus the Elder, founder of the Achaemenian Persian Empire (559–529 B.C.). See Xenophon, *The Education of Cyrus* [*Cyropaedia*] (trans. Henry G. Dakyns, J. W. Dent and Sons, London, n.d., "Everyman's Library").

2. *De conscientia et eius iure vel casibus: libri quinque*, or *Conscience: Its Law or Cases, Five Books*, was first published at Amsterdam in 1630. Like the *Marrow*, it went through many editions and was translated into several languages; see Introduction p. 9.

METHOD AND CHART OF THE
MARROW[3]

3. A modification of the chart found in the 1642 translation (London); it is preceded in the front matter by a lavish "method" of 24 pp. Ames may not have offered such a chart in any of the editions published during his lifetime, but the above is faithful to the method and divisions which he had in mind, Introduction, pp. 41–42. Later editors added charts for two other works, *Opera* (*Amstelodami*, 1658), or *Works*, Vol. V.

72

Theology,
I, i, ii, p. 77,
has two
parts

Faith in God,
I, iii, p. 80.
What may be
known of God
from the
back, so to
speak, I, iv,
3, p. 83, are

Sufficiency,
I, iv, 10, p. 84,
known in his

Efficiency, or
working power,
I, vi, p. 91,
known in his
decree and
counsel, I,
vii, p. 94,
whose parts
are

Essence,
I, iv, p. 83.

Subsistence,
or manner of
being in the
persons of
the Trinity,
I, v, p. 88.

Creation,
I, viii, p. 100.

Providence,
I, ix, p. 107.

**Ordinary
and extra-
ordinary,**
I, ix, 8, p. 107.

**Special for
intelligent
creatures,**
I, x, p. 110,
which relates
to

Man's fall,
I, xi, p. 113,
under which
are to be
considered

Restoration
which con-
tains

Observance,
II, i, p. 219,
whose parts
are

Virtue
II, ii, p. 224.

Good works,
II, iii, p. 232.

Is known
in

Religion,
II, iv, p. 236,
whose act is
worship

**Justice and charity
or love** toward our
neighbor, II, xvi,
p. 300, affecting
him

Divided
into

With ad-
juncts

Directly

Indirectly

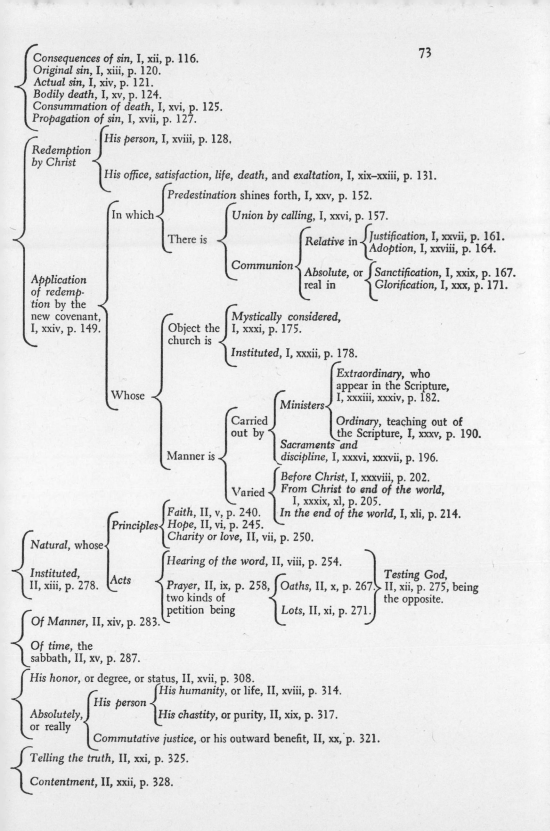

Consequences of sin, I, xii, p. 116.
Original sin, I, xiii, p. 120.
Actual sin, I, xiv, p. 121.
Bodily death, I, xv, p. 124.
Consummation of death, I, xvi, p. 125.
Propagation of sin, I, xvii, p. 127.

Redemption by Christ
— His person, I, xviii, p. 128.
— His office, satisfaction, life, death, and exaltation, I, xix–xxiii, p. 131.

Application of redemption by the new covenant, I, xxiv, p. 149.

In which — Predestination shines forth, I, xxv, p. 152.

There is — Union by calling, I, xxvi, p. 157.

Communion
Relative in — Justification, I, xxvii, p. 161.
Adoption, I, xxviii, p. 164.
Absolute, or real in — Sanctification, I, xxix, p. 167.
Glorification, I, xxx, p. 171.

Whose

Object the church is
Mystically considered, I, xxxi, p. 175.
Instituted, I, xxxii, p. 178.

Manner is

Carried out by
Ministers
Extraordinary, who appear in the Scripture, I, xxxiii, xxxiv, p. 182.
Ordinary, teaching out of the Scripture, I, xxxv, p. 190.
Sacraments and discipline, I, xxxvi, xxxvii, p. 196.

Varied
Before Christ, I, xxxviii, p. 202.
From Christ to end of the world, I, xxxix, xl, p. 205.
In the end of the world, I, xli, p. 214.

Natural, whose

Principles
Faith, II, v, p. 240.
Hope, II, vi, p. 245.
Charity or love, II, vii, p. 250.

Acts
Hearing of the word, II, viii, p. 254.
Prayer, II, ix, p. 258, two kinds of petition being
Oaths, II, x, p. 267.
Lots, II, xi, p. 271.
Testing God, II, xii, p. 275, being the opposite.

Instituted, II, xiii, p. 278.

Of Manner, II, xiv, p. 283.

Of time, the sabbath, II, xv, p. 287.

His honor, or degree, or status, II, xvii, p. 308.

Absolutely, or really

His person
His humanity, or life, II, xviii, p. 314.
His chastity, or purity, II, xix, p. 317.

Commutative justice, or his outward benefit, II, xx, p. 321.

Telling the truth, II, xxi, p. 325.

Contentment, II, xxii, p. 328.

BOOK I

I

The Definition or Nature of Theology

1. Theology is the doctrine or teaching [*doctrina*] of living to God. John 6:68, *The words of eternal life*; Acts 5:20, *The words of this life*; Rom. 6:11, *Consider yourselves . . . alive to God.*

2. It is called doctrine, not to separate it from understanding, knowledge, wisdom, art, or prudence — for these go with every exact discipline, and most of all with theology — but to mark it as a discipline which derives not from nature and human inquiry like others, but from divine revelation and appointment. Isa. 51:4, *Doctrine shall go forth from me*; Matt. 21:25, *From heaven . . . Why then did you not believe him?*; John 9:29, *We know that God has spoken to Moses*; Gal. 1:11–12, *The gospel . . . is not according to man. For I neither received it from man, nor was I taught it, but it came through a revelation*; John 6:45.

3. The principles of other arts, since they are inborn in us, can be developed through sense perception, observation, experience, and induction, and so brought to perfection. But the basic principles of theology, though they may be advanced by study and industry, are not in us by nature. Matt. 16:17, *Flesh and blood has not revealed this to you.*

4. Every art has its rules to which the work of the person practicing it corresponds. Since living is the noblest work of all, there cannot be any more proper study than the art of living.

5. Since the highest kind of life for a human being is that which approaches most closely the living and life-giving God, the nature of theological life is living to God.

6. Men live to God when they live in accord with the will of God, to the glory of God, and with God working in them. 1 Peter 4:2, 6, *That he may live . . . by the will of God . . . according to God*; Gal. 2:19–20, *That I may live to God . . . Christ who lives in me*; 2 Cor. 4:10, *That the life of Jesus may be manifest in our bodies*;

Phil. 1:20, *Christ will be honored in my body, whether by life or by death.*

7. This life in essence remains one and the same from its beginning to eternity. John 3:36 and 5:24, *He who believes in the Son has eternal life;* 1 John 3:15, *Eternal life abiding in him.*

8. Although it is within the compass of this life to live both happily and well, εὐζωία, living well, is more excellent than εὐδαιμονία, living happily. What chiefly and finally ought to be striven for is not happiness which has to do with our own pleasure, but goodness which looks to God's glory. For this reason, theology is better defined as that good life whereby we live to God than as that happy life whereby we live to ourselves. The apostle therefore called it by synecdoche,[4] *The teaching which accords with godliness,* I Tim. 6:3.

9. Furthermore, since this life is the spiritual work of the whole man, in which he is brought to enjoy God and to act according to his will, and since it certainly has to do with man's will, it follows that the first and proper subject of theology is the will. Prov. 4:23, *From the heart come the acts of life;* and 23:26, *Give me your heart.*

10. Now since this life so willed is truly and properly our most important practice, it is self-evident that theology is not a speculative discipline but a practical one — not only in the common respect that all disciplines have εὐπραξία, good practice, as their end, but in a special and peculiar manner compared with all others.

11. Nor is there anything in theology which does not refer to the final end or to the means related to that end — all of which refer directly to practice.

12. This practice of life is so perfectly reflected in theology that there is no precept of universal truth relevant to living well in domestic economy, morality, political life, or lawmaking which does not rightly pertain to theology.

13. Theology, therefore, is to us the ultimate and the noblest of all exact teaching arts. It is a guide and master plan for our highest end, sent in a special manner from God, treating of divine things, tending towards God, and leading man to God. It may therefore not incorrectly be called θεοζωία, a living to God, or θεουργία, a working towards God, as well as theology.[5]

4. A figure of speech in which a part stands for the whole. For other uses of this favorite Amesian device, see I, xxii, 5, p. 142; xxv, 19, p. 154; xxv, 24, p. 154; xl, 31, p. 213; II, ii, 20, p. 227; xvii, 12, p. 309. In I, xxv, 24, p. 154, e.g., predestination is distinguished as a part of election, but on occasions it can be "used in the same sense with election, by synecdoche."

5. Posthumous editions add a third, less forceful term, θεολογία, a speaking or writing on God.

II

The Division or Parts of Theology

1. The two parts of theology are faith and observance. 2 Tim. 1:13, *Hold the express form of the sound words which you have heard from me with faith and love;* 1 Tim. 1:19, *Having faith and a good conscience;* Ps. 37:3, *Trust in the Lord, and do good.* The theology of Paul consisted of these parts: Acts 24:14–16, *I believe all things . . . which are written . . . and I have hope in God. . . . I drive myself to have a conscience without offense.* The same parts made up the theology of Abraham: Gen. 15:6 and 17:1, *Abraham believed the Lord. Walk before me continually, and be untouched.* Christ demands the same of his disciples when he requires, beyond faith, that they *Observe everything which he commanded,* Matt. 28:20. Paul covers the same matters in his Letter to the Romans which manifestly contains the sum of theology. Finally he wanted to have these things taught in the churches. Titus 3:8, *I desire you to affirm these things, so that those who have believed in God may use care to apply themselves in doing good.*

2. It is characteristic of this division (as is required in any art) that it follows from the nature of the object. Since the beginning or first act of the spiritual life, which is the proper concern of theology, is faith and the second act or operation of that principle is observance, it follows that these two are the genuine parts of theology and that no others are to be sought.[6]

3. In the Old Testament (fitted for a legal and servile state) theology appears to be divided sometimes into the fear of God and the observance of his statutes. Eccles. 12:13, *This is the sum: Fear God and observe his statutes, for this is the whole duty of man.* But by metonymy,[7] faith is included in the former, as appears in Prov. 3:5, 7, *Have faith in the Lord with all your heart . . . fear the Lord and turn away from evil.*

6. The distinction between the first act and a second act is made in the scholastic sense that the first act of anything is its being (*esse*) and the second, its working or operation (*operari*).

7. A figure of speech in which the effect may be put for the cause or an adjunct for a subject — or vice versa. Other metonymies are also possible. Ames sometimes identifies the kind of metonymy; more often, the context makes it clear — the above is a metonymy of the adjunct in which "fear of God," an aspect or subdivision, is used in place of "faith," the subject or main topic. See Introduction, p. 41, including n. 88; I, iii, 9, p. 81; ix, 11, p. 108; xl, 31, p. 213; II, vi, 6, p. 246.

4. These two parts are always joined together in use and exercise, but they are distinguished in their nature and in the rules which govern them.

5. They are also distinguished in the order of nature, so that faith holds the first place and spiritual observance the second, for no vital actions or life are forthcoming except where there is an inborn principle of life.[8]

III

Faith

1. Faith is the resting of the heart on God, the author of life and eternal salvation, so that we may be saved from all evil through him and may follow all good. Isa. 10;20, *Lean upon the Lord, the Holy One of Israel, in faith*; Ps. 37:5, *Commit your way to the Lord and trust in him*; Jer. 17:7, *Blessed is the man who has trust in the Lord and whose confidence is the Lord.*

2. To believe signifies ordinarily an act of the understanding as it gives assent to evidence. But since as a consequence the will is wont to be moved and reach out to embrace the good thus proved, faith may rightly designate this act of the will as well. So it is to be understood in this book: *Faith is a receiving* John 1:12, *As many as received him, or who believe.*

3. In this way faith comes by the good which then becomes ours through faith. It is an act of choice, an act of the whole man — which is by no means a mere act of the intellect. John 6:35, *He who comes to me . . . he who believes in me.*

4. Although faith always presupposes a knowledge of the Gospel, there is nevertheless no saving knowledge in anyone — or even a knowledge different from that found in those who are not to be saved

---

8. Posthumous editions add a concluding section to this chapter in which the distinction between faith and observance is held to be similar to the traditional distinction between metaphysics and ethics. Francisco Suarez (1548–1617), *Disputatio I*, or *First Disputation*, v, n. 44 is quoted; see *Opera Omnia* (editio nova, a Carolo Berton, apud Ludovicum Vivès, Parisiis, 1856–78), or *The Complete Works*, Vol. XXV, 50–51. The later editors of the *Marrow* imply, however, that Suarez and other scholastics overemphasized the divisions of theology and philosophy. Faith and observance in the Amesian sense must be understood as different but essentially connected and unified acts. For the text of this addition to the *Marrow*, see *Medulla theologica* (editio novissima, Amstelodami, 1648), pp. 4–5. For other references to Suarez in the original *Marrow* see II, xv (on the sabbath), p. 287, especially n. 11.

— except the knowledge which follows this act of the will and depends upon it. John 7:17; 8:31, 32; 1 John 2:3.

5. True Christian faith which has a place in the understanding always leans upon divine testimony, as far as it is divine. But it cannot be received without a genuine turning of the will towards God. John 3:33, *He who receives his testimony has sealed that God is true*; Romans 4:20, *He was strengthened by faith, by glory rendered to God.*

6. Faith is not more uncertain and doubtful because it leans on testimony alone, but rather more certain than any human knowledge because of its nature. This is so because it is brought to its object on the formal basis of infallibility — yet because of imperfection in the inclination [*habitus*] from which faith flows, the assent of faith often appears weaker in this or that person than the assent of knowledge.

7. Now God is the object of faith, not as he is considered in himself, but as we live well by him. I Tim. 4:10, *We hope in the living God, who is the preserver of all men, especially those who believe.*

8. Christ as redeemer is the mediate but not the ultimate object of faith, for we believe through Christ in God. Rom. 6:11, *Alive to God through Christ*; 2 Cor. 3:4, *We have faith towards God through Christ*; 1 Peter 1:21, *Believing in God through him.*

9. The declarations in the Scriptures, or promises, contain and exhibit the object of faith. The declarations themselves are called the object of faith by metonymy of the adjunct, in the sense that the good to be attained is the end and effect of faith, but not properly the object itself. The true object of faith is the one upon whose strength we lean in pursuing the good. 1 Cor. 1:23 and 2:2, *We preach Christ . . . I determined to know nothing among you except Jesus Christ*; 2 Cor. 5:19, *God was in Christ.*

10. Having this divine faith which looks to the will of God and our own salvation, we must believe not simply any man, but God alone. Rom. 3:4, *Every man is a liar*; 1 Cor. 2:5, *That your faith might not rest in the wisdom of men.*

11. The authority of God is therefore the proper and immediate ground of all truth to be believed in this way. Everywhere the prophets speak solemnly: *The word of the Lord* and *Thus says the Lord.*

12. Hence faith, as it points to the thing to be believed, must finally depend on the authority of God or divine revelation. 2 Peter 1:20–21, *If you first know this, that no prophecy of the scripture is a matter of one's own interpretation*; John 9:29, *We know that God spoke to Moses.* And the final dependence of faith, as it designates the act of believing, is on the operation and inner persuasion of the Holy Spirit. 1 Cor. 12:3, *No one can say Jesus is Lord except by the Holy Spirit.*

13. This faith whereby we not only believe God or about God but in God is true and proper trust. This does not mean a certain and absolute confidence of future good, but rather signifies the choice and appropriation of a good and sufficient means for such confidence and expectation. In this sense men are said to have faith in wisdom, power, friends, and their own riches. Ps. 78:22, *They did not believe in God, and they did not rely on his salvation.*

14. This is declared in all those phrases of Scripture where the true nature of faith is set forth. סָמַךְ; בָּטַח; בְּ, אֶל, and עַל עָשָׂה; πιστεύειν ἐπί, or εἰς — lean upon and rely on, believe in or on. Prov. 3:5; Isa. 10:20; 31:1; 50:10; Pss. 62:7; 37:3 and 5; 71:6; Rom. 10:11.

15. To believe in God, therefore, is to cling to God by believing, to lean on God, to rest in God as our all-sufficient life and salvation. Deut. 30:20, *By cleaving to him, for he is your life.*

16. Hence that general assent which the papists call faith is not faith. By their own confession it can exist without any life in it. Jas. 2:17.

17. That special assent, whereby we declare that God is our God in Christ, is not the first act of faith, but an act flowing from faith. For there is no more certainty of this truth and no truer apprehension of it in you than in another until you have specifically joined yourself to God in faith. Rom. 5:1, 2, *Being justified through faith, we have peace towards God . . . we glory in God.*

18. Since faith is the first act of our life whereby we live to God in Christ, it must consist of union with God, which a mere assent to the truth concerning God cannot effect.

19. Furthermore, one who out of a sense of his misery and the lack of any means of deliverance in himself or others is about to accept the faith must necessarily surrender himself to God in Christ as a sufficient and faithful Savior. But he cannot make that surrender through any assent of the understanding — only through a consent of the will.

20. Although the Scriptures sometimes speak of an assent to the truth about God and Christ as true faith, John 1:50, a special trust is always included. So it is in all places where there are words of saving faith. Either trust is presupposed in the Messiah and only the end pointed to; or it is applied to the person of Jesus Christ; or it is designated as assent as a cause may be designated by its effect. John 11:25–27, *He who believes in me . . . shall live . . . Do you believe this? She said to him, Yea, Lord; I believe that you are the Christ, the Son of God, who is coming into the world.*

21. Trust is rightly said to be the fruit of faith as it looks to God in the future and constitutes a firm hope; but as it looks to God in Christ offering himself in the present, it is faith itself. Hence arise those

names which the Scriptures give to saving faith. πεποίθησις, παρρησία, *Persuasion, boldness*, 2 Cor. 3:4 and 5:6–8; Eph. 3:12; 1 Peter 1:13; 1 John 5:13–14; πληροφορία, *Full conviction*, Rom. 4:21; Col. 2:2; ὑπόστασις, *Substance*, Heb. 11:1.

22. Some place true faith partly in the understanding and partly in the will. This is not quite correct, for it is a single virtue and brings forth acts of one quality throughout, not partly of knowledge and partly of the affections, 1 Cor. 13. The firm assent to the promises of the gospel is called both faith and trust, partly because, as general assent, it produces faith and partly because, as a special and firm assent, it flows from trust as it takes actual possession of grace already received. This firm assent leans on the trust of the heart as a middle or third term [*argumentum*], by the strength of which alone a conclusion about faith can be reached.[9] Moreover, experience teaches that particular certainty of the understanding may be lacking in some at times, even though they have true faith hidden in their hearts.

IV

God and His Essence

1. In the preceding we have dealt with faith. Logic now requires that we deal with God who is the object of faith. That this may be done the more precisely we shall first speak of the knowledge of God.

2. God, as he is in himself, cannot be understood by any save himself. 1 Tim. 6:16, *Dwelling in that inaccessible light, whom no man has seen or can see.*

3. As he has revealed himself to us, he is known from the back, so to speak, not from the face. Exod. 33:23, *You shall see my back parts; but my face cannot be seen.* He is seen darkly, not clearly, so far as we and our ways are concerned. 1 Cor. 13:12, *Through a glass, darkly, after a fashion.*

4. Since the things which pertain to God must be explained in a human way, a manner of speaking called ἀνθρωποπάθεια, anthropopathy, is frequently used.

5. And because they are explained in our way for human comprehension, many things are spoken of God according to our own conceiving rather than according to his real nature.

6. We cannot know him otherwise as we live now, nor do we need to know him otherwise to live well. Exod. 33:19, 20.

9. See Introduction, pp. 45–46, and n. 96.

7. What has been revealed of God suffices us to live well. Deut. 29:29, *The things that are revealed are revealed to us and to our children forever, that we may do all the words of this law.*

8. What can be known of God are his sufficiency [*sufficientia*] and efficiency, or working power [*efficientia*]. Rom. 4:21, *Being fully persuaded that he was able to perform that which he had promised.*

9. These two are the pillars of faith, the bases of consolation, the incitements of piety and the surest marks of true religion, Rom. 4:21.

10. The sufficiency of God is his quality of being sufficient in himself for himself and for us. Therefore he is called all-sufficient, Gen. 17:1.

11. The sufficiency of God is the first reason why we believe in him: He is able to give us life. Rom. 4:20.

12. The sufficiency of God is in his essence [*essentia*] and subsistence, or manner of being [*subsistentia*].

13. The essence of God is that by which he is absolutely the first being. Isa. 44:6, *I am the first and the last; besides me there is no god;* Rev. 1:8, 21:6, and 22:13, *I am Alpha and Omega, the beginning and the end, the first and the last.*

14. This essence is indicated by the name Jehovah, or the Lord. Because the essence of God is what it is, it follows:

15. First, that God is one and only one. Deut. 6:4; 1 Tim. 2:5; Eph. 4:6; 1 Cor. 8:5, 6; Mark 12:32; Rom. 3:29, 30.

16. Second, that God exists of himself, that is to say, not from another or of another or by another or by reason of another.

17. Third and finally, the quality which is called passive is not in him: He is therefore immutable. Ps. 102:26, 27, *Thou remainest . . . thou art the same;* Rom. 1:23, *The glory of the incorruptible God;* Jas. 1:17, *With whom there is no variableness or shadow of turning.*

18. Now because we are not able to take in this essence in one act of comprehension, it is explained as manifold, that is to say, as if consisting of many attributes.

19. They are called attributes because they may more reasonably be said to be attributed to God in the literal meaning of the words, than to be in him.

20. These attributes are God's act [*actus*] — single, most pure, most simple. Hence the nature of the divine attributes may rightly be described in the following propositions as consequences.

21. First, all the divine attributes truly spoken of God apply in the abstract as well as the concrete.

22. Second, those attributes which are in some way common to God and to creatures belong in their substance first to God and secondarily

to the creatures, although the names are taken from creatures and applied to God, and so in one sense belong first to the creatures.

23. Third, for the divine attributes there is no such thing as diminishing, enlarging, abating, or rendering them unequal.

24. Fourth, the divine attributes are not contrary to one another, but agree emphatically.

25. Fifth, all divine attributes are divine perfections. All imperfections which accompany similar properties in the creature are out of the question in speaking of God. Nothing can be conceived to be more perfect than divine perfection.

26. Sixth, divine attributes are in God not only really and eminently, but also formally — though not in the way in which qualities exist in creatures.[10]

27. Seventh, they are in God in a kind of secondary essence, because they do not belong to the formal divine essence. For we conceive God to be, before we are able to think of him as just and good.

28. Eighth, they are distinguished from God's essence and from each other not only in reason reasoning, but also in reason reasoned (as the phrase goes), so that the foundation of the distinction is in God himself.

29. Ninth, those attributes which in their formal sense indicate something belonging to the divine essence, such as omnipotence, immensity, eternity, and the like, are completely incommunicable.

30. Tenth, those that are said to be communicated to creatures apply by analogy, not in the same mode nor with the same meaning as they are said to exist in God.

31. The attributes of God tell what he is and who he is.

32. What God is no one can perfectly define except one who possesses the mind [logica] of God himself. But an imperfect description follows which we can understand and comes close to explaining the nature of God.

33. God is spirit having life in himself. John 4:24, God is spirit; and 5:26, The Father has life in himself.

34. He is called spirit, first (negatively), because he is not a body; second (analogically), because in spiritual substances there are many perfections which adumbrate the divine nature more than any bodily thing can.

10. Ames refers here to a scholastic tradition of citing three ways (modi) in which a quality or an attribute can exist in a substance or thing. A quality may exist really or virtually (virtualiter) when it is found in the potential or capacity of a thing, but not in its act. A quality exists eminently (eminenter) when it exists in a thing as a cause of something else. A quality exists formally (formaliter) when it is found in the very act of the thing or substance, not only in its potential or in its causing power.

35. He is called living, first, because God works by himself, not being moved by another; second, because the vital action of God is his essence; third, because he is the fountain of all being and of vital operation in all other living things. Acts 17:25, 28, *He gives to all life and breath and all things. In him we live, move, and have our being.*

36. He is said to live in himself, because he receives neither being nor life from any other source in any way.

37. Hence the chief title of God, by which he is distinguished from all idols, is that he is the living God, Deut. 32:40; Ps. 84:2; Jer. 5:2.

38. Therefore our faith, seeking eternal life, rests in God alone because God is the fountain of all life, John 5:26.

39. Those properties by which God is distinguished from all other things explain to us who he is.

40. Moreover, these divine properties show how great God is and of what sort he is.

41. With respect to quantity, he is said to be one and infinite because he is immeasurable inwardly and incomprehensible outwardly. Likewise he is said to be eternal.

42. He is said to be one not in kind, but in that perfect unity which is often called numerical and individual in creatures.

43. God is infinite because he is beyond any limitation of essence. Ps. 139:8, *If I climb up to heaven, thou art there, or make my bed in the grave, behold thou art there.*

44. God is immeasurable because he has no material dimension. 1 Kings 8:27, *The heavens and heavens of heavens do not contain thee;* Isa. 66:1, *Heaven is my throne and earth my footstool.*

45. Hence faith does not look just for a certain measure of blessedness to be communicated by God, but an immeasurable glory.

46. God is incomprehensible because he has no all-encompassing boundary.

47. Therefore he is everywhere, because there is no place from which he is excluded and no place where he is included.

48. God is eternal because he is without beginning and end, Ps. 102:25, 26; Isa. 44:6; 1 Tim. 1:17.

49. It is for this reason that our faith apprehends eternal life in God.

50. The properties through which he is said to work set forth the kind of a God that he is. Among these are all the properties of essence and quantity, namely, simplicity, immutability, eternity, and immeasurableness.

51. These may be conceived either as faculties or as virtues which adorn the faculties.

52. The faculties are understanding and will. Faith leans on the one who knows what is needful for us and is also willing to supply it.

53. God's understanding is simple, without composition, argument, or classification. Heb. 4:13, *All things are naked and open to his eyes.*

54. God's understanding is unchangeable. He does not know one thing in a different way from another, or one thing more than another, or better yesterday than now, or now than yesterday. Acts 15:18, *Known to God are all his works from before all ages.*

55. God's understanding is eternal, for it neither begins nor ends, Acts 15:18.

56. God's understanding is infinite because he perceives the whole truth of and reason for everything. Job 11:8, 9, *The wisdom of God is higher than the heavens . . . longer than the earth, wider than the sea*; Ps. 139:6, *Thy knowledge is more wonderful than I can conceive.*

57. We ought to conceive the nature of the divine will in the same way.

58. The will of God is single and totally one in him.

59. The will of God is unchangeable because he always wills the same and in the same manner. Ps. 33:11, *The counsel of the Lord remains forever.*

60. The will of God is eternal because he does not begin to will what he did not will before, nor cease to will what he willed before. Mal. 3:6, *I the Lord do not change.*

61. The will of God may be said to be infinite because it has no outward limitation.

62. The affections attributed to God in scripture, such as love, hatred, and the like, either designate acts of the will or apply to God only figuratively.

63. Virtue is the perfection of the understanding and the will; wisdom, holiness, and the like are virtues of this sort in God.

64. Virtue is attributed to God in so far as it denotes a readiness to act, not as if it were an inclination distinct from faculty and action.

65. But the virtues which arise in man confronting sin and imperfection, such as humility, chastity, shame, and the like, do not apply to God.

66. The perfection of God whereby he is called blessed results from all these attributes, 1 Tim. 1:11 and 6:15.

67. Hence our faith has a firm foundation because it leans on God, the possessor and author of all perfection, blessedness and glory.

V

The Subsistence of God

1. The subsistence, or manner of being [*subsistentia*] of God is his one essence so far as it has personal properties.

2. The same essence is common to the three subsistences. As far as essence is concerned, therefore, the single subsistences are rightly said to exist of themselves.

3. Nothing is attributed to the essence which cannot be attributed to each subsistence in the matter of essence.

4. But what is attributed properly to each subsistence in the matter of subsistence cannot be attributed to the essence.

5. The subsistences are distinguished from the essence, because the modes of subsisting, though consolidated with the essence, are distinguished from it considered by itself.

6. They are distinguished from each other as things connected by certain relative properties, so that one cannot be another, although they are of the same nature. Neither can one be said to be first or last, except in order of beginning and manner of subsisting.

7. These relative properties are, as it were, individual forces in one essence, spiritually and perfectly alive. Hence the subsistences are rightly called persons.

8. Now these properties are not inherent qualities but relative affections which contain all the perfection found in the similar affections of creatures, but none of the imperfection.

9. A relative property in God implies a person, but this is not so in creatures.

10. The subsistences are either breathing, like the Father and the Son, or breathed, like the Holy Spirit.

11. Breathing or sending forth is not a relation which of itself constitutes a person: It is a relation common to two persons.

12. The relative property of the Father is to beget. Ps. 2:7, *You are my son, this day I begat you*; John 3:16, *The only begotten Son*; Heb. 1:6, *The first begotten*. Hence first in order.

13. The relative property of the Son is to be begotten, that is, so to proceed from the Father as to be a participant of the same essence and perfectly carry on the Father's nature. Hence he is second in order. Heb. 1:3, *The brightness of his glory and the character of his person*.

14. The property of the Holy Spirit is to be breathed, to be sent forth and to proceed from both the Father and the Son. John 15:26,

He whom I will send forth to you from the Father, that Spirit of truth who proceeds from the Father; Rom. 8:9, *The Spirit of Christ;* Gal. 4:6, *The Spirit of the Son.*

15. The difference between being begotten, which applies to the Son, and that proceeding which applies to the Holy Spirit cannot be explained in words, except that the Son proceeds from the Father alone, and the Holy Spirit from the Father and the Son (in this instance taken together).

16. Nevertheless, the relationship may be sketched in part by a figure. The Father is, as it were, *Deus intelligens,* God understanding; the Son who is the express image of the Father is *Deus intellectus,* God understood; and the Holy Spirit, flowing and breathed from the Father through the Son, is *Deus dilectus,* God loved. The Son is produced, so to speak, by a mental act or utterance out of the mind or fruitful memory of the Father. The Holy Spirit is produced through the act of loving or breathing from the fruitful will of the Father and the Son. Hence the Son is called Word, wisdom, and image — designations not used of the Holy Spirit. Among creatures there is such a thing as the generation of sons, but there is no such thing as an immediate proceeding from two equally perfect beings (as the Holy Spirit proceeds from the Father and the Son); thus the procession of the Son has a proper designation, but there is no specific manner of procession or particular name for it to be applied to the third person. It is truly said of the Father and the Son that they are spirits and are holy and that the Son in addition proceeds from the Father by spiritual generation.

17. The very name of God — with his proper titles — is given in Scriptures not only to the Father, but also to the Son. Jer. 23:6, *The Lord our righteousness;* John 1:1, *The Word was God;* Rom. 9:5, *God . . . blessed forever;* 1 Tim. 3:16, *God manifested in the flesh;* Rev. 17:14, *Lord of lords and Kings of kings.* It is also given to the Holy Spirit. Acts 5:3, 4, *As you lie to the Holy Spirit . . . you have lied to God;* Acts 28:25 with Isa. 6:9, *The Lord said. The Holy Spirit has spoken;* 1 Cor. 3:16 and 6:19; 2 Cor. 6:16, *The temple of God. The temple of the Spirit.*

18. Divine attributes are affirmed not only of the Father but also of the Son. Isa. 9:6, *The most mighty God, Father of eternity;* John 2:25, *He knew what was in man,* and 3:13, *The Son of man is in heaven,* and 8:58, *Before Abraham was, I am.* And similarly of the Holy Spirit. Ps. 139:7, *Whither shall I flee from thy Spirit?* 1 Cor. 2:10, *The Spirit searches all things, even the depths of God;* Heb. 9:14, *The eternal Spirit.*

19. The acts of God are attributed not only to the Father but also to the Son and the Holy Spirit. For example, election is attributed to

the Son, Matt. 24:31, *His elect;* and the eternal counsel of God is attributed to the Holy Spirit, Isa. 40:13, *Who has weighed the Spirit of the Lord as the man of his counsel?* Creation is attributed to the Son. John 1:3, *All things were made through him, and without him was made nothing that was made.* Creation is also attributed to the Holy Spirit, Ps. 33:6, *By the word of the Lord were the heavens made, and all the strength of them by the breath of his mouth.* The upholding and governing of created things is attributed to the Son. Heb. 1:3, *He who upholds all things by his mighty word.* And to the Holy Spirit. Gen. 1:2, *The Spirit moved upon the face of the waters;* Zech. 4:6, *By my Spirit, said the Lord of hosts.* The special power of working miracles is attributed to the Son. Acts 4:10, *Through the name of Jesus Christ . . . this man stands before you whole;* and 9:34, *Jesus Christ makes you well.* Likewise to the Holy Spirit. Acts 2:4, *They began to speak with other tongues, as the Spirit gave them utterance.* The bestowal of spiritual life and all grace in vocation, justification, adoption, sanctification, and glorification is always attributed as much to the Son and the Holy Spirit as to the Father. The ordaining, sending, and blessing of the ecclesiastical ministry is attributed to the Son. Eph. 4:8, 11, *He gave gifts . . . he gave some as apostles.* And likewise to the Holy Spirit. 1 Cor. 12:11, *One and the same Spirit works all these things;* Acts 20:28, *The Holy Spirit has constituted you overseers.* The very resurrection of the flesh is ascribed to the Son as its author. John 6:54, *I will raise him up.* And to the Holy Spirit. Rom. 8:11, *He shall raise up your bodies by his indwelling Spirit in you.*

20. Divine honor and worship is also given not only to the Father but to the Son. Heb. 1:6, *Let all the angels of God adore him.* Such things are also attributed to the Holy Spirit as when his name is invoked with that of the Father and the Son over those who are to be baptized. Matt. 28:19, *In the name of the Father and of the Son and of the Holy Spirit.* In like manner the Son and the Spirit are invoked in that solemn form of greeting: *The grace of the Lord Jesus Christ and the love of God the Father and the communion of the Holy Spirit be with you all,* 2 Cor. 13:14. And whatever pertains to worship refers as much to Christ as to the Holy Spirit, in the very fact that true worshippers of God are called temples not only of God the Father but also of Christ. Rev. 21:22, *Its temple is the Lord God Almighty and the Lamb;* 1 Cor. 3:16, *Do you not know that you are the temple of God and that the spirit of God dwells in you?* and 6:19, *Do you not know that your body is the temple of the Holy Spirit which is in you?*

21. Finally, the authority and majesty proper to God is attributed to the Son and the Holy Spirit. 1 Cor. 2:8, *The Lord of glory;* 1 Peter 4:14, *That Spirit of glory.* All holy prophecy is attributed to Christ

and the Holy Spirit. 1 Peter 3:19, *Christ in the spirit . . . preached to those spirits who were in prison*; 2 Peter 1:21, *Holy men acted upon by the Holy Spirit spoke*; Acts 28:25, *The Holy Spirit has spoken through the prophet Isaiah*.

22. Now that the Holy Spirit is explained to us in all these ways as a subsisting person, it manifestly appears that life, understanding, will, and power are everywhere attributed to him along with all acts proper to a person.

23. His distinction from the Father and the Son is also clearly taught in such words as *Another . . . sent . . . coming . . . from the Father and the Son*, John 14.

24. Hence God as the object of our faith is in every way sufficient to impart salvation to us. For all love, grace, and those things which pertain to living well come from the Father, Son, and Holy Spirit. 2 Cor. 13:14.

VI

The Efficiency of God

1. The efficiency, or working power [*efficientia*], of God is that by which he works all things in all things. Eph. 1:11, *He who works all things*; Rom. 11:36, *From him, through him, and in him are all things*.

2. Practically speaking the effecting, working, or acting of God, insofar as they are in God in action, are not other than God himself. For no compositeness or mutation of power and action can have a place in God's perfectly simple and immutable nature. Yet they add God's particular relation to the real effect.

3. He works all things in all things, because the efficiency of all things depends upon the first efficient cause not only in the matter of their substance but also in the matter of all their real circumstances. Isa. 45:7, *That I, the Lord, do all these things*; Lam. 3:37, 38, *Who says something and it exists, if the Lord does not command it? Out of the mouth of the Most High do not evil and good proceed?* Whatever has any perfection in conduct is reckoned as partaking of reality — but this is certainly not true of the imperfections which are not part of our true subjection to God.

4. The meaning both of the essence of God and of his subsistence shines forth in his efficiency.

5. The meaning of that efficiency which pertains to God's essence is his omnipotence.

6. The power of God, considered as simple power, is plainly identical with his sufficiency. It is rightly considered part of the nature of God as a being and therefore is prior to his knowledge and will. Rom. 11:23, *For God is able to graft them in again.*

7. But power, pertaining to the execution of God's efficiency, in some way follows after sufficiency and thus follows after his knowledge and will. Pss. 115:3 and 135:6, *Whatever he pleases he does.*

8. The proper order for conceiving these things is, first, to think of God's *posse*, his power; second, his *scire*, knowledge; third, his *velle*, will; and lastly his *efficere potenter*, efficient power (which differs from the effectual will of God only in our thinking). Hence arises that syllogism of faith which is distinctly set forth in Matt. 8:2, 3, *Lord, if you will, you can . . . I will; therefore it is done.* Here the will is shown emerging into power.

9. Thus the very will of God, as the effecting principle, is the cause [*ratio*] of power. Rom. 9:19, *Who has resisted his will?* And omnipotence in action is nothing else than the effecting will of God. Ps. 33:9, *He commanded, and it was done;* Rev. 4:11, *By thy will they are and were created.*

10. Therefore it is an error contradicting the nature of God to say that God properly wills to do many things which by his omnipotence he does not do. Eph. 1:19, 20, *The exceeding greatness of his power in us who believe, according to the working of his mighty power.*

11. The omnipotence of God is that by which he is able to effect all things which he wills or could will. 2 Chron. 20:6, *In thy hand is power and strength, and no one can resist thee;* Luke 1:37, *With God there is no word which cannot be done;* Phil. 3:21, *He is able even to subject all things to himself.*

12. Thus God is called throughout in the Old Testament אֵל גִּבּוֹר, *Mighty God,* Isa. 9:6; Jer. 32:18; also אֵל שַׁדַּי, *God all-sufficient,* Gen. 17:1; 35:11; Ruth 1:20, 21. And in the New Testament he is called παντοκράτωρ, *The Lord Almighty,* 2 Cor. 6:18; Rev. 1.8; and 4:8; and only δυνάστης, *The only potentate,* 1 Tim. 6:15.

13. Practically speaking we say that God possesses power because he has an ability to communicate something to others, having the potency of a cause. But properly speaking, in respect to himself, active power does not apply to God, for it implies that he was at first idle and later moved himself into act. God is rather most pure act, Jas. 1:17.

14. Therefore, it is not to be imagined that there is an active power in God which is different from his essence, for the very

essence of God is that power which makes him powerful. Likewise his very mercy itself is that which makes him merciful.

15. But active power does apply to God in respect to the creature who is rightly said to be able to receive and experience that act of God which before he did not feel and experience. Matt. 19:26, *All things are possible with God.*

16. The omnipotence of God deals with things possible in any sense, i.e., whatever God wills or can will, Matt. 19:26.

17. It is not concerned, therefore, about things which are altogether ἀδύνατα, impossible, and involve a contradiction, either in God or in created things. 2 Tim. 2:13, *He cannot deny himself.*

18. Thus a certain distinction is present in divine omnipotence whereby there is a division into absolute power [*potentia absoluta*] and ordaining or actual power [*potentia ordinata sive actualis*].

19. Absolute power is that by which God is able to do all things possible although they may never be done. Matt. 3:9, *God can of these stones raise up children unto Abraham;* and 26:53, *Do you think that I cannot now pray to my Father, and he shall presently give me more than twelve legions of angels?* Mark 10:27; Eph. 3:20.

20. The ordaining power of God is that by which he not only can do what he wills but does actually do what he wills, Pss. 115:3, 135:6; Eph. 3:11.

21. The meaning of God's subsistence, shining forth in his efficiency is seen, first, in the working together of the divine persons and, second, in the individual manner of their working.

22. Their working together is their doing of the same thing inseparably — for all external actions are common to all the persons. John 5:17, 19, *My Father works, and I work. . . . whatever he does, the same likewise the Son does;* and 16:13, 14, *That Spirit shall not speak of himself, but whatever he shall hear he shall speak . . . he shall take of mine and give it to you.*

23. Each person works by himself in respect to the causal power exercised.

24. There is no preeminence of dignity in this working together, but the greater unity and identity in one and the same cause.

25. Hence equal honor is due from us to all the divine persons.

26. The distinct manner of working consists in each person working according to the particular form [*ratio*] of his subsistence.

27. That distinct form is seen partly in the order of working and partly in the boundary of the action.

28. Concerning the order, the manner of working of the Father is from himself, through the Son and Holy Spirit. Therefore the

beginning of things, or creation, is properly attributed to the Father who in order of beginning is the first person.

29. The manner of the working of the Son is from the Father through the Spirit. Hence the dispensation of things is properly attributed to him, especially redemption and the constitution of all church offices. Eph. 4:11, *He therefore gave some to be apsotles, some to be prophets.*

30. The manner of working of the Spirit is from the Father and the Son through himself. Hence the consummation of things is attributed to the Holy Spirit, such as regeneration, Titus 3:5, the bestowal of all spiritual gifts, 1 Cor. 12:4, and the perfection of natural things themselves, Gen. 1:2.

31. As for the boundary of the action, that aspect in which one person's working or manner of working shines forth most clearly is chiefly attributed to that person. So in the usual appropriation, creation is attributed to the Father, redemption to the Son, and sanctification to the Spirit.

VII

The Decree and Counsel of God

1. In the exercise of God's efficiency, the decree of God comes first. This manner of working is the most perfect of all and notably agrees with the divine nature.

2. The decree of God is his firm decision by which he performs all things through his almighty power according to his counsel. Eph. 1:11, *He does all things out of the counsel of his own will.*

3. God's constancy, truth, and faithfulness appear in his decree.

4. Constancy is shown in that God's decree remains forever immutable. Num. 23:19, *The strong God is not a man that should lie or the son of man that he should repent*; Prov. 19:21, *The counsel of the Lord shall stand.*

5. Truth is shown in his declaring only what he has decreed. Jer. 10:10, *The Lord is a God of truth*; Rom. 3:4, *Let God be true though every man a liar.* Although his words may seem on occasion to sound otherwise, their meaning always agrees with the decree.

6. Faithfulness is shown in that he effects whatever he has decreed and just as he has decreed it. Isa. 46:10, *My counsel shall stand, and I will do all my pleasure.*

7. Every decree of God is eternal, 1 Cor. 2:7; Acts 15:8.

8. His decree involves counsel, Eph. 1:11; Acts 4:28.

9. The counsel of God is, as it were, his deliberation over the best manner of accomplishing anything already approved by the understanding and the will.

10. Counsel is attributed to God because of his perfect judgment whereby he does all things advisedly, i.e., willingly and knowingly, not as a result of inquiry as men make judgments. For God sees and wills all things and everything at once. Therefore his counsel is said to resemble deliberation in the strict sense.

11. Three things concur in the perfection of this counsel: one, the purpose [scopus] or end set forth; two, the mental conception of that end; three, the intention and agreement of the will.

12. The purpose or end of the counsel is the glory of God himself, i.e., the goodness or perfection of God which is manifest in his efficiency and shines forth in his works. Eph. 1:6, *To the praise of his glorious grace.*

13. In every artist, or anyone who expresses himself after taking counsel, there exists beforehand an idea which he keeps in mind as he is about to work so that he may fit his work to it. So also in God, since he does not work naturally nor rashly nor by constraint, but with highest perfection of reason, such an idea is to be understood as preexisting, as the exemplary cause of all things to be done. Heb. 11:3, *Those things we see were made of things that do not appear.*

14. The idea of all things is the divine essence, meaning that essence understood by God himself and imitable by his creatures — at least the image or vestige of that perfection may be expressed in some way in creatures. That is, the creatures themselves, so far as they are conceived in the divine mind, are the idea or image of that nature which they have in themselves.

15. An idea in man, who attains knowledge by analysis, is brought in from things themselves. Things exist first in themselves and then come into the senses of men and finally to the understanding, where they can form an idea to direct a subsequent operation. But God knows all things by genesis and does not require knowledge through analysis of things; therefore all things are first in his mind before they are in themselves.

16. In us the things themselves are the pattern and our knowledge is the image of them. But in God the divine knowledge is the pattern and the things themselves are the image or express likeness of it.

17. An idea in man is first impressed upon him and afterwards expressed in things, but in God it is only expressed, not impressed, because it does not come from anywhere else.

18. From this one foundation all errors of merit and foreseen faith

can be sufficiently refuted. For if a particular decree of God depended upon any foresight then an idea of God would have come to him from somewhere else, which hardly agrees with his nature.

19. An idea in God is single, but since it always relates differently to creatures it becomes manifold. Thus it is true that the idea of one creature is not the idea of another.

20. The idea of any perfection in creatures is in God because all perfection proceeds from his active power [*virtus*]. This is not so with imperfection, properly considered.

21. The knowledge of evil thus depends upon the denying of the good, just as the being of evil consists in the taking away of the good. For all things are known according to their being.

22. There are many divine ideas. Some of them are connected and depend upon each other, and from this arises a certain order.

23. Ideas, considered antecedent to the decree of the divine will, represent an abstraction and only a possible existence. Considered after the determination of the divine will, they represent things which are to come in their actual existence.

24. From these considerations arises a division of divine knowledge into the knowledge of simple understanding and the knowledge of vision.

25. The knowledge of simple understanding refers to all possible things, i.e., all things universal and particular which may be brought into being through the most perfect knowledge in God.

26. The knowledge of vision is the knowledge of all future things, whether they are necessary in their own nature, or free, or contingent.

27. The things which God knows through the knowledge of simple understanding he knows by his all-sufficiency, but those things he knows through the knowledge of vision he knows by his efficiency or by the decree of his own will. Ps. 33:15, *He who frames their hearts observes all their works*; Isa. 44:7, *Who is like me, foretelling and declaring it, or ordering it to me, from the time that I arrange the peoples forever so that the things to come and those which shall come may be declared to them?*

28. A middle knowledge by which God is imagined by some to know by hypothesis before the decree of his will that certain things will be, if such and such free causes meet such and such conditions — knowledge of this kind cannot stand with the absolute perfection of God. For it both supposes that events will happen independently of the will of God and also makes some knowledge of God depend on the object.

29. The divine idea has as many forms as there are varieties of notions of things. In regard to principles it is called *intelligentia*,

understanding, whereby God perceives every particular thing about every particular thing; in regard to the truth of particular things it is called *scientia*, knowledge, which in extent is omniscience; in regard to the being which things have in their own measure it is called foreknowledge; in respect to the interdependence of truths it is called *sapientia*, wisdom, whereby he knows what belongs and what is alien to each thing; in regard to the whole order to be appointed in practice it is called *prudentia*, prudence, whereby he knows the fittest occasion for all things; last, in actual practice it is called *ars*, art, whereby he knows how to accomplish all things most skillfully, Heb. 11:10.

30. These words are often used interchangeably in the Scriptures to explain the perfection of the divine understanding to suit the comprehension of those who have a most imperfect understanding, but in their own nature the words have these distinctions and no others.

31. That conjectural knowledge which some attribute to God about future contingencies is plainly incompatible with the divine nature and perfection.

Of the three things which were set forth as concurring in the perfection of God's counsel, namely, the purpose or end set forth, the mental conception of that end, and the intention of the will, the third remains to be considered — which is called good pleasure.

32. The good pleasure of God is an act of the divine will freely and effectively determining all things.

33. Good pleasure in Scripture designates usually the good will of God, whereby he wills and decrees saving good to his own. Yet because all counsel is well pleasing to God, it is rightly used by theologians for all the counsel of God (also in the Scriptures, Matt. 11:26).

34. This will is truly free, because whatever it wills it wills not by necessity of nature but by counsel.

35. It is most free, completely and absolutely free, depending on nothing else. The freedom of the will of men and angels is shared and less free because of its dependence on God.

36. God's freedom in outward acts is not only concomitant with them, as in the case of inward acts, but also precedes them in principle. What God wills to do outwardly he wills not out of natural necessity but by preceding choice, for there is no necessary connection between the divine nature and such acts.

37. This will is effectual, because whatever he wills he effects in his own time; neither is there anything not done if he wills it to be done. Pss. 115:3 and 135:6, *Whatever he pleases, the Lord does.*

38. The will of God is therefore the first cause of things. Rev. 4:11,

By thy will they are and were created. The will of God as it works outwardly does not presuppose the goodness of the object; but he creates and disposes by willing. Jas. 1:18, *Of his own will he begat us;* Rom. 9:18, *He has mercy on him whom he will.*

39. Properly speaking, therefore, there is no cause of God's will.

40. Here it is rightly said that God wills one thing to exist in order to produce another. But it cannot be said that that one thing is properly a cause whereby the will of God is moved internally to appoint the other thing. God willed that the sun and the stars should exist for the generation, conservation, and corruption of things below; yet the sun and the stars are not the cause of God's willing that those things should be generated, conserved, and corrupted. And so it is with all things which are not God but which among themselves are causes and effects dependent on the divine will. There is no cause of God's will outside of itself.

41. The willing of one thing by God is not the efficient cause in him of his willing another. The efficiency of a cause in regard to its effect and dependence of an effect upon a cause cannot be an event in the will of God, which is God himself truly and simply willing all things together and at once in only one act. Yet the schoolmen rightly say that the passivity of the divine will towards one thing is a passive cause of another, and in this sense it is truly and piously said that God wills one thing because he wills another.

42. Therefore, although he wills many things which will not take place except upon some antecedent act of the creature, God's act of willing does not itself properly depend upon the act of the creature. And it is not right, under the name of antecedent will, to attribute to God that imperfect willing which is called "woulding" [*velleitas*] in the schools. This does not agree with an omniscient, omnipotent, and infinitely blessed nature.

43. Therefore the opinion which holds that God wills something antecedent to the acts of a creature and consequent to the acts does not will the same, but something else, is not to be allowed. This makes the will of God mutable and dependent upon the act of the creature, so that as often as the act of the creature is changed God's will itself is changed.

44. According to the same opinion, that form of speech prescribed in the word of God whereby we commit ourselves and all of ours to God — I will do this or that, if God wills — is not always to be used: It should be turned around to state that God will do this or that, if man wills.

45. God's will determines all things without exception: the greatest, the least, the contingent, the necessary, the free. The Scripture shows

this with respect to all kinds of things, e.g., Jesus Christ is to be glorified and the church saved through him, Pss. 2, 110:4, 40:7, 8, 9; Heb. 7:16, 21; Eph. 5:25; and 2 Tim. 1:9. Concerning Pharaoh, Exod. 13, where God disposed all things that he might move Pharaoh to follow and overthrow the people of Israel, nay, he hardened him that he might follow them, still Pharaoh and Israel worked freely. Likewise in the selling of Joseph, wherein all things happened freely and contingently, God determined it according to his own will. It is the same with the very heart of man, Ps. 33:14, 15; 1 Sam. 10:9, 26; Prov. 21:1. With a man killing another by chance, Exod. 21:13. With the lot cast into the urn, Prov. 16:33. With sparrows falling to the ground, with all the hairs of a man's head, Matt. 10:29, 30. With the lilies, the flowers, and the grass of the earth, Matt. 6:28, 30. And finally with all created things, Job 38; Ps. 104; Isa. 45:7; Jer. 14:22.

46. If God did not determine all things, his will would not be the first cause simply and universally. Those who think otherwise must necessarily presuppose two first principles or more than two, which is plainly far from all truth.

47. The way of working [ratio] is not the same in the will as it is in divine knowledge and power, for knowledge knows all things that are to be known and power can do all possible things — together they are stretched forth beyond those things which actually have been, are, and shall be. By his will, however, he does not will all things which he can, but all things which he judges should be willed, or all things which actually happen. Therefore we say that God is omniscient and omnipotent but it cannot be said that he is omnivolent.

48. In whatever God wills he is universally effectual; he is not hindered or frustrated in obtaining what he wills. For if he should properly will anything and not attain it he would not be wholly perfect and blessed.

49. The will of God does not imply a necessity in all future things, but only a certainty in regard to the event. Thus the event was certain that Christ's bones should not be broken, because God willed that they should not be. But there was no necessity imposed upon the soldiers, their spears, and other secondary causes then present.

50. Indeed it is as wrong to say that the will of God, which attains whatever it wills, urges all things with hard necessity as that it is the prime root and efficient cause of all contingency and freedom in things, on the ground that it effectively foreordains certain effects to follow certain causes.

51. In the things which God wills there is a certain order to be conceived. He wills the end before the means to the end because he works according to the most perfect reason. Among means, he wills

first those which come nearest to the end; that which is first in order of execution is last in order of intention and vice versa.

52. The will of God is partly hidden and partly revealed, Deut. 29:29.

53. Those means through which that will is revealed are the "intention of the sign" [*voluntas signi*] — rightly so called not only by metaphor because they show men what they mean, but also by metonymy because they are the effects or adjuncts or partial declarations of God's own will.

54. There are five signs included in that old verse:

> He instructs, forbids, permits,
> counsels, and fulfills.

Because counseling coincides with instruction, it would have been better to have substituted: He promises.

Thus far we have treated generally of the efficiency of God which, together with his sufficiency, makes him the proper and adequate object of faith. The kinds of efficiency now follow.

VIII

Creation

1. The efficiency of God may be understood as either creation or providence.

2. Creation is the efficiency of God whereby in the beginning out of nothing he made the world to be altogether good.

3. Active creation is conceived as a transitive action in which there is always presupposed an object about which the agent is concerned; it is virtually but not formally transitive because it makes, not presupposes, an object.

4. Passive creation can be understood in the manner of mutation, although it is improperly called mutation.

5. Creation refers to the whole world, i.e., whatever exists outside of God.

6. Hence all things which exist outside of God are created — fully created, that is, in matter as well as in form. Rev. 4:11, *Because thou hast made all things;* Col. 1:16, *For by him were made all things which are in heaven and in earth visible and invisible.*

7. Creation produces in the originative sense because it produces not only being as being, but absolutely every part.

8. Therefore before the creation, creatures had no real being either in existence or essence, although they had being known from eternity in the knowledge of God.

9. Creation then produces out of nothing, that is, out of matter that has had no preexistence but which comes into existence with the thing created. Nothing exists from eternity but God, and God is not the matter or a part of any creature, but only the maker.

10. Some things are said to be created whose matter preexisted. But this creation refers not only to the immediate action whereby such things are brought into existence, but also to the mediate action whereby the matter of which they are formed was brought into existence. So it was in the creation of the plants and the animals, Gen. 1:20.

11. That state of nothing or nonbeing of things preceded their being, not only in the order of nature, for in that case they might coexist with God from eternity, but also in the order of duration, as we conceive things.

12. Hence that beginning in which God is said to have created the world, was the end of the duration of nothing and the beginning of the world's duration.

13. In creation God wanted to show both his perfection in his not needing any creature or outward thing (for otherwise he would have created the world as soon as he could) and his freedom in producing all things without natural necessity (for had he created out of necessity, he would have done so from eternity, Rev. 4:11; Ps. 115:3).

14. The world has not been in existence from eternity nor could it have been according to the present dispensation and ordering of things.

15. The day of creation would not have come to be if infinite days had had to go before. The days going before would never have ended, so that that day could have arrived.

16. Hence it follows that no creature was or could have been a cause, instrumental or principal, in the act of creation.

17. Everything created was very good, because it was made neither rashly nor in vain but for the end which the maker had before him. Gen. 1:31, *Whatever he made was very good;* 1 Tim 4:4, *Whatever God made was good.*

18. The goodness of a thing created is the perfection of its fitness for the use which it serves. Now that use is either particular or universal.

19. The particular is the proper use which anything serves in its own nature.

20. The universal is the use of one thing with others for the perfection of the universe, Pss. 104 and 148; Isa. 40:12.

21. In their goodness all created things naturally tend towards God from whom they came. For secondary being is from primary being and for primary being. Hence those phrases: *From him, through him, and to him are all things,* Rom. 11:36.

22. Now natural things tend towards God, first, in that they declare God's glory, Ps. 19:1; second, in that they give occasion for us both to know and seek God, Rom. 1:20; Acts 17:26; and third, in that they sustain our life that we may live well to God, 1 Cor. 10:31; 1 Tim. 4:3, 4.

23. Time coexists with all created things, as appears in the phrase, *In the beginning,* for that was the beginning of time.

24. Place also coexists with things, i.e., the space in which the extension of the creature is defined, Gen. 1:2.

25. But time and place are not, strictly speaking, created but are concreated or connected with created things. They have only a relative, not an absolute, status.

26. God created all things out of nothing. Therefore our faith rests in him in hope against hope, expecting things which are not as if they were. Rom. 4:17, 18.

27. The creation of the world is divided according to the parts of the world. Although the world is one in numerical unity and in unity of order and end, yet it has parts distinguishable by position and by essence and existence.

28. The creation of these parts of the world did not occur at one and the same moment, but was accomplished part by part in the space of six days.

29. There were created, then, the parts of the world which are absolutely or contingently perfect, Ps. 33:6; Heb. 11:3; Gen. 2:7, 19, 22.

30. The creation of things absolutely perfect is seen in those things which have their material and formal principles implanted at the beginning in a complete existence.

31. These creatures are subject to no essential change, such as generation or corruption.

32. The parts absolutely perfect are the highest heaven and its inhabitants the angels.

33. The highest heaven is the dwelling place of God's holiness, full of all things which pertain to eternal blessedness. Here the majesty of God presents itself to be seen, as it were, face to face, 1 Cor. 2:9; Rev. 21:23; 1 Cor. 13:12.

34. It is called the third heaven, the empyrean, the heaven of heavens, and paradise, 1 Kings 8:27; Matt. 8:11; Mark 12:25; and 2 Cor. 12:2, 3.

35. This is the heaven meant in Gen. 1:1 and Heb. 11:10, 16.

36. The angels are spirits of primary perfection created to minister to God.

37. That the angels were created appears in Col. 1:16 and Ps. 148:5. That they were created on the first day with the highest heaven appears, first, from the likeness of their nature to that of heaven; second, in that they are said to have applauded God, as it were, in the creation of other things Job 38:7. They are also spirits, Heb. 1:14, Luke 24:39, ministers of God, Heb. 1:7, 14, of highest perfection, and of an immortal nature, Luke 20:36.

38. The angels so excel in clear-seeing reason that they are said to be, as it were, full of eyes discerning immediately what God would have them do and how it is to be done. They excel in freedom of will so that they perform their offices with diligence, Ps. 103:20; in perfection of strength so that they are able to do deeds of surpassing power, 2 Peter 2:11; and also in the greatest agility so that they accomplish their commissions quickly as if they had wings, Ezek. 1:6.

39. Their ministry is to celebrate the glory of God and execute his commandments, Ps. 103:20, especially for the heirs of eternal life, Heb. 1:14; Ps. 91:11; and 34:7.

40. They were created pure in holiness and righteousness, Luke 9:26; John 8:44; Jude 6; 2 Peter 2:4.

41. They are many in number, up to ten thousand times ten thousand, Dan. 7:10; Heb. 12:22; Matt. 26:53. They are distinguished among themselves by their offices and the objects of their concern, Eph. 1:21, and they are subject only to the rule of God and Christ.

42. God is known in the creation, but not God the Father, Son, and Holy Spirit, because that efficient power whereby the world was created belongs to the essence of God and not to his personal subsistence.

43. The creation of parts of the world contingently perfect is seen in those things whose principles existed before.

44. Hence such creatures are subject to change and corruption.

45. Those things which are contingently perfect have a double existence: first a rude and incomplete existence and later a complete, distinct, and beautified one.

46. The rude and incomplete existence was in that mass which in the beginning was created without form, void, and wrapped in darkness, which is called the earth, the waters, the deep.

47. It is said to be without form not because it lacked shape but because it had no beauty or adornment, or the fullness of the forms which came forth afterwards.

48. In the creation of the complete existence of things, two matters are most to be considered: manner and order.

49. The manner of creation includes four elements. First, the command of God which produces everything: *Let be,* or *Let this or that be done* — a command in which the power of God shines forth showing that only by his word or will he did all things, Pss. 33:9 and 115:3. Second, his approval, which acknowledges the thing brought forth to be good: *God saw that it was good.* The goodness of God shines forth in that he produced all things to a good end and use, Ps. 19:2. Third, his ordaining power which assigns a use to everything: *Let it be to this or that end.* The wisdom of God shines forth in that he has assigned their particular uses to particular created things in a suitable way. Jer. 10:12 and 51:15, *He made the earth by his power, he established the habitable world through his wisdom and stretched out the heavens according to his prudence.* Fourth, the establishment of law and order, which is to be observed perpetually in the thing to which ordaining power applies. The constancy of God shines forth in that he would have all creatures observe their order, not for days or years but to the end of the world.

50. These four are not all to be found in some kinds of things, because of an imperfection which awaits the perfection of other things. Yet in ordinary thought they are equally in all things.

51. The order of creation was this: In the first day after the constituting of the highest heavens, the angels, and the unformed mass, the most delicate part of that mass was called upward and became light, i.e., a shining fire.

52. On the second day, air was made out of that very delicate part nearest to the light.

53. On the third day the thicker parts of the mass were divided so that the sea stood forth by itself as the greatest part of the waters gathered in hollows. And the earth appeared adorned with herbs and trees.

54. On the fourth day were made the luminaries of heaven to give light to the earth.

55. On the fifth day fishes and birds, living in the water and the air, were brought forth.

56. On the sixth day all terrestrial living creatures were brought forth, first the unreasoning animals and then man. And thus the heavens and earth were perfected and all the numbers of created things.

57. In this order the wisdom, power, and goodness of God shine forth abundantly.

58. His wisdom is seen, first, in that simple elements were created before things elementary, condensed, or compound; second, in that among the simple things the more perfect were made first, being closest to the nature of God; third, in that those things were created first which have only being, then those which have life as well as being, then those that have sense as well as being and life, and last of all those which have reason besides being, life, and sense; fourth, in that simple things were created in order from the more perfect to the less perfect, but compound things in order from the less perfect to the more perfect (plants before men, for example).

59. The power of God shone forth in that he first created the plants, the herbs, and the trees before the sun and stars which customarily are causes in their production.

60. The goodness of God shone forth in that he created dwellings before inhabitants, food before living creatures, and the things useful for man before man himself.

61. Man as the last of the creatures is also the summary of all, being both absolutely and contingently perfect — in the former way in his soul and in the latter way in his body.

62. He was the last of the creatures contingently perfect and was thus of them and above them, in the intention of God.

63. Therefore man is said to be created in a different manner from other creatures; they were brought forth by a word only, *Let there be light, Let there be a firmament,* but man was brought forth, as it were, with greater counsel and deliberation, *Let us make man,* Gen. 1:26.

64. The body was first prepared and afterwards the soul was breathed in, Gen. 2:7. The body was made of elementary matter, but the soul was produced not out of matter existing before, but rather by the immediate power of God.

65. The excellency of man was fixed chiefly in this: He bore the image of God.

66. Three things are required for an image: one, that it be like something; two, that it be formed and fashioned to imitate something as a facsimile; three, that the likeness be either in its specific nature or in its highest perfection.

67. In the inferior creatures the image of God is not properly to be found, but only a shadow and vestige of it.

68. In man the true basis for an image is found, but not a perfect one, for that is only in the son of God, Col. 1:15; Heb. 1:3. Yet the imperfection is the result not of deprival but of denial.

69. This image then is the conformity of man in his measure to the highest perfection of God.

70. This image was natural to man, but for various reasons: in part it was the very nature of man, in part the result of the principles and perfection of nature, and in part and in a way the action of nature.

71. The image of God in man was both inward and outward. The inward is the perfection of body and soul.

72. The perfection of body was seen in its embodiment of beauty and usefulness conforming to God's will, Gen. 2:25; Rom. 6:13.

73. The perfection of the soul consisted in its immortal nature, seen not only in the faculties whereby it has freedom in its actions — in the understanding and the will — but also in its endowment with gifts whereby man is rendered able and fit to live well, that is, in wisdom, holiness, and righteousness, Eph. 4:24; Col. 3:10.

74. The external perfection of man consisted of his dominion over other creatures so that he might use them freely to the glory of God and for his own necessity, Gen. 1:26 and 2:19, 20.

75. Hence the tilling of the earth was committed to him and the obtaining of food from the plants of the earth, Gen. 2:15.

76. Thus arises the coming of the creatures to him as to their master and the placing of names upon them by him as their master, Gen. 2:19.

77. And so he was placed in the garden of Eden as in his palace, Gen. 2:15.

78. In the combination of these things the perfection of man was complete; and from that perfection resulted a certain image of God or of divine perfection.

79. The creation of man was male and female, both of them out of nothing as far as the soul is concerned. The body of the male was made out of the earth mixed with other elements and that of the woman out of the man and for the man so that nothing would be missing for his well-being, 1 Cor. 11:8, 9.

80. From this consideration of creation our faith ascends above the order of nature and *Apprehends the light of the glory of God, to be shown in the face of Jesus Christ, because it is God who commanded the light to shine forth out of darkness,* 2 Cor. 4:6.

IX

Providence

1. The providence of God is that efficiency whereby he provides for existing creatures in all things in accordance with the counsel of his will.

2. This providence extends to all things, not only general but particular, Ps. 145:15, 16; Prov. 16:9, 33; Exod. 21:13. It is not determined by any cause, but determines all causes and hence is both the universal and the particular cause of all things.

3. The providence of God is either direct, whereby God, by himself, as the sole cause, provides for things, or indirect whereby he provides through the use of means.

4. God accomplishes directly all things that come to pass through his power over all being as found in the effect (for the power of God applies to every effect, Deut. 8:3; Isa. 28:26) and also over all things that come to pass through the subject by virtue of the being which it possesses as being. For God who is always and everywhere present, immediately and inwardly, works thus in all things.

5. But in those things in which, because of their nature, secondary causes prevail, God is said to work not directly but indirectly. He works through the mediating subjects and the power of secondary causes.

6. God therefore uses means not because of any lack of power, but because of the abundance of his goodness; he communicates a certain dignity of efficiency to his creatures and in them makes his own efficiency more perceptible. 1 Sam. 14:6, *It is no impediment to the Lord whether he saves by many or by few.* Hence God often uses unlikely means to produce the most worthy effects, 1 Cor. 1:27, 28; Amos 9:5; 2 Chron. 24:24; and he often makes the most suitable means ineffectual, Pss. 33:16 and 127:1, 2; Hos. 4:10.

7. Hence our faith does not look to those means which God uses, nor does it depend on them, but rather to God who alone can relieve all our necessities, either with or without means as it appears good to him. Dan. 3:17, *Our God whom we worship is able to deliver us out of the hot fiery furnace and out of thy hands, O king.*

8. The providence of God is either ordinary and usual, or extraordinary and unusual.

9. Ordinary providence consists in God's observance of the order in things which was appointed from the beginning, an order which

requires that a certain thing go before and that a certain consequence follow. Hos. 2:21, 22, *I will hear the heavens and they shall hear the earth; and the earth shall hear the corn and the wine and the oil and they shall hear Israel.*

10. That order in natural things is the law of nature common to all things, or the very nature of things, in so far as these are established in a certain order. It arises from the force and efficacy of the never revoked word of God given in the beginning, *Let it be made, Let it be, Be it so,* which, adumbrating the shape of the future, signifies perpetuity and constancy. By its force it affects all matters which are normally the result of natural things. Jer. 31:35, 36, *The statutes of the moon and of the stars,* and 33:20, *My covenant of the day and my covenant of the night.*

11. Extraordinary providence consists in God's provision for things beyond the usual and appointed order. Whatever is effected is, by metonymy of the effect, called a miracle.

12. A miracle is a work above the appointed order. True miracles always give evidence of the omnipotence of the doer; hence God only is the author of true miracles.

13. Men can be moral causes of miracles in so far as they obtain God's consent to do them, or as God uses their works as a sign or a token of a miracle to be done by him. Yet they cannot really be efficient causes, or instrumental, much less principal causes.

14. The providence of God is either conservational or governmental.

15. Conservation is God's making all things, universal and particular, to persist and continue in essence and existence as well as in their powers, Ps. 104:19, 20; Acts 17:28; Heb. 1:3. This is suitably called by the Schoolmen, "God's holding in his hand," because by this power God sustains all things as if with his hand.

16. Conservation necessarily comes between creation and the government of things created, because whatever is created is for some end and use to which it ought to be directed and governed. But it cannot reach this end or be directed towards it, unless it be continued and maintained in its being.

17. God's conservation is necessary for the creature because the creature depends in every way upon the creator — not only for its creation, but also for its being, existence, continuance, and operation. Every creature would return to that state of nothing whence it came if God did not uphold it; and the cessation of divine conservation would, without any other operation, immediately reduce every creature to nothing. Ps. 104:29, *If thou hide thy face, they are troubled; if thou take away their breath, they die and return to their dust.*

18. Some things — subject only to God — are conserved directly. This conservation is the same as creation, except that creation has a certain newness which conservation lacks and creation lacks a preceding existence which conservation implies. Conservation is nothing else than a continued creation, so to speak, and therefore it is joined with creation. Neh. 9:6, *Thou hast made . . . and thou preservest all things.*

19. Government is the power whereby God directs and leads all his creatures to their proper end. Ps. 29:10, *The Lord sits as king forever.*

20. The government of things is rightly God's. For things could never attain the ends for which they were created unless governed by the same power which created them. It is a failure in the worker to leave work that he has done to be directed by another.

21. This government includes intrinsically not only suitable means for the end, but also efficient power capable of attaining the end. The nature, therefore, of this government is certain, immovable, and indestructible. The creature cannot wholly withdraw from all government although it may turn away from any particular type, Gen. 50:20.

22. Government is either common or special.

23. Common government is God's direction of all things in a similar manner. To such government belongs, first, the law of nature common to all things which is a participation of the divine law and will in all things from the very beginning. Job 38:12, *Hast thou commanded the morning . . . and made known to the dayspring his place?* Second, a natural inclination or principle of working according to that law. Job 5:7, *The sparks fly upward.* Third, a natural instinct or peculiar stirring up of living creatures to higher activities with a certain show or suggestion of reason. Prov. 6:6, *Go to the ant, O sluggard; behold her ways, and be wise;* and 30:24–28, *These four are small upon the earth, but they are exceedingly wise: the ants . . . the rodents . . . the locusts.. ....the spiders;* Jer. 8:7, *The stork . . . the turtledove, the crane, and the swallow observe the times of their comings.* Fourth, a certain power to obey whereby all creatures tend to obey the command of God. Pss. 103:21 and 148:8, *Doing his pleasure, fulfilling his word.*

24. This government shines forth in the operation of all things. First, everything naturally looks toward an end; it is thus necessary that things be directed and governed by an intelligence which is everywhere present and omnipotent, i.e., by God himself. Job 38:26, 27, *In sending down rain . . . to satisfy the waste place, and bringing forth the bud of the tender herb;* Isa. 55:10, *The rain brings it about that the earth brings forth seed to the sower and bread for him who eats.* Second, the works of nature are ordered so accurately and

intelligently that they cannot but proceed from the highest reason, Prov. 30:25–28. Third, alongside of the ordaining power whereby everything seeks its own perfection, all things cultivate a common society, as it were, and desire the preservation of the whole more than themselves (as seen in heavy things carried upward to fill a vacuum).

25. All secondary causes are predetermined to some extent by the force of this government. First, they are stirred to work by an influence, or previous motion. Some such process is necessary to put into action that which was before only potentially in the creature (before the communication and maintenance of power). Second, the causes are applied to the object towards which they work, Ezek. 21:21, 22; 2 Sam. 16:10. Third, by force of the same government they are given order, i.e., limits and bounds are set to their actions, Job 1:12; 2:6; 38:10. Some good results from their actions, Gen. 50:20.

26. Because the exercise of strength in creatures depends upon the will of God, it can be said that we trust in God alone and not in those creatures through which we derive the bounty of God.

X

Special Government of Intelligent Creatures

In the former section, we dealt with common government; now we consider special.

1. Special government is God's government of rational creatures in a moral way.

2. The unique character of these creatures makes the difference. Since they are created after the image of God, are in some way immortal, and decide their actions in accord with their own counsel, they are to be directed towards an eternal state of happiness or unhappiness in accordance with their own counsel and freedom.

3. This special government does not exclude the basic government of the reasonable creature, which is common to all creatures, but it is rather added to it.

4. This moral government consists in teaching and in carrying out what it has previously taught. Mic. 6:8, *He has shown you, O man, what is good;* Deut. 30:15, *Life and good, death and evil.* The revealed

will of God, which is the rule for the moral life, applies to the rational creature at this point.

5. God governs by teaching partly in making law and partly in establishing it.

6. A law is made by commanding or forbidding.

7. A law is established by promising or threatening.

8. God governs by fulfilling when he carries out the things which he has taught. Jer. 32:19, *Thine eyes being opened do look upon all the ways of men, that thou may give to everyone according to his ways and according to the fruit of his action.*

9. From this special way of governing rational creatures there arises a covenant between God and them. This covenant is, as it were, a kind of transaction of God with the creature whereby God commands, promises, threatens, fulfills; and the creature binds itself in obedience to God so demanding. Deut. 26:16–19, *This day the Lord your God commands you . . . this day you have demanded a guarantee from the Lord [a Iehova stipulatus es sponsionem hodie] . . . the Lord demanded a guarantee from you this day . . . to make you high . . . so that you be a holy people.*

10. This way of entering into covenant is not between those who are equal before the law but between lord and servant. It, therefore, rightly pertains to the government. It is very rightly called the covenant not of man but of God, who is the author and chief executor. Deut. 8:18, *That he may confirm his covenant.*

11. In this covenant the moral deeds of the intelligent creature lead either to happiness as a reward or to unhappiness as a punishment. The latter is deserved, the former not.

12. The proper difference, therefore, between a good work and sin is that a good work expects happiness from someone else as a reward. On the other hand, when this is lacking, evil works become supremely evil.

13. Hence arises the force and reason of conscience which is an intelligent creature's self-judgment in his subjection to God's judgment.

14. The special government of rational creatures applies to angels and men.

15. The special government of angels is either a special injunction or an order for an event to follow.

16. In substance this is the same law as the moral law of the decalogue.

17. The exceptions for angels in the decalogue are those commandments which pertain to the nature of man's body or to the condition of this mortal life. These have no place among angels — the many

things that have to do with propagation pointed to in the seventh commandment (Matt. 22:30), those that have to do with the relation of inferiors to superiors in the fifth commandment, parts of the eighth commandment dealing with the obtaining of food in one's vocation, and finally many duties of the second and fourth commandments required of men.

18. In some angels the ordering of the event to follow took the shape of a continuance in obedience. Hence it is that they were confirmed in good and endowed with full happiness so that they immutably cleave to God with perfect obedience and fullness of glory. Such angels are called *Elect,* 1 Tim. 5:21; *Good and holy,* Luke 9:26; also *Blessed* and *Angels of light,* 2 Cor. 11:14.

19. In others, the ordering of the event was a permission whereby it happened that many abused their liberty and fell into apostasy.

20. From that time they were obstinate in evil and condemned to greatest misery, Jude 6; 2 Peter 2:4. Therefore, the evil angels are called impure spirits and angels of darkness, Luke 8:2 and 9:42.

21. In such different ordering the election of some angels and the reprobation of others by God's free counsel and good pleasure is obvious.

22. Concerning the time of the angels' fall, it only appears that it happened before Adam's fall.

23. As for the kind of the sin first committed by them their first motive was in all probability pride.

24. The Scripture states that their punishment is not yet inflicted in final form but will be inflicted at the end of the world, Matt. 25:41; 1 Cor. 6:3.

So much for the government of angels, now follows that of men.

25. In the special government of men, two things are to be observed (as in the government of angels): the prescribing of a law and the ordering of the event to follow. Yet the reasoning is not wholly the same for angels and men.

26. In the prescribing of the law there is similarity. First, the law prescribed to men and angels has the same moral essence summed up in the decalogue. Second, it is written in the heart in the form of disposition [*habitus*], where the first foundation of conscience called συντήρησις, *synteresis,* is located, Rom. 2:15.

27. But the dissimilarity and difference are great. First, the principles of this law common to angels and men have secondary deductions which apply only to men, such as those which relate to parents, marriage, food, and the like.

28. Second, since man is less perfect than the angels and needs more instruction and practice, something positive was added to

(though of the same basis as) the law of nature. The sanctification of the seventh day is an example.

29. Third, because man in this animal life understands by the senses and is led by the hand, as it were, from sensible to intelligible and spiritual things, outward symbols and sacraments were added to the spiritual law to illustrate and confirm it. These symbols contained a special and positive law, a profession of general obedience to the law of nature put in man before, and a solemn confirmation of promises and threats as sanctions.

30. Fourth, because Adam was the first of mankind, from whom all men come, a law was given to him not only as a private person, as among the angels, but as a public person or the head of the family of man. His posterity were to derive all good and evil from him, Acts 17:26; Rom. 5:18, 19; 1 Cor. 15:21, 22.

31. Fifth, in the sanction of this law there was a promise of continuing animal life, a later exaltation to spiritual life, and a threat of bodily death, which had no place among the angels.

32. Given this interpretation, the law of God or his covenant with man in the creation was, *Do this and you will live; if you do it not you shall die*. In these words there is, first, a command and then a promise — you do it and you shall live — and last a threat — if you do it not, you shall die.

33. In this covenant there were two symbols or sacraments. The reward for obedience was marked by a tree, namely, that of life, and the punishment for disobedience was marked by a tree, namely, that of the knowledge of good and evil. The one was the sacrament of life and the other the sacrament of death.

XI

Man's Apostasy or Fall

We have treated the first part of the special government of men which consists in prescribing a law. The other part deals with the ordering of events.

1. For man there are two things to be considered in the ordering of events: ἀπόστασις and ἀνάστασις, his fall and his restoration, Rom. 5:19; 1 Cor. 15:21.

2. With the angels there was preservation of some and apostasy of others, but no ἀνάστασις, or restoration, of the apostates. But in man preservation and apostasy could not exist together, because all

men were created in one Adam in the beginning, root and head. Some men could not be preserved from the fall and others fall in one and the same Adam.

3. In the angels there was no ἀνάστασις, or restoration, because, first, they fell from the highest excellence; and, second, the angelic nature did not completely perish. But in the sin of the first man all mankind perished.

4. The apostasy of man is his fall from the obedience owed to God, or a transgression of the law ordained by God.

5. In the fall two things are to be considered: the committing of the transgression and its propagation.

6. The committing of the transgression occurred in the eating of the forbidden fruit from the tree called the tree of the knowledge of good and evil. The first motion or step of this disobedience necessarily came before the act of eating, so that it may truly be said that man was a sinner before he did the eating. Therefore, the very desire with which Eve approached the forbidden fruit seems to mark a step, so to speak, in her sin. Gen. 3:6, *When the woman saw that the fruit of the tree was good for food and most delightful to the eyes, and the fruit of the tree to be desired in order to get knowledge, she took and ate.*

7. Therefore the first motion and step in this disobedience was the disordered desire for some superiority due to pride of mind. So that she might obtain this superiority — God's prohibition being laid aside in her unfaithfulness — she willed to test the forbidden fruit to see if it would confer such superiority.

8. Therefore the gravity of this sin, containing not only pride, ingratitude, and unfaithfulness, but also a violation of a most sacred oath showed, as it were, a general profession of disobedience and contempt for the whole covenant. This was the more atrocious, given the near perfection of the sinner's condition.

9. We must understand the causes and consequences in the committing of the transgression.

10. There was one principal cause and other secondary ones.

11. The principal cause was man himself in his abuse of free will, Eccles. 7:29. For he had received righteousness and grace by which he might have remained obedient, if he had so chosen. That righteousness and grace was not taken from him before he sinned, although strengthening and confirming grace by which the act of sinning might have been hindered and the act of obedience effected was not given him — and that by the certain, wise, and just counsel of God. God therefore was in no way the cause of his fall; neither did he lay upon man the necessity of sinning. Man of his own accord freely fell from God.

12. The secondary causes were the devil and the woman.

13. The first sin of the devil was pride. From pride came immediately envy towards God and God's image in man. The devil had lost his ordered superiority by taking on disordered superiority, and so the superiority of others pained him and he was maliciously bent on opposing it. But the devil was not the compelling cause, or the cause of a sufficient, direct, necessary, or certain force in bringing about that sin; he was only the consulting and persuading cause through his tempting. For this reason he has the name of the tempter, Matt. 4:3.

14. The devil's tempting is a fallacious or sophistical argument whereby, under the appearance of what is true and good, he tries to seduce into falsity and lead into evil.

15. In this temptation, the good which he held out and pretended to promise was set forth as if it were the greatest of good things; the way to attain that good was pretended to be simple and easy; and that greatest of evils which hung over man's head was hidden from him.

16. The devil does the same in all the temptations by which he ensnares mankind. Yet in this temptation a special cunning is to be observed full of craft and very subtle.

17. First, he chose to use the serpent, which had a natural aptitude the devil knew how to abuse.

18. Second, he dealt with the woman, 1 Tim. 2:14 — whether in the presence or absence of her husband the Scripture does not say.

19. Third, he established nothing in the first conversation; he only put a question to the woman, as if he were ignorant of the matter. *Has God indeed said?*

20. Fourth, his question was ambiguous, for it might be taken that he was not asking about God's command but about the sense or meaning of that command, perhaps not sufficiently understood by man. If the question applied to the command itself then he might seem to be asking whether God had forbidden them to eat of the fruit of any tree, or, as the woman herself answered, whether he had forbidden them the use of that one tree and had simply not given them permission for all.

21. Fifth, when by his question he had placed God's command in doubt, he so ingeniously impaired its sanction or threat in the now wavering mind of the woman that she could deny the truth, or at least the necessity of it.

22. Sixth, after he weakened the command and its sanction, he made a plainly contrary prediction.

23. Seventh, to confirm that prediction he abused both the name of God and the name which God had given the tree. Gen. 3:5, *God knows that when you shall eat thereof your eyes shall be open, and you shall be as gods, knowing good and evil.*

24. Hence it is that the devil is called a serpent, a liar, a seducer, a murderer. Rev. 12:9; John 8:44; Rev. 20:10.

25. With the devil's tempting was joined a tempting by God whereby he ordered the event so that it might show what was in man. But the tempting by God was not evil nor did it tend to evil.

26. A third tempting followed, namely, man's tempting of God, wherein he made trial, in a way, of the truth and grace of God. He tried to see whether God would save him (although he did not cling to him), and whether he would certainly do what he had threatened.

27. A fourth temptation occurred in this connection in the case of Eve. She accepted the temptation or suggestion of the devil and applied it to herself to her own ruin.

28. From this arose a fifth whereby the woman, as the devil's instrument, tempted Adam. And from this proceeded a sixth, whereby Adam tempted himself in consenting deliberately to the woman and the devil.

29. All or most of these temptations are found in the sins of every man.

30. And so the sin which brought about the fall of mankind was consummated in Adam. He was properly the beginning of mankind, and not Eve, except in so far as she was made for him, and so with him constituted one and the same beginning. We therefore read in the Scriptures of a second Adam, but not of a second Eve.

XII

The Consequences of Sin

In the former section we treated of the fall and its causes; now follow the consequences.

1. The consequences of sin are, first, guilt and the sense of wickedness [turpitudo], second, punishment (properly and strictly so called).

2. Guilt is the obligation of the sinner to undergo just punishment for his fault. Lev. 5:2–5, He is guilty; Rom. 3:9, 19, We have proved that all are under sin . . . all the world is guilty before God; 1 Cor. 15:17, You are in your sins.

3. That distinction between guilt of the fault and guilt of the punishment is a distinction without difference — likewise that distinction of the Papists between remission of the punishment and of the fault.

4. Guilt is not the form of sin but a situation [*affectio*] or consequence, partly separable, partly inseparable.

5. It follows sin, partly by virtue of the law of God assigning punishment to sins and in this sense it has some good and is of God. In this respect God cannot separate guilt from sin. Yet as it flows from sin and punishment is warranted and deserved; it also partakes of the nature of sin and is a vicious thing. Thus it cannot rightly be separated from sin. This double aspect of guilt is intimated in Rom. 1:32, *Knowing the law of God that those who do such things are worthy of death.*

6. A gnawing conscience follows guilt, accusing and justly condemning. And then comes a horror and a fleeing from the presence of God, Gen. 3:8, 10; Heb. 2:15; Rom. 8:15.

7. The sense of wickedness is that spiritual pollution whereby a sinner is made destitute of all dignity and honor and becomes vile, Matt. 15:11; Rev. 22:11.

8. This sense of wickedness immediately follows the offense of the sin and remains in the sinner after the act of sin is past and gone. It is often called the spot of sin, corruption, defilement, baseness, dishonesty, nakedness, impurity, a blot, or sometimes fault.

9. The following come from this condition. First, a *Turning away from God*, Isa. 1:15, which is also called *Abomination* and *Detestation*, Prov. 3:32, especially in respect to the greater sins, Prov. 6:16; Jer. 16:18. Second, the shame of a man to the point of confusion, Gen. 3:7. Such a shame is a fear arising from the self-consciousness of wickedness. Rom. 6:21, *What fruit had you from those things of which you are now ashamed?*

10. Punishment is an evil inflicted on the sinner for his sin.

11. It is called an evil because it is a deprivation of good. But it is not a deprivation of a genuine good, as sin is. It is rather a deprivation of the good of happiness in the sinner who is punished.

12. It is called an evil inflicted, not simply contracted, because it pertains to retributive and avenging justice.

13. It is said to be inflicted for sin because it corresponds in fact and kind with what the sin deserves. Punishment follows upon the offence, because it had been prohibited, and upon the guilt, because the threat of punishment had been such.

14. Therefore punishment, properly speaking, has no place but in intelligent creatures in whom there is also sin.

15. Because sin can be brought into order by punishment and sin itself stands against the goodness of God — but punishment only against the good of the creature — sin has more evil in itself than punishment.

16. So it is that the least sin is not to be condoned, although the greatest punishment might be avoided by refraining from it, or the greatest good obtained, Rom. 3:8.

17. In the ordaining of punishment many attributes of God shine forth, especially holiness, righteousness, and mercy.

18. In its largest sense, the holiness of God is freedom and, as it were, separation from all imperfection, Isa. 6:3; Rev. 4:8. But that holiness of God which particularly shines forth here is his inability to communicate with sin, being pure from any stain of sin. Ps. 5:4, *Thou art not a strong God that delighteth in iniquity; evil shall not dwell with thee;* Hab. 1:13, *Thou art of purer eyes than that thou may behold evil.*

19. The avenging justice of God which shines forth here is his power to inflict evil upon those who do evil. 2 Thess. 1:6, *It is justice for God to render affliction to them that afflict you.*

20. This justice, burning only against sin, is called wrath, Rom. 1:18; Eph. 5:6. As it grows hotter, it is called *Fury*, Deut. 29:20. As it gives sentence to be executed against a sinner, it is called *Judgment*, Rom. 2:5. And as it executes the sentence given, it is called *Vengeance*, Heb. 10:30.

21. The mercy shining forth here is his punishment of sin in less degree than the guilty person deserves.

22. This mercy is either clemency or beneficence.

23. Clemency is his moderation of the punishment due. Lam. 3:22, *It is the Lord's great kindness that we are not consumed.*

24. Clemency appears in patience and long-suffering.

25. Patience is his forbearing endurance of sin and sparing of sinners, 2 Peter 3:9.

26. Long-suffering is long suspension of vengeance, Exod. 34:6.

27. Beneficence lies in his being so rich in goodness that he pours forth many good things even on sinners, Matt. 5:45.

So much for guilt, wickedness, and punishment of sin in general; now we consider punishment in particular.

28. The punishment inflicted on man for sin is death, Gen. 2:17; Rom. 5:12.

29. Death is a miserable deprivation of life.

30. By the life of man is understood both the joining of the soul with the body and all the perfection which belonged to man in that state, whether actually communicated or to be communicated upon a condition. Ps. 36:9, *With thee is the fountain of life; in thy light we shall enjoy light.*

31. Therefore death is ordained by God not in the same way that he ordained nature, but as vengeance on sin. And so it properly comes from sin which has earned it and obtained it.

32. But death is not a simple, bare deprivation of life; it is connected with subjection to misery. It is more than the annihilation of the deserving sinner, for besides the subject of the misery the misery itself is also carried away.

33. A kind of image and representation of this death was the casting of man out of paradise, which contained a symbol of life, Gen. 3:22–24.

So much for death in general. Now follows a special consideration of it.

34. In death — the curse of God that lies upon sinners — there are two degrees: the beginning and the consummation. There are two parts: the punishment which is loss [damnum] or the part of deprivation, and the punishment which is a matter of consciousness [sensus], or the positive part. And there are two kinds of death, spiritual and bodily.

35. The beginning of spiritual death in the form of loss is the defacement of the image of God, i.e., the letting go of grace and original justice. Rom. 3:23, *They are deprived of the glory of God*; Eph. 4:18, *Being alienated from the life of God.*

36. By this letting go of grace man is robbed of all saving gifts. And his nature is weakened, put out of order, or, as it were, wounded.

37. The beginning of spiritual death in the form of conscious realization is spiritual bondage.

38. Spiritual bondage is a subjection to the power of darkness or of spiritually deadly enemies. Col. 1:13, *He has taken us out of the power of darkness*; 2 Peter 2:19, *By what a man is overcome, under the same he is placed in bondage.*

39. This bondage is of the devil and of those who serve him.

40. Bondage to the devil is subjection to his power which he effectively employs among men. He has command over their death, Acts 26:18; 2 Cor. 4:4; John 12:31 and 16:11; 2 Tim. 2:26; Eph. 2:2.

41. Bondage to the devil's servants is bondage to the world and to sin.

42. Bondage to the world is subjection to the evil incitements found in the world, Phil. 3:19; 1 John 4:5 and 2:15, 16.

43. The bondage of sin consists in man's being so captivated by sin that he has no power to rise out of it, Rom. 6:16, 17, 19, 20.

44. Although the freedom of the will essential to man's nature remains, this bondage destroys the freedom which belongs to the perfection of human nature and includes the power to perform acts spiritually good and acceptable — or at least the bondage leaves that freedom remote and dead.

45. From this beginning of spiritual death there follows a multiplication of sin in this present life.

46. Those sins which follow are in a way a punishment for the first sin, Rom. 1:26.

47. These later sins are regarded as a punishment, first, by reason of their effects or consequences, for they increase death among men and promote their misery. Second, these sins are said to be punishment because of the inward suffering to which man is subjected in sinning, whereby his nature is suppressed and made more base. Third, they are said to be punishment for the former sin because the former was the cause of man's loss of that righteousness and grace or divine help, in the absence of which he falls into later sins. Fourth, it may be said that in a way these are punishments of the former sin because the former was a cause disposing and preparing man to commit later sin; in that sense it has brought upon man all these sins and other evils accompanying or following them.

XIII

Original Sin

In the last section the multiplication of sin was stated to be a consequence of spiritual death from its very beginning. This we now detail in the following thesis.

1. The sin that followed upon the first fall is either original or actual.

2. Original sin is a habitual deviation of the whole nature of man, or a turning aside from the law of God.

3. Because it is the corruption of the whole man, the holy Scriptures speak of *The old man,* Rom. 6:6; Eph. 4:22; Col. 3:9; *The body of sin,* Rom. 6:6, 7:24; *A law of the members,* Rom. 7:23; *The members themselves,* Col. 3:5; *Flesh,* John 3:6; Rom. 7:5, 18, 25.

4. It is also found in Scripture that the same corruption is attributed not only to the whole man in general but to each one of his parts. It is attributed to the intellect, as found in Gen. 6:5, *The imagination and thoughts only evil;* Rom. 8:5–7, *They savor the things of the flesh.* To the conscience in Titus 1:15, *The mind and conscience is defiled.* To the will in Gen. 8:21, *The imagination of the heart of man is evil from his childhood.* To affections of every kind in Rom. 1:24, *To uncleanness in the lusts of their hearts.* Last, to the body and all its members as in Rom. 6:19, *Your members yielded to uncleanness and iniquity do commit iniquity.*

5. This sin is said to be a deviation or turning aside in man be-

cause it is a habitual lack of obedience to the law imposed by God on man to guide him in his way.

6. This original corruption [*depravatio*] is called in the Scriptures in a certain special meaning *Sin* or *That sin*, Rom. 6:12; 7:17; 7:8, 20; *The law of sin*, Rom. 7:23; *Sin dwelling in us . . . inhering . . . adhering . . . encompassing us*, Rom. 7:17, 20, 21; Heb. 12:1.

7. This perversion in man has, as it were, two parts, one formal and the other material. Jer. 2:13, *My people have done two evils: they have forsaken me . . . that they might dig cisterns for themselves.* Actual sin reflects original sin, as a daughter her mother.

8. The formal part is an aversion to good. Rom. 3:12, *There is none who does good, no not one.*

9. The material part is a turning and inclining towards evil. Rom. 7:23, *The law of sin.*

10. Because of the original corruption, the will of man in the state of sin (though free in the actions it performs) is captive and servile in its way of performing them. The will is deprived of the power of willing well and takes the form of willing amiss even when the object of the willing is good, Rom. 3:12, 7:14; 2 Cor. 3:5; John 8:34.

XIV

Actual Sin

1. So much for original sin; now we consider actual sin.

2. Actual sin is a deviation of human action or turning aside from the law of God, 1 John 3:4. It follows from original sin as an act follows a habit, or as a person's misdeed flows from a fault of his nature. In this respect original sin is rightly called the tinder for sin.

3. Therefore actual sins, although often having objects opposed to one another and often having different relations to their objects, are tied and knit together at the point of their beginning or foundation, Jas. 2:10; 1 Tim. 6:9.

4. Actual sins are to be understood in several ways. First, in the matter of degree, inasmuch as one sin is greater or less than another. Ezek. 5:6, *She changed my judgment more than the Gentiles themselves;* 8:15, *You shall see yet greater abominations than these;* John 19:11, *He has the greater sin.* Punishment is greater or less; Luke 12:47, 48, *He who knows and does not shall be beaten with many stripes and he that knows not and does shall be beaten with few stripes;* Matt. 11:22, 24.

5. This difference of degree depends upon several considerations. First, upon the person by whom the sin is committed, Num. 12:14. Thus there is a difference between fornication, adultery, and incest. Second, upon the kind and nature of the thing. Matt. 5:21–22, *He that is angry ill-advisedly . . . he that insults . . . he that says, you fool.* Third, upon the strength and weakness of the act. Phil. 3:6, *Concerning zeal, a persecutor of the church;* 1 Tim. 1:13, *A blasphemer, persecutor, and insulter.* Fourth, upon the reason and manner of committing it, for sin may be done out of ignorance or infirmity, or with a high hand. Num. 15:27, 30, *If a soul shall sin through error, he shall offer a she-goat . . . But the soul which commits with a high hand . . . shall be destroyed;* Ps. 19:13, 14; 1 Cor. 6:7, *There is a complete defect in you.* Fifth, upon the circumstances of place, time, and the like. Isa. 26:10, *When favor is showed to the wicked man, he will not learn righteousness; in the land of uprighteousness he does wickedly.*

6. Second, the particular differences in actual sins are relative, depending upon the differences in the virtues of which the acts are the perversions.

7. Therefore the division of sins according to the commandments of God to which they are opposed is quite proper.

8. Third, actual sin is divided into sins of omission and those of commission. These are, as it were, the two parts of original sin, which is a turning from good and a turning to evil, and so actual sin, which derives therefrom, has a double form. When turning from good dominates, the sin is said to be one of omission, and when a turning to evil, a sin of commission.

9. A sin of omission, therefore, is not to do what ought to be done. Jas. 4:17, *He that knows how to do well and does it not, to him it is sin;* Matt. 25:42, *I was hungry and you gave me no meat.*

10. A sin of commission is to do what ought not to be done.

11. A sin of omission is directly contrary to God's commandment and the sin of commission to God's forbiddance. In a sin of commission there is something added to the law of God and in omission something taken away — both are forbidden, Deut. 4:2, 12:32; Rev. 22:18, 19.

12. This division of sin does not bear on the kinds of sin. (*a*) Commission and omission having to do with the same object and with the same intent do not differ in kind. Covetousness, for example, may take either form. (*b*) No moral omission occurs without an accompanying or previous act. (*c*) Omission cannot be voluntary and free without an act — and such an act involves a sin of commission.

13. Fourth, sin is divided according to its subject into sin of the

heart, sin of the mouth, and sin of work. Thus it may be a word, a deed, or a thought directed against the law, Isa. 28:13; Matt. 5:28, 15:19.

14. Fifth, sin is divided according to its object into sin against God and sin against men, Luke 15:18; 1 Sam. 2:25. Yet it clearly does not apply to God and man in the same way. Sin as a transgression of God's law is an offense against God alone; but in a material sense, referring to the loss and wrong sin often inflicts upon men, it is also connected with men.

15. Sixth, sin is divided according to its effect into sin which destroys the conscience and that which does not, into sin which rules and that which is weak, and into sin which is pardonable and that which is unpardonable (these cannot properly be discussed here).

16. This multiplication of sin produces an increase in spiritual death both in the form of loss and in the form of conscious realization.

17. In loss there is a secure feeling and a stupidity, i.e., a lack of the sense of sin and misery.

18. This security comes from the practice of sinning and the soul's obstinacy in sins. For sins, whether they are of commission or omission, when they become customary and old through daily multiplication, beget an evil habit; they cover the will and mind at the same time with a hard skin, as it were. Jer. 13:23, *Can an Ethiopian change his skin or a leopard his spots? Then will you do good who are accustomed to doing evil?* Eph. 4:19, *Being past feeling, they gave themselves to lasciviousness to commit uncleanness with greed.*

19. In the form of conscious realization there is greatest terror of conscience along with desperation, Heb. 10:26, 27; Gen. 4:13.

20. This terror comes from a deep and multiple sense of guilt and of the inevitability of imminent punishment.

21. In this beginning of spiritual death, God imparts a certain moderation, which is either internal or external.

22. Internally this takes the shape of vestiges of God's image, Jas. 3:9. These vestiges appear both in the understanding and in the will.

23. In the understanding, there remain the principles of truth which direct both the theoretical and the practical judgment.

24. The theoretical principles deal with the true and the false, of which all men who have any use of reason have some knowledge, Rom. 1:20; Ps. 19:2, 3.

25. Practical principles distinguish between honest and dishonest, just and unjust — that God is to be worshipped, or that something is not to be done to another which one would not have done to oneself.

26. This is the law written in the hearts of all men. Rom. 2:15, *They show the mark of the law written in their hearts.*

27. From these principles arises a certain force of natural conscience. Rom. 2:15, *Their consciences together bearing witness and their thoughts accusing one another or excusing.* But this conscience, as well as the principles, is corrupt and even dead. Titus 1:15, *Their mind and conscience is defiled.*

28. In the will, the vestiges appear in a certain inclination to dimly known good. Although vanishing and dead, the inclination is found in all people to some degree; for this reason it can be said that at least the shadows of virtue are approved and cultivated by all. 2 Tim. 3:5, *Having a show of godliness.*

29. A restraining power is felt both in the will and the understanding by which excess of sin is curbed in most people so that even sinners abhor the committing of many grosser sins. 1 Cor. 5:1, *Such fornication is not found among the Gentiles.*

30. The external moderation of the misery of sin is by external means, both social and domestic, through which the course of sin and misery can be partly arrested.

XV

Bodily Death

So much for the beginning of spiritual death; now we speak of the beginning of bodily death and the consummation of both.

1. The beginning of bodily death in the sense of loss is either inward or outward.

2. Inward is the losing of the internal good things of the body, that is, health and vigor, Deut. 28:21, 22, 27, 35; 1 Cor. 11:30; Matt. 9:2.

3. Hence mortality is a state and potentiality nearest to death.

4. Mortality is a dissolving or loosening of that bond by which the soul was joined with the body.

5. The outward beginning of death in the sense of loss is the passing of the outward good things whereby life is either enhanced or sustained.

6. The first type (loss of enhancement) is the passing of dominion over the creatures, which after the fall cast off most of the subjection to man under which they had been placed and became his deadly enemies — unless brought into order by the special providence of God. Job 5:22–23, *Be not afraid of the beasts of the earth. For you shall be in covenant with the stones of the field, and the beasts of the field*

shall be at peace with you; Hos. 2:18, *I will make a covenant for them with the beasts of the field.* Second, the disgrace which has come to him both while alive and when dead, Deut. 28:20, 37.

7. Of the second type (loss of sustenance) is poverty, or the loss of things to be used as food, raiment, and possessions, Deut. 28:17, 18.

8. The beginning of this death in the form of conscious realization is also inward or outward.

9. Inward are weariness, Gen. 3:19, pain, and disease, Deut. 28:35.

10. Outward are all those calamities to which the outer life of man is subject, Deut. 28:25, 48.

11. The moderation appearing in this corporal punishment is both inward and outward.

12. Inwardly it is seen in man's having opportunity and due measure of life granted to him by the goodness of God, Gen. 6:3.

13. Outwardly it is seen in certain vestiges of the old dominion over the creatures. Gen. 9:2, *Let the fear of you and the dread of you be upon the beasts of the earth.* Although man fell by his sin from all prior rights of using the creatures to his benefit, yet by concession and divine indulgence he may use them; and thereby he does not sin in simply using them, although he may sin in the manner of use. While life is granted and prolonged to him, there is given the use of those things necessarily required, and in a way due, in life.

14. Even though the creatures were made subject to futility and a curse because of man's sin, Gen. 3:17, 18; Rom. 8:20, 22, they are kept in their condition so that they may supply the necessities of man's life.

XVI

The Consummation of Death

1. The consummation of death is the highest degree of punishment. It endures forever, and is thus said to be infinite in degree.

2. It is infinite only in respect to loss and deprivation, because it is the losing of an infinite good; it is not infinite with respect to consciousness or any definite affliction. It may be said to be infinite in regard to the thing afflicting but not the manner of afflicting.

3. There are degrees in this punishment which correspond to the degrees found in sins. Luke 12:47, 48, *He shall be beaten with many stripes. . . . he shall be beaten with few stripes.*

4. In the matter of duration this punishment is said to be eternal, or never to be ended. Mark 9:44, 46, 48, *Where their worm dies not, and their fire never goes out.*

5. It is eternal because of the eternal permanency of the fault; because of the immutability of the condition, to which punishment of this degree comes; and because there is no such thing as reparation.

6. Thus the incorruptibility of the lost is their immortality in death and to death.

7. The consummation of spiritual death in the point of loss is a total and final forsaking by which a man is separated completely from the face, presence, and favor of God. Matt. 7:23, *Depart from me*; and 25:41, *Depart from me you cursed*; 2 Thess. 1:9, *Who shall be punished with everlasting destruction, being driven from the face of the Lord and the glory of his power.*

8. Then follows a great and eternal hardening in evil and despair of good, Luke 16:26.

9. The consummation of spiritual death in the point of conscious realization is a full sense of bondage to the power of the devil, to which a man is totally delivered, Matt. 25:41.

10. Thereupon comes a full sense of the terrors of conscience and sin. For the lost sin and will sin forever — but not the sins of this life (theft, murder, adultery, and the like) nor under the conditions prevailing while they were alive. They will continue to offend in hatred, envy, indignation, and similar affections produced by the sharpness of the punishment. These sins after death do not have the same reward that they have in this life, because then there is no possibility of avoiding sin, no threat given, and no increasing of punishment.

11. Therefore the sins of the lost have in them more of punishment than the sins of the living. The sins of the living are more connected with offense.

12. Terror of conscience is, it might be said, a perpetually gnawing worm, Mark 9:44; Isa. 66:24.

13. The consummation of bodily death with the spiritual comes first through the separation of soul from body, 1 Cor. 15:42, 43. For some a change of this sort, like death, will occur, 1 Cor. 15:51, 52; 1 Thess. 4:15, 16. It is marked, second, by a casting of soul and body into hell, or that place which God has prepared for the extreme torment of sin, Rev. 21:8.

14. Pains and the greatest agony of soul and body occur, Luke 16:23.

15. There are lamentations, howling, gnashing of teeth and similar marks of greatest agony, Luke 13:28.

16. But concerning the place of hell and the manner of torture and

the nature of the attendant circumstances, the Scripture has said nothing definite, because it is not necessary for us to know.

❦

XVII

The Propagation of Sin

So much for the act of transgression, now we consider its propagation.

1. Propagation is the participation in the condition of Adam by all
human posterity descended from him in a natural manner, Job 14:5;
Ps. 51:7; Rom. 5:14; Eph. 2:3. This has occurred by God's just ordering. The justice of it appears among men in some ways; first, in natural
law by which inbred qualities are passed on from parents to children;
second, in hereditary law by which the burdens of parents are transferred to children; third, in the law of like-for-like by which the rejection of good and the enduring of evil are balanced.

2. The propagation of sin has two parts, imputation and real communication.

3. Imputation means that the individual act of disobedience which
was Adam's becomes ours also.

4. Real communication means that the individual sin, although not
ours, is like ours in meaning and nature.

5. Original sin, being formally a want of original righteousness and
following the first sin as a punishment, has the nature of a punishment before that of a sin. Insofar as, by God's justice, original righteousness is refused, it is a punishment. Insofar as that righteousness
ought to be in us, but through man's fault, is not, it is a sin.

6. Therefore this deprivation carries over from Adam in the form of
a deserved punishment. But it is also a sin in its causative aspect because anyone born a son of Adam is not worthy of righteousness —
and the lack of what one ought to have and does not is a sin in him.

7. Along with this deprivation there is also passed along a certain
ineptness and perversity of all bodily faculties, which in their way are
in conflict with the right way of doing things approved by God.

8. For with the deprivation of righteousness by which all the faculties ought to be controlled, there arises such a defect in them that in
any moral situation their very inclination is morally evil.

9. Out of this condition arises each actual sin, for the mind blinded
by the deprivation of light easily admits errors. And the will being now

turned from God and without God burns with love of itself and evil desire.

10. From this propagation of sin follows a propagation of death both in its beginnings and in its consummation, in the form of conscious realization as well as of loss, bodily as well as spiritual, to all the posterity of Adam.

11. Because of this apostasy of mankind the faith by which we now believe in God is a necessity not only for life but for salvation. It is not sufficient for fallen man that God simply gives him life, but it is also necessary that he should give life to man dead in sins, Eph. 2:1. This was one difference between the question of the rich young man, Matt. 19:16, *What good shall I do that I may have eternal life?* and that of the jailer, Acts 16:30, *What must I do to be saved?*

XVIII

The Person of Christ, the Mediator

After the fall of man, we next consider his restoration.

1. The restoration of man is the lifting from a state of sin and death to a state of grace and life.

2. The cause of this restoration was the merciful purpose of God. Eph. 1:9, *According to his free good will which he purposed in himself.* For there was nothing in man which could provide any power to effect this restoration. There was rather much that made to the contrary: There was sin, in which existed enmity toward God — a fact which of itself commends his love towards us. Rom. 5:8, *But God commends his love towards us in that when we were yet sinners Christ died for us.*

3. There are two parts in this restoration, redemption and its application. The former is, as it were, the first act of restoration and the latter the second; the first is, as it were, the matter and the second the form of our salvation; the first the sufficiency and the latter the efficiency of it.

4. These parts are of one and the same compass. For the end of redemption is its application, and the first reason, rule, and measure of application is the same gracious will of God which brings about the redemption. Eph. 1:9, 10, *He has made known to us . . . the mystery of his will, according to his free good will which he had foreordained in himself that in the full dispensation of those times before ordained, he might summarily gather together all things in Christ.*

5. Therefore redemption applies to each and all for whom it was obtained in God's intention. According to Christ's word in John 6:37, *Whatever the father gives me shall come to me.*

6. Redemption is establishing man in freedom from the bondage of sin and the devil by the payment of a just price. 1 Peter 1:18, *You know that you were not redeemed . . . by corruptible things, as silver and gold, but with precious blood;* 1 Cor. 6:20, *You have been bought with a price;* and 7:23, *You have been bought with a price.*

7. For this liberation was not primarily effected by power or prayers, although these had their force in completing the matter, but rather by the giving of a just price.

8. This price, which could not be paid by man, required the work of a mediator to intercede between God and man making a perfect reconciliation between them. 1 Tim. 2:5; Acts 20:28, *The Church of God which he purchased by his own blood;* 1 Tim. 2:5, 6, *The man Christ Jesus, who gave himself as a price for our redemption.*

9. Now such a mediator is not given only for one age, but for yesterday, and today, and forever: Heb. 13:8, *Jesus Christ is the same yesterday, today and forever;* Rev. 13:8, *The lamb slain from the foundation of the world.* This is true even though he was manifest only in the fullness of time, Col. 1:26; Titus 1:2; 1 Peter 1:20. The mediation was equally necessary in all ages, and it was sufficient and effectual from the beginning because of God's decree, promise, and approval.

10. That mediator is Jesus Christ alone. Acts 4:12, *Neither is there salvation in any other, for among men there is given no other name under heaven by which we must be saved.*

11. In Christ two things are to be considered, the fitness he had to perform the work of redemption and the parts of redemption itself.

12. Fitness consists of his person and the office imposed upon his person.

13. In the person of Christ the mediator, two things are to be observed: the distinction of the two natures and their union in his person.

14. The distinct natures are the divine nature, in that he is the second person of the Deity, and the human, which is similar to ours in all ways (except sin and the mode of subsistence), Matt. 1:23, *Emmanuel . . . God with us;* John 1:14, *The word was made flesh.* The distinction between the two natures holds because they remain absolutely the same in essence and essential properties as they were before they were joined. Therefore the deity in Christ is neither changed, mixed, or in any way confused with the humanity nor the humanity with the deity.

15. The personal union is the taking of human nature by the sec-

ond person of the deity so as to subsist inseparable in the same person, John 1:14.

16. For the second person of the deity has a twofold way of subsisting, although it has but one subsistence; one is in the divine nature from eternity and the other in the human nature after the incarnation. Rom. 9:5, *Of such is Christ, according to the flesh above all, God blessed forever. Amen.* The second way of subsisting belongs to the Son of God in his union with human nature.

17. The union adds nothing to the divine person and nature except a relationship. But in the human nature it effects a change whereby that nature is elevated to highest perfection; this becomes, as it were, a characteristic of the divine person by whom it is assumed. It is, so to speak, an arm [*membrum*] of the same whole θεάνθρωπος, God-man, of which the divine nature is, as it were, another part. In the sphere of subsistence the human nature becomes, as it were, the effect specifically sustained by the divine nature, as well as the subject in which the divine nature specifically dwells, Col. 2:9.

18. We may attempt to describe this union in several logical ways, since it cannot be sufficiently explained by any one.

19. We use all those terms which go to the heart of unanimity and unity to show that it is the closest kind of union.

20. Yet we temper these terms with an " as it were," because the union is mystical and secret, and therefore cannot be plainly expressed but only adumbrated in human words and notions.

21. In the union there is a personal communication of properties which, however, is not a real transfusion, for if it were, the divine nature would take on the properties of the human, the human the properties of the divine, and the human would be divine and the divine human — or divine and human would cease to be. Neither is it a real giving [*donatio*] in which the human nature would use the divine properties as its own instruments. It is rather a communion or concurrence in the same operations, so that things are performed together by each nature but according to the distinct properties of each.

22. So it is that all the acts and sufferings of Christ are rightly referred to his whole person as the one responsible, though some go with one nature, some with the other, depending on their sources and forms.

23. And so follows the communication of properties which are predicates or attributes. The properties of either nature are assigned to the whole person, as when Christ is said to be dead, which is proper only to the human nature, or to have been in the beginning, which is proper only to the divine. Or the properties of either nature may also be attributed to the other nature because of the one person, as when

God is said to be *Taken up in glory*, 1 Tim. 3:16; or *Crucified*, 1 Cor. 2:8. This does not belong to the divine nature but to the human. And those things which are proper to the whole person are attributed to either nature, as when the man Christ is said to be the mediator between God and man, 1 Tim. 2:5. This belongs to Christ not as man but as God and man.

24. Just as this communication properly refers to the person of Christ, and not to the natures considered in themselves, so the communication of predicates applies to God or man in the concrete, and not to deity or humanity in the abstract.

25. The communication of properties is not merely verbal, but neither is it so real that the property of one nature passes into the other for actual possession or use.

26. The examples which are customarily adduced by those who think otherwise, such as the relation between matter and form, between soul and body, and between the iron and the fire, neither apply to this mystery nor prove their position.

27. There were in Christ two kinds of understanding: a divine understanding whereby he knew all things, John 21:17, and a human, whereby he did not yet know some things, Mark 13:32. So there were two wills, one divine, Luke 5:13, and the other human, with a natural appetite, Matt. 26:39. So Christ has a double presence, but the human presence cannot be everywhere or in many places at once.

28. Because God-in-Christ, the θεάνθρωπος, or God-man, has restored life to us, our faith is carried towards Christ.

XIX

The Office of Christ

Thus far we have dealt with the person of Christ; now we consider his office.

1. The office is that which he undertook in order to obtain salvation for men. 1 Tim. 1:15, *This is a sure saying and worthy of all acceptance, that Jesus Christ came into the world to save sinners.*

2. Those who deny that the purpose set forth in this mystery by God and Christ was the salvation of men deprive God and Christ of their honor and men of their comfort.

3. Two things are to be considered: the calling to this office and the office itself. Heb. 5:4–5, *None takes this honor to himself, except he that is called of God, as was Aaron. So also Christ.*

4. The calling is an action of God, κατ' ἐξοχήν, or par excellence, of the Father, whereby he bound his Son to this office through a special covenant.

5. This covenant is expressed in Isa. 53:10, *If he should make himself a sacrifice for sin then he would see his offspring, would prolong his days, and the delight of the Lord would prosper through him.*

6. This calling therefore contains choosing, foreordaining, and sending. Isa. 42:1, *My elect*; 1 Peter 1:20, *Foreknown before the foundation of the world*; John 3:17, *God hath sent his Son into the world.* It is called in the Scriptures a *Sealing*, John 6:27; *Sanctification*, John 10:36; *Anointing*, Isa. 61:1; Ps. 45:7; Heb. 1:9; and *Giving*, John 3:16.

7. Choosing refers to the end; foreordaining to the means; and sending to the performance, which is carried out by grace alone without any condition foreseen in men or in Christ himself.

8. Everything which Christ did or suffered, even all the circumstances, was foredetermined. Luke 22:22, *The Son of Man goes as it is appointed*; Acts 4:28, *That they might do all things whatever thy hand and thy counsel have before determined to be done.*

9. The calling was not accomplished in any ordinary way; it was confirmed with a solemn oath to seal its exceptional quality and its eternity, Ps. 110:4; Heb. 5:6; and 7:24.

10. The office itself to which Christ is called is threefold; namely, that of prophet, priest, and king.

11. The number and order of offices is shown, first, by the necessity of men who are grievously laboring under (*a*) ignorance, (*b*) alienation from God, and (*c*) powerlessness to return to him. The first is met by the prophecy of Christ, the second by his priesthood, and the third by his kingship.

12. Second, this number is shown by the order in which salvation is brought, since it must first be preached, then obtained, and afterward applied. The first is the role of the prophet, the second of the priest, and the third of the king.

13. Third, the order also appears in the appointed way of carrying it out: Christ first taught others, declaring the will of God to them; then he offered himself; and afterward he entered into his kingdom.

14. The prophecy of Christ is his perfect revelation of the whole will of God, which brings salvation. Hence in Scripture he is called not only a *Prophet*, Deut. 18:15; Acts 3:22; a *Teacher*, Matt. 23:7; the *Apostle of our confession*, Heb. 3:1; and the *Angel of the covenant*, Mal. 3:1 — he is also called the *Very wisdom of God*, 1 Cor. 1:24, and the *Treasure of wisdom and understanding*, Col. 2:3.

15. Christ was the principal cause of this prophecy; it was in oth-

ers, whether angels or men, as his instruments. 1 Peter 1:11, *The prophets searched in whom or what manner of time the foretelling spirit of Christ which was in them should declare*; and 3:19, *In which, going to the spirits in prison, he preached.* In Christ it was part of his nature, so that he could reveal all the secrets of God when he wished. To others it came as a single act, in a flash; they could exercise prophecy only at given times when he pleased. Jer. 42:7, *After ten days came the word of the Lord to Jeremiah.*

16. In order that he might be such a prophet, it was necessary that he should be God, John 1:18 and 3:13. And it was necessary also that he should be man, Acts 3:22 (to be compared with Deut. 18:15). For if he had not been God, he would not have understood the will of God perfectly, 1 Cor. 2:11, 16, and would not have been able to reveal it throughout all ages. If he had not been man, he could not have fitly set it forth to men in his own person, Heb. 1:1.

17. The priesthood of Christ is his expiating of the sins of men by sacrifice, and obtaining God's favor for them, Col. 1:20, 22; 2 Cor. 5:15; Rom. 5:10.

18. This priesthood was not legalistic or temporary, but according to the order of Melchizedek, Heb. 7:17. It existed not through a carnal commandment but by the power of an indestructible life, Heb. 7:16, not in an order weak and mutilated but in one which is stable and perfect, Heb. 7:18–19. It lasts not for a time, but forever, Heb. 7:24. Finally, it has room for no successor or vicar, but is perpetual, pertaining only to the everlasting Christ himself, Heb. 7:24–25.

19. In such an office Christ was the priest, the sacrifice, and the altar. He was priest in both natures, Heb. 5:6. He was the sacrifice principally in his human nature, and thus the Scriptures attribute sacrifice not only to the person of Christ but to his body, Heb. 13:12; 1 Peter 2:24; Col. 1:22. It is also attributed to his blood, Col. 1:20, and to his soul, Isa. 53:12; Matt. 20:28. Yet the main reason why the sacrifice became effectual was the nature of God, namely, that the Son of God offered himself for us, Acts 20:28; Rom. 8:3. He was the altar properly according to his divine nature, Heb. 9:14; and 13:10, 12, 15. For it is the function of the altar to sanctify that which is offered upon it and so it ought to be of greater dignity than the sacrifice itself, Matt. 23:17. But Christ by his divine nature also sanctified himself in a way in his human nature, John 17:19.

20. Thus it appears how necessary it was that Christ the mediator should be both God and man. For if he had not been man, he would not have been a fitting sacrifice; and if he had not been God, the sacrifice would not have been sufficient.

21. The kingship of Christ is his power to dispense and administer

all things pertaining to the salvation of man with force and authority, Ps. 2:6; Dan. 2:44; Luke 4:36.

22. The properties of this kingship are, first, its universality. It covers all ages, Matt. 22:43–45. It is relevant to all kinds of men, Dan. 7:14; Rev. 17:14; and it applies to all creatures so far as they in some way further or enhance the salvation of men, Eph. 1:21, 22.

23. Second, it holds sway in the very souls and consciences of men, Rom. 14:17.

24. Third, it dispenses everlasting life and death, Rev. 1:18.

25. Fourth, it is eternal, Dan. 2:44; 7:14.

26. Fifth, it brings the greatest peace and most perfect joy to those who are its heirs, Isa. 9:6; Eph. 2:16; Heb. 7:2.

27. Therefore this kingship is called throughout the Scriptures the kingdom of *God*, the kingdom of *Peace* and *Glory* (see the places above cited). It is also called the kingdom of *Light and glory*, the kingdom of *Heaven*, and *The world to come*, Heb. 2:5.

28. It continues to appear how necessary it was that Christ the mediator should be God and man. If he were not God he could not be the spiritual king of our souls, dispensing eternal life and death, and if he had not been man he could not have been a head of the same nature as his body.

29. All the offices of Christ were patterns. In the prophetical office he even had subordinates who were also called prophets. But his priesthood and kingship do not allow such a subordination; nor was anyone by office ever a spiritual priest or king besides Christ.

30. The reason for the difference is that the declaration of the will of God to men, which is the office of prophets, may in some manner be performed by man alone. But the expiation of sin by sacrifice before God, which is the duty of a priest, and the government of the souls and consciences of men, which is the role of king, is not possible for a mere man.

31. The kings of the nations are not properly subordinated to Christ in their authority, but rather to God.

XX

Satisfaction

1. There are two parts of redemption: the humiliation of Christ as our mediator, and his exaltation.

2. His humiliation is his subjection to the justice of God in order

to perform those things necessary for the redemption of man. Phil. 2:8, *Being found in shape as a man he humbled himself and made himself obedient unto death.*

3. This humiliation does not properly belong to the divine nature, considered in itself, but rather to the mediator θεάνθρωπος, God-man.

4. Therefore the taking of human nature in itself is not a part of this humiliation, because it was the action of God alone. But the condition of a servant which accompanied the taking of human nature was the first and proper basis of the humiliation. By a relation overflowing from this condition, the divine person is rightly said to be emptied, Phil. 2:7, since for the time being he existed in a form which was void of all glory and divine majesty. The divine majesty suppressed and hid itself throughout the time of humiliation, not continuously exercising the dignity which afterward appeared in the exaltation.

5. The end of this humiliation is satisfaction and the achievement of merit.

6. It is called satisfaction because it is for the honor of God as a kind of recompense for the injury done to him by our sins. Rom. 3:25, *Whom God hath set forth to be a reconciliation by his blood . . . to show his righteousness.* This is shown in all those places of Scripture where Christ is said to be *Dead for us.* An efficiency is set forth in that phrase, which cannot be attributed to Paul or Peter in their death, 1 Cor. 1:13. Satisfaction takes away condemnation, Rom. 8:34, and finally brings with it reconciliation to salvation, Rom. 5:10.

7. The same is indicated where it is said that *He was made sin for us,* 2 Cor. 5:21. For he could in no other way be made sin than by inward pollution or outward reputation. But he was most free of pollution; and sin could not in any way be imputed to him other than that he might undergo for us the punishment due to sin.

8. In the same way it is said that *He bore our iniquities,* Isa. 53:4. That phrase does not signify any submission in Christ, for by bearing them he took away the sins of the world, John 1:29. Nor does it signify the sole power of taking away sins, for he carried our sins in his own body on the cross, 1 Peter 2:24.

9. The same force is found in the words, *He paid the price of redemption for us,* Matt. 20:28. No mere deliverance or means of deliverance is set forth in that phrase, because the price itself is named and it is intimated to be like payments of silver or gold for salable merchandise, 1 Peter 1:18. The object to which this price is applied is added, Heb. 9:13–15, *Blood sprinkling those that are unclean,* and 10:22, *Our hearts purged from an evil conscience by sprinkling.* Christ himself is thus a mediator because he made himself the price of re-

demption, 1 Tim. 2:5, 6. And we are partakers of this redemption because Christ gave himself for us, Gal. 2:20; and we believe in him,
John 1:12, and through him in God, 1 Peter 1:21.

10. In the same sense also he is called an *Offering and sacrifice for
our sins*. Eph. 5:2, *He gave himself for us as an offering and sacrifice
of sweet-smelling favor to God*. For he was so true and appropriate a
sacrifice for sin that all other sacrifices which went before were but
shadows of it; and now that it has been offered, it is neither needful
nor lawful to offer any other, Heb. 10:12, 14.

11. The whole mystery depends upon this: Christ is such a mediator
as to become also our *Surety*, Heb. 7:22. He is the common beginning
for those who are to be redeemed, as Adam was for those who are created and lost, Rom. 5:16–18; 1 Cor. 15:22.

12. In the humiliation of Christ there was also achievement of
merit, since it was ordered for our benefit or good in the form of a reward. This is shown in all the places of Scripture where he is said to
have procured righteousness for us by obedience. Rom. 5:19, *Many are
made righteous* (according to the favor of God); Rom. 5:10, *We have
been reconciled to God by the death of his Son* (and have eternal life);
Rom. 5:21, *Life eternal in Jesus Christ*.

13. The achievements of merit and satisfaction by Christ do not
differ essentially, in such a way as to be identified in different actions;
they are two phases of one and the same obedience.

14. Neither should any part of that obedience found in the humiliation of Christ be excluded from the honor and profit that go with it.

15. The exaltation of Christ, however, although it is an essential
part of his mediation, does not belong with his achievement of merit
or satisfaction.

16. The satisfaction in substance was perfect by all standards of
justice. Yet it presupposes grace in that Christ was called to perform
this work, and this work, being performed, was accepted in our name
and for our good. Satisfaction also presupposes grace in that what was
demanded by it was given in a remunerating covenant. John 3:16,
God so loved the world that he gave his only begotten Son. Rom. 3:24,
*We are justified freely by his grace, through the redemption made in
Jesus Christ*; and 5:15, *The grace of God and gift by grace which is
of that one man Jesus Christ*.

17. Thus the greatest justice and the greatest grace are manifested
together and together work in man's redemption. Rom. 5:17, *They
receive abundance of grace and the gift of righteousness*. The fruits
of this satisfaction are rightly called altogether the fruits and effects
of the grace and mercy of God.

18. This satisfaction had sufficient and, in a way, infinite worth,

first, because of the person who offered it, who was God; second, because of the value and excellence of the thing offered, for he offered himself, God and man; third, because of the manner of offering in which there was a certain divine perfection in the personal union.

19. Just as the greatness of an injury increases according to the dignity of the person offended (for it is in one's dignity that a hurt is felt), so the value of satisfaction increases according to the dignity of the one who makes it (as the yielding of honor is in proportion to the dignity of the person yielding it).

20. In satisfaction, not only the act or the suffering, but the person himself who acts and suffers, voluntarily complies with the will of him to whom the honor is yielded. Work always depends on the worker.

21. Here it should also be observed that Christ's dignity, which belonged to his very substance, confers more upon the worth of the work than could the accidental dignity found in some men.

22. Because of Christ's dignity it comes about that the satisfaction was sufficient for substance and superabundant for certain circumstances over which he had no responsibility.

<hr />

XXI

The Life of the Humiliated Christ

1. Christ's humiliation is found in his life and his death.

2. His life has two parts: the first in his conception and birth, and the second in the period after his birth.

3. In his conception two principles worked together, one active and the other passive.

4. The passive was the blessed virgin Mary who is called the passive principle not because she did nothing in the process of bringing forth Christ, but because she did nothing of herself — except to provide the material out of which the body of Christ was formed. Even for that she could not immediately provide fit material (for hers was not pure); it was made fit by a certain supernatural preparation and sanctification. Luke 1:35, *Because that which shall be born of you is holy.* Yet Christ was truly the son of Mary and the seed of the woman promised from the beginning. There are not, therefore, two sonships distinct in Christ, or two sons joined together. The temporal sonship whereby he was linked to his mother was only

to satisfy reason. Indeed the human nature of Christ had a real causal relation to Mary, but his sonship is not a matter of his nature but of his person. Yet there is a relation of his human nature to his person and of Mary to his human nature so that it may truly and rightly be said that Mary was the mother of God.

5. The active principle of the conception was not a man (and, therefore, blessed Mary was a mother and virgin at the same time, Matt. 1:23; Isa. 7:14); it was rather the Holy Spirit. But Christ cannot be called the son of the Holy Spirit, not even insofar as he is a man, for as a man he does not have the same nature as the Holy Spirit, and it is possible only for a person, not a nature, to be a son.

6. From the first instant of the conception, Christ received in his human nature a fullness of grace with regard to first act — John 1:14, *Full of grace and truth;* and Luke 2:40, *He was filled with wisdom —* but also so that it could be increased with regard to second acts and spread to new objects. Luke 2:52, *He grew in wisdom.*

7. Therefore, Christ was enriched with blessedness from the very instant of his conception. But, as pilgrims do, he made progress in it until he came to the highest exaltation.

8. In the birth of Christ there was the humility of greatest poverty and the witness to greatest glory, so that both natures and both parts of the mediation can be declared from the beginning.

9. The earthly accompaniments of the birth of Christ were most humble. But the angels and stars of heaven declared a glory by which all kinds of men were moved — shepherds, wise men, Herod, and the priests with all the people, Luke 2:18; Matt. 2:2, 3.

10. Through this birth he was the son of all the patriarchs of the whole world in the flesh, but he was especially that seed of Abraham in whom all nations were to be blessed, and he was that son of David who was to have a kingdom not of this world, but everlastingly of another. John 18:36, *My kingdom is not of this world;* Luke 1:33, *And he shall reign in the house of Jacob forever; and of his kingdom there shall be no end.*

11. The time, place, and other similar circumstances of his birth manifested the same truth.

12. After the birth, the life of Christ was both private and public.

13. He lived the private life before the public because the human condition to which he had subjected himself required it, because the law of God had so determined it, and because the weakness of man required that the sun of righteousness should appear by degrees and that they be led, as it were, by the hand from every imperfect thing to the perfect.

14. His private life consisted of his infancy and his time of subjection to his parents.

15. In his infancy occurred his circumcision and offering at the temple, the flight into Egypt, and the return.

16. Christ was circumcised and offered because he subjected himself not only to the eternal and moral law, but also to the ceremonial and other laws of God.

17. The ceremonial observances were confessions of sin. Therefore, Christ who was made sin for us fitly showed himself agreeable to them.

18. There were also outward means of divine worship which Christ observed that he might fulfill all righteousness.

19. Last, there had been certain forms which adumbrated Christ. In order that he might fulfill and by this means sanctify them, he wished to apply them to himself.

20. Circumcision was the seal of God's covenant.

21. Offering was the presentation and dedication of the firstborn to God. Therefore Christ was rightly circumcised and offered. He was to confirm that saving covenant by his blood. And among all firstborn, he alone was perfectly holy to God — all others were only types.

22. The flight into Egypt and the return meant that, first, from the very beginning he was born to undergo misery; second, in the condition to which he had submitted he could provide for his life in the manner of men; third, he could show that he was the man to bring us out of a spiritual Egypt into the promised land.

23. In his subjection to parents, which is the subject of the fifth commandment of the decalogue, he showed that he was subject to the whole moral law. For there is the same reason in one commandment as in all and there is no part of moral obedience from which Christ the Lord of heaven and earth might seem to be more free than subjection to men.

24. This legal obedience — required of Christ now made man by law of creation, yet made man not for himself, but for us — was part of the humiliation, satisfaction, and achievement of merit which God demanded and received from him for us.

25. In this subjection two things are to be observed, the exception which he allowed and the effect his subjection produced.

26. The exception was the disputation he had with the scribes when he was only twelve years old.

27. This disputation was a prior testimony to that public calling to which he was ordained and sent as a master and teacher of Israel.

28. It also taught that the knowledge and wisdom with which Christ was endowed were not acquired in the course of time, but conferred or infused by God from the beginning.

29. The effect of this subjection was his manual labor, that is, an

acceptance of the curse that by that labor we shall eat bread in the sweat of our face.

30. His public life was his open manifestation of himself to be the messiah. In this life there was a beginning, a career, and a conclusion.

31. To the beginning belong his baptism and temptation.

32. The baptism of Christ was an inauguration to the public performance of his office; Christ's three offices are affirmed and confirmed in it.

33. They are affirmed by the testimony of the Father publicly announcing that Jesus Christ is his son, and that he has been appointed by him king, and that he is one in whom He is well pleased, that is, a chief priest, who by his intercession should take away the sins of the world; and a chief prophet. Matt. 3:17 and 17:5, *This is my Son, in whom I am well pleased; hear him.*

34. The same offices are confirmed by signs, namely, by the opening of heaven, the descending of the Holy Spirit in the bodily shape of a dove resting upon Christ, and an audible voice sent down from heaven giving the testimony of the Father.

35. They were also confirmed by the testimony of John, who was appointed as a witness, preacher, and forerunner of Christ. He testified to him before others, being enlightened in part by the revelation of the Spirit, and in part by the signs mentioned.

36. By the baptism of Christ our own baptism was confirmed and sanctified. At the same time the person with whom our baptism is connected is declared, showing that all the force of it is to be sought in him.

37. Christ was tempted so that he might show he was much stronger than the first Adam and could overcome temptations, and help us with συμπάθεια, sympathy.

38. His public career took place in the midst of poverty and labor.

39. The poverty of Christ did not involve a particular vow, or begging.

40. The labor of Christ consisted of traveling through various regions, of watchfulness, and the full employment of all his strength to do good.

41. The public career of Christ was given to preaching and working miracles. Grace and authority were always joined to the preaching of Christ. His words either opened or hardened the hearts of others.

42. The object of his preaching was basically the gospel or the kingdom of heaven. Mark 1:14, *Preaching the gospel of the Kingdom of God.*

43. The purpose of the miracles was to demonstrate the person

of Christ, confirm his doctrine, and manifest his spiritual mission.

44. Christ wrought miracles in angels, men, animals, things without life, in heaven, earth, air, sea, in things corporal and things spiritual. This he did that he might show his universal and divine power to be of equal force towards every kind of thing.

45. The conclusion of the life of Christ was the preparation for death itself.

46. His preparation for death was his instructing and comforting his disciples.

47. This instructing and comforting was partly accomplished at his transfiguration. Luke 9:31, *Moses and Elijah appearing in glory told of his departure*. And it was declared by those sacraments which look toward the death of Christ in a special way, namely, the Passover and Lord's Supper. It was given partly by example. John 13:15, *I have given you an example, that you should do as I have done to you*. Partly in his last sermon, John 14:15, 16, and partly in his prayer, John 17.

<hr />

XXII

The Death of Christ

1. The death of Christ is the last act of his humiliation in which he underwent extreme, horrible, and most acute pain for the sins of men.

2. It was an act of Christ and not a mere matter of enduring because he met and endured it purposely. John 10:11, *I am the good shepherd. The good shepherd lays down his life for his sheep*; and 10:18, *No man takes it from me, but I lay it down myself*. For the same reason it was also voluntary and not compelled. The act arose out of power and not merely out of weakness — out of obedience to his father and love for us, not out of his own guilt or deserving. It was designed to satisfy through victory and not to ruin through surrender.

3. It contained the greatest punishment because it equaled all the misery which the sins of men deserved. Therefore, there is an abundance of words and phrases describing this death in the Scriptures. For it is not simply called a death but a cutting off, a casting away, a treading under feet, a curse, a heaping up of sorrows, and the like, Isa. 53; Ps. 22.

4. However, it contained the punishments in such a way that their

continuance, their ordination to the uttermost [*deordinatio*] and other circumstances accompanying the punishments of the sins of the lost were removed from his death. Acts 2:24, *It could not be that he would be retained by death*. There are reasons for this. First, such circumstances do not belong to the essence of the punishment itself, but are adjuncts which follow and accompany those who cannot suffer punishment so as to effect satisfaction by it. Second, there was in Christ both a worthiness and a power to overcome, as it were, the punishment imposed. 1 Cor. 15:54, 57, *Death is swallowed up in victory. Thanks be given to God, who has given us victory through our Lord Jesus Christ.*

5. This death was the consummation of all humiliation. It was by far the greatest part of that humiliation. So Christ's death itself is often spoken of in the Scriptures by a synecdoche of the member as the full satisfaction of his whole humiliation.

6. Within these boundaries, the death of Christ was the same in kind and proportion as the death justly due for the sins of men. It corresponded in degree, parts, and kind.

7. The beginning of Christ's spiritual death in point of loss was the passing of the joy and delight which the enjoyment of God and the fullness of grace were accustomed to bring. He lost this spiritual joy not in principle, not basically, but rather in the act and awareness of it.

8. The beginning of spiritual death in point of conscious realization was the tasting of the wrath of God and a certain subjection to the power of darkness. The wrath of God was most properly signified in the cup which was given to Christ to drink. Matt. 26:39, *My Father, if it be possible, let this cup pass from me.*

9. The object of this wrath was not Christ as such. It was connected only with that punishment which he underwent as our surety.

10. Subjection to the power of darkness was not servitude, but lay in the distress which Christ felt in his mind.

11. Because of these the soul of Christ was affected with sadness, grief, fear, and dread in ἀγωνία, agony, Matt. 26:39; John 12:27; Heb. 5:7; and Luke 22:44.

12. The soul of Christ was affected not only in the part sometimes called lower, but also in the higher; not only nor especially through its συμπάθεια, sympathy, with the body, but directly and intimately; not principally by the compassion which it had for others, but by true suffering which it underwent in our name; not from a horror of bodily death (which many of Christ's servants have also overcome by his power), but from a certain sense of spiritual and supernatural death.

13. There were two effects of this ἀγωνία, agony. First, a strong prayer showing a mind astonished and a nature fleeing from the bitterness of death — yet always conditioned by and subject to the Father's will. Mark 14:35, *He prayed that . . . it might be that this hour would pass from him.* John 12:27, *My soul is troubled. And what shall I say, "Father free me from this hour?" No, for this purpose I have come to this hour.* Second, there was a watery sweat mixed with drops of blood dripping to the ground. Luke 22:44, *Being in agony he prayed more earnestly; and his sweat was like drops of blood falling to the ground.*

14. In this beginning of Christ's spiritual death there was a certain moderation and mitigation in that there was time for those duties which were to be done before his death, namely, prayers, discourses, admonitions, and responses.

15. The moderation was both inward and outward.

16. The inward occurred in the momentary abatements of the pressure and distress he felt in his soul. Thus he thought of the meaning of the office he had undertaken, the glory that would arise to his Father and to himself, and the salvation of those whom his Father had given him. He consciously chose to embrace all the miseries of death in order to obtain these ends.

17. The outward mitigation in this death came through the angel who strengthened him by speaking to him, Luke 22:43, *An angel from heaven appeared to him, comforting him.*

18. There was no inward beginning of Christ's bodily death except that natural weakening and dying which was caused from outside.

19. The external beginning was shown in phases of loss and conscious realization.

20. In the realm of loss he was rejected by his own people and counted worse than a murderer; he was forsaken, denied, and betrayed by his most intimate disciples. By all kinds of men, especially the leaders and those who were considered wise, he was called a madman, a deceiver, a blasphemer, a demoniac, a sorcerer, and a usurper of another's kingdom. He was stripped of his garments and denied necessary food.

21. In point of conscious realization, he was aware of the shameful arrest, the violent hauling away, the denial of ecclesiastical and civil justice, the mocking, whipping, and crucifixion with reproach and injury of all kinds. Yet there was some mitigation in this death: first, in the manifestation of divine majesty through certain miracles, such as the falling of soldiers to the ground at sight of him and at sound of his voice, and the healing of Malchus' ear; second, in the working of divine providence whereby it happened that he was justified by the

judge before he was condemned. Matt. 27:24, *I am innocent of the blood of this just man.*

22. The consummation of Christ's death was the highest degree of the appointed punishment; and in this connection are to be considered the death itself and the continuance of it.

23. The consummation of his spiritual punishment as loss was the forsaking of him by his Father, as a result of which he was deprived of all sense of consolation. Matt. 27:46, *My God, my God, why hast thou forsaken me?*

24. The consummation of his death in conscious realization was the curse whereby he endured the full consciousness of God's judgment on man's sins. Gal. 3:13, *He was made a curse for us.* The hanging on the cross was not a cause of or reason for this curse, but only a sign and symbol of it, *Ibid.*

25. The consummation of bodily death was the expiration of his soul in greatest torment and pain of body.

26. In this death there was a separation of the soul from the body, but the union of both with the divine nature remained so that a dissolution of the person did not occur.

27. This death of Christ was true and not feigned. It was natural, or from causes naturally working to bring it about, and not supernatural. It was voluntary and not at all compelled; yet it was violent and not from internal principles. It was also in a certain way supernatural and miraculous, because Christ kept his life and strength as long as he would and when he desired he laid it down, John 10:18.

28. The continuance of this death was a continuance of the state of lowest humiliation and not of the punishment of affliction, for when Christ said, *It is finished*, it applied to the latter punishment.

29. The continuance was the remaining under the reign of death for three days, Acts 2:24. This state is usually and properly described as existence in Hell.

30. The burial of Christ for three days was a testimony and representation of this state.

XXIII

The Exaltation of Christ

1. The exaltation of Christ is his glorious triumph over his and over our enemies. Luke 24:26, *Should not Christ have suffered these things and entered into his glory?* Eph. 4:8, *When he ascended on high he*

led captivity captive; Col. 2:15, *God has spoiled principalities and powers and made a show of them openly, triumphing over them through him.*

2. He overcame death by enduring, by making satisfaction for sin, and he overcame the devil by depriving or taking the prey out of his hands.

3. The crown and manifestation of this victory is his exaltation. There was a true triumph of merit in his death and in the cross through which Christ is said to be exalted or extolled, John 3:14, not only on the site, physically, but also in meaning and merit. The point of actual triumph, however, was not in humiliation but in exaltation.

4. Christ triumphed on the cross as on a field of victory, but in his exaltation as on a king's throne or triumphal chariot.

5. The glory of this triumph was a change from the humble form of a servant and the attendant abject condition into a state of blessedness altogether heavenly. Phil. 2:9, *Wherefore God also highly exalted him and gave him a name above every name.*

6. Concerning the divine nature, it was only an active manifestation; for the human nature it was a genuine receiving with congruent actions resulting.

7. The human nature received all the perfections possible for created nature. In his soul there was complete fullness of wisdom and grace, not only in principle and disposition but also in act and expression. His body also was beautified with greatest purity, agility, splendor, and strength. Heb. 12:2, *For the joy that was set before him, he endured the cross;* Phil. 3:21, *Who shall transform our vile body that it may be like his glorious body.*

8. As the exalted soul of Christ retained the nature of a soul, so the glorified body did not relinquish the essence and essential properties of a body. Therefore, it cannot be everywhere or in many places at the same time or existing in the same place with another body penetratively. All that have eyes to see may clearly perceive this point in phrases of Scripture. *Being taken from them he was carried up into heaven,* Luke 24:51; *He is not here; he is risen,* Matt. 28:6; and many others.

9. There were three degrees of exaltation corresponding to the same number in his extreme humiliation. His resurrection from the dead is opposed to his death; ascension into heaven to descending into the grave and hell; and sitting at the right hand of God to remaining in the grave and in the state of death or hell.

10. Christ's resurrection pertained to his whole human nature which had fallen by death. For the soul it was a resurrection from hell or from the state and dominion of death to which the soul, so far

as it was a part of the human nature, was subject. For the body it was a resurrection from the dead and from the grave.

11. The soul cannot be said to have risen again, but this can be said of the body and human nature. The body and the man actually recovered their perfection, but the soul recovered the ability to act and move perfectly in the body.

12. There are two parts in the resurrection. The first is internal, namely, a revivification brought about by the uniting of soul and body; the second is external, namely, his departing from the grave to disclose himself in the restored life.

13. To this resurrection the following gave testimony: the angels; Christ himself in many appearances (ten of which are at least mentioned in the Scriptures) and in many proofs drawn from the Scriptures; and men who certified it by seeing, hearing, and touching him.

14. Christ did not rise by the power or permission of another, although this work is attributed to God the Father, Acts 2:24; he rose, rather, by his own power. John 2:19, *Destroy this temple, and within three days I will raise it up*; and 10:18, *I have power to take up my life again*.

15. The time of resurrection was the third day after death and burial, Matt. 28:1; Luke 24:7; Acts 10:40; I Cor. 15:4.

16. The purpose of the resurrection was, first, that he might show himself as the Son of God. Rom. 1:4, *Declared mightily to be the Son of God . . . by his resurrection from the dead*. Second, that he might seal his victory over death. 1 Cor. 15:57, *Thanks be to God, who gives us victory through our Lord Jesus Christ*. Third, that he might fulfill the parts of his office which followed his death. Rom. 4:25, *He was raised for our justification*. Fourth, that he might show himself justified and justifying others. 1 Cor. 15:17, *If Christ has not been raised, your faith is vain, and you are yet in your sins*. Fifth, that he might be the substance, example, and beginning of our spiritual and bodily resurrection. 1 Cor. 15:20, 21, 23, *He is made the first fruits of them that slept. . . . in Christ shall all be made alive*.

17. For Christ as God is absolutely and in principle the cause of our resurrection. As he made satisfaction by his humiliation and death, he is the meritorious cause, but as he rose from the dead he is the exemplary cause and also a demonstration and a beginning for us.

18. The ascending of Christ into heaven is a middle step, as it were, in the course of exaltation by which he leaves the earth and ascends to the highest heaven as to a throne of glory. Acts 1:11, *He is taken up from you into heaven*; Eph. 4:10, *He ascended far above all the heavens*.

19. This was an ascension of the whole person, but it belongs to the

divine nature only figuratively. The divine nature is now joined with the human nature in sublimity and serves as the cause of the ascending — manifesting its glory, once emptied, as it were, when it entered into human nature at the incarnation. The ascension most properly applies to the human nature because it involved a change from a lower place to a higher.

20. His ascension did not occur until forty days after the resurrection (Acts 1:3), because the weakness of the disciples required such a time for the strengthening of their faith by means of the appearances, and for fuller instruction in the things of the kingdom of God, Acts 1:3. He did not ascend later, lest he should seem to be contemplating living on earth.

21. The place from which he ascended was the Mount of Olives, Acts 1:12. It was here also that he suffered his deepest humiliation, Luke 22:39. This occurred so that he might teach that his suffering and ascension pertained to the same thing.

22. He ascended to the empyreal heaven of the blessed, which is not a heaven which is everywhere as some imagine (so that ascension would be only a change of condition and not of place) but the highest above all other heavens, Eph. 4:10, the seat, house, or mansion of God, John 14:2. Thus Christ's specific human nature is rightly and truly said not to be with us in earth, Matt. 26:11. But his person and that spiritual power which depends upon human nature is everywhere with us to the end of the world, Matt. 28:20.

23. The witnesses of the ascension were numerous men and angels, Acts 1.

24. He was the first in order of those who ascended into heaven in the priority of nature, for his ascension was a cause of others' ascension, Heb. 9:8. The souls of others had ascended before, Col. 1:20, and some very probably even ascended bodily, Gen. 5:24; Heb. 11:5; 2 Kings 2:11.

25. The cause of the ascension was identical with that of the resurrection, namely, the power of God, which is the same in the Father and the Son. As related to the Father it is called an assumption but in the Son an ascension, Acts 1:11. His body was in a glorified condition, capable of being carried upward as well as downward.

26. The ascension had these purposes. First, that he might place his human nature now glorified in the mansion of glory. Second, that he might show himself to be the one who could enter the deep and heavenly counsels of God. John 3:13, *How shall you believe if I tell you heavenly things? For there is none who ascends into heaven but he who descends from heaven, namely, the Son of man, who is in heaven.* Third, that he might prepare mansions for all his own in the

house of his Father, John 14:3. Fourth, that he might in the name of his own take possession of the heavenly kingdom, Eph. 2:6, *Has raised us up together, and has made us sit together in heavenly places in Christ Jesus.* Fifth, that by his intercession and power he might take care for those things which are to be performed for their salvation. John 16:7, *If I go from you, I will send a comforter to you.* Sixth, that we may have most certain assurance of our own ascension to heaven. 1 Cor. 15:20, *He has become the first fruits of them that sleep.* Seventh, that we also in thought, attitude, and conversation may pursue heavenly things. Col. 3:1; Phil. 3:20, *Seek those things that are above, where Christ is. We conduct ourselves as citizens of heaven, whence also we look for a Savior, the Lord Jesus Christ.*

27. His seat at the right hand of God marks the highest degree of exaltation in which he enjoys the greatest glory of his mediation. The resurrection and ascension are movements leading to this state. Resurrection and ascension are also, in a certain way, common to us with Christ, but sitting at the right hand of the Father belongs to Christ only.

28. The highest glory with which Christ is endowed in this state is properly and formally a kingly glory. Acts 2:36, *Let therefore all the house of Israel know for certain that God has made this man Lord.*

29. This kingly glory is the fullness of power and majesty whereby he governs all things for the good of his own. Ps. 110:1; 1 Cor. 15:25, *For he must reign until he has put down all enemies under his feet.*

30. This majesty and power belong properly to the person of Christ the mediator. It can also be truly said that the human nature of Christ has now such lofty dignity and sovereign power that he is set in authority over and above all created things, Eph. 1:20–21. But from this height of dignity it is a kind of stupid madness and near blasphemy to conclude that the human nature of Christ, which was created and remains finite, absolutely and abstractly considered has the same omnipotence and omnipresence as God himself.

31. To this kingly dignity belongs the power by which Christ is made judge of men and of angels.

32. The kingly glory of Christ overflows into his other offices so that he exercises a kingly priesthood and kingly prophecy.

33. His kingly priesthood is the pleading of our cause, not by suffering and humble supplication on bended knee, as it were, but by gloriously bringing to mind the things which he did and suffered. Heb. 9:24, *Christ has entered . . . into heaven itself, to appear before the face of God for us.*

34. Christ exercises kingly prophecy while he pours out his spirit upon all flesh, while he sends out his ambassadors, works with them,

and confirms their words by signs that follow, and last, while he gathers his own out of the world and protects, builds up, and preserves them for ever, Matt. 28:18–20; Mark 16:20.

✦━━◆◦◎◦◆━━✦

XXIV

The Application of Christ

So much for redemption; we now consider its application.

1. Application is the making effectual, in certain men, of all those things which Christ has done and does as mediator.

2. This application, if specially designated, is attributed to the Holy Spirit. 1 Cor. 12:13, *By one Spirit we are all baptized into one body.* But it depends, first, upon the Father's decree and donation by which he has given Christ certain men to be redeemed and saved, John 6:39, *This is the will of my Father, that of those he hast given me I should lose nothing,* for those and only those whom the Father has given to Christ come to him, John 6:37. Second, upon the intention of Christ whereby he has made satisfaction for the good of those who have been destined for him by the Father. John 17:9, 11, 12, 19, *I pray for those whom thou hast given me because they are yours.* Third, upon the acceptance of the Father, or his ratification of the satisfaction given for the reconciliation and salvation of those persons. 2 Cor. 5:19, *God was in Christ reconciling the world to himself, not imputing their sins to them.*

3. The agreement between God and Christ was a kind of advance application of our redemption and deliverance of us to our surety and our surety to us. Upon that latter redemption, to be completed in us, it has the effect of a kind of an efficacious example; the former is a representation of the latter and the latter is brought into being by the former.

4. Thus our deliverance from sin and death was not only determined by the decree of God but also granted and communicated to Christ and to us in him before it was known by us. Rom. 5:10, 11, *We have been reconciled to God by the death of his Son . . . through whom we have now received a reconciliation.*

5. Both the Father and the Son are declared to send the Spirit to perform this application. John 14:16 and 16:7, *The Father shall give you an advocate . . . I will send him to you.*

6. Hence every good gift and every perfect good is said to come down from the Father from above, Jas. 1:17. All saving things are said

to be communicated to us *In Christ,* as in the head, *Because of Christ,* as obtained by his merit, and *Through Christ,* as the one through whom they are effectually applied, Eph. 1:3, 5, 11.

7. Therefore, the application is the end result of the obtaining. Since the end is intended by God the Father and Christ the obtaining, as the means to that end, has a firm connection with it. If the redemption of Christ were of uncertain outcome, the Father would have appointed the Son to death and the Son would have undergone it without any certainty whether any would be saved by it or not, and all the fruit of this mystery would depend upon the free will of men.

8. The application plainly has the same latitude as redemption itself, i.e., redemption applies to all those and only to those for whom it was obtained by the intention of Christ and the Father. Yet because of them the same temporal benefits of Christ overflow also to others.

9. As for the intention of application, it is rightly said that Christ made satisfaction only for those whom he saved, though in regard to the sufficiency in the mediation of Christ it may also rightly be said that Christ made satisfaction for each and all. Because these counsels of God are hidden to us, it is the part of charity to judge well of every one, although we may not say of all collectively that Christ equally pleads the cause of each before God.

10. The application by which God fulfills with greatest firmness what was contained in a covenant formerly made and broken is called in the Scriptures the *New covenant,* Heb. 8:8, 10; *A covenant of life, salvation, and grace,* Rom. 4:16; Gal. 3:18. In the same sense it is also called the *Gospel,* Rom. 1:16; *The good word of God,* Heb. 6:5; *A faithful saying and worthy of all acceptation,* 1 Tim. 1:15; *A good doctrine,* 1 Tim. 4:6; *The word of life,* Phil. 2:16; *The word of reconciliation,* 2 Cor. 5:19; *The gospel of peace,* Eph. 2:17 and 6:15; *The gospel of salvation. The word of truth,* Eph. 1:13, *The arm of God,* Isa. 53:1; *The fragrance of life to life,* 2 Cor. 2:16.

11. It is called a covenant because it is a firm promise. In the Scriptures every firm determination, even though pertaining to lifeless things, is called a covenant. Jer. 33:20, 25, *My covenant with the day and my covenant with the night. . . . If my covenant be not with day and night, if I appoint not the statutes of heaven and earth.*

12. Yet because it is a free gift and confirmed by the death of the giver, it is more properly called a testament, not a covenant, Heb. 9:16. This sense is not found in a firm determination, which is not so properly called a testament as a covenant.

13. The new covenant differs from the old in many ways. First, in kind, for the old was a covenant of friendship, so to speak, between

the creator and the creature, but this is a covenant of reconciliation between enemies.

14. Second, in the action, for in the former there was an agreement of two parties, God and man, but in the new only God covenants. For man being dead in sin has no ability to make a spiritual covenant with God. But if two parties are necessary in the strict sense of a covenant, then God is a party assuming and constituting and man is a party assumed.

15. Third, it differs in the object, for the old was extended to all men, but the new belongs in a special way only to certain men. Although from the human point of view it is often offered indiscriminately, by its nature it belongs and with special propriety is directed to those whom God intended, those who are called sons and heirs of the promise and salvation, Gen. 15; Acts 2:39 and 3:25; Rom. 4:16, 13 and 9:7, 8; Gal. 3:21, 29.

16. Fourth, in principle or in the moving cause, for in the old covenant God expressed his wise and just counsel in the form of sovereignty — but in the new there is only mercy. A form of grace was shown in the old by the fixing of a reward for obedience, but it was not truly directed by grace. The new covenant, therefore (and not the old one), was complete, that is, it actually led man to happiness.

17. Fifth, in its basis, for the old was founded on the ability of man himself, but the new on Christ Jesus.

18. Sixth, in the matter or the goods promised, for in the old God promised only life but in this he promises righteousness and all the means of life. Man being dead, a restoration was necessary, not the continuance or perfection of life.

19. Seventh, in the conditions, for the old required perfect obedience of works to be performed by man of his own strength prior to the carrying out of the promise, which would then be in the form of a reward. But the present covenant requires no properly called or prior condition, but only a following or intermediate condition (and that to be given by grace as a means to grace), which is the proper nature of faith.

20. Eighth, in the effect, for the old teaches and shows what is righteous, but the new bestows righteousness in itself. In the old there was a dead letter which was death to a sinner, but in the new there is a quickening spirit.

21. Therefore, the former never wrought salvation to any man, neither could it bring anything to any sinner except death. But the present covenant does not in itself bring death or condemnation to any, but brings assured salvation to all those by whom it is received.

22. Ninth, in duration, for the old is antiquated for those who are

partakers of the new. The present covenant is everlasting, both in its own duration, since it admits of no end or change in substance, and in its application, for the grace of this covenant continues forever with those who are once truly in it.

✦━◈━✦

XXV

Predestination

1. The application of redemption to some men and not to all and the manifest difference which, therefore, arises between men in the dispensation of grace gives to us a first intimation of God's predestination of men.

2. Predestination has existed from eternity. Eph. 1:4, *He has chosen us before the foundations of the world were laid;* 2 Tim. 1:9, *Which grace was given us before all ages.* It operated in the very beginning of God's work, but there is no inward difference in the predestined until the actual application of it. Eph. 2:3, *And we were by nature the children of wrath as well as others;* 1 Cor. 6:11, *And such were some of you.* Predestination before the application of grace puts nothing in the persons predestined but lies hidden only in the One who predestines.

3. Predestination is a decree of God concerning the eternal condition of men which shows his special glory, Rom. 9:22, 23, *Willing to show his wrath and make his power known, he suffered with much patience the vessels of wrath prepared to destruction, in order to make known the riches of his glory for the vessels of his mercy, which he has prepared for glory.* 1 Thess. 5:9, *God has not appointed us to wrath, but to obtain mercy.*

4. It is called destination because there is a sure determination of the order of means for the end. Because God determined this order by himself before any actual existence of things, it is called not simply destination but predestination.

5. It is called a decree because it contains a definite sentence to be executed under firm counsel. In the same sense also it is called a purpose and a counsel, because it sets forth an end to be reached as a result of deliberation.

6. Predestination is accompanied by the greatest wisdom, freedom, firmness, and immutability. These are found in all the decrees of God.

7. The basis of predestination is unmovable and indissoluble. 2 Tim. 2:19, *The foundation of God stands sure, having this seal. The Lord*

knows who are his. On that basis the number of the predestined (not only the formal number, or numerand, as they say, i.e., how many shall be saved and how many not, but also the material number, or numerate, i.e. who the men are) is certain with God not only in the certainty of his foreknowledge but in the certainty of the means he has ordered. Luke 10:20, *Rejoice that your names are written in the heavens.*

8. Predestination does not necessarily presuppose that either its end or object exists; rather it causes it to exist. Predestination orders that it should be. 1 Peter 1:20, *Christ foreknown before the foundations of the world are laid.*

9. Hence it depends upon no cause, reason, or outward condition, but proceeds purely from the will of him who predestines. Matt. 11:26, *Even so, Father, because it pleases thee*; Rom. 9:16, 18, *It is not of him that wills or of him that runs but of God who shows mercy. . . . He has mercy on whom he will and chooses those whom he will harden.*

10. Hence it is not necessary, nor does it agree with the Scriptures, to appoint any previous quality in man which might be considered the formal object of predestination. No condition in any man decides that others should be excluded. It is sufficient only to understand that men, equal among themselves, are the object of the decree; the difference inherent in the decree does not depend upon man, but the differences found in men are the result of the decree.

11. As for intention, there is no foreknowledge which is prerequisite or presupposed for the decree of predestination besides that simple intelligence which relates to all things, since it depends upon no cause, reason, or outward condition, but proceeds purely from the will of him who predestines. Eph. 1:5, 9, *He has predestined us . . . according to the good pleasure of his own will . . . according to his free will which he had purposed in himself.*

12. Properly it is an act of the divine will towards a certain object which it determines to bring to a certain end by certain means. Eph. 1:11, *We were chosen when we were predestined according to the purpose of him who works all things through the pleasure of his own will.*

13. As this decree exists in the mind of God, it presupposes an act of the will and is called foreknowledge. Thus foreknowledge sometimes means the same as predestination, but is less accurate. Rom. 11:2, *He has not cast away his people whom he foreknew.*

14. There is properly only one act of will in God because in him all things are simultaneous and there is nothing before or after. So there is only one decree about the end and means, but for our manner

of understanding we say that, so far as intention is concerned, God wills the end before the means. Rom. 8:30, *Those whom he has predestined, those he called.* As for execution, however, he first wills the means and then directs them to their end. 2 Thess. 2:13, *He has chosen us . . . to salvation, through sanctification . . . and faith.*

15. Some means are also end, and even the causes of other means. John 6:37, *Whatever the Father gives me shall come to me; and he who comes to me I will in no way cast out.* But they are not causes of the act of predestination itself or of all its effects.

16. There are some means which in their own nature relate to the end of predestination. Of this kind are all the revelations of grace in the gospel. Other things are related to these means, as it were, by circumstance, such as naturally good or evil things which, above or beyond their own nature, and through the overruling direction of grace, work together for our salvation.

17. There are two kinds of predestination, election and rejection or reprobation [*reprobatio*].

18. Election is the predestination of certain men so that the glorious grace of God may be shown in them. Eph. 1:4–6, *He has chosen us . . . he has predestined us . . . to the praise of his glorious grace.*

19. Election is one, simple act of the will in God, but for our understanding it breaks up into many acts by synecdoche.

20. The first act of election is to will the glory of his grace in the salvation of some men. 2 Thess. 2:13, *God chose you from the beginning to salvation.*

21. The second act is to designate certain men to partake of this salvation. 2 Tim. 2:19, *The Lord knows who are his.*

22. But the true meaning of election is in this second act which contains: specific love, Rom. 9:13; love relating to supernatural and chief good, Jer. 31:3; Eph. 5:25; love involving a setting apart from others in which, in a comparative or relative manner, there is contained a certain real intention of love, Rom. 9:13; John 17:6; 1 Cor. 1:27, 28.

23. The third act of election is the purpose or intention of preparing and directing means by which the men elected are definitely led to the end of salvation. These means are properly redemption and the application of redemption, John 6:37; 2 Thess. 2:13.

24. This third act is called predestination in a special way, the latter being sometimes distinguished in the Scriptures from election, as applying to the elect alone. Rom. 8:29; Eph. 1:4, 5, *Those whom he foreknew he also predestined . . . As he has chosen us . . . He has predestined us.* Otherwise it is used in the same sense with election, by synecdoche.

25. Predestination is sometimes said to accord with God's purpose, Eph. 1:11, or his purpose to accord with election, Rom. 9:11 (and election is said to accord with the purpose, counsel, and good pleasure of the will of God, Eph. 1:5).

26. Sure knowledge accompanies these acts of will in the divine mind in that God most certainly knows the heirs of eternal life. Therefore, election itself is called knowledge or foreknowledge, Rom. 8:29. This knowledge of God — retaining distinctly the names of those to be saved and the good things appointed for them as if written in his book — is, therefore, called the book of life. Ps. 69:28; Rev. 3:5 and 13:8.

27. God made only one election in Christ, mystically considered, i.e., pertaining to Christ and those who are in Christ. In the same sense there was one creation of all mankind. Yet a certain distinction may be made according to reason whereby Christ may be considered as first elected as head and then some men as members in him, Eph. 1:4.

28. But Christ is not the meritorious or impelling cause of election in itself, although he may reasonably be considered as a cause since all the effects of election follow his being sent.

29. In the work of redemption, Christ himself is rightly said to be an effect in the first act of election. He is the means given for the salvation of man, as this salvation is the action of God. John 17:6, *Thine they were, and thou gave them to me.* Yet considering this salvation as our good, Christ is not the effect but the cause. So it may be rightly said that in the first act of election Christ the Redeemer was the effect and subordinate means, but in the third act of election he is to be considered a cause. Eph. 1:3, *He has blessed us in Christ with all spiritual blessings in the heavens.*

30. Reprobation is the predestination of certain men so that the glory of God's justice may be shown in them, Rom. 9:22; 2 Thess. 2:12; Jude 4.

31. As in election, three acts are to be conceived in reprobation.

32. The first act is to will the setting forth of justice. Therefore, the purpose of God in reprobation is not properly the destruction of the creature, but divine justice which shines forth in deserved destruction.

33. This is the first difference (in reason) between election and reprobation; in election not only the glorious grace of God is an end but also the salvation of men themselves, whereas in reprobation damnation in itself has no relation to an end or a good.

34. The second act is to designate men in whom this justice of God may be made manifest, Jude 4.

35. The act cannot be called election because it is not performed

out of love; it communicates deprivation of good rather than any good. Therefore, it is rightly called reprobation because it rejects or removes those to whom it is directed from the love by which the elect are appointed to salvation. Just as there is love which sets apart in election, so there is a denial of love which sets apart or contrasts in reprobation.

36. This negative setting apart found in reprobation depends upon the setting apart found in election. Therefore, the remote end of reprobation is also the glory of the same grace which is manifested in election. Rom. 9:22, 23, *He allowed the vessels of wrath that he might make known the riches of his glory towards the vessels of mercy.*

37. Because of this setting apart whereby God does not bestow blessedness upon some persons, he is said to *Hate* them, Rom. 9:13. This hatred is negative or privative, because it denies election. But it has a positive content, for God has willed that some should not have eternal life.

38. In this is found, nevertheless, the second difference (in reason) between election and reprobation, namely, that the love in election bestows good on the creatures directly, but the hatred in reprobation only denies good — it does not bring or inflict evil because the creature himself deserves it.

39. The third act of reprobation is the intention to use means by which justice may be manifested in the reprobate. These means, most accurately speaking, are permission to sin and abandonment to sin, Rom. 9:18; 2 Thess. 2:11, 12.

40. Here is a third difference (in reason) between election and reprobation: Election is the cause not only of salvation but of everything causally connected with salvation; reprobation is not properly a cause of either damnation or sin (which deserves damnation) but an antecedent only.

41. There is a fourth disparity, namely, that the means leading to reprobation are not in themselves either cause or effect. For the permission to sin is not the cause of the forsaking, the hardening, and the punishment: The cause of these is the sin itself.

XXVI

Calling

We have dealt with application in general; now we consider its parts.

1. The parts of application are two, union with Christ and partaking of the benefits that flow from this union. Phil. 3:9. *That I may be found in him . . . having the righteousness that is by the faith of Christ.*

2. This union is the spiritual relation of men to Christ by which they obtain the right to all the blessings provided in him. 1 John 5:12, *He that has the Son has life;* and 3:24, *He dwells in him, and he in him.*

3. This union is accomplished by calling.

4. Calling is the gathering of men together in Christ so that they may be united with him. 1 Peter 2:4, 5, *Coming to him;* Eph. 4:12, *The gathering together of the saints . . . for the building up of the body of Christ.* From this union with Christ follows union with God the Father. 1 Thess. 1:1, 2, *To the church . . . which is in God the Father and in our Lord Jesus Christ.*

5. This is the first consideration in the application of redemption. Eph. 1:7–9, *In whom we have redemption . . . after he made known to us the mystery of his will.* And it is the first thing by which a man is actually elected, i.e., the first act of election shown and exercised in man himself. For this reason, calling and election are often taken in the Scriptures in the same sense. 1 Cor. 1:26–28, *You see your calling . . . God has chosen foolish things . . . and weak things.*

6. The calling does not depend on the dignity, honesty, industry, or any endeavor of the ones called, but only upon the election and predestination of God. Acts 2:47, *The Lord did add to the church . . . such as should be saved;* and 13:48, *As many as were ordained to eternal life believed;* Rom. 8:30, *Those whom he predestined he also called;* Titus 3:5, *Not by works of righteousness, but of his own mercy;* Jas. 1:18, *Of his own will he begat us by the word of truth.*

7. The parts of calling are two, the offer of Christ and the receiving of him. John 1:11–12, *He came to his own, and his own received him not. But to as many as received him . . . he gave to them.*

8. The offer is an objective presentation of Christ as the sufficient and necessary means to salvation. 1 Cor. 1:23, 24, *We preach Christ . . . the power of God and the wisdom of God;* Heb. 7:25, *He is per-*

fectly able to save those that come to God by him; Acts 4:12, *There is no other name under heaven given among men by which we must be saved.*

9. Concerning Christ there is absolutely nothing presented, or which ought to be presented, in the calling of men to be believed as true which is not simply and absolutely true. For this is both against the nature of testimony, insofar as it is an object of that faith which has its place in the intellect where the standard is truth; and against the nature of the gospel itself, which is called the word of truth κατ' ἐξοχήν, or par excellence, Eph. 1:13.

10. The offer of Christ is outward and inward.

11. The outward is a propounding or preaching of the gospel or the promises of Christ. Acts 9:15, *That he may bear my name in the sight of the Gentiles.*

12. But so that men may be prepared to receive the promises, the application of the law usually precedes, in order to uncover sin and lead to ἀναπολογία, a sense of guilt, and humiliation in the sinner. Rom. 7:7, *I knew not sin except by the law.*

13. The promises concerning the outward promulgation are given to all alike with one command to believe. But, concerning the peculiarity of the things promised which depend upon the intention of the promiser, the promises belong only to elect who are called the *Sons and heirs of the promise*, Rom. 9:8.

14. The inward offer is a kind of spiritual enlightenment, whereby the promises are presented to the hearts of men, as it were, by an inner word. John 6:45, *Whoever has heard of the Father and has learned . . . comes to me.* Eph. 1:17, 18, *That he might give you the spirit of wisdom and revelation . . . the eyes of your mind being enlightened, that you may know what is the hope of your calling.*

15. This is sometimes and in a certain way granted to those who are not elected, Heb. 6:4; 10:29; Matt. 13:20 ff.

16. If anyone out of malice opposes this illumination, he commits a sin against the Holy Spirit which is called unpardonable or mortal, Heb. 6:6; 10:29; 1 John 5:16; Matt. 12:32.

17. The receiving of Christ occurs when Christ once offered is joined to man and man to Christ. John 6:56, *He . . . abides in me, and I in him.*

18. We say about this joining that we are *In Christ*, 2 Cor. 5:17; *We put on Christ*, Gal. 3:27; *We are dwelled in by Christ*, Eph. 3:17; *The house of Christ*, Heb. 3:6; *The temple of Christ*, 2 Cor. 6:16; *Espoused with Christ*, Eph. 5:23; *Branches of Christ*, John 15:5; *Members of Christ*, 1 Cor. 12:12. And the name of Christ himself is in a certain way given to us. 1 Cor. 12:12, *So also is Christ.*

19. Because of this receiving, calling is termed conversion, Acts

26:20. All who obey the call of God are completely turned from sin to grace and from the world to follow God in Christ. It is also called regeneration or the very beginning of a new life, a new creation, a new creature — and it is often so described in the Scriptures, John 1:13; 3:6; 1 John 3:9; 1 Peter 1:23; and 2:2. The offer itself is properly termed calling, since God effectually invites and draws men to Christ, John 6:44.

20. As for man, receiving is either passive or active. Phil. 3:12, *I apprehend, because I have been apprehended.*

21. The passive receiving of Christ is the process by which a spiritual principle of grace is generated in the will of man. Eph. 2:5, *He has quickened.*

22. This grace is the basis of that relation in which man is united with Christ. John 3:3, *Except a man be born again, he cannot see the kingdom of God.*

23. The will is the proper and prime subject of this grace; the conversion of the will is the effectual principle in the conversion of the whole man. Phil. 2:13, *It is God that works in you both to will and to do of his own good pleasure.*

24. The enlightening of the mind is not sufficient to produce this effect because it does not take away the corruption of the will. Nor does it communicate any new supernatural principle by which it may convert itself.

25. Yet the will in this first receiving plays the role neither of a free agent nor a natural bearer, but only of an obedient subject. 2 Cor. 4:6, *For it is the God who has said that light should shine out of darkness who has shined in our hearts.*

26. Active receiving is an elicited act of faith in which he who is called now wholly leans upon Christ as his savior and through Christ upon God. John 3:15, 16, *Whoever believes in him;* 1 Peter 1:21, *Through him believing in God.*

27. This act of faith depends partly upon an inborn principle or attitude toward grace and partly upon the action of God moving before and stirring up. John 6:44, *None can come to me, unless the Father . . . draws him.*

28. It is indeed called forth and exercised by man freely but also surely, unavoidably, and unchangeably. John 6:37, *Whomever my Father gives me will come to me.*

29. With this faith in which the will is turned to possessing the true good, there is always joined repentance, in which the same will is turned to doing the true good and comes to turn away from and hate the contrary evil or sin. Acts 19:4; Mark 1:15, *Repent, and believe in the gospel.*

30. Repentance has the same causes and principles as faith, for they

are both free gifts of God. Eph. 2:8, *Faith is the gift of God;* 2 Tim. 2:25, *Whether God may at some time give them repentance.* They have the same subject; both have their seat in the heart or will of man. Rom. 10:9; 1 Kings 8:48, *With the heart man believes. They shall come back with all their heart.* They are also begotten at the same time. But, first, they have diverse objects, for faith is properly directed to Christ and through Christ to God, but repentance is directed to God himself who has been offended by the sin. Acts 20:21, *Turning towards God and faith in our Lord Jesus Christ.* Second, they have diverse ends, for faith properly seeks reconciliation with God but repentance compliance with the will of God. Rom. 3:25, *A reconciliation through faith in his blood;* Acts 26:20, *That they should . . . turn to God doing works fit for repentance.*

31. Repentance, so far as it comprises the care, anxiety, and terror connected with the law, precedes faith in order of nature, as a preparing and disposing cause, and is even found in the unregenerate; but insofar as it turns man away effectively and genuinely from sin, by which God is offended, it follows faith and depends upon it as an effect upon its cause and so belongs to those who have faith.

32. Although this repentance always brings with it grief for sins past and present, it does not so much consist of grief as of a turning from and hatred of sin and of a firm purpose to follow good. Amos 5:15, *Hate the evil and love the good.*

33. Repentance is not true and sound when it does not turn a man from all known sin to all known good, or when it does not continue in strength and actually renew itself continually from the time of conversion to the end of life.

34. Repentance is likely to be known before faith, because a sinner cannot easily persuade himself that he is reconciled to God in Christ before he feels himself to have left those sins which separated him from God.

XXVII

Justification

1. Participation in the blessings of the union with Christ comes when the faithful have all the things needed to live well and blessedly to God. Eph. 1:3, *He has blessed us with every spiritual blessing;* Rom. 8:32, *He who spared not his own son . . . how shall he not freely with him give us all things also?*

2. This participation therefore brings a change and alteration in the condition of believers from the state of sin and death to the state of righteousness and eternal life. 1 John 3:14, *We know that we are translated from death to life.*

3. This change of state is twofold, relative and absolute (or real).

4. The relative change occurs in God's reckoning. Rom. 4:5, *And to him who does not work, but believes in him who justifies the ungodly, his faith is imputed as righteousness.* 2 Cor. 5:19, *God was in Christ reconciling the world to himself, not counting their offenses.*

5. The change, of course, has no degrees and is completed at one moment and in only one act. Yet in manifestation, consciousness, and effects, it has many degrees; therein lie justification and adoption.

6. Justification is the gracious judgment of God by which he absolves the believer from sin and death, and reckons him righteous and worthy of life for the sake of Christ apprehended in faith. Rom. 3:22, 24, *The righteousness of God by faith in Jesus Christ in all and upon all that believe. . . . they are freely justified by his grace . . . through the redemption made by Jesus Christ.*

7. It is the pronouncing of a sentence, as the word is used, which does not denote in the Holy Scriptures a physical or a real change. There is rather a judicial or moral change which takes shape in the pronouncing of the sentence and in the reckoning. Prov. 17:15, *He that justifies the wicked;* Rom. 8:33, *Who shall lay anything to the charge of God's elect? It is God who justifies.*

8. Therefore, Thomas and his followers are completely mistaken for they would make justification a kind of physical motion from the state of unrighteousness to that of righteousness in a real transmutation. They consider that it begins with sin, ends in inherent righteousness, with remission of sin and infusion of righteousness the motion between.

9. The judgment was, first, conceived in the mind of God in a decree of justification. Gal. 3:8, *The Scripture, foreseeing that God would justify the Gentiles by faith.* Second, it was pronounced in Christ our head as he rose from the dead. 2 Cor. 5:19, *God was in Christ reconciling the world to himself, not imputing their sins to them.* Third, it is pronounced in actuality upon that first relationship which is created when faith is born. Rom. 8:1, *There is therefore no condemnation to those who are in Christ Jesus.* Fourth, it is expressly pronounced by the spirit of God witnessing to our spirits our reconciliation with God. Rom. 5:5, *The love of God is shed abroad in our hearts by the Holy Spirit which has been given to us.* This testimony of the spirit is not properly justification itself, but rather an actual perceiving of what has been given before as if in a reflected act of faith.

10. It is a gracious judgment because it is given not by God's justice but by his grace. Rom. 3:24, *Freely by his grace.* For by the same grace with which he called Christ to the office of mediator and the elect to union with Christ, he accounts those who are called and believing, justified by the union.

11. It happens because of Christ. 2 Cor. 5:21, *That we may become the righteousness of God in him.* The obedience of Christ is that δικαίωμα, the righteousness, Rom. 5:16, in the name of which the grace of God justifies us, just as the disobedience of Adam was that κρίμα, the offense, Rom. 5:16, for which God's justice condemned us, Rom. 5:18.

12. Therefore, the righteousness of Christ is imputed to believers in justification. Phil. 3:9, *That I may be found in him not having my own righteousness which is of the law but that which is by faith in Christ, the righteousness of God through faith.*

13. This righteousness is called the righteousness of God because it is ordained, approved, and confirmed by his grace to the end that sinners can stand before him, Rom. 10:3.

14. This justification comes about because of Christ, but not in the absolute sense of Christ's being the cause of vocation. It happens because Christ is apprehended by faith, which follows calling as an effect. Faith precedes justification as the instrumental cause, laying hold of the righteousness of Christ from which justification being apprehended follows; therefore, righteousness is said to be from faith, Rom. 9:30; 10:6. And justification is said to be by faith, Rom. 3:28.

15. This justifying faith is not the general faith of the understanding by which we give assent to the truth revealed in the Holy Scriptures, for that belongs not only to those who are justified, nor of its nature has it any force to justify, nor produce the effects which are everywhere in Scripture given to justifying faith.

16. Neither is it that special trust (properly speaking) by which we obtain remission of sins and justification itself. For justifying faith goes before justification itself, as a cause goes before its effect. But faith apprehending justification necessarily presupposes and follows justification as an act follows the object towards which it is directed.

17. That faith is properly called justifying by which we rely upon Christ for the remission of sins and for salvation. For Christ is a sufficient object for justifying faith. Faith justifies only by apprehending the righteousness by which we are justified. That righteousness does not lie in the truth of some proposition to which we give assent, but in Christ alone *Who has been made sin for us that we might be righteousness in him,* 2 Cor. 5:21.

18. Therefore, words are often repeated in the New Testament

which show that justification is to be sought in Christ alone: John 1:12; 3:15, 16; 6:40, 47; 14:1, 12; Rom. 4:5; 3:26; Acts 10:43; 26:18; and Gal. 3:26.

19. Justifying faith of its own nature produces and is marked by a special, sure persuasion of the grace and mercy of God in Christ. Therefore, justifying faith is not wrongly described as persuasion by the orthodox (as it often is) — especially when they take a stand against the general faith to which the papists ascribe everything. But the following should be considered. First, the feeling of persuasion is not always present. It may and often does happen, either through weakness of judgment or various temptations and troubles of mind, that a person who truly believes and is by faith justified before God may for a time think that he neither believes nor is reconciled to God. Second, there are many degrees in this persuasion. Believers obviously do not have the same assurance of grace and favor of God, nor do the same ones have it at all times. But this cannot be said of justifying faith itself, without considerable loss in the consolation and peace which Christ has left to believers.

20. Justification does not free from sin and death directly by taking away the blame or stain or all the effects of sin; rather it removes the guilty obligation to undergo eternal death. Rom. 8:1, 33, 34, *There is no condemnation . . . Who shall lay anything to their charge? . . . who shall condemn?*

21. Nor does it take away guilt so that the deserving of punishment is removed from sin. This cannot be taken away as long as sin itself remains. But justification does take away guilt so that its haunting or deadly effects vanish.

22. The absolution from sins is called many things in the Holy Scriptures — remission, redemption, and reconciliation, Eph. 1:6, 7 — but these all have the same meaning. When sin is thought of as a bondage or kind of spiritual captivity because of guilt, justification is called redemption. When it is thought of as subjection to deserved punishment, it is called remission — also passing by, blotting out, exoneration, taking away, casting away, removing, and casting behind the back, Rom. 4:7; Col. 2:13; Mic. 7:18; Isa. 43:12; 38:17; Ps. 32:1, 2. And when sin is thought of as enmity against God, justification is called reconciliation, Rom. 5:10. Sometimes this is regarded as even a kind of winking at sin, Num. 23:25, and a covering of sin, Ps. 32:1, 2.

23. Not only are past sins of justified persons remitted but also those to come, Num. 23:25. God sees no iniquity in Jacob or perverseness in Israel. Justification has left no place for condemnation. John 5:24, *He who believes has eternal life and shall not come into condemnation* — justification gives eternal life surely and immediately.

It also makes the whole remission obtained for us in Christ actually ours. Neither past nor present sins can be altogether fully remitted unless sins to come are in some way remitted.

24. The difference is that past sins are remitted specifically and sins to come potentially. Past sins are remitted in themselves, sins to come in the subject or the person sinning.

25. Yet those who are justified need daily the forgiveness of sins. This is true because the continuance of grace is necessary to them; the consciousness and manifestation of forgiveness increases more and more as individual sins require it; and the execution of the sentence which is pronounced in justification may thus be carried out and completed.

26. Besides the forgiveness of sins there is also required an imputation of righteousness, Rom. 5:18; Rev. 19:8; Rom. 8:3. This is necessary because there might be a total absence of sin in a case where that righteousness does not exist which must be offered in place of justification.

27. This righteousness is not to be sought in a scattered fashion in the purity of the nature, birth, and life of Christ. It arises rather, with remission of sins, out of Christ's total obedience, just as the disobedience of Adam both robbed us of original righteousness and made us subject to the guilt of condemnation.

XXVIII

Adoption

1. Adoption is the gracious judgment of God wherein he gives the faithful the dignity of sonship because of Christ. John 1:12, *As many as receive him to these he gives the right,* ἐξουσία, *to be made the sons of God, to those who believe in his name.*

2. It is called a gracious judgment because it manifests the gracious will of God towards men. 1 John 3:1, *See what love the Father has showed us, that we should be called the sons of God.*

3. This judgment progresses in the same steps as justification. It was first in God's predestination. Eph. 1:5, *He has predestined us . . . that he might adopt us as sons.* Afterward it was in Christ. Gal. 4:4, 5, *God has sent forth his Son . . . that we might receive adoption.* And then it was in the faithful themselves. Gal. 4:6, *Because you are sons, God has sent forth the Spirit of his Son into your hearts, crying, "Abba! Father!"*

4. It has to do properly with the faithful that are called and justified, John 1:12, for by adoption we are not made just, which would follow if adoption were only a part of justification itself, as some would have it. Neither is it a calling to Christ. Adoption is rather a sublime dignity following from the application of his work. Rom. 8:17, *Heirs together with Christ.*

5. Yet calling and justification are a foundation for this relationship of adoption, for the right of adoption is obtained by faith and the righteousness of faith, John 1:12.

6. Although adoption follows from faith, justification comes in between. Adoption of its own nature requires and presupposes the reconciliation found in justification.

7. The faithful can expect heaven, so to speak, by a double title, namely, the title of redemption through justification and the title, as it were, of sonship through adoption.

8. It should however, be understood that the title of redemption is the foundation of this right and adoption adds to it excellence and dignity.

9. Here is the first difference between divine adoption and human. Human adoption relates to a person who, as a stranger, has no right to the inheritance except through adoption. But believers, though by natural birth they have no right to the inheritance of life, are given it because of rebirth, faith, and justification.

10. There is also a second difference. Human adoption is only an outward designation and bestowal of external things. But divine adoption is so real a relationship that it is based on an inward action and the communication of a new inner life.

11. This adoption takes place because of Christ, for not only did he alone deserve it as redeemer, Gal. 4:5. *That he might redeem them . . . that we might receive adoption,* but since it is applied by faith, he alone is the bond of the union. Rom. 8:17, 29, *Heirs with God, joint heirs with Christ . . . conformed to the image of his Son.*

12. Just as Christ is applied in justification as a garment to cover our sins, so in adoption he is applied as a brother and prince of our salvation. Heb. 2:10–13, *Many sons . . . the prince of salvation . . . For he who sanctifies and they that are sanctified are all one. . . . He is not ashamed to call them brethren . . . Behold, I and the children which God gave me.*

13. This application makes so close a relationship that all believers are said to be the first-begotten of God by the grace of adoption and communion with Christ, although Christ is properly the only natural Son of God and, much more, the first begotten of God. Heb. 12:23,

You have come to the universal assembly and meeting of the first-born who are written in heaven.

14. It appears, therefore, that believers are the sons of God in a very different manner from Adam in the first creation. Although Adam might be called metaphorically the son of God, because of his dependence on God and the likeness and image of him in which he was created, yet he was not the son of God by this mystical union and communion with Christ, who is the natural Son of God.

15. There is a third difference between human adoption and divine. Human adoption was introduced when there were no, or too few, natural sons. But divine adoption is not from any want but from abundant goodness, whereby a likeness of a natural son and mystical union is given to the adopted sons.

16. The dignity of this adoption not only far exceeds the common relation in which God is said to be the Father of every creature, but also that which we had before the fall. That was weak, but our adoption today remains forever in the form of a bond. John 8:35, *The servant abides not in the house forever but the son abides forever.*

17. Therefore, the name of God and of Christ is given to believers by a certain special right and reason, 1 John 3:1. So it was with Jacob who took the sons of Joseph in adoption and had them called by his name, Gen. 48:5.

18. And believers are also taken, as it were, into God's family and are of his household, Gal. 6:10, so that they may always be under God's fatherly tutelage, depending upon him for nourishment, bringing up, and perpetual keeping. It was thus in the old days among the Hebrews for whom adoption meant the nurturing and bringing up by the next of kin, Esther 2:7.

19. Along with the dignity of sons we are also given the status of heirs. Rom. 8:17, *If sons, then heirs also.* But this inheritance which falls to believers is eternal blessedness and therefore adoption sometimes means in Scripture all the glory prepared for the faithful and expected by them in heaven. Rom. 8:23, *Looking for our adoption, the redemption of our bodies.*

20. Therefore, eternal blessedness belongs to believers and is given them not out of justice because of their merit, but out of the grace whereby they are numbered among the sons. Gal. 3:29, *If you are Christ's then you are Abraham's seed and heirs by promise.*

21. Here arises a fourth difference between human adoption and divine. The human is ordained so that the son may succeed the father in the inheritance. But divine adoption is not ordained for succession, but for participation in the inheritance assigned. Both the Father

and his first-begotten Son live forever and this admits no succession.

22. A true part of the adoption is the witness of the Spirit which is given to believers. Herein the dignity is sealed with the expected inheritance; it is called *The spirit of adoption*, Rom. 8:15–16, 23; and Gal. 4:5–7.

23. The spirit is said to be communicated to believers not because faith goes before all operation of the Spirit, as some of the unskilled hold, for the very first regeneration and conversion is plainly attributed to the Holy Spirit by Christ. John 3:5–8, *Born of the Spirit.* The spirit is said to be communicated because only believers, after they have already believed, receive that working of the Holy Spirit whereby they are sealed, as it were, with a sign of their inheritance, Eph. 1:13, 14; 4:30; and Gal. 3:14.

24. And it also appears that assurance of salvation is not, properly speaking, justifying faith but a fruit of such faith. The Apostle expressly says, *After you believed, you were sealed*, Eph. 1:13.

25. The first fruit of adoption is that Christian liberty by which all believers are freed from the bondage of the law, sin, and the world. John 8:32, 36, *If the Son shall set you free, you shall be free indeed*; Rom. 6:22, *Being freed from sin we were made servants to God*; Gal. 4:26, *Jerusalem which is above is free and is the mother of us all*; Heb. 2:15, *That he might set at liberty those who out of fear of death were subject to bondage all their lives.*

26. The second fruit is that believers, partaking of the dignity of Christ, become in their way prophets, priests, and kings through him; Rev. 1:6.

27. The third fruit is that all the creatures and the things the creatures do are either subject to the dominion and use of believers, Titus 1:15; 1 Cor. 3:21, 22; or they minister to them (as it is affirmed of the angels, Heb. 1:14); or at least strive for their good, Rom. 8:28.

XXIX

Sanctification

So much for justification and adoption, which relate to the relative change of state for believers. Now we consider the real change, wherein justification is manifested and its consequences, so to speak, brought into being.

1. The real change of state is an alteration of qualities in man himself. 2 Cor. 5:17, *Old things have passed away; all things are new.*

2. The change is not in relation or reason, but in genuine effects seen in degrees of beginning, progress, and completion. 2 Cor. 4:16, *The inner man is renewed day by day.*

3. This alteration of qualities is related to either the just and honorable good of sanctification, or the perfect and exalted good of glorification. Rom. 6:22, *You have your fruit in holiness and your end in everlasting life.*

4. Sanctification is the real change in man from the sordidness of sin to the purity of God's image. Eph. 4:22–24, *Put off that which pertains to the old conversation, that old man, corrupting itself in deceivable lusts, and be renewed in the spirit of your mind. Put on that new man who according to God is created to righteousness and true holiness.*

5. Just as in justification a believer is properly freed from the guilt of sin and has life given him (the title to which is, as it were, settled in adoption), so in sanctification the same believer is freed from the sordidness and stain of sin, and the purity of God's image is restored to him.

6. Sanctification is not to be understood here as a separation from ordinary use or consecration to some special use, although this meaning is often present in Scripture, sometimes referring to outward and sometimes to inward or effectual separation. If this meaning is taken, sanctification may relate to calling or that first rebirth in which faith is communicated as a principle of new life; a common confusion of regeneration and sanctification hereby arises. The term is rather to be understood as that change in a believer in which he has righteousness and indwelling holiness imparted to him. 2 Thess. 2:13, *Through sanctification of the Spirit.*

7. For God himself witnesses that holiness is a gift of inherent grace. Jer. 31:33, *I will put my law into their mind, and in their heart will I write it;* Ezek. 36:26, 27, *I will give you a new heart, and a new spirit will I put into the midst of you.*

8. Sanctification is distinguished from that change in a man which is linked to his calling in faith and repentance, for in the latter faith is not properly considered a quality but a relationship to Christ, nor is repentance considered a change of disposition (for then it would be the same as sanctification), but a change of the mind's purpose and intent. Sanctification involves a real change of qualities and disposition.

9. It is called a real change so as to distinguish it not only from justification but also from sanctification by institution, which is the case in the sanctification of the seventh day. It is also distinguished from sanctification by association with symbols, such as the sanctifica-

tion of the elements in the sacraments. And last, it is distinguished from sanctification by manifestation, as God is said to be sanctified by men, 1 Peter 3:15.

10. It pertains to the whole man and not to any one part. 1 Thess. 5:23, *Now may the God of peace himself sanctify you wholly; and may your whole spirit, soul, and body be preserved blameless until the coming of our Lord Jesus Christ.* But the whole of the man, or that whole which the man comprises, is not immediately changed.

11. Although the whole man partakes of this grace, it is first and most appropriately in the soul and later progresses to the body, inasmuch as the body of the man is capable of the same obedience to the will of God as the soul. In the soul this grace is found first and most appropriately in the will whence it passes to other faculties according to the order of nature. Deut. 30:6, *The Lord thy God shall circumcise your heart and the heart of your seed so that you will love the Lord your God with all your heart and with all your soul and that you may live;* Rom. 2:29, *Circumcism is of the heart.*

12. It is called a change in man from sin to distinguish it from the sanctification which denotes simply the opposite of the negative, such as that which is attributed to the human nature of Christ which is said to be sanctified or made holy (although the nature of Christ was never defiled by unholiness).

13. The starting point of sanctification is the filthiness, corruption, or stain of sin. 2 Cor. 7:1, *Let us purge ourselves from all filthiness of flesh and spirit, being led to holiness in the fear of God.*

14. Its end is the purity of God's image (said to be fashioned or created once more in *Knowledge, righteousness, and holiness,* Eph. 4:24) or *Conformity to the law of God,* Jas. 1:25; *Newness of life,* Rom. 6:4; the *New creature,* 2 Cor. 5:17 and Gal. 6:15; and the *Divine nature,* 2 Peter 1:4.

15. The end is called a new and divine creature. First, because it is not produced by those principles which are in us by nature, as is characteristic of all the arts pursued with industry and discipline — it comes out of the new principle of life communicated by God to us in our calling. Second, because our natural disposition is of a completely different kind from what it was before. Third, because it takes for its model the highest perfection found in God himself.

16. There are two degrees of sanctification. One occurs in this life which is generally called an *Infancy,* 1 Cor. 13:11, 12; Eph. 4:14; 1 Peter 2:2. The variety found in this life is so great that some who are sanctified when compared with others and even with themselves at different times, may rightly be called *Infants,* and others *Adults* during their life here, Heb. 5:13, 14. But the highest degree

which we attain in this life is only a beginning of the holiness promised and expected. The other degree is called the *Age of manhood and maturity*, Eph. 4:14; 1 Cor. 13:11; Phil. 3:12. In the life to come the movement and progress of sanctification ceases; only rest and perfection is found. So in this life we are more properly said to enjoy sanctification than sanctity, and in the life to come only sanctity and not sanctification.

17. Sanctification has two parts, one known in the term describing its mortification, or beginning, and the other describing its end, or vivification or resurrection, Rom. 8:5, 6.

18. Mortification is the first part of sanctification. It is the wasting away of sin. Col. 3:3, 5, *You are dead. Mortify therefore your earthly members.*

19. The meritorious and exemplary cause of this is the death of Christ. Rom. 6:5, 6, *Being grafted to the likeness of his death . . . we know that our old self is crucified with him.*

20. The principally effective cause is the Spirit of God who communicates to the faithful the efficacy of Christ's death. Rom. 8:13, *If by the Spirit you mortify the deeds of the body, you shall live.*

21. The serving cause is faith itself. Rom. 6:17, *From the heart you have obeyed that form of doctrine to which you were committed.*

22. From this mortification there follows in all who are sanctified a denial of themselves and the world, Luke 9:23; Gal. 6:14.

23. Thus an inner difference arises between the sin remaining in believers and the sin remaining in others. In the others sin reigns, prevails, and dominates; in believers it is broken, subdued, and mortified.

24. Vivification is the second part of sanctification. It is the restoration of the image or life of God in man. Col. 3:10; Eph. 4:24; Rom. 12:2, *Having put on the new man . . . be transformed by the renewal of your mind.*

25. The exemplary cause is the resurrection of Christ. Col. 3:1, 2, *You have been raised with Christ.*

26. The principally effective cause is the spirit of God which raised Christ from the dead. Rom. 8:11, *If the Spirit of him that raised Jesus from the dead dwells in you.*

27. The serving cause is faith. Gal. 2:20, *The life which I now live in the flesh I live by faith in the Son of God.*

28. From vivification there arises among the sanctified a strong tie, or total commitment, to God and Christ. 2 Cor. 8:5, *They gave themselves to the Lord.*

29. Because sanctification is imperfect while we live here as children, all believers have, as it were, a double form — that of sin and that of grace, for perfect sanctification is not found in this life, except

in the dreams of some fanatics. 1 John 1:8, *If we say we have no sin, we deceive ourselves, and there is no truth in us.* Yet all that are truly sanctified tend to perfection, Matt. 5:48; 1 Cor. 13:11; 2 Peter 3:18.

30. Sin or the corrupted part which remains in the sanctified is called in the Scripture the *Old man, outward man, the members,* and *the body of sin.* Grace or the renewed part is called the *New man, the spirit, the mind,* and the like.

31. Two things should be noted. First, a spiritual war is continually waged between these parts. Gal. 5:17, *For the flesh lusts against the Spirit and the Spirit against the flesh; and these are contrary to each other.* Second, there is a daily renewal of repentance.

32. The flesh which remains in the regenerate is not only in the inciting and sensory appetite, but in the will and reason itself, 1 Thess. 5:23.

33. Flesh or inordinate desire [*concupiscentia*] is the true reason for sin in the regenerate themselves, Rom. 7.

34. Even the best works of the saints are so corrupted by this flesh that some remission is needed.

35. But the good works of the regenerate are not to be called sins; rather they are said to be defiled with sin.

36. Because of justification, the defilement of good works does not prevent their being accepted and rewarded by God.

37. The struggle found in wicked men between conscience and will is not the striving of the spirit against the flesh but that of flesh fearing against flesh inordinately desiring.

<hr>

XXX

Glorification

We have spoken of sanctification, one part of the alteration of qualities which relates to a just and honorable good. We now consider the other part, glorification, which relates to perfect and exalted good.

1. Glorification is the real change in man from misery, or the punishment of sin, to eternal happiness. Rom. 8:30, *Those whom he justified he also glorified.*

2. It is called a real change so that it may be distinguished from the blessedness which is only potential in election, calling, justification, and adoption or illustrated in holy works. Rom. 4:6, *David*

declares the man to be blessed to whom God reckons righteousness; Ps. 65:4, *Blessed is he whom thou choosest and bringest to dwell in thy courts;* Matt. 5:3, *Blessed are the poor in spirit.*

3. Since the starting point is misery or the punishment of sin, it is called redemption, 1 Cor. 1:30; Eph. 1:14; Gal. 3:13; Heb. 2:14, 15.

4. Redemption is a real deliverance from the evils of punishment, which is actually nothing but the carrying out of the sentence of justification. For in justification we are pronounced just and awarded the judgment of life. In glorification the life that results from the pronouncement and award is given to us: We have it in actual possession.

5. It is said to be real to distinguish it from the redemption which is the payment of the price of redemption and the application of it to justification, mentioned in Eph. 1:7 and Col. 1:14.

6. In the Scriptures it is often called deliverance and preservation from the wrath of God, from death, and from the kingdom of darkness.

7. The end of glorification is called beatification, blessing, eternal life, glory, glorification, the kingdom of our Lord and Savior Jesus Christ, and an immortal inheritance, Eph. 1:3; John 3:36 and 6:47; 2 Peter 1:3, 11; 1 Peter 1:4 and 5:10.

8. The first stage of beginning glorification is the apprehension and sense of the love of God shining forth in Christ, in the communion of believers with him. Rom. 5:5, *The love of God is shed abroad in our hearts by the Holy Spirit which is given to us.*

9. There comes about a certain friendship between God, Christ, and the faithful. John 15:15, *I have called you friends, because all I have heard of my Father I have made known to you;* Jas. 2:23, *Abraham was called the friend of God.*

10. The second stage is undoubting hope and expectation of the enjoyment of all those good things which God has prepared for his own. Rom. 5:2, *We rejoice under the hope of the glory of God.*

11. For this reason we are free to come to God with trust, Eph. 2:18 and 3:12; Heb. 10:22.

12. Hence also the certainty of perseverance and salvation, Rom. 8:38.

13. This certainty about the thing itself, which is called a certainty of the object, is made fast for all true believers. But the perceiving of it, which is called a certainty of the subject, is not always enjoyed by all. Yet it may be acquired by any without special revelation and it should be sought by all. This trust, rightly grounded, has nothing in common with presumption.

14. This certainty is established and confirmed to believers by the word, by seals, by oath, and by the guarantee of God himself. Heb. 6:17, *God willing abundantly to show to the heirs of the promise the immutability of his counsel, he bound it with an oath so that by two immutable things . . . we might have strong consolation;* Eph. 1:13, 14, *You have been sealed with the promised Holy Spirit which is the guarantee of our inheritance.*

15. This truth is perceived and made certain in us in these ways. First, by a certain spiritual sense in which the grace of God now present becomes known and evident to the believer. Second, by the gift of discernment through which believers distinguish true grace from its shadow. Third, by the whisper and witness of conscience in which grace and salvation are made fast for believers, just as sin and death are for unbelievers. Fourth, the Spirit of God so confirms to believers these ways of perceiving that they have the same certainty as faith itself. Rom. 8:16, *The Spirit himself witnesses with our spirit that we are sons of God;* 1 Cor. 2:12, *We have received the Spirit which is from God, that we may know the things that God has freely given us;* 2 Cor. 13:5, *Try yourselves, to see if you are in the faith. Examine yourselves;* 1 John 4:16, *We know and believe the love which God has towards us.*

16. This certainty follows upon the perceiving of faith and repentance, where the free covenant of God is rightly understood, 2 Cor. 13:5.

17. If either of these is wanting, the certainty (so far as it is conscious) is taken away, so that he who rightly understands the promise of the covenant cannot be sure of his salvation, unless he perceive in himself true faith and repentance. Neither can he who feels himself truly to believe and repent be sure of his perseverance and salvation unless he also understand from the covenant that God will surely preserve to the end those who believe and repent.

18. Therefore, the certainty of salvation cannot be known in any other way nor by any other persons than those who in faith keep a good conscience, and maintain it against any more grievous wound of the sins which debilitate conscience.

19. Therefore, faith and a good conscience flourish or languish in men as this certainty is strengthened or diminished, Ps. 51.

20. Those, therefore, who hope for salvation without any consciousness of or concern for faith and repentance hope by presuming and perish by hoping.

21. From certainty arises consolation, peace, and unspeakable joy, Rom. 5:2, 3; 1 Peter 1:8; Rom. 14:17; 2 Cor. 1:5. These are the first fruits of glory, Rom. 8:23.

22. Consolation is an easing of fear and oppressive grief, 2 Cor. 1:4. Yet it sometimes contains by synecdoche the beginning of all salvation, Col. 2:2.

23. Peace is a quieting of the mind coming partly from deliverance from evil and partly from the presence or hope of good things that are the opposite of evil, Phil. 4:7.

24. When joined with grace in the salutations of the Apostle it denotes all the happiness given to the faithful by the favor of God.

25. Joy is that delight felt in intimate participation in the chief good.

26. Therefore, eternal life itself is called joy, Matt. 25:21; John 15:11.

27. The third stage is the possession of spiritual gifts of grace in overflowing abundance, Col. 2:2, 7, 10, *With all riches of the full assurance of understanding . . . abounding in faith . . . full of life.*

28. Hence the abundance of grace is said to provide a rich entrance into the kingdom of God, 2 Peter 1:8, 11.

29. The fourth stage is the experience of God's benevolence or good will, Ps. 31:19, *How great is thy goodness, which thou layest up for them that fear thee? Ps. 65:4, We are satisfied with the goodness of thy house, with the things of thy holy temple.*

30. With this is involved God's fatherly providence whereby he watches ever over the faithful for good as he watches over the wicked for evil. In this sense, the good hand of God is said in Scripture to be with his own, Neh. 2:8.

31. Hence all things work together for good in those who love God, Rom. 8:28.

32. These all show that the faithful are rooted and grounded in the love of God, Eph. 3:17.

33. Perfect glorification is in the taking away of every imperfection from soul and body and the bestowal of total perfection.

34. This is granted to the soul immediately after the separation from the body, 2 Cor. 5:2; Phil. 1:23; Heb. 12:23. It is not ordinarily to be granted to the soul and body together until that last day when all the faithful shall in one moment be perfected in Christ, Eph. 4:13; Phil. 3:20, 21.

XXXI

The Church Mystically Considered

So much for the application of redemption considered in itself. Now we take up the matter of the subject to which and the way in which it is applied.

1. The subject is the church. Eph. 5:25–27, *Christ loved the church and gave himself for her, that he might sanctify her, being purified by him with the washing of water through the word, that he might make her glorious to himself, that is, a church without spot or wrinkle or any such thing, but rather holy and blameless.* Therefore, election, redemption, vocation, justification, adoption, sanctification, and glorification properly pertain to the same subject, i.e., to the individual men who make up the church. John 17:9–10, *Those whom thou hast given me, for they are thine*; Rom. 8:29, 30, *For those whom he foreknew he also predestined.*

2. The church is both the subject and an effect of redemption. For it is not first actually a church and later joined in union and communion with Christ; it is the church of Christ because it is united to Christ.

3. And this is the reason why we can neither explain nor understand the nature of the church unless we first perceive and explain the things which have to do with the application of Christ.

4. The elect, before they are grafted into Christ, are in themselves not of the church except in terms of that potentiality which in its own time will surely become actual because of God's intention and transaction with Christ. This remote potentiality in which all men are involved will certainly be made actual for the elect by God's determination.

5. Therefore, the orthodox who define the church as a company of the elect mean either those who are called according to election or the church not only as it exists now but also as it will exist hereafter.

6. The church is first of all constituted by calling, whence both its name and definition.

7. The church is indeed the company of men who are called. 1 Cor. 1:24 and 10:32, *Those who are called, both Jews and Greeks . . . to Jews, to Greeks, and to the church of God.* Because the end of calling is faith and the work of faith is a grafting into Christ, and this union brings with it communion with Christ, the church can be defined at once as a company of believers, a company of those

who are in Christ, and a company of those who have communion with him.

8. Faith looks to Christ and through Christ to God; likewise the church which exists by faith looks to Christ as its head and through Christ to God. Therefore, the church is called the *Body of Christ*, Col. 1:24; the *Church of God*, 1 Cor. 10:32; the *Kingdom of Christ*, Col. 1:13; and the *Kingdom of God*, Rom. 14:17.

9. It is called a *Company* because it consists of a multitude joined in fellowship or a community of many (not a single person who is called), thus Eph. 4:16 where it is named a *Body joined and made up of diverse members*. Hence it is often called in Scripture a *House, family, city, kingdom*, or *flock*.

10. This company is limited to men because the good angels, although in a way they belong to the church because of their union with Christ and the saving grace communicated by him, are not the same as the members of the redeemed church.

11. The form or constituting cause of this church must be something found alike in all those who are called. This can only be a relationship, and the only relationship which has this power is that which comes from a primary and intimate affection toward Christ. In man this comes only by faith. Faith, therefore, is the form of the church.

12. Inasmuch as faith is in each believer individually it is the form of those that are called. But seen collectively in all, faith is the form of the company of those that are called, or the church.

13. The same believing men, on the one hand, are individuals called by God; on the other, they are collectively the company which is the church of God.

14. Therefore, all the promises of God containing essential blessings which are made to the church in Scripture belong to each believer.

15. The relationship is so intimate that not only is Christ the church's and the church Christ's, Song of Sol. 2:16, but Christ is in the church and the church in him, John 15:4; 1 John 3:24. Therefore, the church is mystically called *Christ*, 1 Cor. 12:12, and the *Fullness of Christ*, Eph. 1:23.

16. The church is metaphorically called the bride and Christ the bridegroom; the church a city and Christ the king; the church a house and Christ the householder; the church the branches and Christ the vine; and finally the church a body and Christ the head.

17. But these comparisons signify not only the union and communion between Christ and the church but also the relation showing Christ to be the beginning of all honor, life, power, and perfection in the church.

18. This church is mystically one, not in a generic sense, but as a unique species or individual — for it has no species in the true sense.

19. It can, therefore, be called catholic, not as catholic signifies καθ' ὅλου, a genus of something general, but as it describes something uniquely universal (as when we speak of the world). This is so because it embraces believers of all nations, of all places, and of all times.

20. No part of the church can truly be called catholic unless it professes the faith of the catholic church. Thus the ancient authorities called not only that part of the church at Rome catholic but other churches as well. Our church at Franeker may rightly be called catholic since it professes the faith which belongs to the catholic church.

21. The church is divided according to the degree of communion it has with Christ. In this sense it is called either militant or triumphant.

22. The church militant is that which knows only of a communion begun and so still struggles with enemies in the battlefield of this world. 1 Cor. 13:9, 12, *We know in part and prophesy in part. For we see through a glass darkly;* 2 Cor. 10:4, *The weapons of our warfare;* Eph. 6:12, 13, *We wrestle . . . Therefore take the whole armor of God.*

23. The church triumphant is that which is already perfected. Eph. 4:13, *Until we all come . . . to a perfect man, to the measure of the full stature of Christ;* 1 Cor. 15:46, *Afterwards comes that which is perfect.*

24. The militant church is both invisible and visible (that is, to outward sight or sense).

25. This distinction is not a division of genus into species, as if there were one church visible and another invisible, or of the whole into the members, as if one part of the church were visible and another invisible. It relates to phases of the same subject: Invisibility is a condition or mode of the church having to do with its essential and internal form; visibility is a condition or mode of the church having to do with its accidental or outward form.

26. The essential form is invisible both because it is a relation which cannot be perceived by the senses and also because it is spiritual, and so farther removed from sense perception than many other relations.

27. The accidental form is visible because it is an outward profession of inward faith, easily perceived by sense.

28. The visible profession is the manifest communion of the saints which they have with Christ and among themselves.

29. Their acts of the communion with Christ are those by which they present themselves to God in Christ to receive his blessings and to glorify him for those blessings.

30. Their acts of communion among themselves are all those in which they strive to do good to each other. These acts are especially those which directly further their communion with God in Christ.

31. Many acts of this kind are to be performed towards those who are not yet members of the church, for they ought to be judged as belonging to it potentially.

32. The church visible in itself, in comparative relation to others, is divided into the church hidden and manifest.

33. The manifest church is found where a greater number of saints exist and profession is freer and more public.

34. The hidden church is found where the number is fewer and profession less open. This is likely to occur in time of heresies, persecutions, or godless morality.

35. In the same way, the church is more pure or less pure as profession is more or less perfect.

36. Profession depends not only upon confession and the preaching of the word, but also upon the receiving of it and devout obedience to it.

37. Although the church is subject to changes of this kind and may relinquish any part of the world, yet from its gathering it never has totally failed nor shall it fail to the end of the world.

38. For Christ must always have his kingdom in the midst of his enemies until he makes his enemies his footstool.

39. The church never wholly ceases to be visible. Although sometimes there is scarcely a church pure enough to offer the same pure worship at all points, yet the church is still somehow visible in the very midst of the impurity of worship and profession.

XXXII

The Church Instituted

1. The church living upon earth, though it is not wholly visible, is visible in its parts both individually in its single members and collectively in its companies or congregations.

2. The first visibility is in the personal profession of men. This does not make a visible church, except as it exists in these particular

members, i.e., it makes the church's members visible; the church itself, in its integral state, does not become visible in the same place. Acts 19:1, *Paul . . . came to Ephesus where he found certain disciples.*

3. That visibility which is in companies or distinct congregations not only makes a visible church, but, so far as outward form is concerned, also makes as many visible churches as there are distinct congregations. Rev. 1:4, *The seven churches;* 2 Cor. 8:1, 19, *The churches of Macedonia. All the churches.*

4. These congregations are, so to speak, similar parts of the catholic church and partake both of its name and nature.

5. Therefore a particular church, in respect of the nature it has in common with all particular churches, is a species of the church as a genus; but in respect of the catholic church, which has the nature [*ratio*] of a whole, it is a member made up of various individual members gathered together; and in respect of these members it is also a whole.

6. Such a congregation or particular church is a society of believers joined together in a special bond for the continual exercise of the communion of saints among themselves.

7. It is a society of believers because the same thing makes a church visible in profession which in its inward and real nature makes it a mystical church, namely, faith.

8. Because true faith has holiness joined with it, which it keeps effectual, Acts 15:9, and the profession of true faith cannot be separated from the profession of holiness, the church is variously but with the same meaning called a society of believers and a society of saints. Eph. 1:1, *To the saints which are at Ephesus and faithful in Jesus Christ;* 1 Cor. 1:2 compared with 2 Cor. 1:1; Rom. 1:7; and Col. 1:2.

9. Hence visible and particular churches are rightly said to be in God the Father and in the Lord Jesus Christ because of the faith which they profess, 1 Thess. 1:1; 2 Thess. 1:1.

10. Doubtless there is no particular church of this sort in which profession of the true faith is made but there are also to be found in it some true believers.

11. Those who are only believers by profession, while they remain in that society, are members of that church, as they are of the catholic church so far as outward status is concerned. In inward or essential status, they do not belong. 1 John 2:19, *They went out from us, but they were not of us.*

12. The children of those believers who are in the church are to be counted with the believers as members of the church, 1 Cor. 7:14,

Your children are holy. For they are partakers with their parents of the same covenant and profession.

13. Yet children are not such perfect members of the church that they can exercise acts of communion or be admitted to all its privileges unless there is first a growth of faith. But they are not to be excluded from the privileges which pertain to the beginning of faith and entrance into the church.

14. Believers do not make a particular church, even though by chance many may meet and live together in the same place, unless they are joined together by a special bond among themselves. Otherwise, any one church would often be dissolved into many, and many also merged into one.

15. This bond is a covenant, expressed or implicit, by which believers bind themselves individually to perform all those duties toward God and toward one another which relate to the purpose [*ratio*] of the church and its edification.

16. Hence it is that in the Old Testament we very often read of the renewing of the covenant whenever any true reformation of the church is present.

17. Therefore, no one is rightly admitted into the church except on confession of faith and promise of obedience.

18. This joining together by covenant makes a church only as it looks toward the exercising of the communion of saints. For the same believing men may join themselves in covenant to make a city or some civil society when their immediate concern is for the common civil good. But they cannot make a church except as in its constitution they intend holy communion with God among themselves.

19. The same men may make a city or political society and not a church; or a church and not a city; or both a church and a city.

20. Therefore, those meetings that are formally ecclesiastical are said to be held in the name of the Lord, Matt. 18:20; 1 Cor. 5:4.

21. No sudden coming together and exercise of holy communion suffices to make a church unless there is also that continuity, at least in intention, which gives the body and its members a certain spiritual polity.

22. The church is instituted by God and by Christ. Heb. 3:3, 4, *He that built the house . . . For every house is built by someone.* In this sense it differs from the mystical church where the gathering is not prescribed to men but effected directly by divine operation. The gathering of an instituted church, however, is so effected by God that his command and man's duty and labor come first. Heb. 10:25, *Not forsaking the assembling of ourselves together.*

23. It is instituted by God and Christ alone because men have

no power in themselves to institute or frame a church for Christ; neither is any such power committed to them by the revealed will of God. Their greatest honor is that they are servants in the house of God, Heb. 3:5.

24. Man, therefore, does not have power either to take away any of those things which Christ has given his church or to add things of like kind. Yet in every way he can and ought to make certain that the things which Christ has ordained are furthered and strengthened.

25. Christ has so instituted the church that it always depends upon him as the head — considered without Christ it is not a complete body.

26. Therefore, the church may not properly make new laws for itself for instituting new things. It ought to take care only to find out the will of Christ clearly and observe his ordinances decently and with order, with greatest edification resulting.

27. Since the ordinances of Christ always have God's blessing joined with them, various promises of God are made to the church about the presence of Christ, Matt. 18:20; 1 Cor. 5:4. So in a special way he is said to live and walk in the churches, Rev. 2:1; Isa. 31:9. And promises are made about the presence of the Holy Spirit, Isa. 59:21. Thus an ampler and surer blessing of God may be expected in the instituted church of God than is found in any solitary life.

28. Therefore, those who have opportunity to join the church and neglect it most grievously sin against God because of his ordinance, and also against their own souls because of the blessing joined to it. And if they obstinately persist in their carelessness, whatever they otherwise profess, they can scarcely be counted believers truly seeking the kingdom of God.

29. The profession of the true faith is the most essential mark of the church.

30. This profession may in some congregations precede the solemn preaching of the word and the administration of the sacraments.

XXXIII

The Extraordinary Ministers
of the Church

1. So much for the subject of the application of redemption; now we consider the way of application.

2. The way of application consists of those means whereby the Spirit bestows Christ and all his benefits on us for our salvation.

3. The Spirit itself supplies all saving things to us internally, most intimately, and in its own way directly. No external means properly have the power to communicate grace to us in any real sense. Therefore, although external means naturally concur and operate in the preparation of man to receive grace, yet in themselves they do not properly confer grace. It is the Spirit that works together with them. 1 Cor. 3:7, *Neither is he that plants anything nor he that waters, but God who gives power to increase.*

4. The two principal means of this sort are the ministry and the holy signs (or symbols), to which some ecclesiastical discipline must be added.

5. The ministry is an ecclesiastical function in which a man, being singled out, is responsible by special right for holy things. 2 Cor. 4:1, *We have this ministry, having obtained mercy;* 1 Cor. 4:1, *Let a man account us as ministers of Christ and stewards of the mysteries of God.*

6. It is called the ministry because the power which is committed to the men of the church is a power of acting only by command of Christ and out of obedience to him alone, 1 Cor. 4:1, 2.

7. The spiritual or regal power of self-rule whereby one works in freedom and by his own choice does not belong to men, but to Christ alone.

8. Therefore, a minister of the church is bound to execute his office himself, as one who does not have power to appoint anyone in his place — for that would be an action of command, not of obedience.

9. The permanent minister of many churches where vicars must serve is not of God's ordaining, but of man's ambition and presumption.

10. Ministerial power is not absolute but relative, i.e. it is not an absolute power to do anything but consists of a right whereby one has

due power to do lawfully what he could not do before. Therefore, it is called a power of right.

11. But it is a special right because it refers to special duties unlawful for others; and it undertakes certain common duties in a certain special way.

12. The right of ministry depends upon calling. Heb. 5:4, *No one takes this honor to himself except he that is called of God as was Aaron.*

13. Calling is an action which commits an office to someone with authority to minister.

14. Therefore, it is clearly ridiculous to ordain the calling of ministers but not give them power to preach the word without further permission.

15. A necessary part of calling is fitness for the ministry.

16. Those who are altogether unfit to do the work of the ministry, if they are called to it by men, are ministers of men and not of God. Hos. 4:6, *Because you have despised knowledge, I will also despise you so that you shall not be a priest to me.*

17. Fitness arises from a fit measure of gifts and a ready will to undertake and execute the office.

18. The ministry produces a third state of the church. As by faith it has its essential state and by gathering its integral state, so by the ministry it has a certain organic state. It is now made fit to do all the works which pertain to the good of the whole.

19. The course and direction of these operations is ecclesiastical polity.

20. The form of this polity is altogether monarchical in respect to Christ as the king and the head. But in respect to the visible system of administration, it is of a mixed nature: partly aristocratic, so to speak, and partly democratic.

21. Therefore, in the lawful ministry of the church, hierarchy or sacred rule has no place, but rather hieroduly or sacred service.

22. One minister is not subject to the power of another in his responsibility but each one depends directly upon Christ. So it is that the angels who are inferior in office to others are directly subject to God and not to other angels.

23. This ministry is either extraordinary or ordinary.

24. An extraordinary ministry is one which has a certain higher and more perfect direction than can be attained through ordinary means.

25. Such ministers always have extraordinary gifts and assistance so that they minister without error.

26. The authority of an extraordinary minister is given actually

neither by man nor through man but by God alone through Jesus Christ and the Holy Spirit, Gal. 1:1.

27. Therefore, the calling to such a ministry is direct.

28. Yet an extraordinary calling is not so direct as to exclude all ministry of men, as appears in the calling of Elisha and Matthias. It excludes only the ministry which lacks infallible direction.

29. Such an extraordinary ministry was surely necessary for the church because that will of God to which living well to God is directed could not be discovered by human industry or any ordinary means used in other arts and sciences. But it required men who were stirred up and sent by God and to whom he manifested his will in order that they might be in the place of God himself for us. Exod. 4:15, 16, *And you be to him instead of God.*

30. God revealed his will to those extraordinary ministers in several ways. First, by direct speech, Rev. 1:10, to which was often added the appearing and speaking of an angel or of Christ himself, such as the angel of the covenant. Second, by a vision in which the form of things to be declared was shown to the eyes of the vigilant along with the word. Third, by dreams through which like proposals were imparted to the minds of men asleep. Fourth, sometimes by a special familiarity, mouth to mouth, so to speak, without riddles. Num. 12:6–8, *If there be a prophet among you, I will make myself, the Lord, known to him in a vision and will speak to him in a dream. It is not so with my servant Moses . . . With him I speak mouth to mouth and not in dark speeches; and the form of the Lord he beholds.*

31. The mode of this revelation was so powerful that it often took men into ecstasy: They were so caught up above themselves that they knew nothing but what was proposed, and not even that in all its circumstances, 2 Cor. 13:3, 4.

32. Yet it is certain that the divine truth of such revelation is always confirmed and sealed in a special way to those to whom it is revealed. Therefore, it does not need further confirmation. Gal. 1:17; 2:6, *Neither did I return to those who were apostles before me . . . They who were of repute made no difference to me.* Sometimes, however, miracles are added for more abundant confirmation, Judg. 6:36–38.

33. This extraordinary ministry is either for the first instituting of a church, or for the special and extraordinary conservation of a church, or for the extraordinary restoring of a church which has collapsed.

34. The ministry of instituting a church is always accompanied by a testimony of miracles. Heb. 2:3, 4, *Which at first began to be spoken*

. . . God also bearing witness with signs and wonders and many miracles and gifts of the Holy Spirit distributed according to his will.

35. Yet miracles do not provide testimony to any doctrine in the sense that they immediately produce faith. For doctrine which does not agree with the known will of God ought not to be accepted, although it might seem to be confirmed with miracles. Deut. 13:1–3, *Although that sign or wonder come to pass which he foretold you, saying, "Let us go follow other Gods" . . . do not harken to the words of that prophet;* Gal. 1:8, *Though we or an angel from heaven preach to you another gospel besides that which we have preached . . . let him be accursed.*

36. The ministry of conserving and restoring a church although extraordinary and usually confirmed by miracles does not always or necessarily require a testimony of miracles. This appears in many places in the Old Testament and in John the Baptist.

37. The prophets, apostles, and evangelists were extraordinary ministers.

38. Wyclif, Luther, Zwingli, and the others who were the first restorers of the gospel were not, strictly speaking, extraordinary ministers.

39. Yet they are not wrongly called extraordinary by some. First, because they performed something similar to what was done by the extraordinary ministers of old. Second, because as occasion required they received gifts of special magnitude from God. This may also be affirmed of many of the more famous martyrs. Third, because they necessarily attempted some things out of the common course, since the order of the time was disturbed and decayed.

40. It is, therefore, ridiculous to require miracles of those men to confirm the doctrine which they propounded, when such an attestation was not necessary even among the extraordinary ministers.

XXXIV

Holy Scripture

1. Extraordinary ministers were raised up by God to instruct the churches not only orally, but also by divine writings so that there might be a perpetual use and fruit of their ministry in the church even when such ministers no longer remained.

2. Only those could set down the rule of faith and conduct in

writing who in that matter were free from all error because of the direct and infallible direction they had from God.

3. They received from God the command to write. This was partly outward and general, as when they were commanded to teach, and sometimes special, as when specific writing was called for. Deut. 31:19; Rev. 1:19, *Write the song. Write the things which you have seen.* It came partly by the inward impulse of the Spirit. 2 Peter 1:21, *For prophecy came not in former times by the will of man, but holy men spoke as they were moved by the Holy Spirit;* 2 Tim. 3:16, *All Scripture is inspired by God.*

4. They also wrote by the inspiration and guidance of the Holy Spirit so that the men themselves were at that point, so to speak, instruments of the Spirit. 2 Tim. 3:16; Jer. 1:9, *Behold, I put my words in your mouth;* Acts 28:25, *Well indeed spoke the Holy Spirit by Isaiah the prophet.*

5. But divine inspiration was present among those writers in different ways. Some things were altogether unknown to the writer in advance, as appears in the history of past creation, or in the foretelling of things to come. But some things were previously known to the writer, as appears in the history of Christ written by the apostles. Some things were known by a natural knowledge and some by a supernatural. In those things that were hidden and unknown, divine inspiration was at work by itself. In those things which were known, or where the knowledge was obtained by ordinary means, there was added the writers' devout zeal so that (God assisting them) they might not err in writing.

6. In all those things made known by supernatural inspiration, whether matters of right or fact, God inspired not only the subjects to be written about but dictated and suggested the very words in which they should be set forth. But this was done with a subtle tempering so that every writer might use the manner of speaking which most suited his person and condition.

7. Therefore, Scripture is often attributed to the Holy Spirit as the author with no mention of the writers. Heb. 10:15, *Whereof the Holy Spirit also is a witness to us.*

8. Although the inscriptions of the holy books usually bear the names of the authors, there is sometimes deep silence on this matter. However, this does not diminish the worth of such books or lessen their authority.

9. Neither does a book written by some extraordinary servant of God and upon direction of the Spirit become a part of Holy Scripture unless it is publicly given to the church by divine authority and set apart to be its canon or rule.

10. What the authors have committed to writing, in terms of its substance and chief end is nothing else than the revealed word of God, which is the rule of faith and morals.

11. Therefore, all those things which were spoken of in the first chapter as the doctrine of life revealed by God are properly found in the Holy Scripture. For the Scripture is that very doctrine in writing —and as writing it is treated of here rather than then.

12. Therefore, in matter and content, Scripture, i.e., the doctrine revealed from God, existed before the church. But as a writing, in respect of which it is properly known as Scripture it comes after the early church.

13. It is called Holy Scripture, and sometimes κατ' ἐξοχήν, par excellence, *the* Scripture, and its writers are called holy, partly because of its subject and of its object, which is the true and saving will of God, and partly because of the directive influence which governed its writing, Rom. 1:2; Eph. 3:5; 2 Peter 1:21; 2:22; 3:2; Rev. 18:20.

14. Although various parts of the Scripture were written upon a special occasion and were directed to particular men or assemblies, in God's intention they are equally for the instruction of the faithful of all ages, as if specially directed to them. Therefore in Heb. 12 the exhortation of Solomon found in Proverbs is spoken (as to sons) to the Hebrews who lived in the apostles' time; in 2 Peter 3:15 Paul is said to have written to all the faithful in writing to the Romans; and in Heb. 13:5 what was said to Joshua is said to all believers.

15. All things necessary to salvation are contained in the Scriptures and also those things necessary for the instruction and edification of the church. 2 Tim. 3:15–17, *The Holy Scriptures can make you wise unto salvation that the man of God might be complete, perfectly furnished for every good work.*

16. Therefore, Scripture is not a partial but a perfect rule of faith and morals. And no observance can be continually and everywhere necessary in the church of God, on the basis of any tradition or other authority, unless it is contained in the Scriptures.

17. All Scripture was not committed to writing at one and the same time, for the state of the church and the wisdom of God demanded otherwise. But beginning with the first writing, those things were successively committed to writing which were necessary to the particular times.

18. The articles of faith have grown with the times not in essence but only in explication.

19. In form of expression, Scripture does not explain the will of God by universal and scientific rules, but rather by stories, examples,

precepts, exhortations, admonitions, and promises. This style best fits the common usage of all sorts of men and also greatly affects the will by stirring up pious motives, which is the chief end of theology.

20. The will of God is revealed in such a way in Scripture that, although the substance itself is for the most part hard to conceive, the style of communicating and explaining it is clear and evident, especially in necessary matters.

21. The Scriptures need no explanation through light brought from outside, especially in the necessary things. They give light to themselves, which should be uncovered diligently by men and communicated to others according to their calling.

22. Hence there is only one meaning for every place in Scripture. Otherwise the meaning of Scripture would not only be unclear and uncertain, but there would be no meaning at all — for anything which does not mean one thing surely means nothing.

23. There is no visible power established in the church, royal or magistrative, for the settlement of controversies in theology. But the duty of inquiry is laid on men; the gift of discerning truth both publicly and privately is bestowed upon them; and an endeavor to further the knowledge and practice of the known truth according to their calling is enjoined — to all of which is joined a promise of direction and blessing from God.

24. Because the Scriptures were given for the use and edification of the church, they were written in languages which were most common and widespread in the church at the time when they were written.

25. Therefore, all the books written before the coming of Christ were in Hebrew. For to the Jews were committed the sayings of God, Rom. 3:2; 9:4. And for like reason the books written later were put in the Greek language because that was most common in the areas where the church first flourished.

26. Some knowledge, at least, of these languages is necessary for a precise understanding of the Scriptures, for they are to be understood by the same means required for other human writings, i.e., skill and experience in logic, rhetoric, grammar, and the languages. However, there is one exception: The special light of the Spirit must be sought for in the Scriptures by the godly.

27. The Scriptures are not so tied to these first languages that they cannot and ought not to be translated into other languages for common use in the church.

28. But, among interpreters, neither the seventy who turned them into Greek, nor Jerome, nor any other such held the office of a prophet; they were not free from errors in interpretation.

29. Hence no versions are fully authentic except as they express the sources, by which they are also to be weighed.

30. Neither is there any authority on earth whereby any version may be made absolutely authentic.

31. God's providence in preserving the sources is notable and glorious, for neither have they wholly perished nor have they been injured by the loss of any book or blemished by any serious defect — though today not one of the earlier versions remains intact.

32. From these human versions all those things may be known which are absolutely necessary, provided they agree with the sources in essentials. Hence, all the versions accepted by the churches usually agree, although they may differ and be defective at several minor points.

33. We must not rest forever in any accepted version, but faithfully see to it that a pure and faultless interpretation is given to the church.

34. Out of all the books divinely delivered and placed, as it were, in the treasury of the church there is made up a complete canon of faith and morals, whence they have the name, canonical scripture.

35. The prophets made up the canon of the Old Testament and Christ himself approved it by his testimony. The canon of the New Testament together with the Old was approved and sealed by the apostle John with divine authority. Rev. 22:18–19, *For I witness to everyone who uses the words of the prophecy of this book: If any shall add to these, God shall lay upon him the plagues written in this book; and if any shall take away anything from the books of this prophecy, God shall take away his share in the book of life.*

36. The books commonly called among us apocryphal do not belong to the divine canon nor were they rightly joined by men in earlier times to the canonical books as a secondary canon. First, some of them contain manifest fables told and affirmed as true histories, as those of Tobias, Judith, Susannah, Bel and the Dragon, and the like. Second, they often contradict the sacred Scriptures and themselves. Third, they were not written in Hebrew or delivered to or received by the Jewish church to which God committed all his oracles before the coming of Christ, Rom. 9:4. Fourth, they were not approved by Christ, not being among those books which he designated when he commanded his own to search the Scriptures. Fifth, they were never received by either the apostles or by the early Christian church as part of the divine canon.

XXXV

Ordinary Ministers and
Their Office in Preaching

1. The ordinary ministry is that which receives all of its direction from the will of God revealed in the Scriptures and from those means which God has appointed in the church for its continual edification.

2. They are called ordinary because it is according to the order established by God that they may be and usually are called to minister.

3. In their service they have the will of God revealed earlier through the extraordinary ministers as a fixed rule; therefore, they ought not to propose or do anything in the church which is not prescribed to them in the Scriptures.

4. They depend upon the extraordinary ministers and are, so to speak, their successors. Although in manner and degree extraordinary ministers have no successors, ordinary ministers in their essential service perform the same office toward the church as the former once did.

5. The right to this ministry is regularly accorded by men and for that reason the calling of an ordinary minister is indirect.

6. But this is to be understood in the sense that the authority for administering divine things is directly communicated from God to all lawful ministers, though the appointing of persons upon whom the authority is to be bestowed is done by the church.

7. But the church cannot confer the necessary gifts for this ministry, and cannot prescribe for God those upon whom he should confer them. Therefore, the church can only choose those who appear to it in advance to be suitable. For ordinary ministers, unlike extraordinary ministers, are not made fit by their very calling when they were unfit before.

8. Therefore, in an ordinary calling it is required that a lawful examination precede the calling itself. 1 Tim. 3:10, *Let them be first tried then let them minister if they be blameless.*

9. The purpose of the ordinary ministry is to preserve, propagate, and renew the church through regular means.

10. There are two parts in this ministry: First, a minister must do those things which he does for the people in the name of God; second, he must do those things which he does for God in the name of the people.

11. Here the preaching of the word is of utmost importance, and so it has always been of continuous use in the church.

12. The duty of an ordinary preacher is to set forth the will of God out of the word for the edification of the hearers. 1 Tim. 1:5, *The end of παραγγελία, preaching, is love out of a pure heart, a good conscience, and faith unfeigned.*

13. Since first an earnest zeal for the church's edification is required, a man cannot be a fit preacher unless he has *Set his heart to study the law of the Lord and to do it, and to teach his statutes and ordinances in Israel,* Ezra 7:10. For one who teaches another ought before and while he teaches to teach himself, Rom. 2:21. Otherwise he is not prepared to edify the church.

14. This duty is to be performed not only for all hearers in common but also specifically for each status and age — for old men, young men, servants (Titus 2 and 3), teachers (2 Peter 1:12), yea, for each individual. 1 Thess. 2:11, *We exhorted, comforted, and charged each one of you not only publicly but privately;* Acts 20:20, *Publicly and from house to house.*

15. He ought always to have this aim of edification so clearly before his eyes as to take great care not to *Turn aside to vain discussion* (1 Tim. 1:6), *Striving about words* (2 Tim. 2:14), *Unprofitable controversies or speculations of what is falsely called knowledge* (1 Tim. 6:20). *He should hold fast to the faithful word which leads to teaching* (Titus 1:9), *And which cannot be condemned* (Titus 2:8).

16. Since to this end the will of God is to be set forth out of the word, no one is fit for the ministry who is not greatly concerned with the Holy Scripture, even beyond ordinary believers, so that he might be said, with Apollos, to be mighty in the Scriptures, Acts 18:24. He must not put his trust in notes and commentaries.

17. In order that the will of God may be set forth fruitfully for edification two things are necessary: First, the things contained in the text must be stated; second, they must be applied to the consciences of the hearers as their condition seems to require. 1 Tim. 6:17, *Charge those that are rich in this world that they be not highminded or trust in uncertain riches.*

18. Ministers impose upon their hearers and altogether forget themselves when they propound a certain text in the beginning as the start of the sermon and then speak many things about or simply by occasion of the text but for the most part draw nothing out of the text itself.

19. In setting forth the truth in the text the minister should first explain it and then indicate the good which follows from it. The first part is concerned with doctrines and proofs; the latter with applica-

tion or derivation of profit from the doctrines. 2 Tim. 3:16, *All the Scripture . . . is profitable for doctrine, for reproof, for correction, and instruction in righteousness.*

20. Those who invert and confuse these parts make it difficult for their hearers to remember and stand in the way of their edification. Their hearers cannot commit the chief heads of the sermon to memory so that they may afterwards repeat it privately in their families; and when this cannot be done, the greatest part of the fruit, which would otherwise be made available to the church of God through sermons, is lost.

21. A doctrine is a theological principle either in the express words of Scripture or deriving from them as a direct consequence.

22. A doctrine rightly must first be discovered and then discussed.

23. The discovery is made by a logical analysis in which rhetoric and grammar are utilized.

24. Analysis means principally observing the scope or purpose of the text and, by the art of logic, the means by which it is attained.

25. Confirmation must be added by interpreting the doubtful parts in the analysis. Manifest parts, clear in themselves, neither require nor permit needless interpretation.

26. The discussion of a doctrine consists partly in proofs, if it be questioned by the hearers (it is foolish to go to any length to confirm what all acknowledge), and partly in illustration of the things already well proved.

27. Proofs ought to be sought from the clearer testimonies of Scripture, with reasons being added where the nature of the thing will allow. But here the treatment must be adapted to the profit of the hearers.

28. Illustrations may be drawn from almost anywhere they may be found but the contrasting and comparing themes are the most important.

29. Each doctrine when sufficiently explained should immediately be applied to its use. Upon this part, unless there is some special reason against it, great insistence must be made, since this contains the conclusion and the good of the first part, and is closer to the chief purpose of the sermon, which is the edification of the hearers.

30. They sin, therefore, who stick to the naked finding and explanation of the truth, neglecting the use and practice in which religion and blessedness consist. Such preachers edify the conscience little or not at all.

31. Not all the doctrines which may be drawn out of the text are to be propounded or all the uses set forth but only those are to be selected which the circumstances of place, time, and person suggest as

most necessary — and of these especially those which make for the stirring up or strengthening of the spirit of devotion.

32. They sin who do care little about what they say provided it may appear that they may have thought about and spoken many things. They do this frequently, forcing many things out of the text which are not in it and often borrowing for it from other places, bringing anything out of everything. The result is the ruin rather than the edification of the hearers, especially among the untutored.

33. Both doctrine and use ought to be structured, as far as possible, to have some connection between them and to manifest it. For the mind is not drawn from one thing to a different thing without loss; nor is there anything that helps the memory more than logical order.

34. A use is a theological principle deduced from a doctrine which shows the use, goodness, or end of it.

35. The logic of the deduction is to be explained, if it be not clear. To this should be joined a proof or illustration as the necessity of the hearers and the wisdom of the speaker suggests.

36. Use lies in the area either of judgment or of practice, 2 Tim. 3:16.

37. In judgment it provides information and reformation of the mind.

38. Information is the proving of some truth.

39. Reformation is the refutation of some error.

40. Although every truth may be taught upon occasion, every error need not always come up for refutation. For heresies already buried are not to be dug up again just so that they may be refuted, nor wicked blasphemies glibly repeated. This troubles and offends, especially when all is declared, explained, and refuted in a solemn way.

41. Direction, needed in the practice of life, consists of instruction and correction.

42. Instruction is a setting forth of the life which ought to be followed.

43. Correction is a condemnation of the life which ought to be shunned.

44. After the declaration of a doctrine application should follow, and this is so like the derivation of uses that the two may often be made one.

45. To apply a doctrine to its use is to sharpen and make specially relevant some general truth with such effect that it may pierce the minds of those present with the stirring up of godly affections.

46. Men are to be pricked to the quick so that they feel individually what the Apostle said, namely, that the word of the Lord is a two-edged sword, piercing to the inward thoughts and affections and going

through to the joining of bones and marrow. Preaching, therefore, ought not to be dead, but alive and effective so that an unbeliever coming into the congregation of believers should be affected and, as it were, transfixed by the very hearing of the word so that he might give glory to God. 1 Cor. 14:25, *The hidden things of his heart are disclosed; and so, falling down on his face, he will worship God and say that God is among you indeed.*

47. This application is either for an oppressed mind, in consolation, or one that is failing to follow up the good, or to avoid evil, in exhortation or admonition.

48. Consolation is the application of some point that either takes away or mitigates grief and oppressive fear.

49. In consolation, indications are profitably given to a man's conscience to assure him that he shares the benefits with which the minister comforts the conscience of believers. Thoughts to the contrary, which may arise in a pious and troubled mind, are dispelled and refuted.

50. Exhortation is the application of a point which begets, quickens, and excites some inward virtue or furthers the exercise of it.

51. In exhortation to virtue it is profitable to show the means which lead to the begetting of that virtue in us. But let each one be proved by places and examples from Scripture, or by reasons which have a firm foundation in Scripture.

52. Admonition is the application of a point to correct some viciousness.

53. In admonition, or exhortation against vices, remedies may be found from passages which are most likely to be effective against them.

54. The doing of all these things must have in it no show of human wisdom or mixture of carnal affections; it should manifest itself throughout as the demonstration of the Spirit. 1 Cor. 1:17; and 2:1, 4, 13, *Not with skill of speaking, lest the cross of Christ should have no effect. Not with excellence of speech or wisdom, not in persuading words of men's wisdom, but in spiritual and powerful demonstration. Not in words which man's wisdom teaches, but in that which the Holy Spirit teaches.* It is the word of the Spirit, the word of life, which is preached for the building up of faith in God. If anything be not fitly spoken or done to this end, it is as useless as hay and stubble, 1 Cor. 3:12.

55. Therefore, neither human testimonies, no matter what they be, nor stories known only to the learned ought to be mixed in, except on the rare occasions when urgent necessity or sure hope of good results seem to require it (and then the reason for so doing should be made clear). Much less should words or sentences in

Latin, Greek, or Hebrew be used which the people do not understand.

56. The purity, perfection, and majesty of the word of God is violated when it is said to need the admixture of human words. And at the same time a disservice is done to hearers who get so accustomed to human flourishes that they often contract the disease of itching ears, begin to dislike the simplicity of the gospel, and will not endure sound teaching. 2 Tim. 4:3.

57. Consider Paul, who cites only a few, brief sayings of heathen poets, not naming the authors — and that incidentally and by the way — to convince the Gentiles to whom they were known and approved. His example hardly supports those who "of necessity" or "to improve the sermon" frequently and purposely insert human testimonies, commending their authors with the same solemnity used in citing the names of the prophets. And such is done among Christians who only desire to hear Christ; the end result is only a show of learning.

58. Unnecessary and farfetched preambles and plausible words of orators ought not to be used. Nor should ministers indulge in digressions or excursions, for they smack of the human spirit, take time, and shut out other things more edifying.

59. If any introduction is used applying to the subject in hand, it should be either in announcing the text or applying it to use.

60. Speech and action should be completely spiritual, flowing from the very heart. They should show a man well versed in the Scriptures and in pious exercises, who has first persuaded himself and thoroughly settled in his own conscience those things to which he would persuade others, and in whom, finally, there is zeal, charity, mildness, freedom, and humility mixed with solemn authority.

61. Pronunciation must be natural, familiar, clear, and distinct so that it can be easily understood. It should fit the matter in such a way that the affections are moved. Gal. 4:20, *I wish now to be present with you and change my tone, for I am in doubt of you.*

62. There are two voices, among others, which are offensive. The first is heavy, slow, singing, drowsy in which not only the words are separated with a pause, as if by commas, but even the syllables in the same word, producing great hindrance to understanding.

63. The other voice which is most offensive in a sermon is hasty and swift, overwhelming the ears with so much speed that there is no distinct understanding of the subject.

64. Speech, pronunciation, and gestures which would be ridiculous in a senate, in courts of law, and the forum are the more to be avoided in a sermon.

65. The power of the Holy Spirit more clearly appears in the naked simplicity of words than in elegance and luster. Therefore, Paul calls

himself ἰδιώτης τῷ λόγῳ, unskilled in speaking, 2 Cor. 11:6. Yet if any-one has a certain outward forcefulness in speaking he ought to use it with genuine directness.

66. In proportion as affectation appears, effectiveness and authority are lost.

67. The sum of the matter is that nothing is to be allowed which does not contribute to the spiritual edification of the people, and nothing omitted by which we may surely reach that end.

68. A supplement to the sermon is prayer both before and after.

69. In the prayer before it, general matters ought to be set forth: the end and use of the word and of preaching, our wants, our un-worthiness, and our duty, together with the gracious promises of God. All these should be brought to remembrance so that the minds of all will be stirred up humbly to seek and faithfully to observe the will of God.

70. In the prayer following, the giving of thanks should always be included and the chief heads of the sermon turned into petitions.

XXXVI

The Sacraments

So much for the ministry, or the first means of the Spirit in apply-ing Christ and his benefits.

1. The second means is found in the signs, or symbols.

2. A sign is something perceptible to the senses which, beyond the appearance of the thing it brings directly to the senses, at the same time makes something else come into the mind. In this regard the role of a sign is as far-reaching as that of a logical argument.

3. Some signs are natural and others have been instituted.

4. There is such a difference between these two that only an ugly error can confuse them.

5. There is also an ordinary and perpetual sign and another that is extraordinary and temporary.

6. In reference to the thing signified, a sign relates either to things past and is called ἀναμνηστικός, commemorative, or to things pres-ent and is called διαγνωστικός, demonstrative, or future and is called προγνωστικός, annunciative. It may consist of all these, setting forth things present, past, and future.

7. In reference to end and use, it either serves the understanding and is called an informing [notificans] sign; or it serves the memory

and is called a reminding [*commonefaciens*] sign; or it serves faith and is called a sealing [*obsignans*] sign; or lastly it may serve all of these together.

8. Hence a holy sign is either a bare sign, or a seal as well.

9. A bare sign only represents something. A seal not only represents but presents something by sealing.

10. A sign sealing the covenant of God is called a sacrament, Rom. 4:11.

11. It is a sign commemorating, demonstrating, announcing, informing, reminding, and sealing.

12. A sacrament of the new covenant, therefore, is a divine institution in which the blessings of the new covenant are represented, presented, and applied through signs perceptible to the senses.

13. Such a sacrament has the meaning of a secondary divine testimony in which the primary testimony of the covenant itself is specially confirmed for us.

14. Therefore, the special application of God's favor and grace which arises from true faith is very much confirmed and furthered by the sacraments.

15. In a sacrament there is something perceptible to the senses and something spiritual.

16. The former is a sign which represents or applies and the latter is what is represented and applied.

17. Yet the word *sacrament* usually and most properly signifies the outward or perceptible thing itself.

18. The sacramental signs do not include the spiritual thing to which they refer in any physically inherent or adherent sense for then the signs and things signified would be the same.

19. Neither are they bare signs which merely indicate and represent. They communicate and testify to the thing itself; indeed, they present the thing to be communicated.

20. None can institute such a holy sign but God alone. No creature can communicate the thing signified, or make its communication certain to us, or finally add such force to signs that they can confirm faith and confidence, or stir up spiritual grace in us, more than anything else can.

21. The thing itself which is set apart and separated for such holy use is properly called a representing sign, illustrated in the bread and wine in the Supper. But the use of these things is called an applying sign, illustrated in the distributing, receiving, eating, and drinking.

22. Therefore, the sacraments do not properly exist apart from their being used, i.e., they are not revered sacraments either before or after their use.

23. The spiritual thing which is signified by the sacraments of the new covenant is the new covenant itself, or Christ himself with all the blessings which are prepared in him for the faithful.

24. Yet some sacraments more expressly represent some dimension or aspect of this covenant than others, which set forth some other dimension.

25. But all have this in common, namely, that they seal the whole covenant of grace to believers. And they have this use not only at the time they are administered but to the end of life.

26. The form of a sacrament is the union between the sign and the things signified.

27. This union is neither physical nor yet imaginary; it is rather a spiritual relation by which the things signified are really communicated to those who rightly use the signs.

28. Those who partake of the signs do not necessarily partake of the spiritual thing itself, and the same manner and means of partaking do not apply to both.

29. From this union follows a communication of predicates. First, the sign is predicated of the thing signified, as when sanctification of the heart is called circumcision; second, the thing signified is predicated of the sign, as when circumcision is called the covenant and bread the body; third, the effect of the thing signified is predicated of the sign, as when baptism is said to regenerate; fourth, a property of the sign is predicated of the thing signified, as when breaking, which is applicable to bread, is attributed to Christ; fifth, a property of the thing signified is attributed to the sign, as when sacramental eating and drinking is called spiritual.

30. The basis of these relations is found, first, in the likeness or analogy of the sign to the thing signified. Indeed, such a likeness, although not constituting the sacrament itself, is prerequisite for the constituents of a sacrament and becomes as foundation for them. Second, the basis is in the word of institution, consisting of a command and a promise. The command imposes on us the duty of using the creatures of bread and wine to this holy end. The promise leads us to believe that we shall not use them in vain. This word of institution distinctly applied with appropriate prayer is called the word of consecration, blessing, sanctification, and separation. Third, the basis is completely laid in the prescribed observance and use itself, which have such great force that if this or that person pays no heed to them, though he be present in body and receiving, there is no sacrament for him, though for others it is most effectual.

31. The primary end of a sacrament is to seal the covenant. And this occurs not on God's part only but secondarily on ours, for not

only are the grace and promises of God sealed to us but also our thankfulness and obedience towards him.

32. Therefore, mystical signs of holy things cannot be instituted by man without prejudice to and violation of the sacraments, even though they do set forth the duty only of man.

33. Such signs are not properly sacraments; they are rather sacramental signs, that is, they partake of the nature of sacraments. Even as such they cannot be instituted by man.

34. A secondary end is the profession of faith and love. Taking the sacraments symbolizes the union we have with God in Christ and the communion we hold with all those who are partakers of the same union, especially with those who are members of the same church.

XXXVII

Ecclesiastical Discipline

Discipline is associated with the word and sacraments. In summary it has always been considered with them and, therefore, can be fitly treated in this place.

1. Holy discipline is an application of the will of God to persons through censure to guard against offenses or remove them from the church of God.

2. In the preaching of the word, the will of God is set forth and really applied to beget and increase faith and obedience. In the administration of the sacraments the will of God is applied to persons through the seals to confirm faith and obedience. In the exercise of discipline the will of God is also applied to persons in censure to remove the vices contrary to true faith and obedience.

3. Therefore, discipline is usually associated by the best theologians with the word and sacraments in the marks of the church. Although the relationship is not essential and reciprocal (nor is it in the case of the other two), yet it ought to appear in a full consideration of the church.

4. This discipline is ordained and prescribed by Christ himself, Matt. 16:19; 18:15–17. It is, therefore, plainly of divine right and may not be taken away, diminished, or changed by men at their pleasure.

5. Indeed, he sins against Christ, the author and ordainer, who does not do all he can to establish and promote this discipline in the churches of God.

6. It applies, without exception, to members of visible, instituted

churches, Matt. 18:15; 1 Cor. 5:11; it does not apply to others, 1 Cor. 5:12. It pertains to all those, and only to those, who have the right to partake of the sacraments.

7. To such people it applies the will of God, i.e., those means of spiritual reformation which Christ alone has given to his churches, 2 Cor. 10:4. Therefore, punishments and pains of body or purse have no place at all in ecclesiastical discipline.

8. Discipline has to do with sins and offenses in such people; it is a wholesome remedy for the wounds and diseases to which the sheep of Christ are subject, 1 Cor. 5:5.

9. It prevents and takes away offenses, effectually and personally applying the will of Christ, which attacks and abolishes them.

10. But because it effectually enforces obedience towards Christ, a great part of the kingship of Christ by which he visibly governs the church is placed, not without special reason, in this discipline by the best theologians.

11. The true reason why the discipline of Christ is solidly constituted and exercised with doctrine in so few churches is because most of those who would seem to know Christ and to hope in him refuse to receive the whole kingship of Christ and yield themselves completely to him.

12. As discipline is part of the kingship of Christ, so it is also part of the gospel. For it is the holy manner of promoting the gospel ordained by the gospel itself. Therefore, those who reject discipline accept neither the whole kingship of Christ nor the whole gospel.

13. Since every part of the kingship of Christ is necessary to us in its own way and especially that which effectually represses sin, men should not be well content in churches lacking discipline unless that public defect is made up by private watchcare over one another.

14. The parts of this discipline are brotherly correction and excommunication.

15. Discipline consists not only or even chiefly in the thunderbolt of excommunication and anathema, but primarily in Christian correction.

16. The proper end of reproof is not excommunication (although by chance that sometimes may happen) but the prevention of it, so that the sinner by timely repentance may be kept in the church.

17. Correction, rebuke, or admonition ought to be used for every sin where the remedy of discipline applies, but in various ways depending on the variety of sins, hidden and known. In hidden sins those three degrees are to be observed which Christ prescribed in order, Matt. 18:15–17. But in public sin such steps are not necessary, 1 Tim. 5:20.

18. Admonitions should always be sought from the word of God and not from men's opinions; otherwise they will not reach the conscience.

19. Full excommunication is not to be used unless obstinacy be added to sin, Matt. 18:17. The sinner who is rightly admonished must appear either penitent or obstinate; the penitent is not to be excommunicated, only the obstinate.

20. But in the more heinous offenses not as much patience or delay is required to discern repentance or obstinacy as in the more usual faults.

21. When the matter admits of delay, it is agreeable to Scripture and reason that excommunication be first inaugurated by suspension or abstention from the Supper and similar privileges of the church. This is usually called lesser excommunication.

22. Yet the matter must not be left here, for by this means and at that time repentance should be urged. If there is no hope of it, resort must be had at length to a complete severing from the communion of the faithful, which is usually called the greater excommunication.

23. An obstinate sinner cannot be separated from the faithful unless the faithful be separated from him, and this produces a salutary sense of shame, 2 Thess. 3:14. Those who are lawfully excommunicated are to be avoided by all communicants. This refers not to moral and other necessary duties, but to those aspects of social contact which presuppose acceptance and inward familiarity. Speech, prayer, farewell, entertainments, table, are denied.

24. He who is not penitent should not be set free from the bond of excommunication; nor should freedom be denied anyone who is penitent. It is not enough for one to say "I repent; I will do it no more," but not otherwise show true repentance. Such indications of serious repentance ought to be in evidence that the church would be bound to be satisfied by them. Otherwise hypocrisy is nourished and the church mocked, as well as Christ himself.

25. Yet for some sins a weaker repentance (if it appear genuine) may be allowed than for others.

26. The power of discipline (so far as the right to it is concerned) belongs to the whole church of which the offender is a member. Those who have the right to admit have the right to expel. The keeping or cutting off of members concerns the whole body equally, and is, therefore, to be carried out with the consent of the church, and not only with the church's permission but by its approval and determination.

27. The elders have the main role in the exercise and administra-

tion of discipline. This is not only in directing public action and pronouncing sentence but also in giving admonitions beforehand, making up for what they observe to be neglected by individuals.

28. The customary censures of popes, pontifical bishops, and their officers, themselves deserve a heavy censure. For they are profanations of the name of God, supports of an unjust government, and traps for other men's money. They are not spiritual remedies of sin.

29. Indulgences, commutations, and human transactions in those things for which Christ has ordained the discipline of the church are the profits of the great whore.

❦

XXXVIII

The Administration of the Covenant of Grace before the Coming of Christ

1. Although the free, saving covenant of God has been one and the same from the beginning, the manner of the application of Christ or the administration of the new covenant has not always been so. It has varied according to the times during which the church has been in process of being gathered.

2. In this variety there has always been a progression from the imperfect to the more perfect.

3. At first the mystery of the gospel was manifested in a general and obscure way and later more specifically and clearly.

4. The manner of administration of the covenant is twofold: One points to the Christ who will appear and the other to the Christ who has appeared.

5. The Old and New Testaments are reducible to these two primary heads. The Old promises Christ to come and the New testifies that he has come.

6. While Christ was still to appear, all things were more outward and carnal, afterwards more inward and spiritual. John 1:17, *The law was delivered by Moses; grace and truth came by Christ.*

7. The church then had a double aspect: first as an heir and second as a child. Gal. 4:1 ff., *So long as the heir is an infant he differs not at all from a servant, though he be lord of all.*

8. As an heir the church was free; as a child, in a certain way, not free, Gal. 4:1.

9. As an heir it was spiritual; as a child carnal and earthly, Heb. 9:10; Rom. 9:7.

10. As an heir it had the spirit of adoption, but as a child the spirit of fear and bondage. Rom. 8:15, *You have not received the spirit of bondage again to fear, but you have received the spirit of adoption.*

11. The manner of administration of the covenant, in respect to the coming of Christ, was one before Moses and another from Moses to Christ.

12. Before Moses the polity of the church was rude and loose, as it would be in its childhood. There were as many visible churches as there were families of godly people; the ministry was almost always an extraordinary one conducted by prophets. The masters of families and the firstborn had the right to administer certain holy things as ordinary ministers, according to the direction they received from the prophets.

13. And there was some difference of dispensation from Adam to Abraham from that of the time from Abraham to Moses.

14. From Adam to Abraham it should be noted, first, that redemption by Christ and the application of Christ was promised in general. It was to be carried out by the seed of the woman in order to banish the works of the devil, or sin and death. Gen. 3:15; Rom. 16:20; 1 John 3:8, *The seed of the woman shall break the serpent's head. The God of peace will tread Satan under your feet shortly. The Son of God was manifested to dissolve the works of the devil.*

15. Second, calling was evident in the distinction between the seed of the woman and the seed of the devil, and between the sons of God and the sons of men, Gen. 6:2. Third, the way of justification was set forth by expiatory sacrifices offered and accepted for sins. Eph. 5:2, *Christ loved us and gave himself for us, an offering and sacrifice to God for a sweet-smelling savor.*

16. Fourth, adoption was indicated both by the title of sons, common to all the faithful at that time, and by the translation of Enoch into the heavenly inheritance, Gen. 5:24; Heb. 11:5.

17. Fifth, sanctification was expressly taught by the prophets and foreshadowed by typical oblations and rites of sacrifice, Jude 14; Rom. 12.1.

18. Sixth, glorification was publicly sealed by the example of Enoch and the saving of Noah and his family from the flood. 1 Peter 3:20, 21.

19. In this period the building and saving of the ark in the flood was an extraordinary sacrament, Heb. 11:7; 1 Peter 3:20, 21. There was no ordinary sacrament in those times, but in many sacri-

fices there was something like a sacrament, for those who sacrificed commonly partook of a holy banquet at a holy place with joy before God in their sacrifices, Exod. 18:12. This sealed to them in a certain way the grace of the covenant which is present in the sacraments.

20. From the time of Abraham the church chiefly consisted of his family and his posterity.

21. At that time the benefits of the new covenant were all more clearly and distinctly witnessed to than before.

22. First, election was set forth in the persons of Isaac and Jacob who were beloved before Ishmael and Esau, Rom. 9:11–13.

23. Second, redemption along with its application was majestically shown in the person and blessing of Melchizedek — also in the promise and covenant of blessing to come to all nations from the seed of Abraham.

24. Third, a calling came in the leading of Abraham from Ur of Chaldees to a certain new and heavenly country, Heb. 11:8–10.

25. Fourth, justification was illustrated by the express testimony of God that faith was reckoned to Abraham for righteousness, as the father and pattern of all who should believe. The sacrament of circumcision was also given, which was the seal of that righteousness.

26. Fifth, adoption was declared by giving God's name to Abraham and all the sons of the promises, and by assigning the inheritance to the sons of the promises, the family of the free woman through grace, Gal. 4:26, 28, 31.

27. Sixth, sanctification was prefigured by circumcism, which stood for the taking away and abolishing of the corruption of sin and the old man so that a new creature might come in their places, Col. 2:11; Deut. 30:6.

28. Seventh, glorification was pointed to in the blessing promised in the land of Canaan, which was a type of the heavenly country.

29. From the time of Moses to Christ, these same things were further adumbrated by extraordinary and ordinary means.

30. Redemption and its application were extraordinary. They were signified, first, in the deliverance from Egypt through the ministry of Moses, who was a type of Christ, Matt. 2:15, and by the entrance into the land of Canaan through the ministry of Joshua, another type of Christ. Second, in the brass serpent, by looking at which men who were about to die were restored to health, John 3:14; 12:32. Third, in the cloud which shielded the Israelites from all injuries from enemies and from the sky. They also had light provided day and night, along with a refreshing of their strength, 1 Cor. 10:2; Isa. 4:4–5. Fourth, in the passing through the Red Sea where a way was opened to the land of promise, their enemies being overwhelmed and destroyed, 1 Cor. 10:2. Fifth, in the manna from heaven and the

water from the rock whence they received continual nourishment, so to speak, out of God's hand, 1 Cor. 10:3, 4; John 6:32, 33.

31. In the ordinary sense Christ and redemption were foreshadowed by the high priest, the altars, and sacrifices for sins.

32. Justification was shown in many sacrifices and ablutions and in the sacrament of the Passover.

33. Adoption was shown in the dedication of the firstborn to God.

34. Sanctification was set forth in all the offerings and gifts as well as in the observances which had anything to do with cleanliness.

35. Glorification was shown in the inheritance of the promised land and the communion which they had with God in the holy of holies.

36. The church of the Jews instituted by Moses, in point of external coming together, was only one because the whole solemn communion prescribed at that time depended upon one temple and was exercised by public profession and rites.

37. The synagogues were not complete churches, for the total worship of God and the whole sacred communion prescribed at that time could not be exercised in them.

38. Therefore, the church of the Jews was a national church—though in some respect catholic or universal, inasmuch as the believing proselytes of every nation under heaven were bound to join themselves to that one church, Acts 2:5, 6, 8–11; 8:27.

39. The primary ministers were the priest of the family of Aaron in a continued line of succession, and to them were joined the other Levites, Num. 3:6–10.

40. Yet neither priests nor Levites were allowed to minister unless they were first examined, and passed the tests in body, age, and gifts of the mind.

41. The ecclesiastical discipline of that time was ceremonial to a large extent, but sufficient to keep pure all holy things of every kind.

XXXIX

The Administration of the Covenant from the Coming of Christ to the End of the World

1. The manner of administration of the covenant, now Christ has appeared, is twofold: the one lasting until the end of the world and the other at the end itself.

2. From the time of Christ to the end of the world there is an ad-

ministration of one kind which is altogether new and is rightly called the New Testament.

3. It is of one kind without end or alteration because it is perfect; no other is to be expected to which it would give place as to the more perfect.

4. The testament is new in relation to what existed from the time of Moses and in relation to the promise made to the fathers. But it is new not in essence but in form. In the former circumstances the form of administration gave some evidence of the covenant of works, from which this testament is essentially different. Since the complete difference between the new covenant and the old appeared only in the administration which came after Christ, this administration is properly termed the covenant and testament which is new.

5. This differs also from the former administration in quality and quantity.

6. Its difference in quality is in clarity and freedom.

7. Clarity occurs, first in the more distinct expression than heretofore of the doctrine of grace and salvation through Christ and through faith in him (together with other kindred points of the doctrine). Second, it is expressed not in types and shadows, but in a most manifest fashion.

8. In both of these respects, Christ is said to have been set forth earlier under a veil but now to be offered with an open and unveiled face. 2 Cor. 3:12, *We use great evidence in speaking, being not like Moses who put a veil over his face so that the children of Israel could not see the end of that which was now taken away as unprofitable.*

9. Freedom comes, first, in doing away with government by law, or the intermixture of the covenant of works, which held the ancient people in a certain bondage. The spirit of adoption, though never wholly denied to believers, is also most properly said to be communicated under the New Testament, in which the perfect state for believers most clearly shines forth. Gal. 4:4, 5, *After the fullness of time came, God sent forth his Son . . . that we might receive the adoption of sons.* Second, the yoke of ceremonial law is taken away in that it was a mortgage bond held against sinners, forbade the use of some things in their nature indifferent, commanded many burdensome observances of other things of the same nature, and veiled the truth itself with many carnal ceremonies. Col. 2:17, *Which are a shadow of things to come, but the body is of Christ.*

10. Those who force upon the Christian churches Jewish ceremonies or other similar religious and mystical ceremonies offend against the liberty which Christ has obtained for us. Divine ceremonies were not suppressed in order that human ones might supplant them.

Nor is it likely that Christ would leave such mysteries to the will of men after his coming, when he permitted no such thing to his people before that. He might so easily have provided us religious and mystical ceremonies had he judged them necessary or profitable — that is, aside from the very few which he prescribed by name — or at least indicated in a last will to whom he granted such authority — but this he never did. Gal. 5:1, *Stand fast, therefore, in the liberty wherewith Christ has made you free and be not entangled with the yoke of bondage.*

11. In measure this administration differs from the former intensively and extensively.

12. It differs intensively, first, in that the application of the Spirit is more effectual and the gifts of the Spirit more perfect than they were ordinarily in the Old Testament. The old administration and the new are compared to each other as the letter and the Spirit, 2 Cor. 3:6. Second, the new administration produces a more spiritual life, 2 Cor. 3:18.

13. This administration differs extensively, first, in respect of place, because it is not confined to any one people as before, but is diffused through the whole world. It differs, second, in respect of time, since the duration of time before the consummation of the whole mystical church is not set. 2 Cor. 3:11; Eph. 4:13, *That which remains . . . until we all attain to . . . mature manhood, to the measure of the full stature of Christ.*

14. Since this new administration is so perfect, it follows that the communion of saints in the church instituted according to the New Testament should be most perfect.

15. Therefore, in every church of the New Testament the whole solemn and ordered worship of God and all his holy ordinances can and ought to be observed in such wise that all the members of that church may find their communion in them at the same time.

16. It was once ordained of God, in the church of the Jews, that certain more solemn parts of divine worship should be celebrated in one place and others in other places. This is no longer true, for one particular church is ordained in which all holy offices are to be performed.

17. Therefore, all Christian churches together have one and the same right. One no more depends upon another than another upon it.

18. It is, therefore, fitting that a particular church should not consist of more members than may meet together in one place to hear the word of God, celebrate the sacraments, offer prayers, exercise discipline, and perform other duties of divine polity as one body.

19. In some larger cities there are more believers than can hold communion together. It is a gross error leading to all sorts of confusion not to distribute them into several churches, but let them overrun one to such an extent that the edification of individuals cannot be rightly taken care of and furthered.

20. The instituted church since Christ has appeared is not one catholic church in the sense that all believers throughout the world are joined with each other in one and the same outward bond, depending upon one and the same visible pastor or company of pastors. Rather there are as many churches as there are companies or particular congregations of people professing the faith who are joined together in a special bond for the continual exercise of the communion of saints.

21. The mystical church, as it exists in its members, has its divisions and subdivisions, as we might speak of the church of Belgium, of Britain, or of France, much as we name the sea from the shores it washes, i.e., the Belgian, the British, and the French, though it is one and the same sea. Yet the instituted churches are several different species or individuals participating in the same common nature, like several fountains, schools, or families. Many or all might perhaps be called one church because of the quality they have in common, just as many families of a certain noble stock are often designated by the name of one family, such as the family of the House of Nassau.

22. The church instituted by God is not rightly national, provincial, or diocesan. These forms were introduced by man from the pattern of civil government, especially Roman. Rather, it is a parochial church or a church of one congregation; the members are united with each other and ordinarily meet in one place for the public exercise of religion.

23. Such a company and no larger one is properly signified by the word ἐκκλησία, or church; nor does the word have a broader meaning in the New Testament when it refers to a visible designated company. And so it is among more ancient profane authors.

24. Established congregations in the same country and province are, therefore, always called churches in the plural, never one church, even in Judea, which was once one national church, 1 Thess. 2:14; Acts 14:23; 15:41; Rom. 16:4, 5, 16; 1 Cor. 16:1, 19; 2 Cor. 8:1, 18, 19; Gal. 1:2, 22.

25. The particular churches mentioned in the New Testament were each accustomed to come together, ἐπὶ τὸ αὐτό, Acts 2:46; 5:12; 14:27; 15:25; 21:22; 1 Cor. 5:4; 14:23, 26; 11:17, 33.

26. Nothing is read in all the New Testament about the establishment of any larger church upon which lesser congregations depend.

Nor is any worship or holy ordinance prescribed which is not observed in each congregation. Neither is any ordinary minister ordained who is not committed to some one such company.

27. Yet particular churches, as their communion requires, and the light of nature and the rules of orderliness and examples from Scripture teach, may and often should enter into covenant relationship and mutual association in classes and synods in order to enjoy common agreement and mutual help as much as fitly may be, especially in matters of greater moment. But this combination does not constitute a new form of church nor ought it to take away or in any way diminish the freedom and authority which Christ has left to his churches. It should serve only to direct and promote that freedom and authority.

28. Ordinary ministers conform to the instituted church and are not ecumenical, national, provincial, or diocesan bishops, but rather elders of one congregation. In the same sense they are also called bishops in the Scriptures.

29. Those superior members of a hierarchy are merely human creations brought into the church without divine precept or example. They cannot fill the office of pastor in so many various congregations. They rob the churches of their liberty, while exercising a kind of regal or, rather, tyrannical dominion over them and their pastors. They have brought in with them the Roman Antichrist himself as the head, and as the tail of this wild beast the chancellors, suffragans, archdeacons, officials, and similar props of the hierarchy (whose very names are apocryphal and altogether unknown among the first churches) to the utter oppression of the churches of God.

30. The right of calling an ordinary minister is in the church itself which he must serve, Acts 14:23.

31. Yet the direction and help of the elders of the same church and usually of neighboring churches are needed.

32. The essence of the calling is in election by the church and acceptance by the one elected.

33. Preliminary to it comes an examination or test.

34. Consequent to it and consummating it comes ordination, which is nothing else than a solemn introduction of the minister already elected into the free execution of his responsibility. So it is that χειροτονία, the raising of hands to vote, and χειροθεσία, the laying on of hands, often mean the same thing among the ancients.

35. Episcopal ordination of a minister without title, i.e., without a church to which and in which he may be ordained is as ridiculous as trying to imagine a husband without a wife.

36. A minister called to one church cannot leave it of his choice nor be cast out without just cause. Neither can he undertake the like care

of another church or neglect that which he has undertaken by voluntary nonresidence without a sacrilegious breaking of his covenant.

37. Ordinary ministers are either pastors and teachers or ruling elders with whom are associated those who take care of the poor, namely, deacons, deaconesses, or widows.

38. By these offices Christ has sufficiently provided for all the necessities of the members of the church, so that they may be instructed in the knowledge of the truth especially by the teachers, stirred up to the practice of piety chiefly by the pastors, preserved in the course of life and called back to repentance for sins by them and the ruling elders, and helped in their poverty by the deacons.

XL

Baptism and the Lord's Supper

1. The sacraments of the New Testament follow from its nature. They are few in number, easy to prepare and observe, and very clear in their meaning.

2. They were sanctified and instituted by Christ himself. Although the one sacrament was first used by John the Baptist yet by that very fact he became the forerunner of Christ so that he might show that it did not become an ordered institution by the ministry of John but through the institution of Christ himself.

3. The sacraments are baptism and the Lord's Supper. No other sacraments or sacramental signs were delivered to the church by Christ or his apostles, nor can others be appointed by men in the church.

4. Because of God's institution it is of greatest necessity for believers to use these sacraments diligently and devoutly. But they are not so necessary to salvation that the absence or mere lack of them deprives one of salvation. Given the institution, they are not to be celebrated by any who are not lawful ministers or who are outside of a church assembly.

5. Baptism is the sacrament of initiation or regeneration.

6. Although it seals the whole covenant of grace to all believers, when it is specially made our own, it represents and confirms our very ingrafting into Christ. Rom. 6:3, 5, *We have been baptized into Christ Jesus . . . being planted together with him;* 1 Cor. 12:13, *We have been baptized into one body.*

7. From the time of our first ingrafting into Christ by faith a relationship of justification and adoption is entered into. As the sacra-

ment of that ingrafting, baptism stands for the remission of sins, Mark 1:4. And it stands, also, for adoption in that we are consecrated by it to the Father, Son, and Holy Spirit, whose names are pronounced over the baptized.

8. And because holiness always comes from Christ into whom we are ingrafted, to all the faithful, baptism is also the seal of sanctification. Titus 3:5, *He has saved us . . . by the washing of regeneration and the renewing of the Holy Spirit*; Rom. 6:4–6.

9. And since glorification cannot be separated from true holiness it is at the same time the seal of eternal glory, Titus 3:7, *That we might . . . be made heirs, according to the hope of eternal life*; Rom. 6:8, *If we are dead with Christ, we believe that we shall also live together with him.*

10. Because those benefits are sealed by initiation in baptism, it should be noted, first, that baptism is only to be administered once. There is only one beginning of spiritual life by rebirth as there is but one beginning of natural life by birth.

11. Second, baptism ought to be administered to all those in the covenant of grace, because it is the first sealing of the covenant now first entered into.

12. The infants of believers are not to be forbidden this sacrament. First, because, if they are partakers of any grace, it is by virtue of the covenant of grace and so both the covenant and the first seal of the covenant belong to them. Second, the covenant in which the faithful are now included is clearly the same as the covenant made with Abraham, Rom. 4:11; Gal. 3:7–9 — and this expressly applied to infants. Third, the covenant as now administered to believers brings greater and fuller consolation than it once could, before the coming of Christ. But if it pertained only to them and not to their infants, the grace of God and their consolation would be narrower and more contracted after Christ's appearing than before. Fourth, baptism supplants circumcision, Col. 2:11, 12; it belongs as much to the children of believers as circumcision once did. Fifth, in the very beginning of regeneration, whereof baptism is a seal, man is merely passive. Therefore, no outward action is required of a man when he is baptized or circumcised (unlike other sacraments); but only a passive receiving. Infants are, therefore, as capable of participation in this sacrament, so far as its chief benefit is concerned, as adults.

13. Faith and repentance no more constitute the covenant of God now than in the time of Abraham, who was the father of the faithful. Therefore, the lack of these ought not to prevent infants from being baptized any more than it prevented them from being circumcised then.

14. The sign of this sacrament is water, not in itself but in cleansing the unclean by immersing or sprinkling.

15. Water was chosen because nothing in common use more fitly represents the spiritual washing performed by the blood or the death of Christ, nor is the sprinkling or application of the blood of Christ more fitly expressed by anything. For since Christ's death there should be no use of natural blood in holy things.

16. The Lord's Supper is the sacrament of nourishment and growth for the faithful in Christ.

17. It should, therefore, be administered to them often.

18. But the Supper is to be administered only to those who are visibly capable of nourishment and growth in the church. Therefore, it is to be given not to infants, but only to adults.

19. Because the fullest and most perfect nourishment is sealed in Christ, no single, simple sign of nourishing is to be used but a double kind — bread and wine, such as the body requires for its nourishment.

20. Those who take away either of these signs from the faithful in the administration of the Supper take away from the wisdom of God, mutilate the institution of Christ, and grievously lessen or take away the consolation of the faithful.

21. Bread and wine are to be used, for nothing more fitly expresses the very close union we gradually come to enjoy with Christ, a union founded on the sacrifice of his body and the shedding of his blood. This use is closest to the eating of flesh and the drinking of blood, which have no place in holy things now that Christ's sacrifice is accomplished — for eating flesh and drinking blood are abhorred not only by religion but by man's nature.

22. To pretend any transubstantiation or consubstantiation in this sacrament is, more than in baptism, a kind of blind and stupid superstition.

23. The spiritual nourishment in this sacrament does not require that the bread and wine be changed into the body and blood of Christ, or that Christ be corporally present with them. It is required only that they be changed in their application and use, and that Christ be spiritually present with those who receive them in faith.

24. Transubstantiation and consubstantiation are contrary to the nature of sacraments in general, contrary to the meaning of our other sacrament, or baptism, contrary to the most used phrases in the Old Testament, contrary to the human nature of Christ, contrary to his state of glorification, and to the revealed will of God who has declared that Christ shall remain in heaven until the day of judgment.

25. The words of institution, "This is my body," must be under-

stood, like other sacramental phrases encountered everywhere in the Holy Scriptures of which God himself is the clear interpreter. Gen. 17:10, 11, *This is my covenant . . . that it may be a sign of the covenant between me and you.*

26. As far as studied interpretation goes, learned men differ over the meaning of the phrase. Most of our interpreters see in it a figure of speech, that is, a metaphor or metonymy.

27. The Lutherans contend that there is no figure to be found here but only an unusual predicate.

28. Not a few contemporary interpreters say that there is here neither any proper figure nor an unusual predicate. They see rather a mystical predicate, not a proper one.

29. But no sufficient reason is advanced why we should deny that there is a figure in the words. This may be demonstrated as follows. If the predicate were an unusual or not a proper predicate, as they would have it, this unusual or not proper meaning would have to be shown in some word. If this were done, then necessarily that word would be transferred in some way out of its natural meaning and use: And if that happened, the word itself would take on the nature and definition of a figure.

30. No figure is found either in the antecedent *this*, nor in the proper copula, or the word *is*. The figure is in the consequent, namely, the word *body*, which is put for a sign of the body. This does not exclude a true and proper body from the sentence, but rather includes it by the relation which the sign has to the thing signified.

31. There is not only one figure but a threefold one in this word. The first is a metaphor wherein one like thing is put for another; a metonymy of the adjunct is also connected and compounded with this. For the bread is not only like the body of Christ, but also, by God's institution, adjoined to it. The second is a synecdoche of the part for the whole, in which the body of Christ is put for the whole Christ. The third is a metonymy of the subject for the adjuncts, because Christ is put for all the benefits derived from him to us. In the second part, the wine, there are also other figures sufficiently clear.

⟶◦◦⟨◦⟩◦◦⟵

XLI

The End of the World

1. So far we have considered the administration of the covenant before the end of the world. In that end, the application which has only been begun in this life will be perfected.

2. Then the end of calling will be reached by all who are called, for we are called to the eternal glory of God, 1 Peter 5:10. In this the end of faith, or the salvation of souls, is also said to be contained, 1 Peter 1:9.

3. That declaration of justification and redemption which is shown in their effects will then be completed; in this life the faithful are said only to await redemption, Luke 21:18; Rom. 8:23; Eph. 1:14.

4. Then all the adopted will enter into the possession of their inheritance; in this sense the faithful in this life are said to wait for adoption, Rom. 8:23.

5. Then the image of God will be perfected in all the sanctified. Eph. 5:27, *That he might present the church to himself glorious, not having spot or wrinkle or any such thing, that she might be holy and without fault.*

6. Then finally the glory and blessedness hoped for will shine forth in all fullness, not only in the soul but also in the very body. Phil. 3:21, *He shall transfigure our humble body that it may be made conformable to his glorious body.*

7. Because the state of the church then will be one of perfection and not of edification, the ministry, sacraments, and discipline together with the instituted churches themselves will cease, and the mystical church will remain in immediate communion with God.

8. Hence the end of the world should be awaited with all longing by all believers. Phil. 3:20; Titus 2:13, *We expect the savior, Jesus Christ. Expecting that blessed hope and that glorious coming of the glory of the great God and our savior.*

9. This final perfection of administration requires the coming and personal presence of Christ himself, Acts 10:42.

10. The second coming of Christ will be like the first in that it shall be real, visible, and apparent, Acts 1:11. But it will be dissimilar in that: First, it will be attended with greatest glory and power, Matt. 24:30; Titus 2:13; second, it will dispense the greatest terror among the ungodly and the greatest joy among the godly, 2 Thess. 1:7–10.

11. Two events, the resurrection and the last judgment, will finally distinguish between the godly and the ungodly, 2 Cor. 5:10.

12. Resurrection relates to what has fallen. Because man fell from life by the separation of soul from body, it is necessary for his rising again that the same soul be reunited to the same body and that the same man exist in the restored union of the two.

13. That such a resurrection is possible for God appears from the fact that the restoration of a man requires no more power than was manifested in his first creation. Phil. 3:21, *According to that effectual power whereby he is able to subdue all things to himself.*

14. That the resurrection will actually come about cannot be surely demonstrated by any natural reason, *a priori* or *a posteriori* — it is properly a matter of faith.

15. Neither the nature of the soul nor of the body can be the cause of resurrection, for the forming again and raising of the body out of dust is against the accustomed course of nature, for when nature is completely destroyed it is not wont to be restored. The inseparable union of the soul with the body by which man becomes immortal is beyond the powers of nature.

16. Therefore, the raising of the dead properly belongs to Christ, εάνθρωπος, the God-man. The operating principle is Christ's divine omnipotence by which it may be easily accomplished, even in an instant.

17. The role of the angels will not properly be to raise the dead, but to gather the parts to be raised and to assemble the saints when raised.

18. Although all will be raised by Christ, it will not all happen in one and the same way. The resurrection of the faithful is to life and is accomplished by virtue of the union which they have with Christ who is their life (Col. 3:4; 1 Thess. 4:14) and by the operation of his quickening Spirit which lives in them. Rom. 8:11, *He . . . shall also quicken your mortal bodies by his Spirit dwelling in you.* But the resurrection of the others is through that power of Christ by which he will execute avenging justice.

19. Therefore, the resurrection of the faithful is from the life of Christ as the beginning of their own life as the fruit and effect. It is, therefore, called the resurrection of life. The raising up of the others is from the sentence of death and condemnation, which leads to true death and condemnation, and is, therefore, called the resurrection of condemnation, John 5:28, 29.

20. The last judgment is exercised by Christ as king, for the power of judging is part of the office of a king.

21. For the faithful, it comes from grace and is a function of the kingship of grace essential in Christ the mediator. For the ungodly it

is, strictly speaking, a function only of power and dominion, granted by the Father for a certain perfection of mediation, but not essential to it.

22. The sins of the faithful will not come into judgment. In this life they are covered and taken away by the sentence of justification; the last judgment will be a confirmation and manifestation of that sentence. It would not be right that they should again be brought to light.

23. The place of this judgment will be in the air, 1 Thess. 4:17.

24. The day and year of it is not revealed in Scripture and, therefore, cannot be fixed by men.

25. The sentence, to be carried out immediately, will be to eternal life or death, according to the works that have preceded.

26. The sentence to life for the elect will be given according to their works, not as meritorious causes but as effects testifying to the true causes.

27. The sentence to death for reprobates will be given according to their works as true causes.

28. Christ, θεάνθρωπος, the God-man, is the judge — a deputy, as it were — but because of his divine authority and power, upon which depends the strength of the sentence, he is the principal judge.

29. The faithful will also judge with Christ, assisting not consulting, approving by their judgment and will as well as by a comparison of their life and works.

30. Judgment will be rendered not only on wicked men but also on evil angels. The raising up and judging of wicked men by Christ no more argues the universal redemption of such men than it does that of devils.

31. The fire that is destined to purge and renew the world will not precede the judgment but shall follow.

32. Purgatory is no more necessary before the day of judgment than after. Since, by confession of the papists themselves, it will not exist afterwards, it does not exist before.

33. The elements will not be taken away, but changed.

34. After the day of judgment Christ will remain king and mediator forever.

BOOK II

I

Observance in General

We have considered the first part of theology, or faith in God; now we consider observance toward God, the remaining part.

1. Observance [*observantia*] is the submissive performance of the will of God for the glory of God.

2. It holds the will of God as a pattern and a rule, as shown by the words of Christ which both describe our observance, *Thy will be done on earth as it is in heaven*, and explain his own, *Not as I will, but as thou wilt. . . . let thy will be done*, Matt. 6:10; 26:39, 42. So Ps. 40:8, *I delight to do thy will, O my God; and thy law is within my heart.*

3. Observance takes the will of God not as a secret, effectual, or-daining power — for all creatures, including ungodly men and even devils, do the will of God with an obedience common to all of them. It is concerned rather with the will of God which prescribes our duty, Deut. 29:29, *Things that are revealed have been revealed that we may do them.*

4. It means that our will is *Submissive*, Rom. 8:7. Observance applies our will to accomplish the will of God, commanding in accord with his authority. Rom. 8:7, *The mind set on flesh is not subject to the law of God.*

5. It is called obedience when will is made ready to bring the command of God, which has been heard or in some way perceived, into execution.

6. It is connected with service towards God, whence it is that *Obeying God and serving him* are one and the same thing, Luke 1:74. And to serve God is the same as *Serving in obedience and righteousness*, Rom. 6:16, 18, 22. To do the will of God submissively is to serve God. Eph. 6:6, 7, *As servants of Christ, doing the will of God from the heart, rendering service with good will as to the Lord.*

7. Although our obedience towards God as readiness of mind ought

219

to be the obedience of sons, as the strict duty of submission it is the obedience of servants.

8. From this submission to the will of God comes a necessary conformity between the will of God and ours. Rev. 2:6, *This you have, that you hate the deeds of the Nicolaitans, which I also hate.* And so that clear kind of image of divine perfection which God has revealed, he has set forth to be imitated by us. 2 Peter 1:4, *That we might be made partakers of the divine nature.* John 3:21, *For he who does the truth . . . his works are done according to God.*

9. Hence the same observance which is called *Obedience* in respect of submission to the will of God, and *Righteousness* in that it puts the submission owed into effect, is also called *Holiness* because it takes the pure form and shape of that will. 1 Peter 1:14, 15, *As obedient children . . . as he that has called you is holy, you also be holy in all conversation.*

10. Observance looks to the glory of God. *Do all to the glory of God,* 1 Cor. 10:31 — acknowledge his supreme authority and commanding power (1 Cor. 6:20, *You are bought with a price. Therefore glorify God*) and be related to and represent in part the perfection of God. *Set forth his virtues,* 1 Peter 2:9, in the manifestation of which, glory may be given him by us.

11. In submission there is a kind of reverent fear as the authority and power of God is acknowledged. Therefore, fear of the Lord is often put in Scripture for whole obedience. Ps. 34:11, *I will teach you the fear of the Lord.*

12. It is said to be towards God, for he is at once its standard, its object, and end.

13. The principal efficient cause of observance as an inner, abiding principle is indirectly faith and directly sanctifying grace.

14. For faith prepares a way for us to God (*Let us draw nigh . . . by assurance of faith,* Heb. 10:22) and the power to take that way (2 Cor. 1:24, *By faith you stand*). Observance is, therefore, called *The obedience of faith,* Rom. 1:5. And the faithful are called *The children of obedience,* 1 Peter 1:14.

15. Faith brings forth obedience in three ways. First, it apprehends Christ who is the fountain of life and the spring of all power to do well; second, it receives and acquiesces in the arguments which God has set forth in Scripture to induce obedience, namely, promises and threatenings; third, it has power to obtain all grace, especially that grace which occasions obedience.

16. Sanctifying grace is the very power by which we are lifted up to accommodate our will to the will of God. New obedience is, therefore,

always included and understood in the Scripture when mention is made of the new man and the new creature, Eph. 4:24; Gal. 6:15.

17. For since sin came, man cannot of himself do anything acceptable to God, any work of spiritual life, except it be done in Christ through faith and sanctifying grace. John 15:4, 5, *Without me you can do nothing.*

18. Yet these duties are not to be omitted by a man who does not yet believe, for they are good in themselves — they impede the increase both of sin and the punishment of sinners and they are often recompensed with various benefits from God. This happens not through any fixed law of God but through his abundant and secret kindness.

19. The contributory, moving cause has many parts. First, the dignity and majesty of God which is to be respected in itself. Deut. 32:3, *Ascribe greatness to our God;* Ps. 29:2, *Give unto the Lord the glory of his name.* Second, the kindness of God towards us for which we owe him whatever is in us. 1 Cor. 6:19–20, *You should know that you are not your own but are God's;* Rom. 12:1, *By the mercies of God.* Thus, our observance is nothing else than gratitude owed to God, and is rightly explained by theologians under that title. Third, the authority of a commanding God which has universal and full dominion over us. Jas. 4:12, *There is one lawgiver who can save and destroy.* Fourth, the justice and usefulness of the things commanded, which also are in closest agreement with reason. Rom. 2:15, *Their conscience together bearing witness.* This makes for our perfection and blessedness, as put in Deut. 32:47, *It is your life.* Fifth, the reward and promises by which obedience is induced. 2 Cor. 7:1, *Seeing we have these promises . . . let us purify ourselves.* Sixth, the misery incurred by those who do otherwise. Deut. 28:16; Heb. 12:29, *Cursed shall you be. . . . For our God is a consuming fire.*

20. Obedience is the crucial thing commanded by God and is summarily contained in the decalogue. Otherwise, the law of God would not be perfect.

21. The law of God might seem to be, as it were, abrogated among the faithful, since it does not have the justifying power it had in the original state of integrity nor the condemning power it had in the state of sin. But it does have the force and vigor of a directing power; and it also retains a certain force of condemnation, for it reproves and condemns sin in the faithful (although it cannot wholly condemn the faithful themselves because they are not under the law but under grace).

22. The form of observance is our conformity to the will of God,

which has been revealed in order that we may do it. Mic. 6:8, *He has showed you, O man, what is good.*

23. The standard of our obedience is neither the secret will of God nor his every revelation (for Jeroboam sinned in taking the kingdom of Israel, though the prophet told him that God willed it in some way, 1 Kings 11:31, 2 Chron. 13:5–7). It is rather to be understood as the will prescribing our duty which is revealed for the purpose of our doing it.

24. The will of God in this sense is said to be *Good, perfect, and acceptable to God,* Rom. 12:2. It is good because it is worthy in every respect; perfect, because nothing can be sought further for the instruction of life; acceptable to God, because obedience according to this will is approved and crowned by God.

25. Knowledge of this will is necessary for true obedience. Prov. 4:13, 19, *Take hold of instruction and let her not go; keep her, for she is your life. The way of the wicked is like darkness; they do not know over what they stumble.* Therefore, zeal for knowing this will of God is commanded us along with obedience itself. Prov. 5:1, *Attend to wisdom, incline your ear to understanding.* These words apply especially when practice is considered, just as on the contrary all ignorance of what we are commanded to know and do is sin. 2 Thess. 1:8, *Inflicting vengeance on those who know not God and . . . obey not the gospel of our Lord Jesus Christ.*

26. The knowledge of the will of God should be accompanied in this life by dread, a fear of transgressing it. Prov. 8:12, 13, 14, 16, *I, wisdom, have with me the fear of the Lord. The wise man fears and departs from evil.* This is chiefly fear of the offense, but it is also fear of God's anger and the punishment especially of the kind which is separation from God. Such fear cannot be called servile since more than punishment causes it.

27. The primary end is God's glory, for by observance we tend toward him upon whom we lean in faith. Otherwise, observance could not flow from faith. Since faith is our spiritual life, joining us to God in Christ, the actions of faith which are part of observance must also be carried to God, that is, to his glory.

28. The subordinate end is our own salvation and blessedness. Rom. 6:22, *Being made servants to God you have your fruit in holiness and your end in eternal life;* Heb. 12:2, *For the joy that was set before him he endured the cross.*

29. Obedience given only out of fear of punishment or expectation of reward is rightly called mercenary; yet it is not strange for the sons of God nor does it in any way weaken their filial obedience when they

are secondarily roused to duty out of consideration of reward or fear
of punishment.

30. Our observance is not the chief or meritorious cause of eternal
life. For by grace we receive both the right to this life and also the
life itself as a gift of God through Christ apprehended by faith. Rom.
6:23, *The . . . gift of God is eternal life in Jesus Christ our Lord.*
Yet our obedience is in a certain way the ministering, helping, or fur-
thering cause of possessing this life (the right to which we have already been given), and in this sense it is called the way by which we
walk to heaven, Eph. 2:10.

31. It furthers our life because of its own nature which always tends
toward perfection and is thus a kind of step toward that life itself,
and also because God has promised eternal life to those who walk in
his precepts. Gal. 6:8, *He who sows to the Spirit shall reap eternal
life from the Spirit.*

32. Although our obedience while we live here is imperfect and defiled with a mixture of sin (Gal. 5:17, *The flesh lusts against the
Spirit*), yet in Christ it is made acceptable to God so that it is crowned
with greatest reward.

33. Therefore, the promises made to the faithful for their obedience
are not legal, but evangelical (although they are called something of
both by some), Matt. 5:3.

34. The mode of obedience is submission or humility, broadly assumed, by which the creature submits to God to receive and execute
his commands. This should always be accompanied by sincerity in
which every combination of deviating intention or affection is removed
so that the whole man is applied to his duty, 1 Thess. 5:23; 1 Cor.
6:20; and by zeal, or an intensity of pure affection, Gal. 4:18, *It is
always a good thing to love fervently for a good purpose.*

35. The principal subject of observance is the will, as it is in living
faith. Phil. 2:13, *It is God that works in you, both to will and to do.*

36. The sincerity of an approving will appears most in a readiness
of mind — or an eagerness or cheerfulness. Such eagerness is the very
essence of observance. 2 Cor. 9:7; Deut. 28:47, *God loves a cheerful
giver. Because you did not serve your God in joy and cheerfulness of
heart.* Although a proposed work may not be performed, the eagerness
is often pleasing and acceptable to God. 2 Cor. 8:12, *For if there be
first a ready mind, one is accepted according to what one has.*

37. As the zeal of the will consists chiefly in love and hatred, observance acceptable to God is found in a love of good and a hatred of
evil. Ps. 45:7, *Thou hast loved righteousness and hated iniquity.*

38. The effect and fruit of observance is not only a declaration but

also a confirmation of faith and hope. 1 Tim. 1:19, *Keeping faith and a good conscience which, being put away, some have made a shipwreck of faith.*

39. The corollary is a quiet, joyful, and glorifying conscience. Heb. 13:18; 2 Cor. 1:12; 1 John 3:19–21, *For we trust that we have a good conscience, desiring to conduct ourselves well in all things. Our glorifying is the testimony of our conscience. . . . By which we shall assure our hearts.*

II

Virtue

1. There are two elements in observance: virtue and virtuous action. 2 Peter 1:5, 8, *Add virtue to your faith. . . . For if these things are with you and abound, you will become neither barren nor unfruitful in the knowledge of our Lord Jesus Christ.*

2. The division is one of the whole into members, for these two are joined together in their own nature and produce one and the same observance.

3. Thus both virtues and actions are set forth by the same name and are defined in the same way. They are of the same nature just as arguments of logic have the same name and nature whether they are considered alone and by themselves, or in axioms and syllogisms.

4. Virtue is a condition or habit [*habitus*] by which the will is inclined to do well.

5. It is called a habit not to separate it from disposition and to signify a confirmed and perfect constitution of mind, for such a degree of virtue is seldom granted to men in this life. It is called a habit because it is in general a state of mind of various degrees of perfection.

6. It is called a habit not only because one possesses it but also because it makes the subject behave in a certain manner, i.e., it moves the faculty, which otherwise would not be so moved, toward good. In this sense the word is found in Heb. 5:14, *Those who by reason of habit have their senses conditioned to discern good and evil.*

7. It is located in the will for these reasons. First, the will is the true subject of theology since it is the true beginning of life and of moral and spiritual action. Second, the will is that faculty which is truly carried toward a worthy good, Rom. 7:19, 21. Third, virtue is a προαιρετικός, an elective habit, whose direct function is voluntary choice. Fourth, the will commends the other faculties, and so virtue

especially belongs to it that all may be directed correctly. Fifth, the will is not sufficient for good actions, either by itself or with the help of reason, and so it needs its own internal disposition to work correctly. Sixth, the other faculties are subject to outside compulsion and, if virtue were to have its own fixed position in them, one might lose it whether he willed to or not. Seventh, praise is most properly due the actions of the will and those operations of the other faculties which come from and depend upon the will; but only virtue is praiseworthy, as taught not only by the philosophers but also the Apostle. Phil. 4:8, *If there be any virtue, if there be any praise.* Eighth, the understanding cannot be the subject of virtue because intellectual habits, though most perfect, do not make a man good; nor can any sensory appetite be the subject because true virtue is found in the angels whose souls are separated from bodies, thus being void of appetite. But the sensory faculty often possesses some dispositions which make it possible for the will commanding rightly to be more easily obeyed; and so these dispositions partly resemble virtue.

8. Virtue is said to incline towards good. It is distinguished from a vicious habit which inclines men towards evil, Rom. 7:17, 20, 23. It is also distinguished from the perfections of the mind which surely bring light whereby the will may direct itself toward welldoing, but which do not incline it to do right.

9. Therefore, true and solid virtues always make the man good in whom they dwell — not that the very dispositions inhering in us are themselves the grace making us acceptable to God, as the schoolmen say (for that pertains to faith). The dispositions become part of a good man and goodness is thus derived from them into our actions.

10. Hence, virtue as the beginning of action cannot be abused, but men may and do abuse any other possession of the mind.

11. Therefore, those virtues often called intellectual do not have the true meaning of virtue.

12. Then it is said that virtue inclines not only to good but also to doing well; such action is the principal result of virtue.

13. But as with the standard of well-doing so it is with the standard of virtue, namely, that the sole rule in all matters which have to do with the direction of life is the revealed will of God.

14. Aristotle holds to the Lesbian or crooked law that the judgment of prudent men is the rule for virtue. But there are nowhere such wise men under whose judgment we might always stand and, even if there were, they could not always be known or consulted by the would-be virtuous.

15. What is called right reason, if it is to lead to absolute rectitude, is nowhere else to be discovered than where it is — in the Scriptures.

It does not differ from the will of God revealed for the direction of our life. Ps. 119:66, *Teach me the excellency of reason and knowledge for I believe your precepts*. When the imperfect notions about honesty and dishonesty found in man's mind after the fall are truly understood, they will be seen to be incapable of shaping virtue. They do not differ a whit from the written law of God except that they are imperfect and obscure.

16. Therefore, there can be no other teaching of the virtues than theology which brings the whole revealed will of God to the directing of our reason, will, and life.

17. They who think differently have no reasons which move an understanding and sound man. They hold that the end of theology is the good of grace and the end of ethics is moral or civil good (as if no moral or civil good were in any way spiritual or the good of grace). This is to say that the proper good, blessedness, or end of man is not a single good, and that a man's virtue does not lead him to his end and chief good. They say that theology is concerned with the inward affections of men and ethics with outward manners — as if ethics, which they consider the prudence which governs the will and appetite, had nothing to do with inward affections, and theology did not teach outward as well as inward obedience. They also hold that ethics terminate within the bounds of this life and that theology extends into the future — as if the blessed life were not one, or as if for one and the same life there were one rule for the present and another for the future. They say that the subject of ethics is a good, honest, honorable man and the subject of theology is a godly and religious man. But the Apostle expressly teaches that theology instructs us to live not only piously and righteously but also temperately and justly, or honestly and honorably, Titus 2:12. Consider also that the most eager defenders of this contrary opinion acknowledge and contend that moral virtues are the image of God in man and are thus, to a degree, theological virtues, and that moral virtue can be compared to spiritual as warmth to heat or morning light to noonday light. It follows that just as warmth and heat and morning and noonday light are considered to be of the same character, so also moral and spiritual must be.

18. Therefore, the judgment and desire of that greatest master of the arts, Peter Ramus, was no less pious than prudent: "If I could wish for what I wanted, I had rather that philosophy were taught to children out of the gospel by a learned theologian of proved character than out of Aristotle by a philosopher. A child will learn many impieties from Aristotle which, it is to be feared, he will unlearn too late. He will learn, for example, that the beginning of blessedness arises out of man; that the end of blessedness lies in man; that all virtues are

within man's power and obtainable by man's nature, art, and industry; that God is never present in such works, either as helper or author, however great and divine they are; that divine providence is removed from the theater of human life; that not a word can be spoken about divine justice; that man's blessedness is based on this frail life." [11]

19. The same habit which is called virtue in that it inclines towards God in this way is also called a gift, for it is given by God and inspired by the Holy Spirit. And it is called grace because it is freely bestowed on us by the special favor of God. Because of its perfection, together with the profit and delight it brings, it is called fruit. It is called blessedness by some because of the hope it brings of life eternal.

20. Those who make seven gifts of the Spirit out of Isa. 11:2 weary themselves in vain. *Upon him shall the spirit of the Lord rest, the spirit of wisdom and understanding, the spirit of counsel and might, the spirit of knowledge and the fear of the Lord.* They carefully distinguish these gifts from virtues and busy themselves demonstrating the analogy between each one and some virtue. Certainly there are more than seven gifts of the Spirit, although there are no more mentioned here (and indeed, only six); in this passage only the most kingly and important gifts are remembered, Christ himself being spoken of here, with other gifts understood by synecdoche. The gifts mentioned are not to be distinguished essentially from virtues, but by metonymy they involve all virtues as their causes.

21. The χαρίσματα, or gifts, mentioned in 1 Cor. 12:4 are distinguished essentially from virtues, yet grace, when it stands for an inherent perfection in us, denotes either some one virtue or all virtues together at their root, so to speak.

22. Likewise it is in vain to take twelve fruits of the Spirit from Gal. 5:22, 23. *The fruit of the Spirit is love, joy, peace, long-suffering, kindness, goodness, faith, meekness, temperance* — together with the additions made in the Vulgate translation. These are compared to virtues in the same way as the gifts mentioned above. But the fruits of the Holy Spirit set forth in these circumstances and in this passage given the names of the virtues themselves (for virtues are fruits such as are sought and expected by the farmer, corresponding to the kind of seed sown and bringing with them profit and delight when they appear) are not the only ones. This figure points to virtues and what

11. *Petri Rami Veromandui pro philosophica Parisiensis academiae disciplina oratio, ad Carolum Lotharinguum Cardinalem* (Parisiis, 1551), or *An Oration by the French Belgian Peter Ramus on Behalf of the Philosophical Training at the University of Paris, Delivered to Charles Cardinal Lorraine,* p. 40. See also Frank P. Graves, *Peter Ramus and the Educational Reformation of the Sixteenth Century* (Macmillan, New York, 1912), pp. 174–75. On Ramus' importance for Ames, see Introduction, pp. 37–47.

they do in a certain way in relation to God, though the profit is chiefly in relation to us, and it is for this reason that holiness with all the virtues is called not only a fruit of the Holy Spirit but also our fruit, Rom. 6:22. This profit together with the delight are shown in the passage to the Galatians where joy and peace are counted the fruit of fruits.

23. The same reasoning is used by those who think they have found eight beatitudes in the sermon of Christ, Matt. 5. There is but one beatitude, but since it has many signs, all of which are true virtues, the Lord notes certain individual virtues or results of virtues which most agree to his kingdom and are in a way alien to human ideas. In part he urges them as promising blessedness and in part he describes blessedness or blessed men as those who strive after and profess them.

24. The common expressions [*affectiones*] of virtue are the four which are usually called cardinal virtues.

25. But these do not constitute four kinds of virtues, as conceived by many who have done manifest violence to both virtue and reason by referring artificially all individual virtues to these heads. Rather, they are four conditions necessarily required in the disposition that deserves the name of virtue.

26. The first of these is justice. The meaning is in the general sense of an inclination to act rightly by giving every man his own; it may be called the rectitude of virtue. There is a description of virtue set forth by the Apostle in a congeries in Phil. 4:8, *Whatsoever things are true, whatsoever things are honest, whatsoever things are just, whatsoever things are pure, whatsoever things are lovely, whatsoever things are of good report, if there be any virtue, any praise.* Although truth, justice, and purity are virtues of one and the same nature, justice most intimately describes the essence of it.

27. The second is prudence whereby all the force of reason is used to find out what is right and to apply the means of reason rightly. It alone discerns those things which belong to doing right and possesses the force of understanding, knowledge, and wisdom. All those perfections of the mind usually called intellectual virtues in this sense belong to virtue for they direct the will to do right.

28. In the Scriptures prudence is called spiritual understanding and wisdom, Col. 1:9; understanding here appears to describe a general comprehension of good and evil; and wisdom the same comprehension as it applies to individual things considered in the circumstances by which they are surrounded. Understanding says, as it were, "It is right"; and wisdom, "It is expedient" (according to the distinction made in 1 Cor. 6:12 and 10:23). Foolishness is opposed to this. Eph.

5:17, *Be not therefore unwise, but rather understanding what the will of the Lord is.* Ignorance is also opposed to it. Eph. 4:18, *Being strangers from the life of God by reason of their ignorance.* Prudence is also called judgment, 1 Cor. 2:15, and discerning, Phil. 1:9, to which is opposed vanity of mind, Eph. 4:17, and a mind devoid of all judgment, Rom. 1:28.

29. This prudence should be exercised, first, with circumspection, caution, and due diligence, which the Scriptures often commend under the name of watchfulness. Mark 13:33, *Take heed, watch and pray.* Opposed to this is the sleepiness which is said to have seized the foolish virgins, Matt. 25:5, 13. Second, with choices made in due perspective so that the greater duties may be preferred to the lesser and in every duty the proper measure of desire and intensity of strength may be brought to bear. Matt. 6:33; 1 Cor. 12:31; and 14:1, *Seek first the kingdom of God and its righteousness. . . . Desire the greater gifts. . . . Especially that you may prophesy.*

30. The third general expression of virtue is fortitude, which is a firm persistence in doing right, meeting and overcoming all the difficulties which may come about either from the continuation of the required act or from any other kind of obstacle. This virtue is designated in Hebrew by the word, חִיל, or might, even when it is ascribed to women, Prov. 31:10. A mighty strengthening is required in every virtue, Eph. 3:16. Therefore, it contains, first, a confidence commended in Acts 4:29, to which fear is opposed. Phil. 1:14, *They dare to speak the word without fear.* Second, perseverance and constancy. Rev. 2:26, *Whoever shall overcome and keep my works to the end.* To this is opposed any weakening of the spirit and weariness in welldoing. 2 Thess. 3:13; Gal. 6:9; Heb. 12:3, 12, *Let us not be weary. Be not weary. Lest you faint in your minds. Raise up weak hands and feeble knees.* Third, it contains endurance and patience. Jas. 5:7, 8; Heb. 10:36, *Have a patient mind and establish your hearts. . . . For you have need of patience.*

31. The fourth expression is temperance, or the assuaging and restraining of all those desires which divert men from well-doing. Temperance is that which keeps virtue uncontaminated. 2 Tim. 2:4, *No one who makes war implicates himself;* 1 Peter 1:13, *Gird up the loins of your mind, be sober.* In the Scriptures it is often called sobriety in a general sense, 1 Peter 1:13; 5:8. Sometimes *Purity or cleanness of heart,* 1 Tim. 1:5; 1 Peter 2:22. It is also called sincerity, meaning the exclusion of any polluted mixture. The force of this is shown in 2 Cor. 1:12, *With simplicity and godly sincerity, not with carnal wisdom.*

32. Of these four conditions the first orders and constitutes virtue, so to speak; the second directs it and frees it from error; the third

strengthens it against misfortune; the fourth makes it pure and defends it against all allurements.

33. All these expressions appear to be prescribed and explained together and almost by name in 2 Peter 1:5, 6. *Add to faith virtue* (i.e., justice or a universal rightness), *to virtue knowledge* (or prudence rightly directing all your ways), *to prudence continence* (the temperance by which you can resist the allurement of all pleasures which attract and draw men from the right way), *to continence patience* (fortitude with which you may outlast any hardship for righteousness' sake). The words about piety and charity which follow in this verse contain a division of virtue which will be discussed in a more suitable place.

34. Because these various expressions or elements are more conspicuous in certain virtues than in others, special virtues take their name and definition from them. For example, since true rectitude appears most in the number, measure, weight, and value of things mutually received and given by men, justice is usually associated in a special way with things of this sort. And because the most terrible misfortunes are those which are likely to happen in war and similar dangers, the word fortitude is restricted to those situations. Temperance refers almost wholly to the pleasures of the senses which titillate the most. Still, these three, with prudence taken in a general sense, are tied together and involved with each other, as the philosopher observed who first propounded these four heads of virtue.

35. Many thinkers make virtue formally the mean between two extremes. But this cannot be defended by any reason. First, a negation is not of the nature of a habit, and a middle position is nothing but the negation of a defect or excess. Second, a virtue is identified by its conformity to its own standard, but such conformity is not usually or sometimes or ever to be found in any mean. Third, virtue in its formal sense cannot be applied too strongly and, thus, it does not admit of excess, except in the matter with which it deals, which it shares with vices, or in the circumstances in which it operates, as when some functions are exercised when they ought not to be or not exercised when they should be.

36. The mean found in all virtues is none other than their conformity to their standard or measure. By this conformity they are given modes and bounds in which their nature is contained, as it were, so that they may not fall to the right or the left or out of line in any way. But by this definition a middle position has no more to do with virtue than it has to do with anything else known by its form or distinguishing characteristics.

37. Those virtues found in the middle between two vicious condi-

tions are not virtues simply because they are in the middle. If in the middle, they can be called virtues only because conformity to their standard prescribes such a location. The middle position, whether of affirmation or negation, whether relating to experience or to reason, is subject matter, not perfecting form.

38. It is obvious that the mean has no place in some virtues. The love of God is to be praised not when it is not too much, but when it is most ardent. Here the measure is without measure.

39. The same reasoning applies to the true and specific nature of all true virtues. He who gives when he ought not to is not too generous: He simply gives too much, so that in that respect he ceases to be generous, and in his action may be wanting in not doing what he ought to.

40. To be sure, the wise man warns, *Be not overly just*, Eccles. 7:16. But this is not to be understood of justice in its nature for 7:20 states, *There is none just on earth who does good and sins not*. It is rather a reference to the fact that many take too much upon themselves and would have it reckoned to them as justice. But in true virtues we ought always to try to abound more and more, as the Holy Scriptures often tell us.

41. If we consider extending a specific virtue, there can be no such thing as degree. There is no virtue which at least in application does not extend itself to all things contained within the compass of its object. He is not temperate who is moderate in one lust but indulges in others. However, in respect of the subject a particular virtue may be stronger in one person than in another, either because of apter natural disposition, or more frequent use, or more perfect judgment of reason, or finally because of a greater gift of God.

42. It is often said that virtues are increased by daily use and exercise. This applies to true virtues which proceed from sanctifying grace; daily use can be called their disposing cause and, because of the promise of God, in a way their procuring cause. But use does not in principle or properly produce an increase of virtue.

43. Virtues are lessened by opposite evil acts both in the matter of the disposition accompanying them and in their intrinsic worth.

44. To the extent that the acts of virtue, or contrary vices, are more intent, more frequent, and more continual, they bring about either an increase or diminution of virtue.

45. Virtues are, therefore, divided into human and heroic; into cleansing, clean, and exemplary; and those who possess virtue into infants and men of maturity, Heb. 5:13, 14.

46. Virtues are related to each other coordinately or subordinately.

47. All necessary virtues are coordinate in that they cohere together.

First, in their origin, *For every good and perfect gift descends from the Father of lights by the Spirit of grace*, Jas. 1:17; 1 Cor. 12:11. Second, in their common end and intention which are essentially the same, for all virtues look to God and if his authority is violated in one, it is violated in all, Jas. 2:10. Third, it is found in the good they do to each other, for one virtue disposes another to express itself and defends and strengthens the other in its expression.

48. But virtues are not so essentially and intrinsically knit together that each one shares in the essence of the others or necessarily depends upon others as a generating cause.

49. The subordination of virtues is the dependence of the expression of one virtue on the expression and object of another. This may occur either as a means to an end, which is the command of a superior virtue to an inferior one (e.g., religion commands justice, temperance, and the like by referring their expressions to the advancement of the worship and glory of God), or as a cause to its effect, which is found in the relation of each virtue to every other one (e.g., religion is ordained to bring forth and maintain justice).

50. Whenever the expression of one virtue is directed toward another virtue's end, the effectual force and authority can come from only the superior virtue, although its direction depends upon prudence.

III

Good Works

1. An act of virtue is one which flows from the disposition of virtue. Matt. 12:35, *A good man out of the good treasure of his heart brings forth good things.*

2. In the same sense it is called an act or work that is good, right, laudable, and pleasing to God.

3. Such an act requires, first, a good efficient cause or beginning, i.e., a well-disposed will working from true virtue. For good fruit does not grow except on a good tree, Matt. 12:33. Second, a good matter or object, namely, something commanded by God. Matt. 15:9, *In vain they worship me, teaching doctrines which are the commandments of men.* Third, a good end — or the glory of God and whatever redounds to his glory. 1 Cor. 10:31, *Do all to the glory of God.*

4. But the end and the object in both good and evil acts often coincide, especially in the intention and choice of the will where the end

is itself the proper object. For such acts are directed either to the end as matter or object, as is the case in desiring, willing, wishing, loving, and enjoying, or to those things which are related to the end (insofar as they are so related) just as goodness or ugliness is to be judged by reference to the end.

5. The good intention or intention of doing good which is general and ambiguous cannot make a particular action good if other conditions be wanting. Nor can it be said that the intention to do some particular good suffices if the means are evil, as if someone should steal the goods of another man to bestow them upon the poor, or for other pious reasons. Yet an evil intention always makes an action evil and a good intention with other conditions adds much to the making of a good action.

6. To be truly good an action must be referred to God as the chief end, at least in effect.

7. Fourth, a pattern or good standard is required. This is found when the act accords with the revealed will of God.

8. The will of God, as it is apprehended by reason, informs a man's action. The conscience of man is, therefore, a secondary standard for moral actions. Every action must agree with a right conscience; and an erring or doubtful conscience must be taken seriously before a man may act against it, although a lighter scruple or a hesitance of conscience must not in any way put off an action otherwise approved.

9. All the circumstances must be good to make the shape or the mode good. An individual action is always surrounded by circumstances upon which the goodness or evil of it greatly depends.

10. Those circumstances related to an act of the will take on the nature of an object. For when the will takes some action, it wills all that is involved in the action and thus includes all known circumstances, expressly or implicitly. And when a known circumstance is changed, the act of the will is often changed.

11. But the same circumstances applied to the act of any other faculty are only adjuncts.

12. So the end itself is correctly considered a circumstance so far as the other faculties and their acts are concerned, though this is not true for the will.

13. Although many acts are indifferent, in their own nature, or in general, the circumstances make each individual, moral, and deliberate act either good or evil.

14. An act is indifferent in its kind when its object includes nothing which involves the commanding or forbidding will of God. Yet even acts of this sort, if they are truly human and done in deliberate reason, are either directed to the proper end of conformity to the

will of God, and thus are good; or they are not rightly directed, differ
from the will of God, and are thus evil.

15. Besides actions which are good, evil, and indifferent, some distinguish acts which are said to "have an evil sound." Considered by
themselves they have in them a certain lawlessness, but under certain circumstances they appear to be good, e.g., the killing of a man
and the like. But such acts ought to be classified as indifferent, for
they only seem to contain evil. To free a man from danger of death,
for instance, seems to be good in itself, but many who are not evil
are herein deceived, for the true goodness or wickedness of it in such
action depends upon the circumstances and the object. To slay the
innocent or set at liberty the guilty is evil, but to slay the guilty justly
or to deliver the innocent upon just reason is good.

16. All these causes and conditions must together be good to make
an act absolutely good. A defect in any of them makes the act evil
to that extent.

17. Our good works while we live here are, therefore, imperfect
and impure in themselves.

18. They are not acceptable to God, except in Christ.

19. The works of the regenerate do not have any merit worthy of
a reward obtained on the basis of justice.

20. Yet the reward which is given not out of indebtedness but out
of grace, Rom. 4:4, is sometimes assigned to these imperfect endeavors,
Matt. 5:12. Although all our blessedness is solely the gift of God,
Rom. 6:23, yet the fruits of grace abounding in us are entered in the
accounts which give us the certainty of the gift. Phil. 4:17, *I require
that fruit abounding which may be put to your credit.*

21. An act of virtue is either outward or inward. 2 Cor. 8:10, 11,
To will . . . to do . . . to perform.

22. The inward act belongs to the will itself.

23. The outward act belongs to a faculty other than the will,
whether it is the understanding or the sensory appetite (commonly
called internal), or the performing power (usually called external).

24. The internal action of the will has a goodness or evil so intrinsic
that an act cannot maintain its nature without maintaining its manners. An outward act, however, may remain one thing in nature and
yet change in manner, evil becoming good or good becoming evil, as
if one should begin to walk for an honest purpose but persist in
his journey to an evil end.

25. One and the same good or evil comes from an internal act and
the external act set in motion by it. It is one act in manner. For to
will to worship God and to worship God because of that will are not
two acts of obedience, but two phases of one and the same act; the

goodness of the one continues in the other. 2 Cor. 8:10, 11, *Do that very thing . . . that your readiness to will may be matched by performance.*

26. The outward act without the inward is properly neither good nor evil. But the inward can be good or evil without the external, because the goodness of an act depends first and chiefly upon the will, and this is often acceptable to God, although the outward deed is lacking. 2 Cor. 8:12, *If there is first a ready mind, one is accepted according to what he has.*

27. Just as virtue in its nature tends toward action (for it is an inclination to do well and not be idle), so the internal act tends toward the external. The internal produces the external and in it is brought to its end. Jas. 2:22, *You see that faith was the helper of his works, and by works faith was brought to its end.*

28. Still the external act joined with the internal does not properly and by itself increase its good or evil, so far as intention is concerned, but it serves as an accident [*per accidens*], continuing or increasing the act of the will itself.

29. The good or evil of any act which depends upon the object and the circumstances of the act is by its nature in the external before it is in the internal, although in order of existence it is first in the internal. To will to give everyone his own is thus good because giving itself is good, but the goodness exists in the act of willing before the act of giving. It is evil to will to steal because stealing is evil. In intention the exterior act is the cause of the inward, but in execution the inward act is the cause of the outward.

30. The good or evil which depends upon the end is first in the inward act and then in the outward. The very intention to reach the end is the inward act of the will. Thus to forsake the world for righteousness' sake is good because it is good to will righteousness, and to give alms for vainglory is evil because it is evil to will vainglory.

31. Observance which appears in outward actions without the inward is hypocrisy and is not observance in actual deed but a shadow of it.

32. Yet inward observance without the outward is true observance, although incomplete. If there is an effectual will, lacking only an opportunity or ability of executing, it is no less acceptable to God than if it were joined by an external act, 2 Cor. 8:12.

33. Therefore, we must not judge actions to be good or evil by the event. To be sure, it is just, and God himself decrees, that he who is judge of offenses among men be inclined favorably if the event itself is favorable, Exod. 21:21 ff. Yet before the tribunal of

God the inward sin is as great, other things being equal, when neither event nor outward act follow, as when both follow. Matt. 5:28, *Whoever looks upon a woman to lust after her has already committed adultery with her in his heart.*

34. Yet inward obedience is not sufficient by itself because the whole man ought to subject himself to God. Our bodies are to be offered to God, Rom. 12:1, and God is to be glorified in our bodies, 1 Cor. 6:20. Neither can there be true inward obedience when there is no inclination to the external.

35. What are called works of supererogation are the dotings of idle men who know neither the law nor the gospel. With this term the papists boast that some of them perform more excellent works than are commanded in the law of God through the observance of certain counsels which they imagine do not command but only set forth a special perfection.

36. The best works of the faithful have an imperfection which needs restoration, yet the works themselves are not sins.

❧

IV

Religion

1. Observance consists of either religion or justice.

2. This division is made by God in substance in the parts of the decalogue, as explained by Christ, Matt. 2:37. The same division is made in different words in Rom. 1:18, where all disobedience of men is separated into impiety and injustice, which would have no meaning unless all obedience were directed to piety and justice. This is even more plainly explained in Titus 2:12 where, of the three things propounded, righteousness and piety stand for the new obedience, and temperance for the manner or means of performance, which is a denial of worldly lusts.

3. The Christian life has the same division, more frequently expressed by holiness and righteousness, Luke 1:75; Eph. 4:24. And this is the meaning of the division between love for God and love for neighbor.

4. We use the words religion and justice because religion is a most general word including all the duties which we owe to God. Furthermore, it is most expressive because it sets forth the proper and distinct way in which they are owed to God, Acts 26:5; Jas. 1:26, 27. See also the frequent instances in the Letter to the Hebrews.

5. Religion is the observance whereby we do those things which directly pertain to God's honor. Rom. 1:21, *Although they knew God, they glorified him not as God, neither were they thankful.*

6. Therefore, the word is rightly said by some to be derived from *religare*, binding fast, because in this part of observance we directly and immediately turn towards God to cleave and, as it were, be bound to him.

7. Religion takes the first place in observance. First, obedience towards God must necessarily begin with God himself and with those attitudes and deeds by which we are carried towards him. 2 Cor. 8:5, *They gave themselves first to the Lord and then to us by the will of God.* Second, justice towards men must be carried out by force and virtue of religion if it is to be true observance towards God. It would not be observance towards God unless it brought honor to God, and it would not bring honor to God unless it proceeded from a religious attitude. 1 Cor. 10:31, *Do all to the glory of God.* The phrase *In the Lord* or *In the name of the Lord*, Col. 3:17, has this meaning. Also, *As serving the Lord and not men*, Col. 3:23. Third, religion commands the acts of justice and is not only the truly efficient but also the directing and ordering cause of them. Jas. 1:26, *If any seems to be religious among you and does not restrain his tongue but deceives his own heart, that man's religion is vain.* Fourth, religion is in a way the end of all acts of justice in that they open the way to an act of religion as something greater.

8. Justice itself is, therefore, sometimes called religion in the Scriptures. Jas. 1:27, *Religious worship, that is pure and spotless before God and the Father, is to visit the fatherless.* Justice is not only an inseparable sign of true religion, but also something which must be done at the command of religion and have its beginning from it.

9. Thus the duties of religion are primary and the most important. Matt. 6:33; 22:38, *First seek the kingdom of God. The first and great commandement.*

10. As they are first in order, so they must be taken care of first, Matt. 6:33.

11. This is the meaning of the phrase about seeking God early in the morning, encountered everywhere in the Psalms.

12. Religious duties are of greatest moment and are to be cared for above all others. Matt. 10:37, *He that loves father or mother above me is not worthy of me.*

13. The duties of religion should, therefore, be performed with more intensity and dedication than the duties of justice, for the rule, *Love with all your heart, all your soul, and all your mind* (Matt. 22:37), belongs properly to the former and not the latter.

14. This does not mean that all a man's strength is not required in meeting and fulfilling the duties of the second table. But it does mean that such strength is required especially by the duties of religion, which look to God, and not by the duties which directly affect our neighbor. Indeed, a man may strain too much in love for his neighbor in the material act of loving, although this cannot be done in virtue and charity. But we can in no way love God with too much intensity.

15. If the duties of piety and justice cannot be performed together, in just and prudent balance, the duties of piety are to be preferred. Matt. 12:46–48; Luke 2:49, *Behold my mother and my brethren. Why do you seek me? Do you not know that I must go about my Father's business?*

16. But a just balance is found when the greatest are given proportionally the most and the lesser less.

17. God is better worshipped with inward affection than outward deed. But men need the outward deed more. An outward work of religion may, therefore, sometimes be omitted in order that a necessary work of justice and mercy may be done. Matt. 12:1, 3, 4, 7, 10, 12, *I will have mercy and not sacrifice.*

18. Religion is not violated in this way because religion itself commands the omission of an external work in order that a necessary one may be done.

19. The immediate object of religion towards which it is directed is God, and this is so sufficient that no duty of religion may be referred to any other object without gravest injury to God. Thus comes God's title when he is described by the words "jealous" or "of a jealous kind."

20. Religion is related to God through that divine excellency which shines forth in his sufficiency and efficiency. This is not one attribute, but a perfection arising from all the attributes. Exod. 34:6–8, *The Lord, the Lord, the strong God, merciful and gracious, long-suffering, and full of loving-kindness and truth.* All the individual attributes of God have power to beget religion in us; and so in the Scriptures religion is sometimes referred to mercy. Ps. 130:4, *With thee is pardoning that thou mayest be reverently worshiped.* Sometimes to justice. Deut. 4:24; Heb. 12:29, *Let us have grace by which we may so serve God with reverence and fear that we may be accepted by him. For our God is a consuming fire.* And so for all the other attributes.

21. Religion comes directly from the faith by which we believe in God as the sufficient and efficient cause of life.

22. In this way is to be understood the customary saying that religion looks to God as the first beginning and supreme Lord of life. The papists' distinction is empty, when they declare that the acts of

religion which look to God as the first beginning of life are to be performed only to God but that other acts of religion may be directed to creatures. There is no act of religion which does not belong to God as the first beginning of life.

23. The proper act of religion is to bestow honor upon God and is called worship and adoration, Exod. 12:25, 26; John 4:23. It must bear a certain good towards God, otherwise it would not be observance towards him. No intrinsic good can be added to God, but honor is an outward good — a testimony to the virtue of another which adds to his glory or esteem. This is all a creature can do for God.

24. Therefore, a true and worthy esteem of God and other acts manifesting esteem constitute, as it were, the first matter of religion. Every honest, human act making for the honor and glory of God may be the matter or material object of religion. It is one and the same act which as submission to commandment is called obedience and as honor to God is called religion and worship.

25. The proper way of honor or religious worship is to subject to another the soul itself, and the inward affections and acts of the will.

26. In his soul and its inward acts, man is not subject directly and in himself to any creature. But as soul is knit to body, so the inward act is knit to the outward as its necessary condition, and demands the duty of submission to the creature as to a superior.

27. Honor is due to God not only because it is fitting in the sense that we say a thing is due when we give it out of generosity. It is also due because of the right of the one to whom it is given. So strict is this right that, so far as our debt is concerned, it is more than just, although for service rendered it is much less than just.

28. All worship which by its nature or condition, or by law and common custom, or by the mind and doctrine of the giver renders religious honor to another besides the true God at least to that degree fashions a new and false God for itself.

29. He who does not give religious worship to God is profane, and he who gives it to another besides the true God is an idolater, Acts 10; Rev. 19:10; 22:8.

30. Greatest care must be used in divine worship. Among the Latins, therefore, the word religion is sometimes used metaphorically for any anxious care, even in things not sacred. Thus it appears that the heathen by the light of nature recognized that the care of religion is to be placed above all other things.

31. Because the fear of conscience belongs to the worship of religion, any scruple of conscience is commonly called religious.

Hence we may gather that nature itself dictates that the conscience of man first and most properly looks to religion.

32. What gives the church its general standing as it professes a right manner of worshiping God is rightly called the Christian religion because the church comes by its standing and profession by virtue and by the fact of this religion.

33. Those things designated to religious use by special institution, or the instruments of religion, are also rightly called "religious" because of their status or establishment.

34. The peculiar manner of living which monks have chosen in order to exercise a would-be perfection is usually called "religion" by the papists, and such monks are called "religious" — but this is without reason and does wrong to other Christians.

35. He that is not religious is not a Christian.

36. The true religion is only one.

—◦◦◦◦◦◦◦◦—

V

Faith

1. The parts of religion are two: natural worship and voluntary or instituted worship.

2. This distinction is based on Exod. 20:6 in the words of the second commandment, *Those who love me and keep my commandments.*

3. Natural worship is that which depends upon the nature of God. Even though there were no law revealed and set forth by God, if we rightly perceived and knew the nature of God by proper contemplation, with the grace of God helping, we might know all those things which pertain to our duty.

4. Everyone who understands the nature of God rightly necessarily knows that God is to be believed and hoped in, that he is to be loved and called upon, and to be heard in all things.

5. This natural worship is absolutely basic to salvation. Ps. 79:6; Jer. 10:25; 2 Thess. 1:8, *Pour out thy wrath upon those nations that do not know thee and upon the kingdoms that do not call upon thy name.* Although we obtain eternal life neither by merit nor by virtue of our obedience, this part of obedience has such an essential connection with faith resting upon Christ for eternal life that it cannot be separated from it.

6. This worship has been, is, and shall be one and the same, or

immutable. 1 John 2:7, *The old commandment which you had from the beginning.*

7. Natural worship is prescribed in the first commandment because it is both internal and external.

8. First, all observance is the same inwardly and outwardly and, therefore, both inward and outward worship are treated in the same commandment. Second, in the commandments of the second table, inward and outward obedience are prescribed together in each one, as Christ interprets them, Matt. 5, and all the more so in the commandments of the first table, as in' the first and most important. Third, if it were true that the first commandment calls only for inward worship and the second only for outward, then the first commandment would bind only the inward man and the soul to obedience and the second only the outward man and the body. This is contrary to all reason.

9. Natural worship directs itself towards God, either as our good or as good in himself.

10. The worship which directs itself toward God as our good regards him either as he is ours at present, in faith, or as he is to be ours, in hope.

11. Faith is the virtue by which, clinging to the faithfulness of God, we lean upon him, so that we may obtain what he gives to us. John 3:33, *He who receives his testimony has sealed that God is true*; John 1:12, *As many as received him believed in his name.*

12. These five things belong together in divine faith: 1) a knowledge of what God testifies to; 2) a pious affection toward God which gives his testimony greatest force with us; 3) an assent given to the truth testified to, because of this affection toward God who is the witness of it; 4) a resting upon God for the receiving of what is given; and 5) the choosing or apprehension of what is made available to us in the testimony.

13. The first of these is in the understanding. But it does not produce faith because it is common to us along with unbelievers, heretics, apostates, and the devils themselves.

14. The second, fourth, and fifth are in the will and produce faith as the force within and act of religion.

15. The third is in the understanding but only as it is moved by the will. It does not have the virtue of faith, but is rather an effect of it.

16. But the perfection of faith lies only in the choosing or apprehension, and so must be defined by it.

17. The nature of faith is excellently set forth in the Scriptures when the faithful are said *To cleave to God*, Josh. 23:6; Acts 11:23;

1 Cor. 6:17. *To choose the way of truth and to cleave to the testimony of God*, Ps. 119:30, 31.

18. For by faith we first cleave to God and then fasten on to those things which are made available by God. God himself is, therefore, the first object of faith and what is made available by God is secondary.

19. Faith is our life as it joins us to God. But it is also an act of life because it is a virtue and our duty towards God. Therefore, in an earlier section we defined it only in reference to its obtaining of life and salvation, but here we define it as all that God sets forth for us to believe. Therefore, faith is not wholly concerned about God's threatenings in themselves, because they do not make available the good for us to receive; nor about God's commandments in themselves, because they declare the good to be done, not to be received; nor about mere predictions for in the strict sense they make no good available to us. But faith is rooted in the promises, because in them is set forth a good to be embraced. Therefore, our theologians are accustomed to make the promises the primary object of faith.

20. Those who place faith in the understanding confess that there must be some action of the will to secure that assent, just as in human faith it is said to be a voluntary matter to give credit to someone. So if faith depends upon the will, it must be that the first beginning of faith lies in the will.

21. The material object [*objectum quod*] of this faith is whatever is revealed and set forth by God to be believed, whether by spirit or word, publicly or privately. Acts 24:14, *I believe all things that are written in the law and prophets;* John 3:33, *He that receives his testimony.*

22. Therefore, the church is not absolutely necessary as an object of faith, not even for us today, for then Abraham and the other prophets would not have given assent to those things which were revealed to them from God without any intervening help of the church. To hold contrary is both against the Scriptures and sound reason. But such is the position accepted and maintained by the most learned papists so that they may defend the feigned authority of their false church from arguments of this kind.

23. This material object of faith is always some direct axiom or judgment of truth. But that in which faith has its chief end, concerning which and on account of which assent is given by faith to that axiom, is a simple being conceived of as good. Rom. 4:21, *Being fully persuaded that he who had promised was able also to do it;* Heb. 11:13, *Not having received the promises, but seeing them . . . afar off after they were persuaded of them and had embraced them.*

24. For the act of the believer is not directed to an axiom but to

the thing, as the most renowned schoolmen say. The reason is this: We do not frame axioms except to have knowledge of things. Therefore, the chief end towards which the act of the believer is directed is the thing itself, to which the axiom chiefly refers.

25. The formal object of faith is the truthfulness or faithfulness of God. Heb. 11:11, *Because she judged him faithful who had promised.* The formal or, as they say, particular reason of faith is truthtelling, i.e., the truthfulness or faithfulness of God truly revealing something. It is a commonplace that faith depends on the authority of the one who gives the testimony. Faith is thus distinguished from opinion, knowledge, experience, sight, or sense. The authority of God plainly lies in his truthfulness or faithfulness. Titus 1:2, *God, who cannot lie, has promised.* Hence the proposition is most true that whatever we are bound to believe through divine faith is true. Nothing ought so to be believed unless God himself witnesses the truth of it; God testifies as one who is truthful, and the truth in a witness who knows all things cannot be separated from the truth of his testimony. Therefore, it follows that all that we are bound to believe through divine faith is true. The whole matter is clearly confirmed and used by the apostle Paul in 1 Cor. 15:14, 15, *If Christ be not raised our preaching is vain and your faith is in vain. We are even found to be false witnesses of God, because we have testified of God that he raised up Christ.* If the testimony is not true, the witness is false. Unless it is admitted that whatever God witnesses is true, the surest consequence — namely, that God witnesses this or that and therefore it is true — would avail nothing. Thus divine faith cannot be a principle or cause of giving assent to what is false or of making a false assent either directly or indirectly, either by itself or by accident.

26. Therefore, the certainty of faith about the object is most sure. And to the extent that it is confirmed in the subject or the heart of the believer, so much is the glory of God increased. Rom. 4:20, 21, *He did not doubt this promise of God because of unbelief, but he was strengthened in faith giving glory to God and being fully persuaded that he who had promised was able to do it.* It is true that our faith sometimes wavers, but this comes not from the nature of faith but from our imperfection.

27. A sufficient and sure presentation of the objects of faith, that is, both those things which are to be believed and the form in which they are to be believed is made for us in the Scriptures. Rom. 16:26, *It is made manifest and by the writings of the prophets, according to the commandment of the everlasting God, made known to all nations for the obedience of faith.* 2 Tim. 3:15, *The Holy Scripture can make you wise to salvation by faith which is in Christ Jesus.*

28. The light and witness of the Holy Spirit stirring up faith in us

is necessary in the subject, or our hearts. Yet for the object itself which is to be received by faith absolutely nothing is required — neither the things to be believed nor the incentive nor reason for believing — which is not found in the Scriptures.

29. Therefore, divine faith cannot be reduced or resolved into the authority of the church or into any simple external arguments, often called motives, which by persuasion and inducement prepare us for faith. Faith goes back to the Scriptures themselves, to the authority which they bear from the author God, the first and proper cause of the things to be believed, and to the operation of the Holy Spirit, which is the proper cause of the believing act itself.

30. So the first principle from which faith takes its start and into which it is finally resolved is the conviction that the Scriptures are revealed from God for our salvation as a sufficient rule of faith and morals. 2 Peter 1:19, 20, *You must first know this, that no prophecy of the Scripture is a matter of private interpretation.*

31. Faith is partly implicit and partly explicit.

32. Implicit faith is the believing in the truths of faith in their common principle, not distinctly in each separately.

33. The common principle of all things to be believed in this way is the Scriptures, not the church. Acts 24:14, *Believing all things which are written in the law and the prophets.*

34. He who believes that the Scripture is true in every way believes implicitly all things which are contained in the Scripture. Ps. 119:86, compared with verses 18, 33, *All the precepts are truth itself . . . Open my eyes that I may see the wonders of the law. Teach me, O Lord, the way of your statutes which I will keep to the end.* David believed that these were wonderful and should be sacredly kept even though he did not yet sufficiently understand them.

35. This implicit faith is good and necessary but it is not in itself sufficient for salvation; nor does it possess the true meaning of faith if it stands alone. The will cannot embrace a good which it does not know distinctly, nor will it be effectively moved by it. Rom. 10:14, *How shall they believe in him of whom they have not heard.*

36. Explicit faith is the believing in the truths of faith in particular, not only in general.

37. Explicit faith must necessarily be held concerning those things given to our faith as indispensable means of salvation. Heb. 6:1; 2 Cor. 4:3, *The foundation of repentance from dead works and of faith in God. If our gospel be hid, it is hid to them who perish.*

38. A more explicit faith is required now after the coming of Christ than before, 2 Cor. 3:18. It is also more required in those who are set over others in the church than in the common people, Heb.

9:12. Last, it is more required of those who have occasion to be well instructed than of others, Luke 12:48, *To whom much is given, of him much shall be required.*

39. The outward act of faith is the confession, profession, or manifestation of it, which in their order and place are necessary to salvation, Rom. 10:9, 10. These are always necessary for the preparation and disposition of the mind, 2 Peter 3:15. And they are necessary for the act of faith itself when the glory of God and the edification of neighbor require them.

40. Persistence in confession of the faith leading to the loss of temporal life testifies to the truth and brings the greatest honor to God. Therefore, κατ' ἐξοχήν, at its height, it is called μαρτύριον, martyrdom, and those who engage in it are called μάρτυρες, witnesses, Rev. 2:13. This is as necessary in its place as confession of faith when it cannot be refused without denying Christ, Matt. 10:33, 39; 16:25.

41. Infidelity, doubt, error, heresy and apostasy are opposed to faith.

42. Infidelity is a dissent from the faith in a man who has not yet professed the true faith, 1 Cor. 14:22, 23.

43. Doubt occurs in one who has made profession but whose assent is now diminished or taken away.

44. Doubt that only diminishes assent may coexist with a weak faith, 1 Cor. 8:10, 11. But doubt which takes away assent cannot, Jas. 1:6–8.

45. Error in faith puts forth an opinion contrary to faith, 1 Cor. 15:46.

46. Heresy adds stubbornness to error, Titus 3:10, 11.

47. Apostasy taken absolutely adds to heresy all the errors contrary to faith, 1 Tim. 1:19, 20; 2 Tim. 1:15.

48. These things are opposed to faith not only because they cut off the understanding's assent, which is necessary to faith, but also because they take away the choice and apprehension of faith which is in the will.

VI

Hope

1. Hope is a virtue which leads us to expect things which God has promised us, Rom. 8:25.

2. Hope looks towards God in these ways. First, as the object which it expects, for the principal object of hope is God himself and

those acts by which he is joined to us. 1 Peter 1:21, *So that your faith and hope are in God.* All those things which lead to God like steps and means are less principal objects. 1 Peter 1:13, *Hope in the grace which is brought to you.* Thus God himself is called the *Hope of Israel,* Jer. 14:8, and the *God of hope,* Rom. 15:13. This is not so much because he is the author and giver of hope as because it is he for whom we hope. Second, hope looks to God as the author and giver of all the good it expects. Ps. 37:5, 6, *Commit your way to the Lord and trust in him for he shall bring it to pass.* As it turns toward God for the attainment of good, so it looks toward obtaining it by his own grace. Jer.17:7, *Blessed is the man who trusts in the Lord and whose hope is in the Lord.*

3. The true reason why we should not hope in creatures as we hope in God is because the formal object of hope is not found in creatures. Ps. 146:3, *Trust not in princes nor in any son of man, in whom there is no salvation.* Although some power of helping us and doing us good is given by God to the creatures, yet the exercise of this power always depends on God. Ps. 107:20, *Sending his word he healed them;* Ps. 127:1, *Unless the Lord builds the house, they who labor build it in vain; unless the Lord keep the city, the watchmen watch in vain.*

4. Therefore, when someone says that he hopes for this or that from a man, he either means that he has hopes from God through that creature, or he expresses a human not a divine hope, or what he says is not Christian.

5. Like faith, hope in God looks to the grace of God and Christ as the only sources of good to be bestowed. 1 Peter 1:13; Col. 1:27, *Hope . . . in the grace. Christ . . . the hope of glory.*

6. But divine hope not only looks to God and eternal blessedness but in God and from God it looks to all the things which faith sees in the promises of God, even though in their own nature they may be temporal, Heb. 11:1; 2 Cor. 1:10. But hope still looks mainly towards eternal life and for this reason in Scripture it is often called by metonymy of the adjunct salvation itself or life eternal hoped for, Gal. 5:5; Rom. 8:24; Titus 2:13. Sometimes salvation is also called hope of salvation by metonymy of the subject. Eph. 6:17; in comparison with 1 Thess. 5:8, *The helmet of salvation. . . . For a helmet the hope of salvation.* Usually this is put as the proper object for hope. 1 Thess. 5:8; Titus 3:7, *The hope of eternal life;* Rom. 5:2, *The hope of glory.*

7. The conditions which normally characterize an object of hope — that it be good, that it lie in the future, that it be difficult, probable

— are all found in the promises of God. He always promises the greatest good things which shall not come about without his help, but by virtue of his promise they will not only probably but surely come to pass.

8. The act by which divine hope is turned toward its object is called expectation; this is not merely uncertain or probable conjecture, as with human hope, but of great certainty. Rom. 8:25; Phil. 1:20, *If we hope for what we see not, we expect it with patience. According to my earnest expectation and hope.* Everywhere in the Old Testament where the word מִקְוֶה, usually translated hope, is used, it properly means expectation.

9. Certainty is given to hope by faith, for faith is the foundation of hope. Nothing is to be hoped for which is not believed before in faith. Gal. 5:5, *For through the Spirit, by faith, we wait for the hope of righteousness.*

10. Since faith apprehends the promise and hope expects what is promised, the difference between faith and hope is the difference between what is present and what is to come.

11. Therefore, the distinction of the papists is empty and vain, in holding that the faithful may be certain of their salvation with the certainty of hope but denying that they can ever by ordinary means be certain of it with the certainty of faith. There is one and the same certainty for faith and hope. For this reason hope in the Scriptures, especially in the Old Testament, is frequently used for faith.

12. The expectation of good things to come found in the angels and the spirits of just men in heaven does not differ from our hope because one is certain and the other uncertain. It differs rather in that, first, our hope is grounded upon faith which sees God in the promises, as *Through a glass darkly,* 1 Cor. 13:12. But their expectation comes from clear vision. Second, our hope is attended with labor and effort but their expectation is free of difficulty. Third, our hope is imperfect expectation, but their expectation is perfect hope.

13. Therefore, although hope and faith alike are usually said to be done away with in the life to come, this is to be understood as meaning that they cease to exist not in their essence but only in the measure and degree of their imperfection, 1 Cor. 13:10. Properly, only their imperfection is to be eliminated, but faith and hope themselves are to be perfected in their essence.

14. Christian confidence, looking to the good which is to come, is nothing else than hope confirmed. For it necessarily refers to one of the theological virtues mentioned by the Apostle, 1 Cor. 13:13, *Faith, hope, and love.* But confidence cannot refer to faith, because faith ap-

prehends something now present to which it gives substance, Heb. 11:1. Nor does it refer to love because love does not relate to a good which is ours, 1 Cor. 13:5. Confidence, therefore, refers to hope.

15. The natural fruit of hope is joy and delight in God. Heb. 3:6, *The hope whereof we rejoice;* 1 Peter 1:3, 6, *A lively hope. . . . In this you rejoice.* Hope regards the best things not only as possible and probable, but also as certain of coming. They are with us in a certain way when by hope we are assured that they shall in fact be with us in the future. Rom. 8:24, *We are saved by hope.*

16. The manner of the act depends upon the object's being in the future and promised. Formally hope is not directed to things which are seen. Rom. 8:24, *Hope, if it be seen, is not hope. For why does a man hope for that which he sees?*

17. The fruit and companion of hope is, therefore, patience toward God whereby we constantly cling to him seeking and expecting blessedness, though in this present life we confront many evils without the consolation we desire. Isa. 8:17, *Waiting on the Lord, who hides his face . . . and looking for him;* Rom. 8:25, *But if we hope for that which we do not see, we expect it with patience;* 2 Thess. 3:5, *That patient expectation.*

18. One fruit of this patience is the silence in which we rest on the will of God and repress all carnal thoughts which stir us up to lose patience or struggle against it. Ps. 37:7, *Be silent before the Lord, and without ceasing wait on him.*

19. Hope is strengthened and increased by all evidences which assure us that the good hoped for belongs to us. Rom. 5:4, *Experience produces hope.*

20. The inward signs of divine grace have first place among such evidences. 1 John 3:14, 19, *We know that we are translated from death to life, because we love the brethren.*

21. Therefore, what the papists say is most false, namely, that our hope is grounded partly upon the grace of God and partly on our own merit. However, it can be truly affirmed that hope is strengthened, increased, and stirred up by faith, repentance, good works, and a good conscience. True and lively hope exists through these, so to speak, antecedents Heb. 10:22, 23; 1 Peter 3:15, 16.

22. The effect of hope is a confirmation of the soul as a *Safe and firm anchor,* Heb. 6:19. Luke 21:19, *Whereby we possess our very souls.*

23. There always follows from this confirmation of soul a zeal for holiness. 1 John 3:3, *Whoever has hope in him keeps himself pure, even as he is pure.*

24. First, by way of defect, a fear of the evil of punishment stands

opposed to hope, Ps. 27:3. For as hope is the expectation of good, so fear is the expectation of evil.

25. If fear is moderate and tempered by faith, even though always materially opposed to hope, it is not formally opposed to hope and virtue in man as a sinner so that it can simply be called a vice. Rather it may be considered to have the character and nature of virtue. 2 Chron. 34:27, *Because your heart was tender and you cast yourself down before God when you heard his words against this place.* This is because the orientation is not the same: Hope looks to the grace of God and fear looks to the just merit of our sins.

26. More directly, by way of defect, desperation is opposed to hope, for it is a privation of hope accompanied by a sense of the privation and a knowledge that the thing hoped for is either not possible or at least not to be. Such was in Cain, Gen. 4:13–14, and in Judas, Matt. 27:4, 5.

27. Such desperation is always a grievous sin. It is not just a lack of the hope which men are accustomed to have in themselves or other creatures and which is generally a commendable introduction to divine hope, but it is a lack of divine hope. It always has its beginnings in unbelief, just as hope has its beginning in faith.

28. Desperation in the devils and the damned has the character not of sin but of punishment. For desperation may be considered either as a positive lack, when one refuses to hope for what he should and when he should, or negatively as a mere cessation of hope. In the former but not in the latter sense it is always a sin, being contrary to the law.

29. There are many reasons for despair. Either the grace of God is not considered sufficient to bestow good on us, or God himself is not willing to bestow it. Desperation grounded on the first is always a sin, but not so in the latter sense, if one could be certain of that will of God.

30. But because it is seldom or never shown ordinarily to anyone before the end of this life that God will not make him a partaker of grace and glory, there is no human desperation in this life which is not sin.

31. Second, by way of excess, presumption is opposed to hope because in it we have a rash expectation of some good. Deut. 29:19; Jer. 7:4, 8, 9, 10; *Let there not be any man who, when he has heard . . . blesses himself.*

32. This rash presumption in expectation of good is sometimes a dependence upon creatures, Jer. 17:5; 1 Tim. 6:17. Sometimes it depends in a way upon God, but perversely, without promise and without faith. Thus, a man may expect pardon and salvation but remain unrepentant, or remain determined to live in his sins, or expect something from God which is contrary to his nature or revealed will.

33. But we do not sin in presumption when we hope too much from God in a true and religious hope, for this cannot be done. But he is presumptuous who hopes too lightly and rashly, without basis, or hopes for things which are not to be hoped for.

34. Third, by way of result, *Personal shame* and *Confusion*, Ps. 25:2, 3, are also opposed to hope.

VII

Charity or Love

1. Charity or love is the virtue whereby we love God as the chief good. Ps. 106:1; 118:1; 136:1, *Praise the Lord . . . for he is good, for his kindness endures for ever.* The joy of praising, which is an effect of love, has the same primary object as love, which is this joy's own proper cause. The goodness of God which is manifest specifically in the effects of his kindness is the proper object of love, as it is of praise.

2. Charity or love follows faith and hope in natural order as effect follows cause. We love God in charity because by faith and hope we taste in some measure how good he is and know that his love is shed abroad in our hearts. 1 John 4:16, 19, *We have known and believed the love which God has towards us. We love him because he has loved us first.*

3. Therefore, not love but faith is the first foundation of the spiritual building of man. This is so not only because faith is the beginning, but also because it sustains and holds together all the parts of the building. It has the nature of a root in that it gives power to bring forth fruit.

4. An unclear and remote inclination toward God precedes faith, a certain shadow of which is found to some degree in all creatures. Acts 17:27, *That they may seek the Lord, in the hope that they may find him by seeking him.* But since this is inefficacious, it is an ineffectual "woulding" (as they say) to love God, rather than true love.

5. The distinction of the schoolmen between the natural and supernatural love of God by which they make one love of God the beginning and end of nature and the other the beginning and end of grace is idle imagining. Nor can it be said that since the fall man by natural strength without faith can love God above all — not even with the love they call natural.

6. The love which is charity is love of union, of satisfaction or contentment, and good will. These are, as it were, the parts of love and

they are always found in it if it is true — the desire for union, the enjoyment of satisfaction, and the mark of good will.

7. The love of union is that affection by which we will to be joined with God. 2 Cor. 5:8, *It is our desire to be absent from the body and to be present with the Lord.*

8. God also has a love for union with us. Eph. 2:4, 13, *He loved us with much love. . . . You who were far off are made near.* But his love is out of the abundance of his goodness; he expects no benefit from us, for we are unprofitable servants to him, Luke 17:10; Job 22:2, 23. But our love towards him is out of a want of goodness, for we stand in need of him. 2 Cor. 5:4, *We groan being burdened . . . what is mortal may be swallowed up by life.*

9. Since our love is a desire of union with God it comes in part from what is called concupiscence or appetite. We desire God for ourselves, because we hope for benefit and eternal blessedness from him.

10. The highest end of this love should be God himself.

11. The love which is satisfaction is that affection by which we approve of all that is in God and rest in his supreme goodness. Rev. 7:12, *Blessing, glory, wisdom, thanksgiving, honor, power, and strength unto our God forever and ever! Amen.*

12. God also has a love for satisfaction with us, Heb. 13:16. His satisfaction with us lies in those good things which he gives to us. But ours lies in that goodness and divine perfection which in no way depend upon us.

13. The love which is good will is the affection which bids us yield ourselves wholly to God. We will and endeavor that all things which pertain to his glory shall be given to him. Rev. 4:10, 11, *They fall down . . . and cast their crowns before the throne, saying, Thou art worthy, O Lord, to receive glory, honor, and power;* 1 Cor. 10:31, *Do all to the glory of God.*

14. In his good will toward us God makes us good by conferring on us the good which he desires to bestow upon us. But we cannot properly bestow any good upon him; we can only acknowledge his goodness with the heart, publish it in words, and declare it in some measure by deeds.

15. The mutual love between God and the faithful is something like friendship. John 15:15, *I have called you friends, because I have made known to you all things which I have heard from my Father.*

16. In this friendship, although there is not the same equality as among men who are friends, the equality which is possible appears in certain inward communion between God and the faithful. In this sense God is said to reveal his secrets to the faithful, Ps. 25:14; John 15:15, and to be, as it were, intimately conversant with them. Rev.

3:20, *If anyone shall hear my voice and open the door, I will go in to him and sup with him, and he with me;* John 14:23, *If anyone love me, he will keep my word, and my Father will love him, and we will come to him and dwell with him.*

17. An implicit part of charity is the keeping and fulfilling of all the commandments of God, Rom. 3:10; 1 John 2:5; 3:18. For he cannot truly love God who does not strive to please him in all things and to be like him. 1 John 4:17, *Herein is our charity made perfect . . . that as he is we are also.*

18. In manner our charity looks to God as the highest good and end; neither God nor the love of God depends chiefly or ultimately on anything else, for such love would be mercenary. John 6:26, *You seek me . . . because you ate of the loaves and were filled.*

19. Yet we may love God as our reward, Gen. 15:2, and, in consideration of other good things, as rewards, Gen. 17:2.

20. Love toward God ought to be the highest love in the following ways: First, objectively (as they say) — because of the nature of the object, for whom we should desire greater good than for any other. Second, appreciatively (as some say) — because of our esteem, seen in our preference for him and his will above all other things, even our own life, Matt. 10:37; Luke 14:26. Thus we should choose to die rather than to transgress even the least of his commandments. Third, intensively — all the faculties being fervently applied to loving God. Deut. 6:5, *You shall love the Lord your God with all your heart, with all your soul, and with all your strength.*

21. According to this description of love it is rightly said by some theologians that only God is to be loved, simply by himself and according to all the parts of love, i.e., in good will, in desire for union, and in the enjoyment of satisfaction. Our neighbor is to be loved in a certain respect, but with another objective and without such esteem or intensity.

22. Opposed to love stands the tormenting fear which comes from the presence of God and the fear of punishment inflicted by him. 1 John 4:18, *Perfect love casts out fear. For fear has torment.*

23. When love is perfected it does cast out fear (1 John 4:18), for the latter is a horror rooted in the sense of evil caused by the presence of God. It is thus opposed to love which is related to God as to the absolute good.

24. Second, opposed to love is estrangement from God, called by some the hatred which is abomination. Ps. 14:3; John 3:20, *They have all gone astray. . . . He hates the light.* Just as love is a desire for union so this estrangement is disjunction. The hatred of God most contrary to the love of God is called the hatred which is enmity. John

15:23–25, *They have hated both me and my Father.* Just as the friendship of love is in good will so this enmity against God lies in the evil that ungodly men wish to do to him, and would do if they could, to destroy him or at least to make him other than he is.

25. If God is known as he is in himself he cannot be the object of hatred. Yet when he is known as one who takes vengeance on sinners to that extent he can often be hated by impious sinners because he is starkly against them. John 3:20, *Whoever does evil hates the light, and does not come to the light, lest his deeds be reproved.* Just as the love of God causes the godly to hate impiety against God, so the love of iniquity in the ungodly causes them to hate God as the one who opposes their iniquity.

26. The stages by which men ascend to the height of ungodliness are as follows. First, sinners have an inordinate love of themselves. Second, they will what they please, although it is contrary to the law of God. Third, they hate the law because it is contrary to their desire. Fourth, they oppose God himself who is the giver and author of such law.

27. Opposed to love toward God is the love of this world, for the world does not agree with God and his will. 1 John 2:15, 16, *If anyone loves the world, the love of the Father is not in him. Because whatever is in the world . . . is not of the Father.*

28. As the perfection of love is found in the mind's resting in God, so it is necessarily hostility to love when the mind rests in what is contrary to God.

29. Love is no more the form of the other virtues than any virtue which commands or orders the expressions of another can be its form. Yet, some deeds which do not look to God are referred to him in his love, and in him are perfected. So by a metaphor love may rightly be called the form of these deeds and of the virtues from which they arise.

30. But love cannot be the intrinsic form of faith because it naturally follows faith as an effect follows a cause, and does not precede as a cause an effect.

31. Neither is faith outwardly directed towards God by love; in its own intrinsic nature it looks to God as its object.

32. Justification by faith does not in any way depend on love, as the papists maintain; it depends on the true object of faith.

33. Faith is said to work through love, Gal. 5:6. This is not because the whole effectiveness of faith depends upon love as a cause but because faith manifests and exercises its power by stirring up love.

34. The preposition *through* does not here indicate a formal cause, but rather a kind of instrumental one, as when God is said to regenerate us *through* the word.

35. Faith which is without works is said to be dead, Jas. 2:26. This is not because the life of faith flows from works but because works are subsequent acts necessarily flowing from the life of faith.

36. Faith is said to be perfected by works, Jas. 2:22. This is not an essential perfection, in which an effect is completed by its cause, but rather a complementary perfection, in which a cause is perfected or made actually complete by producing its effect.

37. The object of love is the very goodness of God in itself, but faith and hope look to God as he is manifested for our understanding. Therefore, the inclination of the mind towards God which belongs to love appears in weak believers more evidently and constantly than special deeds of faith or hope. For the goodness of God by itself is more manifest than the way of apprehending it, which is presented darkly to us in this life.

VIII

The Hearing of the Word

1. From faith, hope, and love, the virtues of religion referring to God, there arises a double act which bears on the spiritual communion exercised between God and us; the hearing of the word and prayer.

2. The reason or basis for this division is that in religious worship we relate ourselves to God when we give him due honor either by receiving what he offers or by offering what may be received by him in his perfection. In both respects we do what is immediately and directly honorable to God.

3. The first act of religion, therefore, concerns those things which are communicated to us from God. The other concerns those things which we yield to God.

4. Hearing the word is the devout receiving of the will of God.

5. Hearing here, therefore, means any receiving of the word of God whether it be communicated to us by preaching, reading, or any other way. God is accustomed to work in his own way and by his own institution by the preaching and hearing of the word.

6. The word *hearing* ought not to be taken so literally and strictly as to mean always necessarily the outward sense of hearing; it denotes any perceiving of the will of God, and especially inward receiving and submission.

7. The receiving of the word consists of two parts: attention of mind and intention of will.

8. Attention is applying the understanding to perceive the revealed will of God. Acts 16:14, *The Lord opened the heart of Lydia that she might attend to the things spoken by Paul.* It is often called in the Scripture, especially in the Old Testament, a seeking of the will of God or a seeking of God himself. It refers to the great desire we should have to know God's will, as though it were something we could not at all do without. Isa. 58:2, *Yet they seek me daily, and delight to know my ways, as . . . a nation which does righteousness and does not forsake the judgment of its God; they inquire of me the ordinances of justice, they delight in approaching God.*

9. In this attention we need that prudence which will discern what the will of God is. Rom. 12:2, *That you may prove what is the good, pleasing, and perfect will of God.* When this is perceived, we must not deliberate further whether it be good or is to be obeyed or not, for the will of God is itself the final end of all religious inquiry. Gal. 1:15, 16, *When it pleased God to reveal his sign in me . . . I did not consult with flesh and blood.*

10. Intention is the application of our will to the devout observance of the will of God now known. Ps. 119:106, *I have sworn . . . and will perform it, that I will keep thy righteous judgment.*

11. The purpose of the intention ought to be so strong and firm that we are ready without exception to obey whatever God commands. Jer. 42:5, 6, *The Lord be a true and faithful witness between us if we do not act according to all the things with which the Lord thy God sends you to us. Whether it be good or whether it be evil, we will obey the voice of the Lord our God.*

12. In the form of this intention, the law of God itself is said to be in the heart of a believer, Pss. 40:8, 9; 119:11; Jer. 31:33; Heb. 8:10.

13. In order to be correct, the hearing should come from faithful observance, bringing submission of the inward acts and inclinations of the mind. Rom. 6:17, *From the heart you obeyed that form of doctrine to which you were committed.*

14. To be truly religious, it is necessary, first, that it arise from faith, for by faith we believe the word of truth is that which God reveals to us and are accordingly influenced by it. Heb. 4:2, *The word being heard did not profit them, for it did not meet with faith in them that heard it;* Luke 24:32, *Did not our hearts burn . . . while he spoke to us?*

15. By this faith we cling to the word, Ps. 119:31, and the word itself clings to us and is ingrafted for salvation. Jas. 1:21, *The ingrafted word.*

16. Second, this hearing must come from the hope by which we embrace what God has promised as the word of life and from it also

expect life. Deut. 32:47, *It is your life, and you shall live long in the land;* John 5:39.

17. In hope the faithful bring forth fruit with patience, Luke 8:15.

18. In like manner, there must be joined to it love, with which we cleave to the word or to God revealing himself to us in the word as absolutely good. Ps. 119:97, *How I love thy law;* 2 Thess. 2:10, *They did not receive the love of truth in order that they might be saved.*

19. Because of this love, the word of God dwells bountifully in the faithful, Col. 3:16. And they are transformed into its form and pattern, Rom. 6:17.

20. Such a hearing of the word of God is the true and proper worship of God. First, it bestows spiritual honor on God immediately and directly. For although the act of hearing is most properly directed to our receiving of the will of God, yet because we subject our consciences to God in so receiving we honor him as the possessor of power and divine truth, the acknowledgment of which is the basis of religious worship. Second, it contains a direct and immediate exercise of faith, hope, and charity in which the essential worship of God is chiefly found.

21. Therefore, no word or sentence of men ought to be mingled with the word of God or transmitted in the same manner lest by chance we worship men instead of God.

22. Most definitely opposed to hearing is, first, the pride by which one dwells on his own excellence. Such a person does not wish to submit to the will of God. Pride is always contrary to the humility of religion and to religious observance or obedience in general but it seems most surely opposed to them in this act of religion. A proud man is so far from subjecting himself to the will of another as to a law that he wants to have his own will in place of the law. Jer. 13:15, *Hear and give ear; be not proud, for the Lord has spoken;* Jer. 5:5, *They have broken the yoke, they have burst the bonds.*

23. The real act of pride is a contempt of either God or the will of God and its observance. 2 Sam. 12:9, *Why have you despised the word of the Lord in doing what is evil in his eyes?*

24. Pride is said to be the cause of all other sins for two reasons. First, all sins have something to do with that occupying of first place which pride has, as it were, for an end. Second, pride casts aside contemptuously the authority of the word in which alone the power of sin is to be avoided.

25. There is something of pride in every sin but especially in those which are committed deliberately.

26. Opposed to the hearing of the word is, second, all taking advice from the world, the flesh, or wisdom of the flesh in the things of religion, Rom. 8:7; Gal. 1:16.

27. As in pride men refuse to submit themselves to the will of God; so in taking counsel which is not of God they seek other gods, as it were, to whom they may be subject.

28. Third, the most wicked opposition to the hearing of the word is consultation with the devil. Isa. 8:19; Deut. 18:11–15. Herein religious faith and hope due only to God is transferred in a way either explicitly or implicitly to the enemy of God.

29. Hence it is that faith is likely to be required in those who indulge in such consultations by those who are the masters of these arts.

30. By virtue of this faith there is a certain covenant and a kind of religion entered into with the devil — if not openly and expressly, at least secretly and implicitly.

31. One may not have a direct intention to ask counsel of the devil, yet he is made a partaker of such a sin, if he does something that implies, either in its own nature or in its practical application, a calling on the devil for help or counsel.

32. Therefore, all arts introduced by the influence of the devil for the knowing of secrets are in this respect to be condemned.

33. All divination which is not grounded upon the sure revelation of God or the course of nature ordained by God in creation is to be condemned.

34. All application of things or words to prediction or any functions to which they are not appointed by either nature or God's ordinance is to be condemned.

35. If the help of the devil is sought in such ways, he is in a certain way invoked, and the invoking of God is shut out. And since a kind of revelation is expected, or a submission of mind to receive and execute his commands, this is opposed to the hearing of the word of God.

36. Communion with the devil, therefore, is not only unlawful because it is connected with fraud and seduction, but also because in its own nature it is contrary to true religion.

37. We do not have human communion or fellowship with the devil. And we cannot have religious communion, as formerly some had with the good angels who were ministering spirits sent by God for our good.

38. Therefore, any association with the devil, apart from resistance to him as the enemy of our souls, leads to the violation of true religion and is itself a kind of perverse religion.

39. If he appears at times to be subject to the command of men by some kind of enchantment, it is only a facade of submission so that he may more easily rule them. This does not prevent but only colors the religious submission which men render him in such association.

40. All participate in such sins who by words, images, and other similar things of no sufficient virtue try to cure diseases in others, or who tolerate such doings to that end on behalf of themselves or their families.

41. Sympathies, antipathies, and the special virtues which are found in some things differ from such enchantments in that, as the common experience of all men shows, some faith is required for the former but none for the latter.

42. In many people a strong imagination may perhaps reinforce the efficacy of the media of enchantment, and even this often arises from a kind of religious faith; but it cannot transmit any effect from parents to children or from men to cattle unless a diabolical force is operative.

43. They who most care for the hearing of the word care least for these arts and see the least fruit in them.

❖⟞⟐⟞❖

IX

Prayer

1. Prayer is a devout presentation of our will before God so that he may be, as it were, affected by it.

2. It is an act of religion because by its nature it acknowledges in him who is prayed to that sufficiency and efficiency of knowledge, strength, and goodness which belong to God.

3. It cannot be directed to any other besides God without open idolatry.

4. It arises first from faith. Rom. 10:14, *How shall they call on him in whom they have not believed?* We mean the faith whereby we believe, first, that God knows all things, including the inward affections and motions of our hearts, wherein especially the essence of prayer is found. Second, that God is omnipotent and so can do what he wills in fulfilling our desires. Third, that he is the author and giver of every good thing; and, fourth, that he approves and accepts our prayer through Christ.

5. All our prayers, therefore, are to be offered to God in the name and through the mediation of Christ by the power of justifying faith. John 14:13, 14; 16:23, *Whatever you ask of the Father in my name.*

6. Prayer also arises from hope — whereby we expect the fruit of

our prayers from God. Rom. 8:23, 26, *We . . . groan expecting the adoption. . . . The Spirit intercedes for us with groans that cannot be expressed.*

7. Last, it arises from love — in which we desire to partake of and celebrate the goodness of God. Ps. 34:3, 8, *Magnify the Lord with me, and let us exalt his name together! Taste and see that the Lord is good! Blessed is the man who trusts in him.*

8. Love toward our neighbors is necessary in prayer that is acceptable to God — hence the fifth petition of the Lord's Prayer.

9. Prayer differs from the hearing of the word in that hearing is oriented to the will of God but prayer to our will. In hearing the word we accept God's will but in prayer we offer our will to God to be accepted by him.

10. But it is not a simple willing or desire, but a matter of the whole will, i.e., the will itself exhibited and presented to God. It is not enough for prayer to desire something, for then profane men would pray most since they desire most. Required are the desire to obtain something from God, the will to seek it from him, and finally the presenting or placing of the desire before God.

11. This presenting takes place first and essentially in the will itself when, turning to God, it represents its inclination and desire by an act extended, so to speak, towards God.

12. The prayers of the godly are called in the Scriptures, Desires, Ps. 10:17, and, *Sighs too deep for words,* Rom. 8:26.

13. The presenting is made, second, by the understanding in the form of a sign or definite expression. The understanding expresses the affections of the will before God when it conceives the inner word for them.

14. Thus prayers of the faithful are also called words and sayings because they speak to God first and foremost not outwardly but inwardly. Hos. 14:2, *Take with you words and turn unto the Lord; say unto him, Pardon.*

15. Prayer is, therefore, formally an act of the will with an *antecedent* act of the mind by which we understand what, of whom, for what, and how we must pray; and a *consequent* act by which we conceive and express in what may be called a mental word the prayer itself.

16. Besides the intention or act of the will there is also required attention to God to whom we pray, to the thing about which we pray, and to the prayer itself. For we must not only pray with the spirit but with understanding. 1 Cor. 14:15, *I will pray with the spirit but I will pray with the mind also.*

17. The presenting must be submissive and humble; otherwise it would not be a devout prayer directed to the highest Godhead [*supremum Numen*] and creator by a subject creature. It would be rather either a command of a superior to an inferior or like a familiar consultation, as it were, among equals. Gen. 18:27, *Behold, now I would speak to the Lord, although I am dust and ashes*; Ps. 95:6, *Come, let us bow and fall down and bend the knees before the Lord, our Maker!*

18. The general end of prayer is, as it were, to affect or move God. Therefore, the faithful in their prayers are said to prevail in a way with God, Gen. 32:28, Hos. 12:4, 5, and to *Strive*, Rom. 15:30.

19. Some rightly distinguish between the prayers directed to men and those directed to God: Those who pray to men affect those to whom they pray and have a part in disposing them to what is desired, but those who pray to God do not affect God as much as themselves and dispose not God but themselves to the things desired. Yet God is pleased to commend the force and efficacy of prayer to us by declaring himself to be affected and, as it were, moved by it. Our prayer is the means by which, and not otherwise, God is willing to communicate many things to us. Therefore, those who ask something of God are said to be giving help to effect it, 2 Cor. 1:11.

20. Therefore, we do not pray to God in order that we may make known desires till then unknown to him, for he *Knows our thoughts afar off*, Ps. 139:2, that is, when they are not yet in our own mind. Nor do we pray to him in order to convert him from an opposing to our own point of view, for *In him there is no change or shadow of turning*, Jas. 1:17. We pray to him in order to obtain by our prayer what we believe he wishes to grant. 1 John 5:14, *This is the confidence we have in God, that if we ask him anything according to his will he hears us.*

21. The firmness and immutability of God's providence, therefore, do not take away but establish the prayers of the faithful. The certain apprehension of providence by faith does not make true believers slothful but stirs them up the more to pray, 1 Chron. 17:25–27, *Thou, my God, hast revealed to the ear of thy servant that thou wilt build him a house; therefore thy servant has been bold to pray before thee.*

22. Therefore, we must pray earnestly and continually — earnestly because prayer is a necessary medium of God's glory and our good — continually because such a disposition of the will is never to be cast off and the particular act of prayer is to be performed daily as occasion is offered us.

23. The adjuncts of prayer are a confession and a promise to God, for these two are expressly or implicitly used in every acceptable prayer to God and in every part of it.

24. In prayer we have recourse to the mercy of God as to the fountain of all good granted or to be granted to us, and in so doing we confess that we are miserable in ourselves and void of all good in the attempt to affect and move God by our desires. We profess that our minds are duly concerned about the matters presented and promise that they will be concerned for the future. Such manifestations cannot be absent from our prayers without a certain mocking of God.

25. Confession is a humble and penitent acknowledgment of our offense, guilt, and misery, Ps. 32:5.

26. The end and reason for this confession is, first, that God may be justified and may have glory in his judgments, Ps. 51:6; second, that we may be disposed to obtain the grace of God, Ps. 32:5; and third, that the grace which is granted may appear more clearly.

27. The manner of it varies according to the condition of the sinners. Sins that are not known are to be confessed in general, Ps. 19:13, but sins that are known should be specifically confessed according to the nature and gravity of each one, Ezra 9:14.

28. The promise required in prayer is the testifying to a purpose agreeable to prayer.

29. This purpose is the will's earnest determination to see to it that what we pray to God for is done, Ps. 119:106, 112. (Compare with the verses following.)

30. We carry through in what we pray for both by means which in their own nature are necessary to the end and by other means which depend on contingent circumstances and our own choice.

31. A promise of the latter kind clearly made to God after deliberate consideration is, in a way, made one's own, and called a vow.

32. So a vow must be, first, something neither impossible nor simply necessary, but which may be freely performed according to our will by the ordinary grace of God. Second, something neither evil nor vain, but lawful and good in all circumstances. Third, it must refer only to God as the object of the vow and to his honor as the primary end, although it may redound to our own edification and benefit and that of others.

33. The manner of prayer may be either a short outburst of desire, during which moment the mind is not wholly or for any length of time engaged in prayer, Ps. 129:8; Neh. 2:4. Or it may be a continued chain of prayer.

34. The first ought to be more frequent since it cannot be hindered by ordinary business. The second must be at set times as it is more solemn and does not admit of distraction by other thoughts.

35. Either may be mental or audible.

36. Mental prayer is that which takes place in the will, mind, and

affection without any outside sign purposely used, Neh. 2:4; 1 Sam. 1:13.

37. Audible prayer is that which expresses the inward desire of the mind in words, Hos. 14:2.

38. The voice is the human organ of articulate speech which is often necessary to express, stir up, continue, and increase an inward affection of the mind. Even though the affection ought to precede the utterance, and the utterance conform to the affection, yet when the affection is religiously expressed by the voice, the expression has a certain reaction on the mind itself whereby it is kindled to a greater extent and has more power. Furthermore, the voice is in a way necessary so that the body and the soul may work together in this area of religion.

39. Speech, therefore, is not to be used which the one who prays does not understand and which cannot express his thoughts. Such repeating of unknown words is not truly the speech of a man because it is no more formed out of his inward thoughts than the words sometimes uttered by a parrot; it cannot express clearly the mind's inner feelings whereof prayer should primarily consist.

40. The speech should not be long nor repeat the same things often, Matt. 6:7 — unless from an abundance of the heart, for then neither long prayers nor repetitions are vain and purposeless. They are most acceptable to God, as sufficiently appears in proved examples of such prayers in the Scriptures.

41. Finally, there ought not to be such care of words as would deflect due attention either from God, the subject matter, or the inward affection of the mind.

42. In solemn audible prayers bodily attitudes are required which befit the majesty of God, our own baseness, and the matter at hand.

43. Audible prayer is either in prose or in meter.

44. Singing is metrical and, therefore, it requires greater care for speech and tone than prose.

45. The melody of singing is ordained for a certain spiritual delight whereby the mind is held in meditation on the thing that is sung.

46. Here more distinct meditation comes between the words and the lifting up of the heart than in other prayers; so the first and immediate fruit of a sung psalm is our edification in faith and in observance.

47. The lifting up of the heart to God is required along with the thing sung and following it — this is also the goal of the meditation. We are, therefore, said to sing in our hearts to the Lord, Col. 3:16. Sung psalms are a kind of prayer.

48. Because this religious melody is a kind of prayer it is hardly

fit that the decalogue and the like which are not in the nature of prayer be put into meter and sung in place of psalms.

49. Furthermore, because singing is directly connected with our edification and displays in its own nature the joy of the mind, Jas. 5:13, the same bodily attitudes which are becoming to other prayers are not required in these.

50. Prayer is either solitary or with others.

51. If prayer with others is in prose, one person leads with his own voice and the others follow in feeling and faith, which they ought to declare at the end by saying *Amen,* Neh. 8:6; 1 Cor. 14:16.

52. Antiphonal alternation of prayers, with parts divided between minister and people, and the voice of the people repeating words spoken by the minister is not to be approved.

53. The melody of singing leads to our mutual edification, attention, and the stirring up of pious affections towards one another, Col. 3:16, so all join their voices together, 1 Chron. 16:35; Mark 14:26.

54. In prayers which are said with others, speech must be used which is understood by others, 1 Cor. 14.

55. Broken music which the mind cannot follow should be kept out of holy exercises, at least in those which we have with others.

56. There are two kinds of prayer, petition and thanksgiving. Phil. 4:6, *In everything let your requests be made known to God in prayers and in supplication with the giving of thanks.*

57. Petition is a prayer to obtain something lacking. Matt. 7:7, *Ask, and it shall be given you; seek, and you shall find; knock, and it shall be opened unto you.*

58. What we ask is always lacking wholly or in part, in our perception, or in what we have done or are continuing to do.

59. Therefore, a sense of emptiness and need along with an apprehension of the sufficiency which can meet our insufficiency is necessarily required to make a true petition.

60. The virtue and efficacy of petition lies not in deserving or satisfying, as the papists would have it, but only in obtaining.

61. To "obtain" one must have the means to procure some good freely from another.

62. All good works or all observance flowing from faith have a certain power to obtain blessings from God as a free reward, because of the promise he has given. Hence a good work is called by some, though somewhat improperly, real prayer, distinct from audible and mental prayer. Yet petition obtains its desire in a special way not only because it is a prime part of observance, but because it has this end and use as its own nature. It is a true act of faith and hope through which we receive all good things from God.

63. But obtaining is connected properly not with the justice of God, but rather with his mercy and his kindness.

64. Therefore, we receive every good thing we ask from the hand not of justice but of grace.

65. Petition comes, in a quite formal sense, from faith and hope. Thus it has the same relation to the good things sought as those virtues have to their secondary objects. That is, the things which the virtues apprehend are to be communicated to us from God.

66. Hence only those things are to be asked which are absolutely necessary for the glory of God and for our salvation. But other things may be asked with a tacit submission to the wise disposition of God.

67. Neither the manner nor the particular time to communicate this or that ought to be prescribed to God in our prayers. Yet it is lawful to pray that God should hear us quickly. Ps. 102:2, *Hear me speedily*. He has promised to do this. Luke 18:8, *He will avenge them quickly*. Still it is not ours to define the suitable time for this quick hearing.

68. Since petition also flows from love those things are most to be desired and asked in prayers which most make for the celebration of the glory and goodness of God.

69. We ask not only for ourselves but for all others who are or may be partakers of the divine goodness, 1 Tim. 2:1-3.

70. The patriarchs and the prophets in their blessings not only prayed well, speaking their desires; they also promised well in the name of the Lord. The blessings contain Hebrew words meaning both, *Let God give* and *God shall give*, Gen. 27:28.

71. We should not pray specially for the dead because such prayer has no precept or commended example in the Scriptures nor any use or end. Neither should we pray that every living thing collectively should be saved, because we know the contrary has been determined by God. Yet we should not at all reject any particular living man from the communion of our prayers either from enmity, or from conjecture, or regarding probable signs of his reprobation.

72. Petition is twofold according to the object or thing which is asked. It is praying either for or against — either apprecation or deprecation.

73. Apprecation is petition for the bestowal of good things.

74. Deprecation is petition that evil things be removed. Intercession is connected with these, 1 Tim. 2:1, and is a special form of supplication occurring when the evil we desire to be removed lies in some injury done by men.

75. Plaint and lamentation are part of supplication.

76. Plaint is the expression of our grief over miseries inflicted by men.

77. In our plaint we sometimes call down evil on those who are the authors of the misery. But this is not ordinarily lawful except when it is a prayer to remove a greater evil by the evil we call down. The imprecations of the prophets were also predictions.

78. Lamentation is a sign of our grief over miseries sent by God.

79. Sometimes fasting is added to deprecation as an external accompaniment.

80. Fasting is abstinence from the helps and comforts of this life in which humility is shown in genuine confession and by which we are better equipped to make effectual prayers, 1 Cor. 7:5; Joel 1:14–16; Dan. 9:2, 3.

81. Fasting by itself is not a good work nor part of our obedience towards God, but it helps us make free, ardent, and more continued prayers.

82. The same manner and time for fasting are not equally profitable and necessary to all.

83. Finally, fasting is most religious when the whole mind is so attentive to seeking God that it is called away from the thought and care of the things of this present life.

84. Thanksgiving is prayer about those things we have received, in order to give honor to God. Ps. 50:15, 23, *I will deliver you, that you may glorify me. He who offers praise . . . glorifies me.*

85. It is prayer or praying no less than petition, for in giving thanks to God we make a religious submission of our will to God to influence or move him, as it were, yet the point of it is to refer something to God which we have received, and not to receive something.

86. Thanksgiving relates most to those things we have received, for we must have a sense of benefit before we can thank God.

87. Thanks are to be given not only for what we have actually and tangibly received, but also for the things we apprehend by faith and hope. This is so because the promise of these things is a benefit which in a way is already bestowed, and partly because the things promised are apprehended with such certainty that they act upon the mind as if they were at hand.

88. The giving of praise to God is also part of thanksgiving. We praise those perfections which are in God himself and shine forth in his works, and in a certain way have to do with what we have received; since those perfections are arguments proving that what we have received is good and that we have received it. Rev. 4:8, 9, *Holy, holy, holy . . . Lord God almighty . . . the living creatures give glory and honor and thanksgiving to him who sits upon the throne.*

89. Therefore, the right kind of thanksgiving requires, first, a knowledge of God's blessings; second, an applying them to ourselves through faith and hope; third, a true esteem of them with fitting gratitude.

90. The proper end of thanksgiving is to honor God for all the things we have received, Ps. 50:14. For if we simply accept the good things we have received, resting in them or glorying in ourselves, or ascribing them only to secondary causes, thanksgiving is spoiled.

91. Thanksgiving is thus a secondary end of every religious petition. He who rightly asks anything of God not only asks that he may receive (much less that he may spend it upon his lusts, Jas. 4:3), but also that he may relate what he has received to the glory of God who gave it. 2 Cor. 1:11, *You must help us by prayer, so that for the gift bestowed upon us by many persons, thanks may be given by many on our behalf.*

92. Hence in every petition, thanksgiving for the benefit sought is expressly or implicitly promised.

93. Thanksgiving is more perfect in itself and more excellent than petition, for in petition our good is often sought but in thanksgiving only God's honor.

94. Therefore, in the Scriptures thanksgiving is more often ascribed to the angels and to blessed spirits than is petition.

95. Through this act we are said not only to praise and celebrate God, but also to extol, bless, magnify, and glorify him and the like. These are to be understood as meaning not that they effect what they describe but that they declare the fact.

96. If thanksgiving is solemn, there should be a cheerful solemnity about it, Esther 9:19. Just as fasting over a greater evil both makes our himiliation greater and testifies to it, so in solemn joy for some particular good outward mirth, if it be moderate and within the bounds of temperance, makes the good greater and testifies to it.

97. Evils as evils can be the object neither of petition nor of thanksgiving. Yet afflictions which are ordered by God for our good may be the object of both.

X

Taking Oaths

1. There are two kinds of petition to be used on occasion which were introduced because of man's weakness: oaths and lots.

2. Because they were introduced as occasional, they must not be used often, but only when human necessity requires and a grave and just cause is involved.

3. An oath is the requesting of God's witness to confirm the truth of our witness. Heb. 6:13, 16, *Men swear by him who is greater than themselves, and a confirming oath is to them an end of all strife.*

4. Oaths were necessary after the fall, because man lost by sin both the credit due to his simple witness and that due to the witness of others.

5. The weakness of man in his failure to give credit to the witness of others is so great that it was in a way necessary for God to demean himself by confirming his testimonies in the form of an oath, Heb. 6:13, 17. This was more than was needed of God's faithfulness, but not more than was needed for human weakness.

6. Since God has no one greater or a judge higher than himself (Heb. 6:13) he cannot properly swear. Nevertheless swearing is attributed to him metaphorically because all the perfection of confirmation in the oaths of men is found most perfectly in the testimonies of God.

7. God's witness is rightly called upon to confirm truth because he is the highest truth, neither deceiving nor being deceived. Heb. 6:18, *It cannot be that God should lie.*

8. Therefore, religious worship is given to God in an oath because he is the acknowledged author of truth and conscious of all our thoughts. Things are naked and open to his eyes which are most secret to creatures; he rewards truth and falsehood and provides for all things by wonderful providence. He is the living God. Deut. 6:13, *Fear the Lord thy God and worship him and swear by his name.*

9. We may swear not by any creature, but only by God who alone is omniscient, the law giver, and the rewarder of conscience. Only he is to be worshiped religiously, Matt. 5:34, 35; 23:21, 22; Jas. 5:12.

10. But everything in an oath is not the worship of God for it does not lead directly to the giving of honor to God. Its purpose is to confirm the truth. Yet the petition made in an oath is worship and that part of swearing by the true God is sometimes called in Scrip-

ture true worship, Deut. 6:13; Isa. 48:1. The oath itself is ordinarily called worship.

11. In seeking the witness of God he who swears subjects himself to God's vengeance and curse, if he gives false testimony, that is, if he knowingly deceives. Therefore, in every oath there is contained implicitly or explicitly the utterance or calling down of a curse. Neh. 10:29; 2 Cor. 1:23, *Entered into a curse and an oath. I call God to witness against my soul.*

12. This aspect of swearing is frequent in the Old Testament, e.g., *So God do to me and more also.* In these words there is contained a general or indefinite curse, the way of inflicting the punishment being left to God.

13. Therefore, there is sufficient religion in an oath to shut out equivocation or mental reservation. These may be used in play or lighter jest but they cannot be used in the worship of God without great impiety, for they amount to nothing less than mockery of God's judgment.

14. Furthermore, no man can give a proper release from, commuting of, or dispensation and absolution from an oath (although some oaths unlawful either at the beginning or later to become so may by men be pronounced void).

15. Since an oath is witness to something done or to be done, it can be either an assertive or a promissory oath.

16. An assertive oath relates to something past or present, 2 Cor. 1:23. A promissory oath, in which an element of threat is contained, relates to a future matter, 1 Sam. 20:12–14.

17. An assertive oath, relating to something already done, does not bind one to do anything; it only confirms the truth of what has been done.

18. But such an assertion bears directly on the judgment of him who swears, being grounded on arguments usually called infallible. Thus an oath which agrees with such a judgment is to be accounted honest even though it may differ from the fact, for it reaches the fact only through the medium of judgment. In this way the Romans used that considerate phrase, "I think" [*arbitror*]; even when they were using an oath about things of which they were sure.

19. A promissory oath has the force of an assertive oath since it testifies to a present firm intention of the mind. But, in addition, it binds the swearer to do what is declared as intention.

20. It binds only as far as one can bind himself, i.e., to what he can actually and rightfully perform. It must, therefore, refer always to something lawful and possible.

21. This oath binds a man to fulfillment, even though the oath

was unlawful in manner or the thing promised may bring damage to the one who makes the promise, Josh. 9:19; Ps. 15:4.

22. But if the oath is against the commandments of God it does not bind, for an oath ought not to be a bond of iniquity.

23. Yet some oaths made against the promises of God do bind on occasion; as when, for example, the Jews to whom freedom had been promised, swore to be subject to the foreigners in whose power they found themselves.

24. A promissory oath which promises something to a man only as a favor ceases to bind if the man either cancels or takes away the basis upon which it was made.

25. An oath is lawful and honorable for Christians because, first, it is part of the natural or moral law which is not abrogated; second, it involves God's honor and love for one's neighbor; third, there are commendable examples of oaths used even in the New Testament, 2 Cor. 1:23; Rev. 6:10.

26. Christ in the fifth chapter of Matthew does not condemn every oath — but only those which are rash and indirect, sworn in the name of creatures.

27. Jas. 5:12 condemns the same abuse of an oath, but not all swearing. The construction shows that the repeated words of Christ, "Do not swear," form one sentence with those which follow, "either by heaven, or by earth." They are to be taken together and not separated.

28. Verily, verily is not a form of swearing but only a strong affirmation. The words in Heb. 6:14, Surely I will bless you, contain only the matter not the form of the oath found in Gen. 22:16, 17. The word verily does not appear there either in the Greek or Hebrew, as some have rashly asserted.

29. The words of an oath are to be interpreted in the inner court of conscience according to the meaning of the one who swore, if he acted simply and sincerely; but if he did not so act, then according to the meaning of the one whom he wanted to deceive or to whom he swore. In the outward court of human society, however, the words of those who swear are to be taken as commonly understood.

30. A man does not perjure himself, properly speaking, unless he swears against his conscience or knowingly and willingly departs from what he has lawfully sworn.

31. A promise that is confirmed by a lawful oath is to be kept, provided the circumstances remain the same, even to enemies, thieves, and pirates, for if the respect of persons does not make the oath unlawful, it cannot take away its force.

32. An oath that is extorted by fear does not for that reason cease

to bind, for acts extorted by fear, if they have reason behind them, are wholly voluntary, though not absolutely spontaneous.

33. Those who do not use reason to understand the nature of an oath are not capable of an oath.

34. To seek an oath from one who swears by a false God is not in itself a sin, Gen. 31:53.

35. An oath of a Christian concerning his innocency, which cannot be undercut by any arguments, ought to put an end to controversy on the matter, Exod. 22:11; Heb. 6:16.

36. An oath made only in simple words binds as much as the most solemn one.

37. The rite of touching or kissing a book used in some places is equivalent to the lifting up or the clasping of the hand. It signifies a consent to swear and agreement with the oath itself.

38. The putting of a hand under the thigh of the one asking an oath, Gen. 24:2, was not a mystical sign of Christ but a sign of subjection.

39. Adjuring is the act, properly speaking, of leading another either to swear, Gen. 24:8, or to respect the use of one's religious element in his oath, Num. 5:21; Matt. 26:63, 1 Thess. 5:27.

40. It, therefore, most properly belongs to those who have the right to require an oath of others although it also, to a degree, is part of the religious entreaty which inferiors sometimes use towards superiors and equals among themselves.

41. To adjure demons is to exercise command over them. It is not right, therefore, to exercise such adjuring unless one has received special power from God for the purpose.

42. Exorcisms used before baptism, even in the time of the Fathers, were superstitious.

43. The adjurings or exorcism of inanimate things and consecration of them to supernatural use, as the papists do with their holy water, temples, bells, and the like, are superstitious incantations.

44. The adjuring of a man to accuse himself for any crime brought against him (which is used in the oath called the oath of inquisition or the oath *ex officio*) has no ground in the Scriptures and is against the law of nature.

45. An indefinite adjuring to answer all things which shall be demanded is simply inadmissible.

XI

Lots

1. A lot is the asking of divine testimony to be manifested through a purely contingent event so that a controversy may be decided. Prov. 16:33, *The lot is cast into the lap, but the whole judgment is of the Lord;* 18:18, *A lot makes contentions cease and decides among the mighty.*

2. We call it an asking because the benefit which it expects comes from God alone, and so is directly related to his providence.

3. We call it a contingency so that we may avoid the error of those who commonly understand a lot to be an efficient cause which works by luck [*fortuna*].

4. There are many causes involving luck which differ completely from a lot, e.g., when one finds gold while digging for coal. Also there are many lots in which luck is no acting cause, e.g., when a lot depends upon the flying of birds or some similar effect produced by a cause which works of its own power.

5. It cannot be logically defended that the very cast of a die or any similar action in a lot is always outside the intention or purpose of the agent, but this is necessarily required for anything fortuitous.

6. But we place lots not in the category of contingencies in general, but in that of pure contingency, for there are three degrees of contingencies, some happening often, some seldom, and some, as far as we can understand, equally divided between these possibilities. In other contingencies, there is room for skillful conjecture, but not in pure contingency.

7. Therefore, it is not a fortuitous functioning of the efficient cause which controls a lot. The determining power is either that blind fortune which was made a goddess by profane men and placed in heaven, or the special providence of God working a way that is hidden to us.

8. Since the determination of some question or controversy is sought in a lot and since it is sought by pure contingency, plainly undetermined in itself, so far as we are concerned, it naturally follows that the very determination (whatever the actual intention of men may be) is to be sought from a higher power which can direct such contingencies according to a certain purpose. Therefore, the use of a lot is an appeal either to the true God or to some feigned power designated by many by the name of fortune or luck.

9. Thus, when our theologians teach that a certain extraordinary providence of God presides over lots, they are not to be understood as saying that those who use lots always look directly and distinctly to providence, or that God correspondingly always exercises a personal providence. They are saying that the lot of its own nature has a certain relationship to a singular and extraordinary providence of God which controls a purely contingent event. In this sense their judgment is most true.

10. The common consent of all expects some judgment in a lot. Yet there is no power of rendering judgment in contingent events themselves and no other fortune judging them than the sure providence of God; so it follows that judgment must be expected in a special way from God's providence.

11. Pure contingency itself cannot be a principal cause in deciding any question, nor can the man for whom the event itself is purely contingent direct it to such an end. Therefore, such direction is rightly to be expected from a superior power.

12. Add to this that when a man seeks an answer and has no certain means in his power for determining it, he turns to a superior power. Here the lot fits his purposes.

13. A man who works by counsel, having a certain end or purpose in view for certain reasons, cannot subject his work either to fortune or to pure contingency as such. For then counsel would be without knowledge and undetermined indifference would be a means to effect a determined cause.

14. Expectation of and regard for this singular providence of God is clearly taught in Prov. 16:33, where the action of every lot is affirmed as pure contingency for every man. *The lot is cast into the lap*, but with true discernment *the whole judgment* and its disposition are referred to God.

15. Although all things are in other ways referred to God's providence in the Scriptures, nothing is likely to be referred to it so distinctly unless there is a sure connection.

16. The Hebrew word מִשְׁפָּט, judgment, is sometimes used to signify something besides judgment. But this is not an objection, for the context must always be considered, and there is a certain function of judgment given to lots by all who describe their nature.

17. Hence a lot is not to be used rashly or in sporting or light ways or in those vain controversies which can be decided properly by ordinary means.

18. A lot is not to be used in ordinary affairs or without special revelation for divining, and not to determine a right nor, ordinarily, an action that is past. Its use is to settle a division or to effect a

choice, which otherwise could not be made, between two lawful alternatives. No other determination is possible without causing displeasure to the ones concerned.

19. Those who defend the use of lots in games are sufficiently refuted by one argument, namely, that a lot is held unanimously to have a natural fitness for asking counsel of God's providence in a special manner. It cannot be that one and the same action should by nature be specially adapted to so sacred a use and at the same time be fit for sports and gambling.

20. It does not follow, as is contended, that a lot can be used in a light and sporting way because it is lawful in civil controversies of lesser moment. Although the civil controversies in which a lot is used may not be of great significance, they become great by the consequences joining or adhering to them. The same cannot be said of contests for sport.

21. The determining of the tithes of animals (Lev. 27:32), and of the orders of priestly and Levitical administrations (1 Chron. 26:13, 14; Luke 1:9), might not have been feasible without some divine judgment. They were accordingly fixed by lot by divine institution.

22. The nature of lots does not fit them well for the lightest matters. We should not expect God's special determination unless we have done as much as is in us to decide the question before us, using ordinary means. But if our endeavor does not remove weightiness from the controversy, neither does it remove the need to decide the issue by lot.

23. Like an oath, the very nature of a lot is holy and has no need for special sanctification from any special institution. Although contingency, which is, as it were, the matter of a lot, is not of its own nature holy, as neither bread nor wine are, properly understood, yet in its use it takes on a kind of sanctity, as do the words of an oath and the elements in the sacraments.

24. Christians are free to use the creatures to the ends which they are naturally suited, or made to be suited. But pure contingency is not suited to determine any question, neither does it receive suitability from the consent of those who use it so. Even in those lots which are called extraordinary and acknowledged to depend upon God and not upon men, this consent is similarly involved but it adds nothing to the lot.

25. No one can show that a lot has no religious quality unless he can first demonstrate that there is no special appeal to God's providence in it.

26. Although the realm of sport is not tied to this or that type

of nonreligious action, yet it has natural boundaries which place it outside those things which uniquely pertain to communion with God.

27. It is quite vain to object that a lot often repeated will have various results. This is not likely to happen if a lot can be rightly repeated; and further, every appeal to God's providence does not necessarily bring with it his special action. And it is read that God sometimes in an extraordinary way has given various answers to those by whom he has been unreasonably tempted. Num. 22:12, 20, *Go not with them. . . . arise, go with them.*

28. It is even more vain to object (in place of an argument) that God cannot be induced at our pleasure to exercise an extraordinary providence. In spite of the objection, we may appeal to his extraordinary providence whenever it pleases us.

29. Therefore, diceplaying is repugnant to religion not only because of accompanying accidental circumstances but by its inner nature and of itself.

30. Under the name of dicing fall those sports grounded on pure contingency, although they may be governed in a secondary way by wit, industry, or skill — as in table dice and cards.

31. But human exercises grounded upon skill though in part subject to chance in their development are very different from dicing.

32. Men in playing dice are accustomed to swear, curse, and blaspheme more than in other activities. This happens partly because of the nature of the play itself — the lot being often repeated and failing the expectation of the players, they think the power which they imagine to govern the lot is against them.

33. For the same reason it happens that those who indulge in these games can scarcely put an end or a bound to them. This occurs because those who lose have no reason to despair of their lot and persist in a determined hope and expectation of success.

34. So the losses and harmful effects which corrupt other games as attendant circumstances depend in dicing partly upon the very nature of the play.

XII

Testing God

1. Any testing of God is opposed in a special way to prayer and the hearing of the word. Ps. 95:8–9, *Today if you will hear his voice, harden not your hearts in contention as in the day of trial in the wilderness, when your fathers tested me and proved me, though they had seen my works.* In hearing the word and in godly prayer we have communion with God according to his will; if we seek some similar communion beyond his will, then we are properly said to be testing him.

2. To test God is to seek some divine perfection in an unlawful manner, Ps. 95:9.

3. A trial is sometimes made of God's power. Ps. 78:18, 19, *They tested God in their heart. . . . And speaking against God they said, Can God prepare a table in the wilderness?* Men sometimes circumscribe God's power and set bounds to it at their pleasure, counting him omnipotent only if he does this or that which they want him to do. Ps. 78:41, *They tested God again and circumscribed the Holy One of Israel.*

4. Sometimes men test God's knowledge by doing something secretly and doubting whether God knows it or not. Ps. 94:7, *Saying, The Lord does not see; the God of Jacob does not perceive.*

5. Sometimes God's presence is tested. Exod. 17:7, *They tested God saying, Is the Lord among us or not?*

6. Sometimes God's providence is tested, as when men relinquish ordinary means appointed by God and expect him to provide for them at their wish, although he has promised no such thing, Matt. 4:7.

7. The testing may be of God's anger, justice, and vengeance. 1 Cor. 10:22, *Do we provoke the Lord to anger?* This kind of testing lies in all murmuring and strife against God or those sent by God. 1 Cor. 10:9, 10, *Let us not test Christ . . . do not murmur.* For this reason Massah and Meribah, or Proof and Contention, were names of the same place, Exod. 17:7.

8. Trial of God is occasionally made with the clear intention of a test, as in the unlawful casting of lots. It also occurs whenever we presume something of God which he has not promised.

9. Sometimes it is made with a secret and implied intent, namely, when that which is done of itself and in its own nature becomes a testing of God, although he who does it has no such thought.

10. This is done in two ways. First, when a person desires and expects something but refuses the means necessary for it, as a person does in the world of nature who desires health or continuance of life and yet rejects medicine or food. It occurs also in the world of the spirit when a person desires grace and life, but neglects the word of God, the sacraments, and similar means of grace and salvation. Second, when a person needlessly exposes himself to a danger from which he cannot or can hardly be delivered except by a miracle from God. So it is often in natural things when a person seeks vain glory in disdaining death and in spiritual things when a person seems, as it were, to love the occasions and enticements of sin.

11. This sin sometimes flows from doubt or unbelief, for he who tests God does not sufficiently trust the revealed word of God. He wants to undertake a new way of knowing the will of God. This is opposed to the hearing of the word insofar as it is to be received by us in faith.

12. Sometimes this sin flows from despair. Not expecting the promises of God, men wish to tell God in inordinate haste, as it were, when and how he may satisfy their expectations. And this is opposed to the hearing of the word insofar as it nurtures divine hope in us.

13. Sometimes it flows from a low esteem and contempt of God, as when a person plays and jests to see if God will show himself according to his desire. This is opposed to the hearing of the word insofar as it contains love and fit esteem for God.

14. It is based also on a certain arrogance and pride in which we refuse to subject our wills to the will of God and attempt to make his will subject to our lust.

15. But this sin comes most often from presumption whereby a person is confident that God will do something which he has never promised, or at least has not promised in the manner and by the means expected. So it is that some refer all testing of God to presumption. This arrogant attitude is opposed to prayer in which we humbly present our wishes to God to be carried out by him as he pleases.

16. Indeed, this sin is opposed to all acts of religion in which we depend upon the will of God — for when we test God we do it in such a way that God seems to depend upon our will.

17. We try God when we desire some special sign from him without any special reason, inspiration, or insight. Matt. 16:1, *The Pharisees and Sadducees testing him, required him to show them a sign from heaven.*

18. Yet to refuse a sign offered by God is to try or weary him. Isa. 7:11–13, *Ask a sign . . . I will not ask, neither will I tempt God*

. . . *you weary my God.* A believer may sometimes without sin humbly seek a sign from God about some special necessary thing which would otherwise be not clear. Gen. 15:8, *How shall I know that I shall inherit the land?*

19. The proving or purging of a suspected offense by the use of a hot iron, scalding water, and the like is a testing of God. For a miraculous showing of God's power is thereby expected or demanded to prove a hidden truth without good reason, for there are other means of finding out men's faults — and if these fail, the faults may go unknown without blame.

20. Of the same nature are single duels or monomachies, which were once permitted by public authority and still occur too often. Here, without any basis, the righteousness of a cause is committed for decision to a special providence of God bestowing success, as is thought, in accordance with his justice, and this without any good and sufficient reason.

21. Besides these testings, which are in the nature of a trial, there is also a test by inducement, so to speak, in which help is required or expected from God in committing some impious deed.

22. Such inducements may rightly be called a testing by trial, for the will of God is actually tried. They differ from others only in that the object about which the will of God is tried is an unlawful action in itself, and so the honor of God is especially hurt and violated. To testing is thus joined a kind of disgraceful mocking of God.

23. The testing or proving of God is sometimes done in good faith and by command. Mal. 3:10, *Try me now in this, says the Lord of hosts.*

24. But such a testing is an act of faith, leading us to obey and practice the things which God has commanded with the expectation of the fruit and blessing he has promised.

25. This lawful testing of God repels all the temptations of the devil.

26. The unlawful testing of God lays us open to the temptations of the devil; in fact, we are never overcome by any temptations of the devil unless we test God in some way.

XIII

Instituted Worship

1. Instituted worship is the means ordained by the will of God to exercise and increase natural worship.

2. The means ordained by God are wholly set forth in the second commandment, which forbids all contrary means of worship devised by men under the words, *graven image* and *likeness*. Since these were once the chief inventions of men for corrupting the worship of God, they are rightly used for all devices of man's wit pertaining to worship (by a synecdoche constantly used in the decalogue).

3. Worship does not depend in kind [*in specie*] and directly on the nature of God or on that honor which we owe to God because of creation. It depends rather upon the free institution of God.

4. Hence this worship has varied as the structure of the church has varied. It had one form before Christ and another afterwards.

5. Instituted worship is related to natural worship, otherwise it would not be worship, for one cannot give the honor due to God in any way other than by faith, hope, and love (so far as the essence of the act is concerned). Thereby, in due subjection, we receive from God what he sets forth for us and with the same subjection we offer all that may be offered to his honor. These acts of offering are themselves performed in a special manner by means which God has instituted for his honor. Therefore, a kind of secondary worship takes place in them and they share in a way with the acts of receiving.

6. Instituted worship is related to natural worship as an effect to a cause. It is a means and instrument by which faith, hope, and love function — and these are the components of natural worship. It is an auxiliary cause by which these are furthered; and it is an adjunct of natural worship, of which they form the substance.

7. It is most rightly called worship since it serves as a means and auxiliary cause for primary, natural worship.

8. By the command of God instituted worship depends upon and flows from the primary worship of God. This gives the reason and force of those arguments for they are based on the inward and really essential manner of worshiping God, as found in the second commandment, *They that love me and keep my commandments*; Deut. 10:12, 13, *What does the Lord require of you, but that you fear the Lord your God, walk in all his ways, and that you love and worship*

*the Lord your God with all your heart and all your soul, observing
the precepts of the Lord and his statutes.*

9. The rule of interpreting the Scriptures usually given by some is
not universally true, namely, that all duties are moral and immutable
which have moral and immutable reasons joined to them — unless
this is understood to mean that such duties follow from such reasons
if no special command intervenes. Lev. 11:44, *I am the Lord your
God, so sanctify yourselves, and be holy, as I am holy. Defile not
therefore yourselves with any creeping thing.*

10. No instituted worship is lawful unless God is its author and
ordainer. Deut. 4:1–2; 12:32, *Keep all things which I shall command
you. . . . Add not to the word which I command you, neither take
from it. . . . Everything which I command you observe to do. Add
not to it, or take from it.* 1 Chron. 10:14, *Our Lord broke in on us
because we did not seek him rightly.*

11. This is declared in those words of the commandment, *You
shall not make for yourself,* i.e., by your own cogitation or your own
judgment. Although the phrase, "for yourself," sometimes has another
or broader meaning, here the brief and strict style of the commandments excludes any broadening of the meaning; and it is also clear
that dependence upon man's vain cogitation is prohibited in other
places of Scripture relating to the same matter. Amos 5:26, *Which
you made for yourselves;* Num. 15:39, *Follow not your own heart and
your own eyes, after which you follow a-whoring.*

12. The same is also brought out in the universality of the prohibition in the commandment, including all *Of the things which are
in heaven above, in the earth beneath, or in the waters under the
earth.*

13. For no one besides God can know what will be acceptable
to him and impart that virtue to worship to make it effectual and
profitable to us. Nothing can honor God unless it comes from him
as the author. Finally, we do not read that the power of ordaining
worship at one's pleasure was ever given to any man by God. Matt.
15:9, *In vain do they worship me, teaching for doctrines the precepts of men.*

14. Therefore, implicitly and by God's own interpretation, we make
God ours and give him due honor in religious worship. We subject
ourselves to his authority and ordinances.

15. In this sense men are sometimes said to worship the devil
when they follow the worship which the devil introduced, 1 Cor.
10:20; Lev. 17:7; Deut. 32:17.

16. But we must follow the worship which God has appointed

with the same zeal with which we receive his word or will and call upon his name, Deut. 6:17, 18; 12:25, 28; 13:18; 28:14.

17. Some of the means so ordained by God lead directly to the exercise and increase of faith, hope, and love, e.g., the public and solemn preaching of the word, celebration of baptism, the Lord's Supper, and prayer. And some are for the right performance of these very acts, such as the gathering of the faithful into congregations or churches; the election, ordination, and ministry of ministers ordained by God; and the care of ecclesiastical discipline.

18. The first-named acts belong most properly to the instituted worship of God. The others are also worship, not only in the general sense that every act is one of religious worship which in any way comes from or is guided by religion, but also in their special nature, for their end and use is equally that God should be rightly worshiped.

19. All of these means, therefore, ought to be observed by us both in general and in particular because they are appointed by God. God must be worshiped by us with his own worship, wholly and solely — nothing must be added, taken away, or changed, Deut. 12:32.

20. That is a most empty distinction which some people make to excuse their additions to worship: "Only corrupting and not conserving additions are forbidden." For every addition as well as every subtraction is a departure from the observance and keeping of the commandments of God, and a corruption of them, Deut. 12:32.

21. Of the same nature is the evasion which is made when it is said that only the addition of essentials is forbidden, not accidentals. Although there are some "accidents" or adjuncts in worship, there is no worship which may simply be called accidental, because all worship has in it its own essence. Furthermore, as the least commandments of God even to jots and tittles are to be observed religiously, Matt. 5:18, 19, so additions that seem very small are for the same reason rejected. Last, Moses seals even those laws of place and manner of divine worship, of abstinence from blood, and the like (which are certainly accidental to worship), with the caution not to add to or take away from them, Deut. 12:32.

22. This worship is called obedience for a special reason, because in it we do that which seems right in the eyes of the Lord, although something else might seem more right in our own eyes, Deut. 12:25, 28.

23. Opposed to instituted worship is will-worship which is devised by men and is unlawful, Matt. 15:9; Col. 2:23.

24. The sin committed in will-worship is generally called superstition.

25. Superstition occurs when improper worship is given to God.

26. In superstition God is always the object and in some way the end, but the worship itself is unlawful.

27. It is called improper worship either because of the manner or measure or because of the matter and substance of the worship. The Pharisees offended in the former way on the matter of the sabbath when they urged its observance by the stopping of work beyond the manner and measure appointed by God. And they offended in the latter way by observing and pressing for their own tradition, Mark 7:8.

28. Therefore, superstition is called an excess of religion not in regard to the formal virtue of religion (for no one can be too religious), but in regard to the acts and external means of religion.

29. Excess of this sort is found not only in positive acts involving the use of things, but also in abstinence from things such as meat, which are held to be unclean or unlawful, and the like.

30. Abstinence from lawful things (although they may be considered unlawful) is not, properly speaking, superstition unless some special worship or honor is intended for God by the abstinence.

31. This improper worship stands either against the worship wherein instituted worship is set forth and exercised — hearing the word, celebrating the sacraments, and prayer — or against that worship which deals with the means of instituted worship.

32. The hearing of the word is opposed, first, by teaching through images devised by men, Deut. 4:15, 16; Isa. 40:18; 41:29; Jer. 10:8, 15; Hab. 2:18. Second, it is opposed by a vaunting of traditions which are propounded as rules of religion, Mark 7:8.

33. Religious teaching by images is condemned, first, because they are not sanctified by God to such an end; second, because they can represent to us neither God himself nor his perfections; third, because they debase the soul and call our attention away from the spiritual contemplation of the will of God; fourth, because once admitted into the exercise of worship, by the perversity of man's mind, the worship itself is transferred, at least in part, to them. This is declared in the words of the commandment, *Thou shalt not bow down to them nor worship them.*

34. Similar to images are all ceremonies instituted by men with mystical or religious meanings.

35. Such ceremonies have no fixed power of teaching given by nature or divine institution, and they can receive no power from human institution because man cannot create this by his command, since it is beyond his authority, or by his demand, since God has promised no such thing to the asker.

36. Men cannot arrogate to themselves the authority for instituting such ceremonies because all churches are commanded to do all things

decently and in order, 1 Cor. 14:40. Respect for order and decency requires not that any new holy things should be instituted, but that those instituted by God should be employed in the manner becoming their dignity. Order and decency pertain not only to holy things but also to civil duties — for in each case confusion and unseemliness are vices opposed to the right and necessary way of attaining of the ends and uses for which each are intended.

37. Opposed to the sacraments are, first, sacrifices properly so-called, whether they be bloody or, as the papists say about their mass, bloodless. For since the coming of Christ, all former sacrifices are abrogated; and there is to be no new ordinance because the sacrifice of Christ once offered removes the need of other types, save only those which manifest and seal Christ for our benefit — as is sufficiently done in the sacrament according to God's ordinance — without sacrifices.

38. The institution and use of new seals or ceremonies confirming some grace of God is also opposed to the sacraments, for the one who gives grace can alone seal it.

39. Prayer is opposed by the use of representative images at or before which God is worshiped, even though the worship is referred not to the images themselves — subjectively, as some say — but objectively to God alone.

40. Superstition of this type is called idolatry, Exod. 32:5; Ps. 106:20; Acts 7:41.

41. If idols are themselves worshiped instead of God, this is the idolatry which violates the first commandment. If the true God is worshiped at an image or in an image, this is the idolatry which violates the second commandment.

42. Although such a worshiper does not in intention offend against the primary or highest object in worship, yet from the nature of the thing itself he always offends against the formal worship of God. In his mind a new God, who is delighted with such worship, is imagined as the object of his adoration; religious worship is also given to the image itself. This occurs even when the worship is not considered to be ultimately bound up with the image but is directed to God himself.

43. Therefore, we must shun this kind of idolatry as well as the absolute idolatry of the first commandment. We must also shun the very idols, and the idolothytes or things dedicated to idols, and all the mementos of idols, 1 John 5:21; 1 Cor. 8:10; 10:18, 19, 21; 2 Cor. 6:16; Num. 33:52; Deut. 12:2, 3; Exod. 23:13.

44. Superstition of the second kind is found in the human forms of the church, such as churches that are visibly, and organically ecumenical, provincial, or diocesan, brought in by men. Superstition is also found in the hierarchy which goes with such churches, in the or-

ders of the religious found among the papists, and in their acts and judgments.

45. Intolerable is the audacity of the men who, in order to· save their images, either omit the second commandment altogether or teach that it ought to be so shorn of its meaning that the reading under the New Testament should now be: You shall not adore or worship any likeness or image.

XIV

The Manner of Divine Worship

1. The circumstances of worship to be especially observed are the manner [*modus*] which is described in the third commandment and the time which is commanded in the fourth.

2. These are such close adjuncts of religious worship that in a secondary sense they partake of the meaning and nature of it. Observance of them promotes not only the honor of God which is found in both the natural and the instituted worship of God, but also a certain special honor to him in that their observance is connected with natural and instituted worship by his command and in a direct and immediate way.

3. In general the way to worship is to use lawfully the things which pertain to God.

4. Lawful use consists in the handling of all things in worship in a way agreeable to the majesty of God.

5. The third commandment contains the prohibition: *You shall not take the name of God in vain.* By the name of God is understood all those things by which God is made known to us or reveals himself, just as men are known to one another by their names. Therefore, the name of God embraces all those things which pertain to the worship of God, natural or instituted. Acts 9:15, *That he may bear my name among the Gentiles;* Deut. 12:5, *The place which the Lord . . . shall choose . . . to place his name;* Mic. 4:5, *We will walk in the name of the Lord our God;* Mal. 1:11, 12, *My name shall be great among the Gentiles.*

6. To take this name in vain is to take it rashly — that is, without any purpose, without a just and fitting end; or to take it in vain — that is, not in a manner demanded by the just end, which is the honor of God. It is also commanded that we sanctify the name of God, or

use all holy things in the manner which is suitable to their holiness and dignity, Isa. 1:13.

7. That suitable manner is found when the circumstances are established which the nature of religious things requires.

8. We define this manner in terms of circumstances because the essential manner of the powers and acts of religion is contained in the powers and acts themselves and is directly enjoined in the same commandments with them. The accidental manner of the circumstances, however, is set forth specially in the third commandment, for though it is in a way separable from the acts of religion, they need it to be acceptable to God.

9. These circumstances are either inward or outward.

10. The inward are antecedent, concomitant, or consequent.

11. The antecedent circumstances are a desire and stirring up of the mind or preparation in appropriate meditation on the things which pertain to the holy matter to be handled. Eccles. 5:1, 2, *Take heed to thy feet when thou enterest the house of God. . . . Be not swift with thy mouth, and let not thy mind hasten to utter a thing before God.*

12. This preparation relates chiefly to the more solemn acts of religion. For meditation by which the mind is stirred up, though it is an act of religion, does not itself require previous preparation, or there would be an infinite regress; those acts which by their nature are less perfect ought to give way to the more perfect and more solemn ones.

13. Therefore, before the public and solemn hearing of the word and prayer, private prayer is required, and before private prayer, if it be solemn, there is required some meditation on those things with which our prayers have to do, whether about God to whom we pray or about ourselves who are about to pray or about the things which are to be prayed for.

14. The concomitant circumstances are reverence and devotion.

15. A certain general reverence for God is part of any obedience which respects the commanding authority of God. But this particular reverence properly has to do with those acts of religion which stress the holiness of the things we do.

16. Such reverence contains, first, a due prizing of the worth of such things, second, a fear of too much familiarity by which such things might be desecrated.

17. Devotion also contains two parts. First, a certain special readiness to perform those things which belong to the worship of God. Ps. 108:1-3, *O God, I will sing with a fixed heart . . . I will awake right early.* Second, a proper delight in performing them. Isa. 58:13, *If you shall call the sabbath a delight.*

18. Hence a greater and different concern is called for in hearing the word of God than in receiving the edicts of princes — and in calling upon the name of God than in making supplication to any man.

19. The consequent circumstances are two, first, to retain the force and, as it were, the taste of the worship in our minds, second, to fulfill its purpose and put it to use with full effort.

20. The outward circumstances are those which belong to order and decency. 1 Cor. 14:40, *Let all things be done decently and in order.*

21. The general rule is that these be ordered in a way to make for the most edification, 1 Cor. 14:26.

22. Such circumstances are place, time, and the like, which are adjuncts common to religious and civil acts.

23. These circumstances are likely to be called by some religious and ecclesiastical rites and ceremonies, but they have nothing proper to religion in their nature. Religious worship is not found in them; but the holiness of religious worship is in some way violated by their neglect and contempt. The common matter of order and decency which is equally necessary to religious and civil actions cannot be severed from religious worship without some loss of dignity and majesty.

24. Such circumstances, therefore, which are civil or social in their own nature are not specially commanded in the Scriptures partly because they are part of men's common sense and partly because it would be beneath the dignity and majesty of the law of God that such things be prescribed one by one. On such a procedure many ridiculous things would have been handled by special law, e.g., that in the church assembly one should not sit on another's lap, spit in another's face, or make faces during worship. But the circumstances in question are to be counted as being in accord with God's will. They are commanded, first, under the general law of order, decorum, and edification; second, most of them necessarily follow from the things expressly appointed by God. When God prescribed that the faithful of all sorts should meet together to celebrate his name and worship he ordained thereby that they should have some fit and suitable place to meet, an assigned hour when they could all be present; and when a minister is appointed by God to teach publicly, it follows that it is also appointed that he have a place to live and bodily conditions fit for his functions.

25. These matters of order and decency, therefore, are not left to man's choice so that on that score he may foist whatever he pleases upon the churches. They are determined partly by the general precepts of God, partly by the nature of the things themselves, and partly by the circumstances of the occasion.

26. The various circumstances of order and decency are such that, though they have not been historically instituted, their principles must

be observed by everyone. Indeed, men cannot forbid them without sin.

27. But ordinances about such circumstances as place, time, and the like are rightly said by the best authorities to be partly divine and partly human. They are grounded in part upon the will of God, because of their chief and primary purpose, and partly upon man's prudence, insofar as a special observation agreeable to God's will is concerned. If no human error is made in this matter, the ordinance is to be held as wholly divine. It is the will of God that the church meet at the most convenient hour of the day, all circumstances considered. If, therefore, no error occurs in estimating the circumstances, the hour assigned for meeting after due consideration must be acknowledged as if appointed by God.

28. The special manner of the worship of God is to be determined as the individual nature of each religious act requires.

29. So must be determined the right manner of hearing the word of God, calling upon his name, sharing the sacraments, exercising ecclesiastical discipline, and performing all those things which belong either to the natural or instituted worship of God, Ezek. 33:31; Matt. 13:19; 1 Cor. 11:27, 29; Isa. 66:5.

30. With oaths, since the manner of swearing is held especially important, reference is made by many (not without all reason) to this passage in the third commandment, although oaths by their nature pertain to the first, Lev. 19:12; Matt. 5:34; 2 Chron. 36:13.

31. Contrary in kind to the proper manner is, first, the vice called by some acedia, in which one is apathetic to things divine and spiritual, 2 Tim. 4:3. This stands against the desire we should have for spiritual things, 1 Peter 2:2.

32. Second, the slothfulness in which one refuses the eagerness and labor that are required for divine things, Rom. 12:11. This is opposed to the stirring up and fervor of the mind with which we should pursue divine things, Rom. 12:11; Ps. 57:8, 9.

33. Third, the neglect and contempt of holy things and the abuse of them to a base, ludicrous, and frivolous level — all of which are opposed to the reverence due to holy things, Luke 19:46.

34. Fourth, torpor and wandering of mind in exercises of worship, Heb. 5:11; Ezek. 33:31. This stands against devotion, such as was found in Cornelius, Acts 10:2.

35. Fifth, rashness or frivolousness in using either the name of the titles of God or the things which have special reference to him, Jer. 23:34; Luke 13:1. This is opposed to the pursuit of the just end, which ought to be present with reverence in the use of such things, 1 Cor. 11:17.

36. Sixth, forgetfulness (mentioned in Jas. 1:24, 25) which is op-

posed to reaping the benefit and keeping the power, as we ought to do after acts of religion.

37. Seventh, confusion, which is opposed to order and decency, 1 Cor. 14:33.

XV

The Time of Worship

1. The most solemn time for worship is now the first day of each week, called the Lord's Day, Rev. 1:10; 1 Cor. 16:2.

2. It is called the Lord's Day for the same reason that the holy supper of the Eucharist is called the Lord's Supper, 1 Cor. 11:20. It was instituted by our Lord Jesus Christ and is to be referred to one and the same Lord in its end and use.

3. Natural reason dictates that some time be set apart for the worship of God, for man needs to have time for all his actions, especially his outward ones, and he cannot conveniently attend divine worship unless he cease from other works during the time.

4. To this extent, therefore, the time of worship is based upon the same precept as worship itself. When God created the whole world he is said also to have created time with it. In the same way, when he commanded and ordained religious actions he also commanded and ordained a certain time as a necessary circumstance.

5. That some particular day should be set apart for the more solemn worship of God is a natural moral law [jus]. It is not unknown to the heathen, who have had set and solemn feast days in every age.

6. Positive law decrees that this holy day should occur at least once in a week, or in the compass of seven. But this is also by unchangeable institution so that for our duty and obligation the day has the same force and reason as those which by their nature come under moral and natural law. So the day is rightly said by the schoolmen to come under moral law not by nature, but by custom.

7. That the institution of the day was not ceremonial or temporal appears sufficiently from the fact that it was not specifically for the Jews, or given for the time of the ceremonial law. None can or dare deny that such a fixing of the day might at least have been for a moral reason and benefit. For though natural reason does not dictate the fixing of it as necessary, it does dictate it as appropriate. It apprehends that it is fitting for the worship of God to be frequently exercised, and

for this reason it must acknowledge that the fixing of the day, so far as frequency is concerned, is fitting.

8. That it was not ceremonial appears in the beginning account of the creation where, though there was no place for ceremonies pointing to Christ the Redeemer, the seventh day, or one day out of seven, was set apart for the worship of God, Gen. 2:3.

9. Some contend that the seventh day was mentioned as a prolepsis or anticipation, so that it was sanctified in the mind and purpose of God but not yet in execution, or that a foundation was then established for a sanctification to come but not the obligation or law itself. This position may be refuted by various arguments. First, this idea of anticipation never entered the mind of any man except one who had first anticipated the observance of the Lord's Day with prejudice. The Jews of old never dreamed of it. Their received opinion was that this feast was πάνδημον . . . καὶ τοῦ κόσμου γενέθλιον, among all nations from the beginning of the world (Philo, Περὶ κόσμου, or *Concerning the World*, sec. 89).[12] In the New Testament no such anticipation is taught or implied. Even the authors of this opinion grant that some observance of the seventh day probably existed from the very beginning, Suarez, *Feast Days*.[13] The best interpreters (Luther, Calvin, and the like), none of whom, as all admit, offended in giving too much to the Lord's Day, simply and candidly acknowledge that the seventh day was sanctified from the beginning of the world. Second, no example of such anticipation occurs in all the Scriptures. Although the names of some places are sometimes used in an anticipatory fashion, especially in the Book of Genesis, there is no mention of such a proleptic institution either in that book or in any other of the whole sacred Scripture.

Third, the words and phrases of Gen. 2:2, 3 show the contrary, for the perfection of creation is twice plainly joined with the sanctification of the seventh day in the same manner and phrase as the creation of other creatures and of man himself is joined with the blessing of them,

12. Philo Judaeus (c. 20 B.C.–A.D. 50), the most important philosopher and biblical exegete among the Hellenistic Jews.

13. The full title is *De sacrorum seu festorum dierum observatione et praecepto*, or *The Observation and Teaching of Sacred or Feast Days*, which is Bk. II of *Tractatus primus de nature et essentia virtutis religionis in tres libros divisus*, or *First Treatise on the Nature and Essence of Religious Virtue, Divided into Three Books*, in *Opera omnia* (editio nova, a Carolo Berton, apud Ludovicum Vivès, Parisiis, 1859), or *The Complete Works*, Vol. XIII. Hereafter Bk. II of the *Tractatus primus* will be cited as Suarez, *De diebus festis*, or *Feast Days*, which is Ames's form of reference.

Francisco Suarez (1548–1617), the Spanish Jesuit who taught at a Jesuit college in Rome where Bellarmine was his colleague, exerted a mighty, if not controlling, influence on Ames's theory of law. See especially Suarez, *De legibus ac de Deo legislatore*, or *Laws and God the Lawgiver*, in *Opera Omnia*, Vols. V–VI.

Gen. 1:21, 22, 27, 28. Fourth, neither the purpose of God nor the actual basis for the seventh day gives ground and support for the use of such words of sanctification and blessing. For, if this idea of anticipation were followed, God could be said to have sanctified water, bread, and wine for the sacraments of the new covenant from the time that he gave the promise of bruising the serpent's head by the seed of the woman, Gen. 3:15. (It can only be said that God planned then to seal the covenant of grace by such seals, the sealing being based partly in the promise itself and partly in the creation of the things which might actually be used in the sealing.) Fifth, from the foundation laid in the first creation the prophet finds a perpetual rule and law. Mal. 2:15, *Did he not make one . . . and why one? To produce godly offspring.* So we may ask: Did not God rest on the seventh day — and why the seventh day? To sanctify the seventh day to himself. Sixth, the argument of the Apostle in Heb. 4:3–5, 7–9, appears to rest upon the point of a double rest in the Old Testament. The godly partake of both in this life: the one referring to the sabbath day and the other to the land of Canaan. And David in Psalm 95, promising rest, speaks neither of the sabbath day because that had been in existence from the beginning of the world, nor of the rest of the land of Canaan which was past and not *today* to be expected; he understands rather a third rest, eternal in heaven.

10. There is no record in the history of Genesis that the first patriarchs held to the observance of the seventh day as holy — but this is no hindrance. First, all and everything observed by them for fifteen hundred years neither could nor ought to have been set down in particular in so short a history as that found in Genesis. Thus, though the law of the sabbath was delivered by Moses, no mention is made of its observance in the Book of Judges and other histories. Second, even if it is granted that the observance of this day was for the most part neglected, this would in no way cast doubt on its first institution. Polygamy of the same age no more demonstrates that the sacred laws of wedlock were not instituted at the time of the very first marriage. Third, before the promulgation of the law on Mount Sinai the observance of the sabbath is set forth and urged not as a new thing but as ordained of old, Exod. 16:24–30. Although the same may be affirmed of sacrifices and other ceremonial observances, yet in the sabbath there seems to be a reference, for reasons already given, to the first institution at the time of man's creation. Note the past tense of verse 29, *The Lord has given you.* Fourth, even among the heathen there was always a trace of the observance of the seventh day; it is more than probable that the observance of the seventh day was delivered to them from the patriarchs who were their forefathers. Josephus in his last

book *Against Apion* states that "no city of the Greeks or the barbarians can be found which has not adopted the custom of rest from labor
on the seventh day." [14] Clement of Alexandria in the *Stromateis*, or
Miscellaneous Studies, Book V, indicates the same: ἀλλὰ καὶ τὴν
ἐβδόμην ἱερὰν οὐ μόνον οἱ Ἑβραῖοι, ἀλλὰ καὶ οἱ Ἕλληνες ἴσασι, "Not only
the Hebrews but also the Greeks observed the seventh day." [15] Eusebius, in *De preparatione evangelica*, or *Preparation for the Gospel*,
Book XIII, chapter 13, affirms that "Not only the Hebrews but almost
all philosophers and poets knew that the seventh day was more
holy." [16] Lampridius in *Alexander Severus* tells that when he was in the
city on the seventh day he went up to the Capitol and frequented the
temples.[17] For a somewhat similar purpose holy days were regularly
granted to children in schools on the seventh day, Lucian in *Pseudolo-
gista*,[18] and Aulus Gellius, Book XIII, chapter 2.[19] And some heathen

14. *Against Apion*, Bk. II, par. 40. For a later edition, see *The Works
of Flavius Josephus* (trans. and ed. William Whiston and A. R. Shiletto,
George Ball and Sons, London, 1890), Vol. V, 258. Josephus, born A.D.
37–38, priest and Pharisee from an aristocratic Jewish family and a Roman
citizen, is known chiefly for his *Antiquities of the Jews*. Among his last works
were two essays which vindicated the Jewish people from the calumnies of
Apion, an anti-Semitic Alexandrian scholar.

15. *Stromateis*, Bk. V, ch. 14. For a modern edition, see *Ante-Nicene
Fathers* (Alexander Roberts and James Donaldson, eds., William B. Eerd-
mans, Grand Rapids, 1956), Vol. II, 469. Clement of Alexandria (c. 150–
c.215), an Athenian and convert to Christianity, became head of the cate-
chetical school at Alexandria in 190. The Greek and Latin of the section
of the *Stromateis* quoted here may be found in *Patrologia Graeca* (J. P.
Migne ed. Parisiis, 1857), or *Writings of the Greek Fathers*, Vol. IX, pt. 2,
cols. 161, 162. Hereafter cited as *Patrologia Graeca*.

16. An apologetic work, quoted as Bk. XIII, ch. 7, in Suarez, *De diebus
festis*, p. 244. Eusebius (c. 260–c. 340), bishop of Caesarea, is often considered the "father of church history."

17. Aelius Lampridius lived in the fourth century during the reigns of
Diocletian and Constantine the Great. His attributed *Alexander Severus* dealt
with Marcus Aurelius Severus Alexander (208–35), the "open-minded em-
peror" who had busts of Orpheus, Abraham, Apollonius of Tyara, and Jesus
Christ in his private chapel. For a modern edition, see *Scriptores historiae
Augustae* (trans. David Magie, G. P. Putnam's Sons, New York, 1924), or
Writings of the Augustan History, Vol. II, 178–313.

18. Ψευδολογιστὴς ἢ περὶ τῆς ἀποφράδος κατὰ Τιμάρχου, or *The Mistaken Critic, or A Discourse on the Word Nefandous, against Timarchos*, in
Luciani Samosatensis Opera (ex recensione Guilielmi Dindorfii, editore Am-
brosio F. Didot, Parisiis, 1842), or *The Works of Lucian of Samosata*, pp.
622–31. Lucian of Samosata, born c. 120, died after 180, settled in Athens at
about age 40; he turned from Sophistic rhetoric to the study of philosophy and
developed a variety of satiric dialogue, the form of which was derived from
earlier writers, especially Plato.

19. *Noctes Atticae* (ex recensione Martini Hertz, sumptibus et typis
B. G. Teubneri, Lipsiae, 1871), or *Athenian Nights*, Vol. I, 71–72. This
major work of Gellius (c. 123–c. 165), lawyer and student of literature, dealt
in 20 volumes with such diverse topics as grammar, law, history and antiquities, biography, textual criticism.

professors were accustomed to dispute only upon the sabbath, as Suetonius relates of one Diogenes, Book III.[20] See also Hesiod, *Works and Days*, Book II, ἕβδομον ἱερὸν ἦμαρ, "The seventh is a holy day"; [21] and Linus, ἑβδομάτη δ' ἠοῖ καὶ οἱ τετύκοντο ἄπαντα . . . . ἑβδόμη εἰν ἀγαθοῖσι, καὶ ἑβδόμη ἐστὶ γενέθλη, "Among good days is the seventh day. . . . The seventh is among the prime, and the seventh is perfect." [22] Fifth, forgetfulness or carelessness and neglect regarding this day is clearly reproved by the hortatory word used in the beginning of the fourth commandment, *Remember*.

11. But the law regarding this institution and its moral authority is primarily based on the express command in the decalogue. For it is a sure rule, accepted by all the best theologians, that moral precepts were distinguished from ceremonial and judicial ones in their transmittal in that all and only moral laws were publicly proclaimed before the whole people of Israel from Mount Sinai by the voice of God himself and later written, as it were, by the finger of God himself on tablets of stone to declare their perpetual and unchangeable duration. Christ also testifies expressly that not one jot or tittle of this law should perish, Matt. 5:18.

12. The matter of the fourth commandment is not in degree or mode of the same moral nature as that of almost all the other commandments, for it is part of positive law and not natural law. The three previous commandments are negative and forbid the vices to which we are prone because of our depraved nature. This fourth commandment is propounded first affirmatively by declaring and commanding our duty and then negatively by forbidding the things repugnant to our duty. The admonition specially placed before the precept, *Remember the sabbath day*, or remember to keep this day (as

20. *The Life of the Caesars* (J. C. Rolfe trans. G. P. Putnam's Sons, New York, 1920), Vol. I, Bk. 3 (on Tiberius), pp. 340–41. Tranquillus Gaius Suetonius (c. 69–c. 140) was secretary to the Emperor Hadrian; after dismissal from imperial service he devoted his life to biographical studies. Diogenes, a famous grammarian during the time of Tiberias Caesar (42 B.C.–A.D. 37), lectured every sabbath at Rhodes. Instead of admitting Tiberias' when he came to hear him on a different day, Diogenes sent a message putting Tiberias off until the seventh day. Later when Diogenes waited before the emperor's door to pay his respects, Tiberias bade him return seven years later.

21. *Patrologia Graeca*, Vol. IX, pt. 2, cols. 161, 162. Hesiod, generally thought to have lived shortly after Homer, wrote his Ἔργα καὶ ἡμέραι, or *Works and Days*, as a poem of moral admonitions; it includes an account of the so-called "five ages of the world."

22. For the quoted part of the *Linus*, a traditional, mournful-sounding song, see *Patrologia Graeca*, Vol. IX, pt. 2, cols. 163, 164. Ames probably thought Linus was a person. Callimachus (c. 305–c. 240 B.C.), the Alexandrian teacher and elegist, is the author. See Eusebius, *De preparatione evangelica*, or *Preparation for the Gospel*, in *Patrologia Graeca*, Vol. XXI, Bk. 13, ch. 13, cols. 1119, 1120.

explained in Deut. 5:12), also in part illustrates the fact that the commandment belongs to positive law more than other duties which are more natural, since as such it could more easily slip into oblivion. Yet the positive law upon which this ordinance is grounded is divine law and is unchangeable so far as man is concerned.

13. Those who turn the fourth commandment into allegories of cessation from sin or from the troubles of this life and the like, propounding a fourfold or fivefold sabbath, typical of those who play with allegories, attribute to this member of the decalogue nothing which does not as well and even better fit with many Jewish ceremonies now abrogated.

14. And those who would make this commandment ceremonial (as they would make the second too), besides being refuted by the arguments above, contradict the express witness of Scripture which affirms that ten words or moral precepts are contained in the decalogue, Exod. 34:28; Deut. 4:13; 10:4. They would have only nine, or even eight.

15. Those who claim that the moral sense of the precept is only that some time or certain days be assigned to divine worship do not make the ordinance any more moral than the building of the tabernacle and the temple among the Jews. For by the latter it was declared simply that according to the perpetual will of God some fit place always be set aside for church meetings and public exercises of divine worship. There is nothing more moral in a precept concerning time of worship than in one concerning place; "You shall observe feast days" (which is all they leave in the fourth commandment) ought no more to be put in the decalogue than "You shall frequent the temples."

16. Furthermore, they argue that annual feast days, new moons, and similar ordinances which were merely ceremonial are alike in general and still teach us that some suitable days should be appointed for public worship. Their reasoning leads to a belief that this precept contains no command at all for men collectively or individually. The setting apart of days in their opinion is only commanded directly and private men do not have the power to ordain certain days for public worship. On this score nothing at all would be ordered except by those who are in public office. No particular commandment is given to them, but only a general one, so that they may act according to their own wisdom in setting apart days for public worship. If it seems good to them to appoint one day out of twenty or thirty for this use, they could not thereby be reproved for the sin of breaking this commandment.

17. If there was ever anything ceremonial in the observance of the

sabbath, it is to be understood as an addition or something extrinsic to the nature and first institution of the sabbath. And thus nothing stands against the particular moral significance of the institution of the seventh day. Ceremonies of one type or other were likewise added to other commandments; for example, the authority of fathers and the firstborn in families, based on the fifth commandment, in a way adumbrated Christ the firstborn among the sons of God.

18. Moreover, it does not clearly appear in the Scriptures that any ceremony, or a type of it, properly speaking, existed in the observance of the seventh day. Heb. 4:9 mentions a spiritual keeping of the sabbath based on an earlier type, but as a type it refers only to the rest promised in the land of Canaan and by comparison to the rest of God. In no way or with any significance is there a reference to the rest commanded in the fourth commandment as a type or foreshadowing.

19. In Exod. 31:13, 17 and Ezek. 20:20, the sabbath is called a sign between God and his people, but it cannot be made into a type or representation of any future grace. First, a sign often connotes the same thing as a proof or documentation, as the most learned interpreters note in Exod. 31:13, *It is a sign . . . between me and you,* i.e., a documentation. Thus our mutual love is a sign that we are disciples of Christ, John 13:35, but it is not a type. Second, the sabbath in those places is said to be a sign not of something to come but of something present as every visible concomitant adjunct is a sign of a present subject. For in the observance of the sabbath there is a common and public profession of the communion between God and us. As all solemn profession is a sign of what is professed, in this same sense the sabbath is called a sign.

20. And this is the true reason why the observance of the sabbath is so greatly urged and the breaking of it so severely punished in the Old Testament. In the sabbath there was a common and public profession of the whole of religion. This commandment closes the first table of the law and in summary contains the whole worship of God by setting a certain day for the exercise of it, Isa. 56:2.

21. There are many ceremonies ordained for the observance of the sabbath, but the sabbath was no more made ceremonial by them than it was made judicial or political because of juridical laws which made certain that the sabbath should be celebrated in all sanctity, Exod. 31:14.

22. The accommodation of the fourth commandment to the special state of the Jews (found in the observance of the seventh day from the very beginning) no more makes the precept ceremonial than the promise of the land of Canaan to the people of Israel, Deut. 5:33, *That you may live long in the land which the Lord your God giveth you,*

makes the fifth commandment ceremonial; or than the preface, Deut. 5:6, *I am the Lord your God which brought you out of the land of Egypt,* makes all the commandments ceremonial.

23. To be sure, a more strict observance of the sabbath was commanded in those days of tutelage and bondage which is not binding in all ages. Yet this does not prevent the observance from being plainly moral and common to all ages.

24. Yet nothing can be brought out of the Scriptures which was at any time commanded the Jews for the strict observance of the sabbath which does not likewise pertain to all Christians — except the kindling of fires and the preparing of ordinary food, Exod. 35:3; 16:25. And even these precepts seem to have been special for a particular occasion; for nothing is said about the kindling of fires except in the building of the tabernacle, which God wanted to indicate to be a work not so holy but that it might and ought to be interrupted on the sabbath day. Neither is there any mention of the preparing of food except when manna was miraculously sent from heaven, food which was also miraculously preserved on the sabbath day. And from the life of Christ it appears very likely that he approved of preparing food by the kindling of a fire on the sabbath day. For when he was invited by the Jews to a feast held on the sabbath he did not refuse, Luke 14:1.

25. Sometimes the reason for the sabbath seems to be referred to the deliverance of the people of Israel from captivity in Egypt, but this does not turn the sabbath into a ceremony. First, all the commandments are in some way referred to this deliverance, as stated in the preface of the decalogue. Second, it does not appear that the sabbath itself had any special relation to the deliverance, except that mention is made of the deliverance from Egypt in Deut. 5:15. This passage argues only, however, that the Israelites who had once been servants in Egypt ought readily and willingly to grant this time of rest to their servants.

26. The last day of the week was formerly observed because this was ordained by God at the time of the first creation when he ceased from the work of creation on that day.

27. Divine not human authority has now changed the last day of the week to the first day — only he can change the day of the sabbath who is the Lord of the sabbath, namely, Christ, Matt. 12:8. Therefore, the first day, which has succeeded, is properly called the Lord's Day.

28. Even though the Lord's Day is granted to have been of apostolic institution yet the authority on which it rests is nonetheless divine, for the apostles were guided by the Spirit in holy practices just as they were in propounding the doctrine of the gospel by word of mouth and writing.

29. Since this institution was not temporary, based on a special situation of short duration, it follows that it was the mind of the ordainers that the observance of the day should be perpetual and unchangeable.

30. But it is more likely that Christ himself instituted the practice in his own person. First, Christ was no less faithful than Moses in ordering his whole house, or the church of God, in all things generally necessary and useful, Heb. 3:2, 6. No Christian can reasonably deny that the observance of the day is useful and in some way necessary for the churches of Christ. Second, Christ himself often appeared upon this very day to the disciples gathered together in one place after the resurrection, John 20:19, 26. Third, the Holy Spirit came upon them this very day, Acts 2:4. Fourth, in the practice of the churches at the time of the apostles when mention is made of the observance of the first day, Acts 20:7; 1 Cor. 16:2, it is not remembered as some recent ordinance but as something long since accepted by the disciples of Christ. Fifth, in all things the apostles delivered to the churches what they had received from Christ, 1 Cor. 11:23. Sixth, this institution could have been deferred not more than one week after the death of Christ if God's own law of one sanctified day per week were to remain firm — a law that was demonstrated above to be perpetual. The placing of the holy sabbath of the Jews on the seventh day was abrogated by the death of Christ. It is read that the apostles were occasionally present in the assemblies of the Jews on the Jewish sabbath, Acts 13:14; 16:13; 17:2; 18:4, but the reason was that this was the most fit occasion to preach the gospel to the Jews. Likewise later the Apostle greatly desired to be in Jerusalem on the day of Pentecost, Acts 20:16, because the greatest gathering of Jews would then occur there. Seventh, if the institution of the Lord's day had been deferred until the apostles broke from the Jews and had separate meetings, as some would have it, Acts 18:6, 7; 19:8–9, then in all the time between the death of Christ and the separation (more than three years) the fourth commandment would have bound no one to the observance of any day. For the Jewish day was already abolished and according to this idea there was nothing new put in its place. Thus only nine commandments would have been in force during that time. Eighth, the reason for the change by the consent of all is the resurrection of Christ which is itself a confirmation. On this day the creation of a new world or of a world to come, Heb. 2:5, wherein all things are made new, 2 Cor. 5:17, was completed, and God in Christ's rising from the dead ceased and rested from his greatest work. Just as in the beginning God rested from his work and blessed and hallowed the day wherein he rested, so also it is right that the very day wherein Christ rested from his labors should be hallowed. This is not easily rejected, as some of the ancients urge from Ps. 118:24, *This is the day which the Lord hath made,* for

in that very place Christ's resurrection is treated as Christ himself interprets it in Matt. 21:42. Ninth, it was also most appropriate that the day of worship in the New Testament should be ordained by him who ordained the worship itself and from whom all blessing and grace is to be expected in worship.

31. There is sufficient refutation for those who would make the observance of the Lord's Day an unwritten tradition. First, nothing of such importance as the observance of the Lord's Day, a practice accepted by common sense and the consent of nearly all Christians, depends upon unwritten tradition. Second, this argument becomes a door through which many superstitions and human inventions are brought into the church of God, or it becomes a method of propping them up when they are brought in. Third, many papists are ashamed of this invention for although all papists are accustomed to depend too much upon ecclesiastical traditions in order to hide their superstitions, the sense of divine authority in the observance of the Lord's Day has compelled not a few of them to ascribe the practice to divine and not to any human law. See Bannes, author of *Supplementum ad summam Pisanam, Supplement to the Pisan Summa*, under "Lord's Day" in Book II, ii, question 44, article 1.[23] See also Abbas in the chapter on the allowed days of rest, note 3; Angelus' phrase "days of rest," note 3; and Sylvester's "Lord's Day," question 1.7.[24] Alexander III, pope of Rome, also affirms in the canon law itself in the chapter on the allowed days of rest that "the pages of the Old and the New Testament have specially set aside the seventh day for man's rest." Such is the interpretation of Suarez in chapter one of *Feast Days*: "Both Testaments approve the custom of setting aside a seventh day of the week for man's rest. This was to set it aside formally, though actually the same day was not always set aside. In this way the seventh day in the old law was the sabbath and in the new is the Lord's Day." [25] Fourth, those who count the Lord's Day among the unwritten traditions assign the baptism of children to the same rank and category, and with greater

23. As quoted in Suarez, *De diebus festis*, p. 254. Bannes or Bannez, a Spanish Dominican (1528–1604), was a noted commentator on the works of Thomas Aquinas and a onetime confessor or spiritual director of St. Theresa (1515–82).

24. As quoted or referred to in Suarez, *De diebus festis*, p. 254. Abbas, Angelus, and Sylvester were medieval glossators on canon law. The section of p. 254, *De diebus festis*, which refers to Bannes, Abbas, Angelus, and Sylvester is taken by Suarez from a later, combined gloss on canon law, *Decretalium Gregorii Papae IX compilatio*, in *Corpus juris canonici* (E. L. Richter and E. Friedberg, eds. ex officina Bernhardi Tauchnitz, Lipsiae, 1881), or *Compilation of the Decretals of Pope Gregory IX* [1145–1241], Bk. II, title ix, "De feriis," or "The Days of Rest," ch. 3, cols. 271–72.

25. The quotations from Alexander III (d. 1181) and Suarez are taken from Suarez, *De diebus festis*, p. 248.

show. But our theologians who have answered the papists on these examples of tradition have always contended that these institutions and all others of the same usefulness and necessity are found in the Scriptures themselves.

32. The points which are often advanced from the Scriptures to the contrary (Rom. 14:5; Gal. 4:10; Col. 2:16) do not deny this truth. First, in all these passages the observance of some day for religious use by the action of Christ is no more condemned or denied than the choice of certain meat for religious use by the action of the same Christ. But no Christian would reasonably conclude from those passages that the choice of bread and wine for religious use in the Lord's Supper is either unlawful or not ordained by Christ. Nothing, therefore, can be drawn from the passages against the observance of the Lord's Day on the authority of Christ. Second, the Apostle in Rom. 14 expressly speaks of the judgment about certain days which then produced offense among Christians; but the observance of the Lord's Day which the Apostle himself teaches had already taken place in all the churches (1 Cor. 16:1, 2) and could not be the occasion of offense. Third, it is most probable that the Apostle in this passage is treating of a dispute about the choosing of days to eat or to refuse certain meats, for the question is put in Rom. 14:2 about meats only and in verses 5 and 6 the related problem of duty is discussed; and in the remainder of the chapter he considers only meats, making no mention of days. Fourth, in the Galatians passage the discussion relates only to the observance of days, months, and years as an aspect of bondage to weak and beggarly elemental spirits (4:9). But it was far from the Apostle's mind and altogether strange to Christian faith to consider any commandment of the decalogue or any ordinance of Christ in such a vein. Fifth, in Col. 2 the sabbaths mentioned are specially and expressly described as new moons and ceremonial shadows of things to come in Christ. But the sabbath commanded in the decalogue and our Lord's Day are of another nature entirely, as has been shown.

33. Christian liberty is not at all diminished in this conception (as some seem to feel without cause), for it is not liberty but non-Christian license which results if any think themselves free from the observance of any commandments of the decalogue or the institutions of Christ. Experience also teaches that license and the neglect of holy things more and more prevail when due respect is not given to the Lord's Day.

34. Neither was Adam in bondage because he was tied to the sanctification of the seventh day by special observance.

35. Just as the beginning of the old sabbath occurred in the evening because the creation also began in the evening (the formless earth be-

ing created before the light) and the cessation of the work of creation also began at evening, so also the beginning of the Lord's Day appears to begin in the morning because the resurrection of Christ was in the early morning, Mark 16:2; John 20:1.

36. The correct observance of the day requires two things: rest and the sanctification of that rest.

37. The rest required is the cessation from all work which might hinder divine worship. We must, therefore, abstain on that day from all works properly called servile, for such works were formerly excluded by name in all other solemn feasts (Lev. 23:7, 8, 25, 31, 36; Num. 28:25) and they are excluded all the more from the sabbath.

38. It is ridiculous, however, to interpret servile works — as some do in a kind of allegorical game — as meaning sins, mercenary good works, or those done for reward as in the case of servants. For sins are not forbidden and unlawful at certain times but always and everywhere. And the fourth commandment hardly deals with all sins to be forbidden, although in some sense it may be granted that some sins are to a degree aggravated if committed on such a holy day, Isa. 58:4. Evil deeds which are committed from fear or hope (i.e., altogether servile) are in manner the same as other sins.

39. Servile works are those to which servants or servile men are accustomed — all mechanical work and those in which great bodily labor is required, such as plowing and digging. In addition to these particular works, all of our usual work is forbidden, as is gathered from the opposite concession in the fourth commandment, *Six days you shall labor and do all your work.*

40. Therefore, we may conclude from the subsequent words of the commandment, *On the sabbath you shall not do any work,* that all work which may be properly called ours is forbidden although it may not be, strictly speaking, servile or mechanical.

41. All work is included which pertains to our use of life, i.e., work which concerns natural and civil things and leads to our gain and profit. So work which of its own nature is not servile but befits a freeman, such as studying and the pursuit of the liberal arts, is prohibited. Especially included are those which are common to free men and servants, namely, traveling and handling business affairs.

42. In this sense the words in Isa. 58:3 are to be explained, *You do that which delights you and oppress all your workers,* i.e., you do your own work with care as in verse 13, *Going your own ways.* In this chapter Isaiah treats chiefly of wicked actions and the works which are unlawful at all times (as appears in verse 6); some godly divines, therefore, would seem to be mistaken when they conclude from this passage that every human word or thought or any that pertains to men is to

be counted as sin on the Lord's Day. Not all human words, deeds, or thoughts on the day in question (whether a sabbath properly so-called or a solemn fast) are judged inappropriate and in that respect reprehensible — but only those which concern our wealth and profit, or are simply unlawful and repugnant to the exercise of worship, as appears in verses 3 and 6. Regarding servile and common work there is such a strict law that on the sabbath day men may not go on with their work, even in plowing season or harvest time, that is, even in those times which are most profitable and seemingly necessary for man's life, Exod. 34:21. Likewise forbidden is work which either directly or remotely pertains to such holy things as the building of the tabernacle, Exod. 31:13, and much more the undertaking of an ordinary journey, Exod. 16, or the visiting of markets or fairs, Neh. 13.

43. There are, however, exceptions. First, all those works are permitted which are part of honorable conduct. At all times we ought to live and act honestly and decently, and especially on the day dedicated to divine worship. All things which look simply to this are clearly allowed. Second, those things are permitted which are imposed upon us by special necessity, Matt. 12:11. We should eliminate all those things which men make or pretend to make necessary. But there are still those which in the providence of God are unexpected, necessary, and unavoidable, e.g., when a necessity allowed by the Scripture is present as a sufficient cause for doing ordinary work. Third, all work is permitted which directly affects the worship and glory of God, Matt. 12:5; John 5:8,9. For such work which of its own nature is servile passes into the nature of a holy work and is not properly our work but God's.

44. This rest in itself is not and never was a part of worship. Yet so far as it is commanded by God as necessary for worship and is directed to worship, it is part of observance pertaining to religion and the worship of God.

45. Sanctification of this rest, as of the day itself, is in our special devotion to the worship of God upon the day prescribed in the phrases, *He sanctified that day* and *It is a sabbath to thy God.*

46. On this day public worship ought to be the chief matter and for this reason the sabbath is called a holy convocation, Lev. 23:3; Acts 13:14; 15:23; 16:13. The public convocation of the church ought to be held both before and after noon on the Lord's Day; the double burnt offering of the sabbath in the morning and in the evening, Num. 28:9, is the ample precedent.

47. The rest of the day is to be spent in pious activity. Formerly there was an offering peculiar to the sabbath, but the continued or daily offering with its drink offering was not to be omitted, Num. 28:10.

48. Public worship, which is to be celebrated most solemnly, neces-

sarily requires Scripture reading, meditation, prayer, holy discourse, and contemplation of the works of God wherein we may be more open to public worship and worship may become truly effective in us.

49. Opposed to the ordinance of the Lord's Day are all feast days ordained by men when they are considered holy days like the Lord's Day.

50. It conforms with the day's first institution and the writing of the apostles that only one day in the week should be sanctified.

51. The Jews had no formally sanctified feast days except by divine institution.

52. Any day may be piously turned into an occasion for advancing the worship of God.

53. When God calls us by special judgment to more solemn fasting, such days are to be considered extraordinary sabbaths.

54. Also contrary to the observance of the day are all business, trade, feasts, sports, and other activities which draw the mind of man away from the exercises of religion.

XVI

Justice and Charity toward Our Neighbor

Thus far we have considered religion. Justice now follows, as described in the second table.

1. Justice is the virtue by which we are inclined to perform our duty to our neighbor. That children should obey their parents is thus said to be just, Eph. 6:1. And the way that masters should treat servants is named just and fair, Col. 4:1. And all those things which we owe to our neighbor are carried out in just living, according to Titus 2:12.

2. But justice in this chapter is not to be taken generally as every man's duty to another, for it would then embrace even religion itself. General justice is nothing else than virtue in general, as declared before when we showed that justice was chief among the general expressions of virtue. Neither must this justice be particularly understood as related to the quantity of the thing deserved or received (if so, it would embrace only a few of the duties of the second table, or those in which like is returned for like). It is used here in a certain middle way by which it sets forth the mutual duty between those who

are bound by the same law; in this sense it contains all the force of the second table.

3. Its object is our neighbor. This means everyone who is or may be a partaker with us of the same end and blessedness, whether he is man or angel, Luke 10:36, 37.

4. Thus no holy men whatever and no angels can be objects of religion or of the religious worship commanded in the first table. They are objects only of the justice or duty due our neighbor as contained in the second table. The arguments taken from the nature of the thing also exclude any adoration of the creatures. Acts 10:26, *Rise, for I myself also am a man*; Rev. 22:9, *See that you do it not, for I am a fellow servant with you and your brethren the prophets, and with those who keep the words of this book. Worship God.*

5. In this class and company everyone is included, even by analogy oneself, for everyone is first a neighbor to himself and then to others. No single commandment is given to order a man's relation to himself, for if he is rightly ordered towards God and towards his neighbor, he is also rightly ordered towards himself. The disposition by which one becomes fit to do his duty to God and to his neighbor is a means to his own perfection, but there is a distinction here: Though he must have the same duties to his neighbor as to himself, he does not have the same duties to God as to himself.

6. Because that manner by which these duties are to be exercised toward our neighbor is with respect and desire for their good, this virtue is called love toward our neighbor, Matt. 22:39; Mark 12:31.

7. In this love there is always desire for union, satisfaction, and good will, just as in love toward God, and there is often added mercy when we consider the misery of our neighbor, though this has no place in love toward God.

8. This bond of justice and affection of love ought to flow and derive always from our religion toward God. Religion gives chief honor to God and brings about obedience to his will in the things which directly affect creatures; thus all who neglect their duty toward men deny honor to God and actually show him scorn, 1 Sam. 2:30. The love toward God contained in religion of its own nature produces love toward men, for they are in some sort partakers of the image of God. Therefore, we are said to love God in men and men in God, which is one reason for the phrase, *Beloved in the Lord.*

9. And thus nothing is properly owed to man which is contrary to religion, Acts 4:19; 5:29, *Whether it be right in the sight of God to obey you rather than God, you judge. We must obey God rather than men.*

10. The truth of religion cannot stand with the neglect of justice

and love toward our neighbor. Jas. 1:27, *Religious worship pure and undefilable before God the Father is this: to visit the fatherless and widows in their affliction;* 1 John 4:20, 21, *If anyone says, I love God, and hates his brother, he is a liar. . . . This commandment have we from God, that he who loves God should love his brother also.*

11. Therefore, finally, religion is best proved and tried by justice, as frequently set forth in the Scripture. This argument can be more easily negated than affirmed if it is thought of as referring to outward works and offices of justice, because such works of justice may exist where true religion is lacking. But when true religion is present, they are never wholly absent.

12. In the same way, unjust works more easily argue that a man is ungodly than just works argue that a man is godly. Thus the works of the flesh are said to be *Manifest*, Gal. 5:19, but this is not affirmed of the fruits of the spirit, verse 22.

13. This is the order of love: God is first and chiefly to be loved and is, as it were, the formal reason of love towards our neighbor. After God, we are bound to love ourselves with the love of true blessedness, for loving God with love of union, we love ourselves directly with that greatest love which looks toward our spiritual blessedness. Secondarily, as it were, we ought to love others whom we would have to be partakers of the same good with us. For others may be deprived of blessedness without our fault, but we cannot be. Thus we are more bound to desire and seek it for ourselves than for others.

14. Hence it is that the love of ourselves has the force of a rule or measure for the love of others, *You shall love your neighbor as yourself.*

15. It is never lawful to commit sin for another's sake, although our transgression may seem small and be a chief good which we seek for the other. He that knowingly and willingly sins hates his own soul. Prov. 8:36; 29:24, *He who sins against me offers violence to his own soul. . . . He who partakes with a thief hates himself; he hears the curse, but declares it not.*

16. No man capable of blessedness ought to be removed from the embrace of our love. If we love God above all, no enmities will so prevail with us but that we may love our very enemies for God. Matt. 5:39; Rom. 12:17; 1 Thess 5:15; 1 Peter 3:9.

17. Some men are more to be loved than others, namely, those nearer to God and in God to ourselves. Gal. 6:10, *Let us do good to all, but especially to those who are of the household of faith.*

18. Those who believe are more closely joined to God and to us spiritually than those who do not as yet believe, and so they are more to be loved.

19. Yet this state is for the present time and immediate personal relationships. We may will as much or more of the same good to others in the future, the grace of God and faith entering in. In this sense the Apostle voices affection toward the Israelites, Rom. 9:3.

20. If among those to be loved there is no apparent disparity in relation to God or to ourselves, they are to be loved equally.

21. But if there is any disparity, either in their being joined to God or to ourselves, then those who are most closely joined are more to be loved. This is to say that when we cannot exercise our love actively toward all, we are bound to love those whom God has commended to us by some special joining or communion more than others. Although we ought equally to will the salvation of others, yet the exercise and concern of this will ought chiefly to be for those who are joined to us in a special way. It is the same with a soldier who should wish well to all his fellow soldiers but is yet bound to take most care of those in the same division or joined in the same rank. This appears in the example of Paul who desired the conversion of the Israelites more fervently than any other nation. He gives this one reason: They were his brethren and kindred in the flesh, Rom. 9:3.

22. In this prerogative of love we must wish to those who are joined to us only the good things pertinent to our association, spiritual things for those most closely joined to us spiritually and natural good things for those with whom we have a natural nearness. These good things are not to be separated in our desires; yet the very type of association is a nod from God, so to speak, whereby he bids us direct our efforts chiefly in this or that direction.

23. It follows: First, that our blood kin, other things being equal, are to be given more love than strangers through the good things of this life — and, among our kin, especially those who are the nearest to us.

24. Second, a special friend is to be given more love than an ordinary blood kinsman (at least through those things which belong to the common duties of this life), for friendship may bring a greater nearness than consanguinity alone. Prov. 18:24, *For a friend is nearer than a brother.*

25. Third, parents are to be loved more than any friend. The nearness of parents is greater than that of friends in the communication of what is most intimate to us. 1 Tim. 5:4, *If any widow have children or grandchildren, let them learn first to show piety towards their own house and to recompense their parents; for this is honest and acceptable in the sight of God.*

26. Fourth, parents are to be given more love than children through the good things which ought to flow back to the cause from the effect,

such as honor, esteem, reverence, thankfulness, and the like. Children are to be given more love than parents through the things which flow from cause to effect, such as sustenance, advancement, oversight, and the like.

27. Fifth, husbands and wives are to be given more love than parents and children in the matter of association and union in this life. It is said of this greatest nearness, *They shall be one flesh*, Gen. 2:24, and *Therefore a man will leave his father and mother and cleave to his wife, and they shall be one flesh*, Matt. 19:5.

28. Sixth, those who have deserved well of us are more to be loved than others and among them the ones who have bestowed spiritually good things upon us are to be most loved. *Let him who is taught the word communicate to him that taught him all good things*, Gal. 6:6.

29. Seventh, a community or whole society is more to be loved than an individual member of it, because a joining of a part with the whole is greater than a joining with another part. A prince whose life and safety is necessary or most advantageous for the common good is to be given more love than any of the common people, even more than ourselves in the matter of temporal things. 2 Sam. 21:17, *You shall go no more with us to battle, lest you quench the light of Israel*; Lam. 4:20.

30. The two acts of love toward our neighbor are praying for his good and working for his good. Matt. 5:44, *Love your enemies, bless them who curse you, do good to those who hate you, and pray for those who hurt you and persecute you.*

31. Since this prayer concerns the honor of God, it is part of religion in the first table. Since it concerns the good of our neighbor, it belongs to the justice and love toward our neighbor commanded in the second table.

32. We must pray for all the things which our religion commands us to wish for him, whether they be spiritual or corporeal.

33. Included in this prayer is not only petition, but also thanksgiving by which we praise God for the good things he has bestowed on our neighbors, Rom. 1:8–10.

34. Opposed to this prayer is any calling down of evil which tends to the hurt of our neighbor — called cursing, Matt. 5:44.

35. The working for our neighbor's good is an endeavor on his behalf which is called A *doing good*, Matt. 5:44, and *Love in deeds*, 1 John 3:18.

36. Working is distinguished from praying because the latter is not immediately concerned about our neighbor, being directed toward God, although it tends to the good of our neighbor.

37. Endeavors which concern other creatures for our neighbors' sake must be included in this working, for such actions have the same result as if they were exercised directly for our neighbor himself.

38. Such endeavor consists either of moral persuading or positive action.

39. The endeavor of moral persuasion lies in proposing good by arguments which will stir the neighbor to good.

40. This is done by admonition and good example.

41. Admonition, as generally understood, is any warning in words, whether it be to procure and perfect good for our neighbor or to drive away and repair hurt.

42. It, therefore, includes our duty to *Teach and admonish*, Col. 3:16; *Watch over others that we may urge them to love and good works*, Heb. 10:24; *Exhort them daily*, Heb. 3:13; *Comfort them* in sorrow and grief, 1 Thess. 4:18; and *Correct them in a brotherly manner, if overtaken with some offense*, Gal. 6:1 and Lev. 19:17.

43. Brotherly correction is to be used when we know certainly that the evil to be corrected has been committed and when we have hope of some fruit or good following our correction. The fruit comes either through the amendment of the way of our fallen brother or by saving others from the same sin. Finally, correction must take place when the time, person, and such circumstances are right.

44. Consent or communion with others in their sins is opposed to admonition, Eph. 5:7, 11.

45. A man is said to be partaker of another's sin in nine ways, indicated by the following:

Command, counsel, consent, flattery, retreat,

Participating, nodding, not opposing, not making public.

[*Jussio, consilium, consensus, palpo, recursus,*

Participans, nutans, non obstans, non manifestans.]

Or, in sum, consent is given to sinners by counseling, defending, helping, permitting what we might hinder, and being silent when we might profitably speak, Rom. 1:32.

46. A good example is doing a good work which may stir others to do the like, 1 Tim. 4:12; Titus 2:4, 7; Matt. 5:16; 1 Peter 2:12.

47. A scandal is the opposite of a good example. 1 Cor. 10:32, 33, *Give no offense to the Jews, to the Gentiles, or the church of God.*

48. A scandal is the showing of an evil work which may stir others to sin, in which sense it is called πρόσκομμα, a cause of stumbling; or a work which may hinder or retard others from doing good, in which sense it is called ἀσθένεια, a cause of weakness, and is properly called scandal. 1 Cor. 8:9, 10, *Take heed that your liberty be not an occa-*

sion of stumbling for the weak; Rom. 14:21, *Wherein thy brother stumbles or is offended or is made weak.*

49. In every evil work which others learn about there is material for scandal. Matt. 18:6–8, 15, *Whoever shall be an offense . . . If your hand, foot, eye causes you to offend . . . If your brother sins against you.*

50. Sometimes there is scandal in a work which though in itself lawful is inexpedient for others. 1 Cor. 8:13, *If food offends my brother, I will never eat flesh, lest I offend him.*

51. An indifferent thing is said to be expedient or inexpedient depending on whether it contributes to the glory of God and the edification of our neighbor or not.

52. No human authority can make an action lawful in which scandal is given our neighbor.

53. A scandal is said to be given either when a manifest sin (or that which has the evident form of sin) is committed and recognized by others, or when something not required by God's command is rashly done and brings spiritual hurt to others. The action is much more a scandal if the perverting or troubling of our neighbor is directly intended by the deed.

54. But if offense results not from our work but from the pure malice of others, then it is called an accepted scandal, as with the Pharisees, but the sin is not ours but the sin of those who are offended. Matt. 15:12–14, *Do you know that the Pharisees were offended at that saying? . . . Let them alone; they are blind leaders of the blind.*

55. Although we cannot avoid such an accepting of scandal, the giving of scandal may be avoided and should be. For God never lays upon us a necessity of offending.

56. That scandal by which one is said metaphorically to offend himself or give the occasion of sinning to himself is by analogy to be considered offense given.

57. A positive action or procuring of good for our neighbor occurs when we do something which tends to the good of our neighbor in itself without his help. Heb. 13:16, *Neglect not to do good and distribute.*

58. Although all acts of justice contain love, there are some in which justice shines forth more and others where love rules.

59. Therefore, the distinction arises whereby some duties are said to belong to justice, strictly speaking, and some to love. Christ is the author of this difference and formal distinction, Luke 11:42, *You neglect justice and the love of God.*

60. Acts of justice have in themselves the sense of obligation and the feeling of equality towards others.

61. Acts of love relate more to another's good than our obligation.

62. The duties of justice are prior and of more binding obligation than those of charity (or love).

63. Therefore, we have a greater obligation to pay our debts than to give away anything of our own. And he who offends another has a greater obligation to seek reconciliation than he who is offended.

64. In many situations there is a double meaning for justice. The one meaning concerns the immediate end and words of the law and is called justice in the strict sense; the other concerns the remote end and the reason for the law and is called equity, or ἐπιείκεια.

65. Justice has two parts. The first is distributive justice, which gives to each one his own; the other may be called emendative justice, which restores to each one his own.

66. Distributive justice can follow only from a right judging of things and persons and a fit comparison of things to things and persons to persons. Hence arises that sense of proportion called geometrical.

67. The preference of one person to another in the distribution of a due good without just cause is opposed to distributive justice.

68. Emendative justice is either commutative or corrective.

69. Commutative justice results when there is equality between what is given and what is received.

70. Corrective justice presupposes an injustice; it is either civil or criminal.

71. Civil justice chiefly corrects the injustice of things.

72. Criminal justice chiefly corrects the injustice of persons.

73. Punishment and restitution belong to corrective justice.

74. Punishment is an act of corrective justice by which penalty is inflicted on a violator of justice.

75. The end should be the amendment or restraint of the offender, peace and admonition to others, and the preserving of justice and God's honor. Deut. 13:11; 17:13; 19:20; 21:21, *All Israel may hear, and fear, and do no such iniquity in the midst of you.*

76. Restitution is an act of corrective justice in which a person is given possession of something of his own which was unjustly taken away.

77. Hence an act which calls for restitution is against justice strictly so-called and not only against love.

78. Injury is opposed to this justice.

79. An evil will is opposed to love whether it arises formally from direct intention or has the force of intention by interpretation.

80. Unjust discord goes with this ill will. If it results in secession, especially in religious matters, it is properly called schism.

XVII

The Honor of Our Neighbor

1. Justice toward our neighbor affects him directly or as the result of some action.

2. Justice which affects our neighbor directly relates to his status per se or to the degree of his status.

3. When justice relates to the degree, it is called honor, and is commanded in the fifth commandment (called the first commandment with promise, Eph. 6:2, either because it is the first of the second table or because it is the first and only one in all the law which contains its own special promise).

4. Here human society is presupposed and sanctified — private and domestic as well as public and political. Within this society men are to serve each other in the mutual duties of justice and love so that they may exercise and show forth the religion which they profess in the worship of God.

5. The solitary life which some hermits have chosen as angelic and others embrace for different reasons is so far from perfection that it is wholly contrary to the law and will of God, unless dictated by some extraordinary reason (which can avail only for a time).

6. Human society provides the foundation to all the offices of justice and love commanded in the second table of the law. Transgressions which lead directly to the disturbance, confusion, and overthrow of this society are more grievous sins than breaches of the individual commandments.

7. Political society as well as domestic has been sanctified by God, but, whereas a certain form has been prescribed for domestic (and ecclesiastical) society, it is not so for the political. The latter is left to men's liberty so that, acting as a unit with power, they may ordain the society which best makes for the establishment of religion and justice among themselves.

8. And one reason why there is mention only of parents in the fifth commandment is because only domestic society, being clearly natural, is to remain one and the same throughout all ages and nations. It is primary, the fountain and seed bed of all society, and thus the authority of all superiors is at once set forth and mitigated when they are called fathers, 2 Kings 2:12; 5:13; 13:14; Gen. 41:8, 43; 1 Sam. 24:11; 1 Tim. 5:1.

9. Honor is an acknowledgment of the dignity or excellence of another with proper testimony to it.

10. The terms acknowledgment and testimony are both used because it is expressed neither in outward nor in inward observances alone, but in both.

11. It is said to be concerned with excellence and dignity because we are affected with reverence only when we apprehend some excellence.

12. Therefore, the duty owed those who are placed above us in any eminence is commonly and most properly described by the word *honor* in the sense of respect, but by synecdoche the word also designates our duty to every man in respect of his dignity or excellence, whether this be of the same grade as ours, or less. Rom. 12:10, *In honor outdoing one another*; 1 Peter 3:7, *Let men likewise dwell according to the knowledge of God, giving honor to the woman as to the weaker vessel*; 1 Peter 2:17, *Honor all men.*

13. Honor has first place among the duties owed to our neighbor. First of all, it is nearest to the nature of religion and piety through which we worship God himself; it is even called religion or piety by profane writers as well as by the Scriptures on occasion. 1 Tim. 5:4, *Let him learn first to show piety to his own family.* Second, it is the bond and foundation of all the other relationships of justice to be maintained towards our neighbor. Because of this duty and its degrees, *Men lead a quiet and peaceable life, with all piety and honesty,* 1 Tim. 2:2. This also seems to be the reason for the promise joined to the fifth commandment, namely, that we may prolong our days on the earth, for without a mutual observance of honor between superiors and inferiors it could not be expected that the life of man should continue.

14. Honor as it relates to others' knowledge and opinion of the man to be honored is called *Reputation*, Eccles. 7:1, or a *Good name*, Phil. 4:8.

15. Therefore, honor as an external good of man does not really differ from reputation, except in its connotation.

16. The duty of honor which we owe to all is to preserve their state of dignity unhurt.

17. All offenses which hurt the reputation of our neighbor are opposed to this duty.

18. The reputation of our neighbor is hurt, however, when the esteem due him is diminished. 1 Cor. 4:13, *Being slandered, we pray*; 2 Cor. 6:8, *In honor and dishonor, in evil report and good report.*

19. We may diminish it either by thinking ill of him by ourselves, without just cause (which is called rash judgment), Matt. 7:1; 1 Cor. 4:3, or by doing so among others.

20. The reputation of our neighbor is lowered among others by words, actions, gestures, and other signs.

21. This happens as a result either of what we do itself or of the

circumstances accompanying — sometimes directly and formally with an intention to hurt and sometimes indirectly and only in effect.

22. When the reputation of someone is hurt by an imputation of blame or fault, it is called either insult, derision, or slander, if done in his presence. If done in his absence, it is called detraction.

23. Detraction does our neighbor direct evil in four ways: first, when he is falsely accused of a fault; second, when a secret fault is made public without just cause; third, when an actual fault is exaggerated; fourth, when an act is not condemned but the intention is.

24. Indirectly it affects the good of our neighbor also in four ways: denying the good which is due him; hiding it; lessening it; and praising it coldly.

25. The former ways are contained in the verse, *Imponens, augens, manifestans, in mala vertens* — imputing, magnifying, declaring, turning into evil.

26. The latter in the verse, *Qui negat aut minuit, tacuit, laudatque remisse* — he who denies, lessens, keeps silent, or praises weakly.

27. The reputation of our neighbor is restored by retracting, asking pardon, and sometimes also by compensation.

28. There are duties of honor which belong to unequals and those which belong to equals.

29. Among unequals, superiors should excel in deserving well and inferiors in respect and gratitude.

30. Inequality lies in some simple quality or in authority and power.

31. Inequality in a simple quality is a matter of age or of gifts.

32. Those who are older than others should excel them in setting a good example. Titus 2:4, *That old women teach the younger women to be sober.*

33. Those who are richer in gifts should make them readily available for the profit of others. Rom. 1:14, *I am a debtor both to the Greeks and barbarians, to the wise and the unwise.*

34. Those who have the right to govern others are superior in power; hence power is often called jurisdiction. Their duty is to administer justice and give love to others in what might be called a superior way according to the power given them. Job 29:14, 15, *I put on justice and my judgment covered me as a robe and as a diadem. I was as eyes to the blind, and as feet to the lame;* Col. 4:1, *Masters, do that which is right and equal for your servants.*

35. Such justice is administered in love in protecting and ruling.

36. Protection is the use of power to defend others from evil. Isa. 32:2, *And a man shall be as a hiding place from the wind, and a*

covert from the tempest. Protection also includes the care which provides necessities for others, 1 Tim. 5:8.

37. Ruling is a use of power to further the good of others. Rom. 13:4, *He is the minister of God for your good;* 1 Tim. 2:2, *That we may lead a peaceful and quiet life in all godliness and honesty.*

38. This ruling is exercised through the medium of directing and rewarding.

39. Directing is a setting forth of what is right and good so that it may be observed. Eph. 6:4, *Fathers . . . bring up your children in the nurture and admonition of the Lord.*

40. To such directing belongs the making and promulgation of good laws in any human society.

41. Rewarding is recompensing obedience given or refused according to direction. 1 Peter 2:14, *To take vengeance on the wicked and to praise them who do well;* Rom. 13.

42. Here distributive and emendative justice are best displayed for although justice in other men is the same as that exercised by superiors, it manifests itself most when administered with fitting power.

43. Therefore, the right of punishment does not properly belong to any except those who are supereminent in power, Rom. 13:4; 1 Peter 2:14. When it is rightly exercised, it is not the punishment of men but of God. 2 Chron. 19:6, *Take heed what you do, for you judge not for man but for the Lord, who will be with you in judgment.*

44. Those in higher authority ought to provide for the needs of those under them — the means of salvation for their souls, Eph. 6:4, and food, clothing, and fit housing for their bodies.

45. Those in authority may be either private or public persons.

46. Those who are private include the husband in relation to his wife, parents in relation to their children, and the master in relation to his servants. The power of the husband is moderated by a certain equality; the power of the master is for command alone; but the paternal power is a kind of mixture.

47. Those in public authority are either ministers or magistrates.

48. The difference between magistrates and ministers of the church is, first, that magistracy (of this kind) is an ordinance of man, whereas the ministry is from God, as declared in the Scriptures. Although the power of magistracy is ordained by God, Rom. 13:1, it is still called a *Human creature,* 1 Peter 2:13, which hardly fits the lawful ministry of the church. Second, magistracy is an ordinance of God the Creator and belongs to all kinds of men, but the ecclesiastical ministry is a gift and ordinance of Christ the Mediator and properly and commonly belongs only to those who are of the church of Christ. Third, as a part of his rule, a magistrate has administrative power and, if he is the

supreme magistrate, he may upon just cause make and abolish laws and delegate authority to others. But the ministers of the church as such have only mandated power. They have none of their own. Whatever they do lawfully, they do in Christ's place who gives them the mandate; they, therefore, cannot make laws or pass on to others the mandate they have received. Fourth, magistrates have the duty of securing the common good, both spiritual and corporal, of all those in their jurisdiction by political means and coercive power, 1 Tim. 2:2. But it is the duty of ministers to secure the spiritual good of those committed to them by ecclesiastical means, Acts 20:28; Heb. 13:17.

49. The magistracy and the ministry cannot be exactly distinguished in the things, persons, or causes with which they are concerned. There is no thing, person, or cause so ecclesiastical that it does not belong in some way to the jurisdiction of the magistrate. And no member of a church does anything so secular that the church takes no notice of it in the light of his obligation to God.

50. For this reason the exempting of ecclesiastics (as they are called) from the jurisdiction of the civil magistrate, and also the freeing of them from obedience to magistrates and even parents — distinctions introduced by papists under the pretense of religious perfection — are precisely contrary to the perfect law of God.

51. To the rule based on the power of superiors, inferiors owe subjection and obedience. Heb. 13:17, *Obey your leaders and submit yourselves.*

52. Subjection is acknowledgment of the superiors' authority, 1 Peter 2:18; Eph. 5:22.

53. Obedience is the performance of the things prescribed, Eph. 6:1, 5.

54. Obedience should always be bounded by the limits of power possessed by the superior.

55. Therefore, we must not obey men in things which are against the command of God, for we must obey *In the Lord*, Eph. 6:1; and *In the fear of God*, Col. 3:22 — or in things which are against the command of superiors of greater authority than the ones commanding.

56. So obedience must not be blind or without examination of what is hidden. An inferior ought to inquire as far as is requisite for the matter in hand as to whether the precept be lawful, fitting, and obligatory, Acts 4:19.

57. If the precept is not lawful then the enduring of the punishment wrongfully inflicted counts for and has the force of obedience, 1 Peter 2:19–20.

58. For the good communicated either by the gifts or the power of superiors, inferiors owe submissive gratitude.

59. Gratitude is a desire to compensate for the benefits received.

60. It is a kind of benevolent affection resulting from and in proportion to a benefit received from another. It should not be exhausted in the emotion itself, but should be manifested in fitting endeavor.

61. Gratitude is, of course, the common duty of all men who have received any benefit from others. But there is a special kind of gratitude of inferiors towards superiors which is described when gratitude is said to be submissive.

62. This follows from the relief of their needs, whether in substance, help, or counsel, Gen. 45:9.

63. Gratitude towards those by whose benefits under God we subsist, namely, our parents and our country, or those who take their part with them, is called *Piety*, 1 Tim. 5:4.

64. The duty of equals toward equals is that one should prefer the other in honor, Rom. 12:10; Eph. 5:21.

65. Friendship is the bond inviting some in closer love [*amor*] and communion, Prov. 18:24.

66. The beginning of all honor given to our neighbor, especially that which is due superiors and equals, is humility.

67. Humility is a virtue which calls for the moderation of one's self-esteem so that he will attribute nothing to himself in any way beyond what is fitting. Phil. 2:3, *In humility of mind, thinking everyone better than himself.*

68. Pride and envy stand opposed to humility.

69. Pride is an inordinate affection for one's own excellence.

70. This affection for one's own excellence is called boasting when it is directed toward the good things we have. Directed toward the things which we pretend to have, it is called arrogance. If it seeks fame and esteem from others, it is called vainglory; if it is concerned for dignity, it is called ambition; if it undertakes matters beyond our strength, it is called presumption.

71. Envy is dejection about a good enjoyed by our neighbor because it seems to diminish our own excellence, Num. 10:29.

72. If we are dejected by another's good because we see evil likely to come from it either to others or ourselves, it is not envy but honest fear, Prov. 28:28.

73. If the cause of our dejection is not that another has a good, but that we do not have it and wish we had, then it is not envy but emulation, Rom. 11:14.

74. If the cause of our dejection is the unworthiness of the one who

enjoys the good, then it is not properly envy but indignation, Prov. 29:2.

75. Yet all these emotions, if excessive, are customarily noted in the Scriptures under the name of envy, Ps. 37:1, 7; Prov. 3:31.

❖━━◦◉◦━━❖

XVIII

Humanity toward Our Neighbor

1. Justice directed toward our neighbor's situation concerns either his person or his outward possessions.

2. Justice toward his person concerns either his life or its purity.

3. That which relates to his life is humanity and is commanded by the sixth commandment. The meaning of this commandment is that human life — as the Scripture describes it in Gen. 9:5, 6, *The soul of man and the blood of man* — should be properly cared for. The duty treated here is rightly and wholly embraced under the name of humanity.

4. This commandment, properly speaking, does not include the life of the brute creatures because they are in man's power, Gen. 9:2, 3, and do not have common society with him. Yet a just disposition toward the life of man implies a respect for the image of him found in other living creatures, and cruelty toward them either shows a certain inhuman attitude or little by little grows into it. Therefore, kindness and unkindness toward the brute creatures may be regarded as a subject appended to this commandment.

5. Humanity is the virtue by which we are inclined to preserve the life of our neighbor and his tranquility through lawful means.

6. This is done in two ways — by supplying things helpful and preventing things hurtful.

7. Since the life of man which ought to be preserved is a double one, spiritual and corporal, the duties of humanity are likewise some of them spiritual and some corporal.

8. The spiritual duty is to do everything in our power to promote the edification of our neighbor.

9. It includes prayer, good example, and admonition, and these are required of all.

10. With regard to their immediate end, these are the general duties of charity, but with regard to their indirect and remote end, they have to do with the maintenance of our neighbor's spiritual life, Jas. 5:20.

11. Likewise giving up duties which look to our neighbor's salvation, consenting with others in their sin, and giving offense to others — all sins opposed to our duties — always hurt the spiritual life of our neighbor, Ezek. 3:18; 13:19; 33:6, 8; Rom. 14:15; 1 Cor. 8:11.

12. Just as the soul is more noble than the body, so the spiritual life is of greater worth than the corporal. Sins against the spiritual life of our neighbor are greater (in equal comparison) than those which hurt the body, yet they do not in themselves constitute a hurt to our neighbor. Bodily hurt and death itself are brought on men against their will by outside force, of necessity, but spiritual death cannot be induced in another unless the other is in some way willing and consenting, so that his own action becomes the immediate cause of it.

13. Humanity is required of superiors in power and authority; they should try to further the salvation of their inferiors by their authority.

14. There are various degrees of duty toward our neighbor in his corporal life so that it may be kept tranquil and safe.

15. The first is found in those virtues which restrain us from any hurt of our neighbor.

16. Meekness, patience, long-suffering, and placableness or forgiveness of wrong are of this sort.

17. Meekness is the virtue which moderates anger. Prov. 17:17; 1 Cor. 13:4; Num. 12:3, *Now the man Moses was very meek, above all men who were on the face of the earth.* Gal. 5:22, *The fruits of the Spirit, are restraint of . . . anger, goodness . . . gentleness.*

18. Dullness and wrath are the opposites of meekness.

19. Dullness is the lack of just anger, 1 Sam. 12:13.

20. Wrath is the inordinate stirring up of anger. Gen. 49:7, *Cursed be their anger, because it was fierce; and their wrath, because it was cruel;* Eccles. 7:9, *Be not hasty in your spirit to be angry, for anger rests in the bosom of fools.*

21. The degrees of wrath are being provoked, growing hot, and hatred.

22. Patience is the virtue which moderates anger stirred up by grievous wrong, Luke 21:19; Col. 1:11; 1 Thess. 5:14.

23. Long-suffering is the continuance of patience, although the hurt is prolonged, Prov. 14:29; 15:18; 16:32.

24. Placableness is the virtue by which we easily forgive a wrong done to us, Matt. 18:21, 22; Luke 17:3, 4.

25. The second degree of this duty is found in the virtues which cherish human society, such as concord and benevolence joined with courtesy, affability, and equanimity.

26. Concord is the virtue of ready agreement with others about the things which are good, Phil. 1:27; 2:2; 4:2.

27. Benevolence is the virtue of wishing every prosperity to others.
1 Cor. 13:4, *Charity is . . . kind.*

28. Discord, dissension, enmity, and the like are contrary to these
virtues, Gal. 5:20.

29. A third degree is found in those endeavors by which the very
life of our neighbor is defended, furthered, and strengthened.

30. The attempt to defend, promote, and strengthen the life of
our neighbor involves all the duties which make us agents of the conservation of human life, Prov. 20:10, 11.

31. Fierceness, cruelty, and the like which hurt man's life are
opposed to this, Prov. 24, 10, 11.

32. All such fall under the name of homicide.

33. Homicide is the killing of a man unjustly.

34. Killing and even hurting are unjust when they are not done by
a just authority, that is, a public authority or its equivalent. They are
also unjust when done in an unjust cause or without just order, or
with an unjust intention. These four conditions must always be met for
any killing to be justified. If any one is lacking, homicide is committed.

35. Rash anger also must be counted with homicide, inasmuch as it
tends to the hurt of our neighbor's life. Matt. 5:22, *Whoever is angry
with his brother ill-advisedly.*

36. But from this it is to be inferred not that all anger is condemned, but only that which is rash, having no just cause or measure.
In other respects the state of anger is commended, as in zeal for God,
Gen. 30:2; Exod. 11:8; 16:20; 32:19; Num. 16:15; 31:14; 2 Kings
13:19. So even hatred itself, Ps. 139:21, 22.

37. All this belongs for the most part to the sixth commandment.
Things which are forbidden may in a different context be sometimes
not amiss and sometimes even well and rightly done in obedience to
God.

38. Thus he who kills another without due cause by accident, while
about his lawful work at a lawful time and in a lawful place, provided
he has exercised due care, does not sin, Deut. 19:5.

39. The same reasoning applies to necessary defense as long as
there is no desire of revenge. This kind of defense carries no blame
with it and is allowed to everyone.

40. Sometimes killing is in obedience to God, Deut. 13:9. This
occurs by divine authority and command, 1 Sam. 15:18, 19.

41. No man has power from God, in common law, to kill with
set purpose a man whose innocency he knows.

42. Neither is there any human power which can give sufficient
authority to a subject to slay a man whom he knows to be innocent
and undeserving of death.

43. A war, therefore, can never be just on both sides, for there cannot be a just cause for death to both sides.

44. Nor is it lawful in war to intend the killing of those who are not in some way participants in an unjust cause.

45. If a lawful cause exists along with a just authority and intention and a just method, neither the war itself nor the military service runs counter to religion, justice, or love, Num. 31:3; 1 Sam. 18:17; 25:28; 1 Chron. 5:22; Luke 3:14; Rom. 13:4; 1 Peter 2:14.

46. When these conditions are observed it is lawful for those who have skill in weapons to offer and make available their ability to lawful generals for making war, 1 Chron. 5:18; Ps. 143:1; Luke 3:14; 1 Cor. 9:7.

47. There is no law of God permitting anyone to kill himself.

48. Yet it is sometimes lawful and just for a man to expose himself to certain danger of death.

49. There are sometimes circumstances in which one may and should offer to die, Jonah 1:12.

❖━━◄❂►━━❖

XIX

Chastity

1. Justice which relates to the purity of our neighbor is chastity.

2. Chastity is the virtue of preserving a person's purity in the things of procreation, 1 Thess. 4:3, 4, 5.

3. The parts of chastity are two: the sense of shame and the sense of honor.

4. The sense of shame is that part of chastity which draws back from impurity and, in this sense, may be called decency.

5. The sense of honor is that part of chastity which leads to actions that go with purity.

6. The sense of shame and the sense of honor lie fundamentally in the inward choice of a man but they show in his outward life.

7. Chastity is known especially as decency when it puts away the outer signs of impurity and as honor when it puts on outer signs of purity.

8. Modesty primarily refers to the sense of shame and dignity to the sense of honor.

9. Modesty is the virtue of containing ourselves within the bounds of bodily desire.

10. Dignity is the virtue of observing the decorum of purity.

11. Chastity is virginal, conjugal, or vidual.

12. This division is not of the genus into species but of the adjunct into subjects.

13. For the essence of chastity is the same in all but it has accidental differences according to the different states of those observing it.

14. Virginal chastity is that which should be kept by a maid until she undertakes honorable marriage, 1 Cor. 7:34.

15. Conjugal chastity is that which should be kept in wedlock, Titus 2:5.

16. Vidual chastity is that kept by widows, 1 Tim. 5:7.

17. A marriage lawfully contracted and observed goes with conjugal chastity, Matt. 19:6; 1 Tim. 2:14; Heb. 13:4; 1 Peter 3:1, 2, 4.

18. The difference between the single and married states is that the single state itself contributes nothing to chastity (though chastity may and must be observed), whereas marriage of its own nature has a certain purity as an ordinance from God and by virtue of that ordinance becomes the means to preserve purity and chastity.

19. Marriage is the individual joining of one man and woman by lawful consent for a mutual communication of their bodies and community of life together.

20. It is of one man with one woman, Gen. 2:22; Mal. 2:15; Matt. 19:4, 5; 1 Cor. 7:2; Lev. 18:18.

21. The perfection of friendship and the mutual duties of marriage cannot be reached except between one and one.

22. Therefore, polygamy, even that which prevailed with the ancient fathers, was always a violation of the laws of marriage. It was not tolerated of old by God in any sense except as his cutomary toleration of man's infirmities and ignorances and as a way to turn them to him.

23. For lawful consent it is required, first, that the persons to be joined are suitable. Second, the consent itself must be agreeable to the nature of the thing and the law of God.

24. The right distance of blood is required for persons to be suitable, Lev. 18.

25. Nearness of flesh and blood hinders marriage because of a certain special reverence for our own flesh and blood, which is contrary to conjugal familiarity. This is meant in the sentence: *Do not uncover her nakedness*, Lev. 18:6, 7, and ff.

26. The distance in degrees of relationship either by blood or marriage propounded in Lev. 18 is based on common and unchanging law. Its violations were among those abominations by which the gentiles themselves are said to have polluted the land, Lev. 18:27, 28.

27. Yet the moral law is not so universal that it precludes exception,

either out of sheer necessity as at the beginning of the world, or by special command of God, Deut. 25:5.

28. So-called spiritual kinship or nearness between the one who baptizes, or the godfather, and the godson (as they say) or goddaughter baptized, introduced by the papists as an impediment to lawful matrimony, is an empty and tyrannical device of superstition.

29. Second, maturity of age is required in a person contracting marriage, 1 Cor. 7:36. When this is wanting, even agreements of less moment cannot be made — much less this important one.

30. In order that the consent should be fitting to the nature of the situation, first, the consent of parents is required beforehand if the persons are still under their authority, 1 Cor. 7:36–38.

31. Second, consent of the contracting parties should proceed from sure and deliberate counsel without compulsion or deceit.

32. The joining is said to be individual because it has by its nature the same ends as a human life, Rom. 7:1–3; 1 Cor. 7:39.

33. Concubinage contracted for a time is not marriage instituted and approved by God, but is a shameful escape from it.

34. The perpetuity of marriage does not depend only upon the will and covenant of the persons contracting, for then by consent of both a covenant so begun might be broken, as is the case between master and servant. Rather, the rule and bond of this covenant is the institution of God and thus it is sometimes called in the Scriptures the covenant of God, Prov. 2:17.

35. The institution of God which establishes the individual companionship of husband and wife looks toward the good of mankind and its rightful conservation through the raising up of children and their hereditary succession. This cannot be without the individual joining of parents.

36. Lawful marriage cannot be undone before death without the most grievous fault of the one who causes it.

37. Not even lack of faith or heresy on either side is just cause for separation, 1 Cor. 7:12, 13.

38. But if one party separates with obstinate resolution, the other party is free, 1 Cor. 7:15.

39. The joining is for bodily communication because in marriage godly offspring are first sought, Mal. 2:15. Marriage secondarily offers a remedy against the carnal desires which many without a special gift for continency have had since the fall of Adam; and these desires are so unbridled that unless help comes from this remedy men burn, so to speak, making them unfit for pious duties. They run headlong into unlawful and evil unions, 1 Cor. 7:2, 9.

40. Therefore, the body of the husband is said to be in the power

of the wife and the body of the wife in the power of the husband. They should honestly consult each other's good, 1 Cor. 7:3–5.

41. The vow of celibacy, as it is known among the papists, is not a vow of chastity but of diabolical presumption, a snare to the conscience, and a bond of impurity.

42. Among the ends of marriage is a community of life or that most intimate sharing for mutual comfort and help. Because a man must leave his father and mother and cleave to his wife, Gen. 2:24, and because woman is said to be a helper suited to man, Gen. 2:18, this community of mutual help is not only for the propagation of the human race but for all the amenities of this life.

43. All these are mutual for husband and wife and should be observed equally in all essential and principal matters, provided that that difference of degree between husband and wife — that the husband govern and the wife obey — be observed in all, 1 Peter 3:7; 1 Cor. 11:7–10; Eph. 5:23.

44. Dissipation is opposed to chastity in the stricter sense, in that it is the illicit use of the things pertaining to procreation. In this sense it is called *Impurity, inordinate affection, evil concupiscence*, Col. 3:5; *Lasciviousness*, Rom. 13:13; and the *Disease of concupiscence*, 1 Thess. 4:5.

45. Dissipation includes all auxiliary causes of it, effects of it, and signs of it, such as unchaste glances (Job 31:1; Prov. 9:13; 2 Peter 2:14; Matt. 5:28), nods, kissing, embracing, fondling, dancing, shows, songs, gestures and the like, Gal. 5:15.

46. Auxiliary causes of dissipation are gluttony and drunkenness, Rom. 13:13; Ezek. 16:49; Prov. 23:31, 33.

47. Lasciviousness and lascivious dress are effects and signs of it, Prov. 7:11, as well as obscene speech, Eph. 5:4.

48. There are various kinds of dissipation: first, whoredom, or the union of an unmarried man with an unmarried woman, 1 Cor. 6:16, whether it be lewdness, the deflowering of a woman otherwise honorable, or fornication, which involves a dishonorable woman or prostitute. Second, adultery, in which at least one of the offending persons is married or betrothed. Third, incest or a union of those who are near in the flesh. Fourth, rape, when force is added to dissipation. Fifth, any coition against nature.

49. Adultery is most truly and essentially opposed to marriage, for by its very nature it breaks the bond and covenant of marriage. It is the proper and just cause of divorce, which cannot be said of any other sins although they be more grievous.

50. A just divorce dissolves the very bond of marriage.

XX

Commutative Justice

1. Justice which concerns the outward benefit of our neighbor is called, with a certain appropriateness, commutative justice, because it relates chiefly to commutations or exchanges of goods.

2. This justice is a virtue whereby every man is given his own in external benefits.

3. That which is called one's own is that over which he has lawful possession.

4. Possession is the right to make a complete disposition of a thing as far as laws permit, Matt. 20:15.

5. There are two parts of perfect possession, ownership and use, Luke 20:9; 10:1; 1 Cor. 9:7.

6. These are occasionally separated so that ownership is in one person and use in the power of another for a time.

7. Justice is called for in acquisition and use.

8. The justice of acquisition depends upon the occasion of the possession.

9. The occasion and reason for the possession is called the title.

10. Just title is a just occupation, inheritance, gift, payment, or contract.

11. Just occupation is a lawful taking of things which have belonged to no one but may become someone's.

12. Things are said to belong to no one which are not owned or possessed by anyone.

13. All things are said to have been common at the beginning of the world and also after the flood, in the sense that no man owned or possessed them in a particular way. They were available in common for anyone who would first take or occupy them. This explains the blessing of God upon mankind: Gen. 1:28, *Fill the earth and subdue it. Bear rule over every beast and over all the birds of the heavens and over all the beasts that creep upon the earth.* This is also repeated after the flood: Gen. 9:7, *Be fruitful, increase and fill the earth.*

14. The islands of the sea and the parts of the continent which have never been inhabited are in the same situation.

15. The same principle applies to those things which once belonged to someone but later ceased to do so and are, therefore, customarily called voided or abandoned.

16. Things that are lost, however, are not so considered unless due diligence has been used to find the true owner. If the owner has been sought, the things are rightfully possessed in will and mind, even though they have not been actually received from the other.

17. Wares cast into the sea to lighten a ship or brought to shore from a shipwreck are not to be considered voided or abandoned.

18. Capture, or occupation by right of war justly undertaken, is within the general sense of occupying.

19. Inheritance is a succession to the goods of another by his just will, Lev. 25:45, 46; Num. 27:8–11.

20. A gift is the free bestowal of a good, 1 Kings 10:10, 13.

21. A payment is recompense for work done.

22. A contract in this connection is the giving of a good in accordance with a binding agreement. The form is, "I give that you may give," or, "I give that you may do," or, "I do that you may do," or, "I do that you may give."

23. Possessing by contract includes buying, when something is had at a certain price; letting out, when the use of a thing is permitted for a certain payment; loaning [mutuum], when something is taken, the equivalent of which will later be freely returned; and lending [commodatum], when the return will be in kind, for which a pledge and deposit may be added.

24. Every man's lawful occupation or course of life involves him in these matters, with the exception of those who enjoy public office, of whom we have spoken before in the consideration of the fifth commandment. Although these occupations of life in their nature look to the common good and should be so directed by men, at the same time they look also to the private good of getting and keeping the benefits of this life, Eph. 4:28; 2 Thess. 3:11, 12.

25. All must have some occupation of this sort who are not occupied in or preparing for a higher office, 1 Tim. 5:13; Gen. 3:19. According to the words of the Apostle, *If any will not labor, let him not eat*, 2 Thess. 3:10.

26. It is not enough that one should simply work: He must work for what is good, Eph. 4:28. Quietly and diligently let him follow an occupation which agrees with the will of God and the profit of men, 1 Thess. 4:11, 12; 2 Thess. 3:12. Laziness, voluntary beggary, worthless, irrelevant, unclean arts, and an unnecessary concern for other people's business — the work of the so-called πολυπράγμων, busybody — are the opposite of real work.

27. To what particular kind of occupation a person should apply himself depends partly upon his inward endowments and inclinations,

1 Peter 4:10, and partly upon outward circumstances which may lead him to one course of life rather than another.

28. Because a certain particular providence of God governs such matters, 1 Peter 4:10, everyone is rightly said to be assigned to this or that kind of life, as it were, by the nod of God.

29. Because of this divine providence, a man's particular life occupation is called vocation, analogically, by certain theologians. But this does not mean that men are set apart by God in their ordinary pursuits as a man of faith is set apart to live well, or as a minister of the word is set apart to fulfill the work of the ministry. For nowhere in the Scriptures is any such thing indicated or the title of vocation given to a common occupation simply for itself.

30. The Apostle in 1 Cor. 7:20 mentions vocation but he does not set forth any particular occupation of life (for circumcision and uncircumcision, service and freedom are not occupations of life or legitimate callings). He rather distributes the idea of the calling of the faithful, as it were, by subject; some are called who are servants and some who are free, as appears in v. 24, where he describes the variety of calling by the many states and conditions in which the called are found. In that passage he does not command that everyone remain in the state in which he was called, for he allows a servant to aspire towards freedom, verse 21. But he teaches only that there is no difference between a free man and a servant in relation to Christ and Christian calling, verse 22.

31. Poverty consists in the absence of possessions and riches in their abundance, 1 John 3:17.

32. Riches lawfully obtained are still the good gifts of God, although in their own nature they are not moral goods, Prov. 22:4.

33. And poverty has the character of punishment or affliction, Prov. 21:17.

34. Therefore, there is no perfection in casting away or forsaking wealth unless the special will of God requires it, Acts 20:25.

35. But an evangelical poverty which is spiritual may exist with great riches as in the case of Abraham, Job, and others.

36. Ownership, and differences in the amount of possessions, are ordinances of God and approved by him, Prov. 22:2; 2 Thess. 3:12.

37. In this law of God commutative justice is involved in both getting and using. The sum of it is that we possess our own not another's and do it without hurt to others.

38. The basis of this justice lies in the lawful keeping of the things we have.

39. Parsimony and frugality are required for this keeping of them, Prov. 21:15.

40. Parsimony is the virtue of spending only what is worthy and necessary.

41. Frugality is the virtue of conducting our affairs with profit and benefit.

42. The perfection of this justice, which strictly speaking comes from Christian love, is found in generosity.

43. Generosity is the virtue of being inclined to share our benefits freely with others in accordance with the will of God, 2 Cor. 8:14; Rom. 12:13; Lev. 25:35; Ps. 37:19.

44. Generosity embraces not only free giving, which includes the forgiving of a debt, but also free lending, Luke 6:34, and hospitality, Rom. 12:13; 1 Peter 4:9.

45. Alms properly so-called are part of this generosity when it results from taking pity on the calamity of our neighbor.

46. Theft in the larger sense is contrary to a just title of ownership.

47. Theft is an unjust taking of what is another's against his will, Eph. 4:28.

48. Taking here includes accepting, keeping, and losing.

49. A thing is said to be another's because of his ownership of it, power over it, or possession of it.

50. In various cases the owner for humanitarian reasons is supposed to consent to the giving away of some part of his goods, although he has not actually done so. In such an instance, there is no charge of theft, Deut. 23:24, 25.

51. Another man's goods may be taken away either secretly or by force; here there are two kinds of sin, namely, theft specially so-called, and rapine or robbery, Exod. 22:1; Hos. 6:8, 9; Luke 8:12; 1 Cor. 6:8, 9.

52. Theft includes any fraud used in buying or selling or in any other unlawful acquiring of things.

53. Theft in the state is the embezzlement of public funds, when things belonging to the community are stolen — and artificial inflation, when the buying and selling prices of corn or other things are raised through monopolies or like devices to an unjustly high level.

54. Rapine includes oppression, Isa. 3:14, and extortion, Luke 3:14; 1 Sam. 2:12.

55. Lavishness, or the immoderate bestowing of the things we have, is opposed to parsimony and frugality.

56. Covetousness, or the immoderate keeping of the things we have, Prov. 11:24, is opposed to generosity. So is avarice, or the greedy desire for things we do not have, 1 Tim. 6:9.

XXI

Telling the Truth

1. The justice which affects our neighbor indirectly is truth telling and contentment. The former affects our neighbor through his belief; the latter through some work or action of ours ordered by one of the previous commandments.

2. Truth telling is the virtue of heeding the truth in giving testimony, Matt. 23:22; Eph. 4:25; Ps. 15:2.

3. The ninth precept deals specifically with this telling truth in giving testimony. It treats not only of things which pertain to the good name of our neighbor (the honor of our neighbor being the subject of the fifth commandment), nor only of the riches and benefits of this life (handled in the eighth commandment, Prov. 22:1). A true or false testimony applies not alone to the good name of others but to their possessions and their very life, Prov. 30:14.

4. It is also manifest from its very wording that this commandment refers chiefly to judicial trials, Num. 35:30; Deut. 17:6; 19:15, where many other things are handled besides libel; but it should also be extended to all public, private, political, and sacred testimonies, 1 Cor. 15:15; John 1:7, 8, 15, 19, 32, 34.

5. Therefore, court proceedings find not only their ground, but also their direction in this commandment. Judgment should always be based on fit testimony (unless there be such evidence that testimonies are not required) or at least on strong and (as they say) vehement presumptions equivalent to testimonies.

6. The words of a testimony must always be used in the sense in which they are understood or thought to be understood by those whom the witness attempts to convince, without equivocation, ambiguity, or mental reservation.

7. Truth in a testimony is threefold: It occurs a) when what is said conforms to the matter in hand, b) when it conforms to the mind of the speaker, and c) when it conforms to both.

8. The second instance is the chief concern in witnessing and truth telling. The third must be invoked for matters in which we are either thought or profess to have certain knowledge.

9. Truth telling takes the form of either a simple assertion or a promise.

10. Truth in an assertion at least requires that our affirmations accord with our mind and judgment.

11. Sometimes an assertion itself is necessary. This is when either justice or love requires it of us.

12. Justice demands assertions in public trials from the judge, the plaintiff, the defendant, the witness, the defendant's lawyer, the notary, and the plaintiff's lawyer. Assertion is also required from us, out of court, when we are bound to bear witness for some special reason.

13. Love requires an assertion from us when good would result to our neighbor from it without equal hurt to ourselves or others.

14. Truth in a promise is called good faith.

15. Good faith is the virtue of maintaining firmly the trust imposed in us.

16. Such good faith is the basis of civil justice and all agreements and contracts (a contract being a reciprocal promise).

17. A lie is the opposite of truth in a testimony, Eph. 4:25.

18. A lie is properly a testimony by which one says something that is not in his heart, Acts 5:3. Therefore, comes that phrase in Scripture, a *Double heart*, said of a man who is a liar, Ps. 12:2.

19. To say something involves not only outward words but chiefly their meanings. Hence the same words which are true in one sense are a lie in another, Matt. 26:61.

20. Irony, stories, jests, repetitions of false things and the like are not lies for they are not testimonies. They are not testimonies because they are not confirmed by the credit and authority of the speaker.

21. An intention to deceive, although usually accompanying false testimony, is not of the essence, neither is it necessarily required, of a lie. For if one knows that a person cannot be deceived by his lie, yet he still intends to affirm what is false, he lies just as if he had a hope of deceiving.

22. An intention to hurt certainly increases the mischief of a lie but it does not constitute the nature of it. For if a man out of jest or a desire to please or be obliging lends his credit to something which he knows to be false, it is a lie, pernicious in its own nature to the author himself if not to others. So it is with those who are given to flattery and boasting and delight in confirming monstrous stories or fictions to others.

23. An intention to say what is false constitutes a lie even though what is spoken is most true.

24. The assertion of an uncertain thing as certain is counted a lie, even though we think it may be true.

25. Keeping silent so that one does not speak the truth when required by justice or love partakes of the nature of a lie.

26. But when neither justice nor love requires us to give testimony,

then the truth or a part of it may be concealed without sin, Jer. 38:27.

27. The more heinous lies are those in which the testimony is solemn as in courts of law (where the words of the ninth commandment are especially applicable), in sacred matters and the like, Matt. 26:59; 1 Cor. 15:15.

28. Hence the signing of one's name, any testimony, or commendatory letter against the known truth are foul lies.

29. Pretense in signs or acts, rather than words, is not properly a lie unless by their nature or by some definite convention they are used as and have the force of speech, 1 Sam. 20:20–22; Matt. 26:49. Acts and signs which are not verbal have no definite and determined meaning and thus lack the force of testimony.

30. Such dissembling is sometimes lawful, as in the strategems of war, Josh. 8.

31. But it is unlawful when as end or means it opposes religion, justice, or love.

32. Perfidy or faithlessness is contrary to good faith.

33. A lie is involved in a promise if there is no intention of doing what is promised; faithlessness is involved if there is no fit endeavor to do it. Thus a lie and faithlessness may be found together and they may also be separated.

34. When testimony towards our neighbor is confirmed by oath, the oath is an accessory of the testimony. The oath in itself relates to God only, but in this use it relates to our neighbor also.

35. Therefore, perjury in such a testimony is directly and immediately a sin against the reverence we owe God, and indirectly a violation of the justice due our neighbor.

36. Asseveration is a mode of testimony wherein is declared the sincerity of the witness and his sure knowledge of the thing witnessed. It is not unfitly called by some protestation, because it produces testimony by explanation.

37. Therefore, in asseveration there is no second attestation added to the first as in an oath. It is another example of one and the same thing.

38. In mere asseveration there is no calling upon God, which is essential to an oath.

39. Yet asseveration is not fitting except for more serious testimonies. It is a kind of middle degree between a simple testimony and an oath.

40. In ordinary speech we must above all abstain from asseverations which resemble an oath.

XXII

Contentment

1. The virtue of contentment is the acquiescence of the mind in the lot God has given, 1 Tim. 6:6; Heb. 13:5; Phil. 4:11.

2. This contentment is ordered in the tenth commandment as appears from the words themselves. It is not at all proper to refer this precept to the inward and original purity of righteousness, which is the fountain of all obedience; such purity is not commanded in any one commandment but in all. And the precept no more belongs to the second table where it is situated than to the first.

3. Of all the virtues contained in the second table, however, none is more internal or intimate to vital righteousness than contentment. By it we are, as it were, led by the hand to contemplate and seek righteousness. And so righteousness in its purity is fitly handled here.

4. Joy for the prosperity of our neighbor, as if it were our own, is part of contentment, Rom. 12:15.

5. In contentment and joy are found the height and perfection of all love towards our neighbor. Hence contentment is in a way the perfection of godliness and of a godly man. 1 Tim. 6:6, *There is great gain in godliness, μετ' αὐταρκείας, with contentment* (or, that which produces the perfection of contentment).

6. Therefore, the last commandment stands at the end of an order which proceeds from the less to the more perfect and from the better known to the less known.

7. For this is our most perfect duty and yet least known to us by nature: Whatever we conceive or will should be joined with the good of our neighbor.

8. Although by its nature this is first among duties to our neighbor as the foundation of all the others, it is commanded in the last place, because it is the last to come into being for corrupted man.

9. Covetousness is opposed to contentment, Heb. 13:5.

10. Covetousness does not mean the power and faculty of desiring and seeking what is natural; or the act of that natural faculty, or its lawful operation, which is also natural; or the whole inclination of our corrupt nature (not specially condemned in any one precept but in the whole law); or the actual inordinate primary lusts (for the most part contrary to religion and condemned in the first table); or last, lusts which tend to the hurt of our neighbor (for those having a deliberate will and purpose behind them are condemned in the other commandments). Covetousness means that desire which first insti-

gates and excites the mind to yearn for the good things of our neighbors although it has not yet occurred to us to get them by unlawful
means, 1 Kings 21:2; Mark 10:19.

11. The affinity or close connection which these primary motives
of injustice have with original corruption (whence they arise) has
led many to confuse the two. But the following should be considered. First, original sin is an inborn disposition [*habitus*], so to speak,
perpetually and continually with us during this life, and always in
the same manner while we live here, but those motives are transient
expressions of the disposition. Second, the sin in us is no more an
original than a general principle of all vicious action, while the
expressions of it which are condemned here are plainly limited to
those which affect only our neighbor.

12. The Apostle himself in Rom. 7 clearly explains this commandment by a figure describing the operations of sin. *Concupiscence*,
verse 7, is the same as the *Passions of sinners*, verse 5, and as *Concupiscence effected by sin*, verse 8, and must be distinguished from *Indwelling sin*, verse 7.

13. It is no marvel that the Pharisees (of whom Paul was one) did
not acknowledge the first motives of covetousness to be sins. The
same refusal is stiffly made by their cousins, the papists.

14. Those who divide this last commandment about covetousness
in two, one part about coveting the house and the other about coveting the wife and other objects have forsaken all reason in this
matter. They are forced either to abandon the second commandment
of the first table or to turn it into a needless appendix of the first
commandment so that they may in some way retain the number ten.
Or rather, as is evident with many of them, obscuring the force of
the second commandment in order with some show to separate from
it themselves and their superstitions, they tear apart this tenth commandment. They have no choice about which is the ninth and which
the tenth commandment because in the repetition of the law, Deut.
5:27, coveting the wife is put before coveting the house. They cannot say it is clearly wrong to join together these two types of coveting
when they themselves in explaining the decalogue always join or
rather confuse the ninth and tenth commandments. Last, the very
words of the decalogue plainly show that it is one commandment,
when they forbid one act (*You shall not covet*) and have a common
object (*Anything that is your neighbor's*).

15. An inordinate love of ourselves is a cause of covetousness,
16. This φιλαυτία, self-love, is the source and origin of all sins not
which is called φιλαυτία, 2 Tim. 3:2.
only against our neighbor, but against God himself, 2 Tim. 3:4.

17. Covetousness is divided by John into that of the flesh, having

to do with food and lust, that of the eyes, having to do with outward delight and profit, and the pride of living, having to do with the glory and pomp of this world, 1 John 2:16.

18. *Envy* or an *Eye being evil* is opposed to joy and pleasure in the prosperity of our neighbor, Matt. 20:15. Likewise opposed is any ἐπιχαιρεκακία, rejoicing over the hurt of our neighbor, Ps. 70:3, 4; Obad. 12.

19. In the last commandment that perfection of righteousness is commanded which is in a way central to the whole second table, just as in the first commandment of the first table all parts of religion are in a way commanded. The first commandment of the first table contains the first and great commandment, *You shall love God with all your heart* and the second commandment, like unto it, *You shall love your neighbor as yourself*, is contained in the last commandment of the second table.

20. From the perfection which shines forth in any one of these commandments it is manifest that a complete and accurate fulfilling of the law is impossible even to the faithful by the grace bestowed upon them in this life. The rule and measure of our obedience (as has been well said) is in affirmatives, *You shall love with all your heart* and in negatives, *You shall not covet*, both of which are impossible in this life. It necessarily follows that no one can satisfy exactly the law.

21. In this life we know only in part, 1 Cor. 13:9, and, therefore, act only in part. We receive only the first fruits of the Spirit, Rom. 8:23. Therefore, we cannot precisely observe a law wholly spiritual, Rom. 7:14. We carry about us flesh that lusts against the Spirit, Gal. 5:17, and we cannot obey without covetousness, inclining and drawing us another way. Finally we are not perfect, Phil. 3:12, and we cannot render perfect obedience. We always need to have that petition in our heart and on our lips, *Forgive us our debts*.

22. Yet it is rightly and truly said that the *Yoke of Christ is easy, his burden light*, Matt. 11:30, and *His commandments not grievous*, 1 John 5:3. Here the yoke is considered, first, as the law is actually observed by the faithful who delight in it, Rom. 7:22; Ps. 119:14, 16, not as it ought to be observed. Even this kind of observance by the faithful brings rest to their souls, Matt. 11:29, although the imperfection which still cleaves to them is grievous and troublesome to them. Second, the yoke is here considered in relation to the spirit and not the flesh, Matt. 26:41. Third, it is here united with the remission of all the sin and imperfection which cling to our endeavors. Fourth, the yoke is light and not grievous in comparison with the letter of the law which kills. Fifth, it is a preparation for the reward

appointed by God for obedience begun, though imperfect — in which sense all afflictions are counted light, 2 Cor. 4:17. The ease and lightness of the law of God is not in proportion to our strength: It comes from the grace of our Lord Jesus Christ and the love of God, with the gift of the Holy Spirit which is with all those who love the law of God. Amen.

INDEX

338   INDEX